DIABLO® II

ULTIMATE STRATEGY GUIDE

BY BART G. FARKAS

BRADYGAMES STAFF

Director of Publishing
David Waybright

Editor-In-Chief
H. Leigh Davis

Creative Director
Robin Lasek

Marketing Manager
Janet Eshenour

Assistant Marketing Manager
Susie Nieman

CREDITS

Senior Project Editor
David B. Bartley

Translations/Foreign Rights
Mike Degler

Screenshot Editor
Michael Owen

Book Designer
Dan Caparo

Production Designer
Bob Klunder
Jane Washburne
Tracy Wehmeyer

BRADYGAMES ACKNOWLEDGEMENTS

We'd like to extend our sincere gratitude to everyone involved in this project for an outstanding job. Were it not for the uncanny authoring prowess of our friend and colleague, Bart Farkas, and the tremendous effort and cooperation from everyone at Blizzard, especially Melissa Edwards, this guide would not have been possible.

AUTHOR ACKNOWLEDGEMENTS

Because books like this require a team effort to put them together accurately and in a timely manner, there are plenty of folks to thank both at Blizzard Entertainment and at BradyGAMES. I'd first like to say a huge 'thank you' to everyone, then I'll list each person that who contributed individually.

Blizzard North

These gentlemen were all part of the design and production of the game. Together and individually, they provided me with invaluable information. Matt Householder deserves a special thanks for reviewing the book and managing information flow from Blizzard North.

Matt Householder
Max Schaefer
Tyler Thompson
Pete Brevik
Mike Murphy
Anthony Rivero
Marc Tattersal
Alex Munn
Fred Vaught
Michio Okamura
Ken Williams
Mike Scandizzo
Ted Bisson

Blizzard Entertainment Headquarters

As with other Blizzard titles, this is the location where all of Blizzard's extensive QA testing takes place. The many people in QA, as well as the other portions of Blizzard Headquarters, all deserve a huge round of thanks. Special thanks needs to go out to Jason Hutchins, Carlos Guerrero, and Brian Love from QA, as well as the QA Manager Ian Welke, who made my visits to Blizzard run smoothly. Also from the QA Department, Dean Lee deserves a special thanks for his extensive work on the skill combinations for both of the new character classes. I'd also like to thank *all* Blizzard employees for makings such great games, and anyone else behind the scenes that helped with the creation of this book. Perhaps the single greatest effort came from Geoff Fraizer—the brains behind the Chaos Sanctuary and the Arreat Summit (Blizzard's online strategy guides). Geoff compiled and filtered information to me, and played a significant role in the creation of this guide. That said, thanks to:

Bill Roper – Senior Producer
John Lagrave – Producer
Melissa Edwards – Business Development Associate
Elaine Di Iorio – Senior Manager of Business Development
Christian Arretche – Blizzard North liaison
Geoff Fraizer – Innumerable contributions
Carlos Guerrero – Diablo II Test Lead
Derek Simmons – Past contributions
Justin Parker – Skills
Les Douglas – Quests Lead Tester
Jason Hutchins – QA Assistant Manager, numerous contributions
Ian Welke – QA Manager
Dave Fried –Level Designer
Roger Eberhart - Tips
Eric Dodds – All around great guy
Brian Love – Monsters, Monsters, and more Monsters
Ilya Berelson - Game Tester
Eric Straus – Game Tester
Ed Kang - Macintosh Lead Tester
Roger Eberhart - QA Multiplayer Team Lead
Rob Foote - Game Tester
Jeanette Clausen - Game Tester
Chris Van Der Westhuizen – Game Tester
Ron Frybarger – Game Tester
Ted Barken – Game Tester
Michael Backus – Game Tester
Dean Lee - Game Tester
Manuel Gonzalez – Game Tester
Ray Laubach – Game Tester
Matt Lee – Game Tester
Kelly Chun – Damages

BradyGAMES

The entire staff at BradyGAMES was most excellent to work with (as usual). BradyGAMES is the premiere strategy guide publisher in this industry, and their love of games shows through in all facets of their work. I'd like to thank you all for your support and help throughout the project, but special thanks needs to go out to David Bartley, whose editing skill and easy-going nature makes every project a pleasure.

DEDICATION

For Derek (diablo two)

CONTENTS

INTRODUCTION 4

CHAPTER 1: THE BASICS 5
- The Diablo Story 6
- Expansion Set Charges 6
- Major Characters 9
- Battle Chest Basics 10
- Weapons & Armor 13

CHAPTER 2: THE CHARACTERS . .21
- **NECROMANCER 21**
  - Poison & Bone 26
  - Curses 30
  - Summoning & Control 33
- **AMAZON 38**
  - Bow & Crossbow 40
  - Passive & Magic 44
  - Javelin & Spear 48
- **PALADIN 52**
  - Combat 54
  - Offensive Auras 58
  - Defensive Auras 61
- **SORCERESS 64**
  - Fire 66
  - Lightning 69
  - Cold 72
- **BARBARIAN 76**
  - Combat Skills 78
  - Combat Masteries 82
  - Warcries 83

THE EXPANSION CHARACTERS 87
- **ASSASSIN 87**
  - Martial Arts 90
  - Shadow Disciplines 95
  - Traps 100
- **DRUID 108**
  - Elemental 110
  - Shape Shifting 113
  - Summoning 118

CHAPTER 3: ACT QUESTS 125
- **Act I** 127
- **Act II** 136
- **Act III** 144
- **Act IV** 150
  - Diablo 154
- **Act V** 155
  - Baal 164

CHAPTER 4: THE LISTS 165
- **BESTIARY**
  - Diablo II Monsters 166
  - Expansion Monsters 186
- **ITEMS LISTS 198**
  - Charms 198
  - Gems 205
  - Set Items 206
  - Runes 218
  - Jewels 218
  - Unique Items 218

CHAPTER 5: MULTIPLAYER 219

APPENDIX 227
- Runes 228
- Rune Word Enhanced Items 229
- Crafted Items 230
- Jewels 230
- Magic Items Prefixes 232
- Magic Items Suffixes 238
- Character Skills Tables 245
  - Necromancer 245
  - Amazon 251
  - Paladin 257
  - Sorceress 263
  - Barbarian 269
  - Assassin 275
  - Druid 281

DIABLO® II ULTIMATE STRATEGY GUIDE

Brady Publishing
An Imprint of Pearson Education
201 West 103rd Street
Indianapolis, Indiana 46290

Printing Code: The rightmost double-digit number is the year of the book's printing; the rightmost single-digit number is the number of the book's printing. For example, 01-1 shows that the first printing of the book occurred in 2001.

07 06 28

Manufactured in the United States of America.

INTRODUCTION

In 1996, the original *Diablo*® was released to the world and immediately (like all Blizzard Games), it reshaped the computer gaming landscape. *Diablo* was a real-time role-playing game that had compelling gameplay—something that had previously been unheard of. Not only was it a great single-player game, it also offered a unique way of playing with other gamers from all over the world with its revolutionary Battle.net® system. After *Diablo*'s release, all similar games were destined to be compared to it, and in most cases the efforts were not even worthy of comparison. Even to this day, the original *Diablo* is still played by gamers the world over. Now, more than four years after *Diablo* came onto the scene, *Diablo*® *II* and *Diablo*® *II: Lord of Destruction*™ (the expansion set) are available and are wowing gamers and critics alike with an engrossing story, spine-tingling special effects, gut-wrenching battles, and gameplay that is second to none.

What makes the *Diablo II* Realm such a special place for gamers is the loving attention to detail that Blizzard has put into balancing all aspects of the gameplay so that each of the 210 skills has value in the game. Indeed, the largest section in this book is *Chapter 2: The Characters*, where you can learn all about each of the skills, including strategies specific to certain areas of the game and even multiplayer action. The complexity of the seven character classes and their skill sets is astounding, and this is the primary reason why the *Diablo II* Realm is a place where gamers want to return again and again. Of course, the item sets, the unique weapons, and thousands upon thousands of magically enhanced items make this game equally rich.

When the expansion set was released, the millions of rabid *Diablo II* fans were at last able to continue their quest, following the path of Baal, the last of the Prime Evils and the brother of Diablo, into the Barbarian Highlands of the north. *Lord of Destruction* also added a massive number of new items and wrinkles to the gameplay (covered in *Chapter 1: The Basics*). This perfect addition to the *Diablo II* Realm seamlessly put together both the old and the new into what can only be described as an uber-game that will continue to dominate the hearts and minds of gamers for years to come.

NOTE

All of the statistics (Character Skill numbers, monster stats, etc.) are based on the Final Gold Master release of the game (the same version included in the Battle Chest). These numbers are totally accurate in single-player mode. However, balancing issues are being addressed by Blizzard on a daily basis, so you will likely notice some descrepencies in the stats when playing Battle.net. Indeed, everytime you download a new patch on Battle.net, you will be altering the multiplayer game stats in this way. So get all of your single-player game information here, but visit Blizzard's web site regularly (the Chaos Sanctuary and the Arreat Summit) to keep up with the ever-changing world of Battle.net!

This Ultimate Guide draws upon the wisdom and experience of the entire Blizzard crew that helped to create and test both *Diablo II* games included in the Battle Chest. Many long hours were spent on-site at both Blizzard North and Blizzard Headquarters in Irvine consulting with the resident 'experts' who specialize in each of the game's various aspects. In creating this book, we attempted to make it as useful to the reader as possible; therefore, there was a heavy emphasis placed on each of the skills, and the basic flow of the quests. The Bestiary in *Chapter 4: The Lists* gives you what you need to know about all of the hideous monsters you'll meet in the *Diablo II* universe, including the Bosses and Unique monsters. The many tables in this chapter (and the *Appendix*) provide essential information on the myriad of items and weapons in the game. *Chapter 1: The Basics* identifies and explains changes that occurred between *Diablo II* and the expansion set, as well as providing the low-down on the potions, scrolls, difficulty levels, and even the effects of each of the Shrines that you'll encounter in the game.

Let this book be a reference to guide you whenever you have a question or are having difficulty. After all, the *Diablo II* Realm is so rich, complex, and huge that there will certainly be times when even the most independent of gamers will need to grab a hint or two from this guide!

Chapter 1

THE BASICS

THE DIABLO STORY

In the first game, Diablo spent two centuries slowly working to corrupt the Soulstone that imprisoned him. In time, he was able to extend his influence into the surrounding area and corrupt both King Leoric and his archbishop, Lazarus. The King proved too strong to fully control, so the Demon took possession of his son, Prince Albrecht. Diablo then began to shape an outpost of Hell within the catacombs that ran beneath the town of Tristram. By spreading terror into the surrounding countryside, the Demon was able to attract many heroes who came to cleanse the land of evil. By the time the strongest of these heroes reached his goal, though, he had become fully influenced by the will of Diablo. In his twisted state, this adventurer believed that the only way to fully control the Demon was to plunge the shard of the Soulstone into his own head. This, of course, was exactly what Diablo had planned as the Demon now had an even stronger body to use in the completion of his ultimate plan.

In *Diablo® II*, Diablo has headed east to the desert outside of the city of Lut Gholein, intent on freeing his brother, Baal. The possessed body of the fallen hero has taken on an increasingly demonic appearance. For this reason, the Demon brought with him a mortal companion to go amongst the people of the city, listening for information, and securing what mundane necessities the Lord of Terror still required. Diablo soon found himself pursued by even greater mortal heroes as he raged across the lands to wake his brothers.

Diablo II begins here, with you choosing a character from one of five (or seven if the expansion pack is installed) character classes: Amazon, Barbarian, Necromancer, Paladin, Sorceress, (and the expansion's Druid and Assassin). After selecting a character, you work your way through four Acts (of the original *Diablo II*) and 21 quests while en route to destroy Diablo. Along the way, you'll go through many sets of armor and weapons. You'll also meet hideous monsters, valued allies, and evil overlords.

In *Diablo® II: Lord of Destruction™* you continue on and follow the path of Baal, the last of the Prime Evils and the brother of Diablo. The quest to destroy Baal leads into the Barbarian Highlands of the north. The Lord of Destruction intends to corrupt the powerful Worldstone, which protects the whole of the mortal plane from the forces of Hell. It will be up to you to defeat Baal and stop the forces of evil before they turn the world into a permanent Hell on Earth!

EXPANSION SET CHANGES

Diablo II: Lord of Destruction is much more than just another Act added to the end of *Diablo II*. In fact, *Lord of Destruction* changes the *Diablo II* world in many ways to effectively create an entirely new and refreshed gaming experience. The expansion set must be played from the beginning of the *Diablo II* game—that is to say, if you wish to play as the Druid or the Assassin, you must complete the first four Acts before you can play the fifth Act. If you choose to play Act V with your current character, you must play to the end of *Diablo II* to open the portal to a new adventure.

The new 800x600 resolution is awesome!

What's so great about the expansion set is that it adds many more layers to the gameplay of the original *Diablo II*. Of course, there are two new character classes, the Druid and the Assassin, but that's only the tip of the iceberg when it comes to what's new with the *Diablo II* universe. There's a slew of new items that affect everything from high-level Battle.net® characters to low-level characters experimenting with socketed weapons, shields, or even armor (another new addition).

The team at Blizzard has worked hard to incorporate plenty of new wrinkles into the gameplay to make *Diablo II* and the expansion set highly replayable for years to come. Here's a list of improvements and changes that will keep you coming back for more.

EXPANSION FEATURES

- **The Mini-map:** There are two modes now; one that saves space and appears in the upper corner of the screen, and the traditional overlaid translucent map.
- **Bank Account:** The amount of money that can be kept in the Stash has been increased.
- **The Stash:** It's now *twice* as big.
- **Weapon Swapping:** You can now carry two weapon sets and switch between them with a keystroke! This enables you to have two very different weapon configurations, such as a ranged weapon like a Crossbow with Bolts in one set, and a melee pair like a Bastard Sword and Shield in the other. Pressing one key automatically switches these weapon sets.
- **More Hotkeys:** Instead of just eight, you now have sixteen hotkeys for spells and skills.
- **More Items:** Thousands of new items are now at your disposal due to the hundreds of new prefixes and suffixes available.
- **Crafted Items:** A new class of items made in the Horadric Cube using Runes and other objects.
- **Elite Items:** A new class of items found only in Hell difficulty.
- **Ethereal Items:** Translucent items with an improved fundamental ability. They cannot be repaired and will degrade unless socketed with the Zod Rune.
- **More Sets:** There are now 16 new Sets, for a total of 32, making Set hunting/trading more complex and fun.
- **Character-specific Items:** There are many new items like Shields, Helms, Shrunken Heads, Orbs, Claws, and Katars that can be used only by certain characters.
- **Charged Items:** Some new items have set charges in them. For example, a ring might have 15 charges of Frost Nova. This enables a non-Sorceress to use Frost Nova. Of course, these items open up many new doors for gameplay.
- **New Socketed Items:** Armor may be enhanced by placing gems into the sockets—some have as many as six sockets.
- **Two New Classes of Gems:** You can now put Jewels and Runes in sockets. There are 33 Runes that can be placed in socketed items. They're even more powerful if placed in a specific order in certain items.
- **Arm Hirelings:** They can now wear armor and use weapons that *you* give them!
- **Heal Hirelings**: They can now be healed with potions by dropping a potion on their portrait. Hirelings can even be resurrected after they die (for a price).
- **Keep Hirelings:** What's exceptional about the new way Hirelings are handled is that they gain experience as they stay with you, and you can carry them over between Acts. This way, you can develop a trusty sidekick who can stay with you through the entire game!

NOTE

We recommend installing Diablo II: Lord of Destruction and playing Diablo II from the start with the expansion set enabled. This will give you access to all of the great features that the expansion introduced.

EXPANSION MODIFICATIONS

As noted by Blizzard's staff, there were many changes implemented with the addition of the *Diablo II: Lord of Destruction*. These changes affect the *Diablo II* Realm only if you've installed the expansion set.

- Gambling prices are now based on the character level.
- You can no longer Gamble for Set or Unique Items.
- Items Gambled can be Exceptional and Elite Items once a player has reached certain character levels.

- Rings and Amulets are always listed on the Gambling Screen.
- Boss monsters now do 30% less damage than before to Hirelings and minions.
- Monsters now display "Undead" or "Demon" when highlighted. If nothing is listed, they are an "Animal" type.
- Maximum monster level is now level 70 in Nightmare and level 90 in Hell.
- Monsters in Nightmare/Hell difficulty have higher Resistances and Hit Points, and lower Attack Ratings than before.
- Poison Damage attacks from monsters inflict more damage than before.
- Mana and Life stealing effects are reduced by half in Nightmare and Hell.
- Retrieving your corpse where you died in Nightmare and Hell restores 50% of any experience lost at death.
- Increased amount of Gold that can be held in a character's Stash.
- Increased the power of all Gems/Skulls and added level requirements.
- Increased the power of all throwing potions and added level requirements.
- Increased the resistance penalty in Nightmare difficulty to -40 and Hell difficulty to -100.
- Looting corpses in multiplayer is now available only in Hardcore games.
- In multiplayer, you may go hostile only once per minute with each player in your game.
- New Party Experience Bonus to players in a Party in multiplayer.
- Crystal Swords have increased durability.
- Scepter class items have increased damage.
- Diablo is harder in Normal difficulty.
- Unique monster types will appear more often in Nightmare and Hell.
- The Diablo countdown timer has been removed (after you destroy Diablo in Act IV).
- Normal Unique Items now have Level Limits.
- You can now carry up to 250 bolts and 350 arrows.
- You can now carry up to 12 Keys in one stack.
- Bone Shields and Helms can now have sockets.
- Total Chance to Block is now dependent on Dexterity, Character Level, and Chance to Block Items.
- Flawless quality Gems now drop.
- Exceptional Items can now drop in later stages of Normal difficulty, depending on Character Level and Monster Level.
- New Normal Set Items that have not been converted may have additional magical bonuses and abilities, depending on how many pieces of the Sets are worn or which pieces are used in combination with other Set Items.
- Bosses now do not always give a guaranteed Rare/Set/Unique, but still have a good chance.
- Item drop rate has been increased for single player and for Parties.
- Item drop rate for soloing in multiplayer games is the same as single player.
- Gold from items sold to vendors is now shared with Party members in the same Act. (This gold sharing has been eliminated in the first expansion patch.)
- Monsters are sometimes immune to certain attacks and now list immunities. As difficulty increases, monsters have more immunities and a greater number of monsters possess immunities.
- The Super Unique Monster, Flamespike the Crawler, has been removed from the Inner Cloister Waypoint.

MAJOR CHARACTERS

These are the major characters in the *Diablo II* storyline, as outlined by the game's designers at Blizzard North. This is not a detailed listing of each character's motivations and personality, but rather, is merely meant to tell you a little about each character so that you can identify where they 'fall' in the plot as you work your way through the game.

ANDARIEL

Lesser Evil. Maiden of Anguish.

BAAL

The last of the Prime Evils. Brother of Diablo. Lord of Destruction.

DIABLO

Prime Evil. Lord of Terror.

DURIEL

Lesser Evil. Prince of Pain.

IZUAL

Angel. Bore the rune blade "Azure Wrath" in an assault on the Hell Forge and was corrupted. First gave the demons information about the Soulstones. Now serves as a lieutenant in Hell.

JERED CAIN

Horadric leader that pursued and captured Diablo.

MEPHISTO

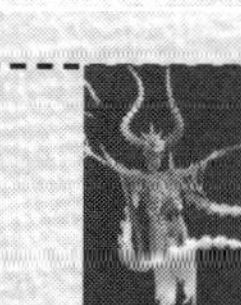

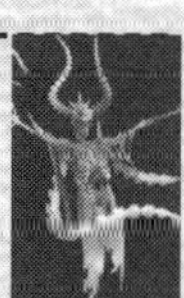

Prime Evil. Lord of Hatred.

TAL RASHA

Horadrim mage who was in the group pursuing Baal. Voluntarily imprisoned himself with Baal to supplement the power of the shattered Soulstone. Was eventually corrupted and thus revealed the secret of the Worldstone to the three Prime Evils.

TYRAEL

An Archangel in the ranks of Heaven. He has always been especially concerned for the welfare of humanity, and may have erred on the side of being too compassionate toward mortals. He has also dealt quite a bit with the Soulstones and the Worldstone itself over the ages. It was he who forged the angelic rune blade "Azure Wrath" which Izual used in his tragically doomed attack on the Hell Forge.

BATTLE CHEST BASICS

This section covers the essential core elements of the *Diablo II* experience, including some key differences between *Diablo II* and the expansion set—so read on, brave warrior!

EXPANSION SET HIRELINGS

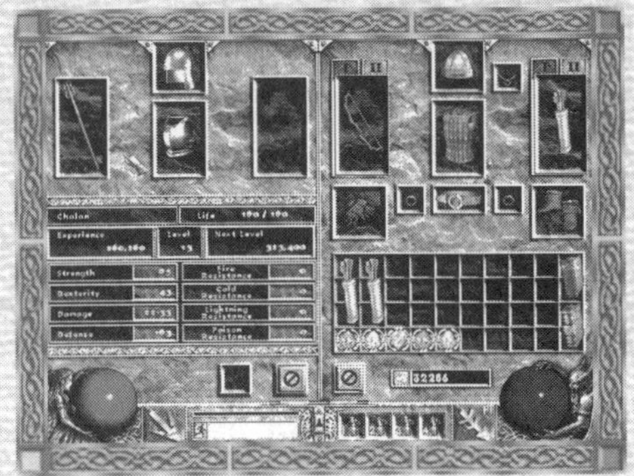

The expansion set allows you to equip Hirelings with items from your Inventory!

As mentioned earlier, the Hirelings in the expansion set are considerably different than in the original *Diablo II,* where Hirelings were confined to specific Acts and could not be healed with potions or armed with weapons. However, in the expansion set, you can get a Hireling from Kashya in Act I and have that Hireling follow you through the entire game; your Hireling will gain experience as you do, and accompany you from Act to Act (if you want). Secondly, you can equip your Hireling with Magical or Socketed Armor and Weapons, and continually upgrade their equipment as the game wears on. Lastly, you can heal Hirelings by dropping a health potion on their icon. No doubt many gamers will want to keep one Hireling and stay loyal to them, building them up as they enhance their own skills and characteristics. If the Hireling is vanquished, not to worry, you can grab him/her back if you have enough gold, even if it's later in a game after you've saved and exited several times!

NOTE

You can equip your Hirelings with certain helms and body armor, but not shields.

Here's a breakdown of the Hirelings and how they may be used throughout the five Acts:

Act I

The Rogues may be equipped with Bow-class weapons only. All Rogues cast the Inner Sight spell, and some have Fire Arrow or Cold Arrow, as well.

Act II

The Guardsmen in Act II may be equipped only with Spear or Javelin-class weapons. If they are labeled *Combat*, they use the Jab attack; if they are labeled *Defense*, they use the Defiance aura; and if they are labeled *Offensive*, they use the Blessed Aim aura. Defensive Guardsmen also get Holy Freeze and Offensive Might once they reach higher levels.

Act III

The Iron Wolves can be equipped with both a Sword (one-handed only) and a Shield. Iron Wolves labeled *Lightning* attack with Charged Bolt and Lightning Bolt, those labeled *Cold* use Frozen Armor and Glacial Spike, and those labeled *Fire* use Fireball and Inferno.

Act IV

There are no Hirelings in Act IV, but you can bring a Hireling with you from a previous Act.

Act V

The Barbarians can be equipped with a one- or two-handed Sword and use either of the skills Bash or Stun.

GAMBLING

Gambling occurs when you buy an item from one of the NPCs that allows you to gamble. The 'Gamble' part of it refers to the fact that you may be paying 10,000 gold pieces for an incredible item that's worth over 50,000 gold, or you might just have thrown away that money for an average item that you could find almost anywhere. If you have the extra money, it's definitely worth gambling, but keep in mind that in *Diablo II: Lord of Destruction* Set and Unique Items can no longer be obtained by gambling!

Gambling can be a good way to get high-end items—if you have the money to Gamble with in the first place.

Managing your Inventory and making sure that you are well equipped are essential to your success. (Larger expansion set Inventory and Stash shown here.)

INVENTORY

Your Inventory is a limited space that houses everything from potions and scrolls to the weapons and armor that you pick up as you work your way through the game. The items that you gather as you kill monsters can either be used, sold, or stored. Selling items is a great way to obtain gold, especially if you sell a Unique or magically enhanced weapon that you otherwise have little or no use for. Of course, the Inventory is a finite space, and you'll soon run out of room for the new items that you find. Frequent trips back to town via Town Portals or Waypoints is highly recommended because all of those average items that you sell will eventually add up to one very expensive and powerful item!

 TIP

Once you have obtained the Horadric Cube, you can keep it in your main Inventory. Although it takes up four squares, the Cube itself holds 12 squares inside it, so you can actually gain eight storage spaces by keeping items inside the Horadric Cube!

Since your Inventory fills up quickly, it's nice to have another storage place for your extra items—the Private Stash. This is a permanent storage chest that appears in each of the towns and allows you to store some extra goodies. The downside to the Private Stash is that the space is also limited, but at least it's protected from others, even if you die! It's a good idea to sell or trade what you don't need and keep the really cool items (like pieces of a Set you're collecting) in your Private Stash for later use.

 WARNING

When you die in Hardcore Mode, you lose everything—character, inventory, and your stash!

HORADRIC CUBE RECIPES

Since the release of the original *Diablo II*, the Horadric Cube has been a source of much conjecture over what could or could not be created by using its Transmuting abilities. Fortunately, the Horadric Cube is even more important in the expansion set with the addition of Crafted Items. These items are created inside the Horadric Cube with the aid of Transmuting. Below are also several Cube Recipes. For Crafted Items Recipe Tables, see the *Appendix* in the back of this guide.

The Horadric Cube is now more valuable (and versatile) than ever.

NOTE

In the first patch of the game, Blizzard has changed the recipe that generated a new Rare item and added two new recipes dealing with Rares:

CHANGED: 6 Perfect Skulls + 1 rare item ➡ 1 randomly selected low-quality rare item of the same type

NEW: 1 Perfect Skull + 1 rare item + 1 Stone of Jordan ➡ 1 randomly selected high-quality rare item of the same type.

NEW: 3 Perfect Skulls + 1 rare item + 1 Stone of Jordan ➡ adds 1 socket to the rare item.

HORADRIC CUBE RECIPES

- Staff of Kings + Viper Amulet ➡ Horadric Staff
- Khalim Flail + Khalim Heart + Khalim Eye + Khalim Brain ➡ Super Khalim Flail
- 1 Wirt's Leg + 1 Town Portal Book ➡ Portal to Cow Level
- 3 Health Potions + 3 Mana Potions + 1 Gem ➡ Full Rejuvenation Potion
- 3 Health Potions + 3 Mana Potions ➡ Rejuvenation Potion
- 3 Small Rejuvenation Potions ➡ Full Rejuvenation Potion
- 1 Perfect Gem of Each Type + 1 Amulet ➡ Prismatic Amulet
- 1 Ring + 1 Ruby + 1 Exploding Potion ➡ Garnet Ring
- 1 Ring + 1 Sapphire + 1 Thawing Potion ➡ Cobalt Ring
- 1 Ring + 2 Topaz ➡ Coral Ring
- 1 Ring + 1 Emerald + 1 Antidote Potion ➡ Viridian Ring
- 1 Axe + 1 Dagger ➡ Throwing Axe
- 1 Spear + 1 Arrow Quiver ➡ Javelins
- 3 Rings ➡ Amulet
- 3 Amulets ➡ Ring
- 3 Chipped Gems + 1 Sword ➡ Magic, Socketable Long Sword
- 1 Magic Small Shield + 1 Spiked Club + 2 Skulls ➡ Small Shield of Spikes
- 4 Health Potions + 1 Ruby + 1 Magic Sword ➡ Long Sword of the Leech
- 1 Diamond + 1 Kriss + 1 Staff + 1 Belt ➡ Savage Bardiche
- 1 Strangling Gas Potion + 1 Health Potion ➡ Antidote Potion
- 2 Arrows ➡ Bolts
- 2 Bolts ➡ Arrows
- 3 Gems of the same type and grade (lower than Perfect) = 1 Higher Grade Gem of the same type
- 3 Perfect Gems of any type + 1 Magic Item ➡ 1 New Magic Item of the same type
- 6 Perfect Skulls + 1 Rare Item ➡ 1 Low-quality New Rare Item of the same type
- Perfect Skull + 1 Rare Item + Stone of Jordan➡ 1 High-quality New Rare Item of the same type
- 3 Perfect Skulls + 1 Rare Item + Stone of Jordan➡ add 1 Socket to Rare

'MOUSING' OVER

If you ever want to know something about any item in the game, you need only move your mouse cursor over the item (or button) in question and a dialogue box will pop up that contains all the information about it. The exception to this rule are items that have yet to be identified. The descriptions for unidentified items appear in red and you won't be able to equip them until they have been identified by a Scroll of Identify (or by Deckard Cain once you earn this option).

WEAPONS & ARMOR

This is a no-brainer: If you have Armor in your Inventory that could be equipped (put on your body) to improve your defense rating, then by all means equip it! You never know when a few extra points of defense will mean the difference between a close call and a gruesome death, so always equip the best set of Weapons and Armor that you have in your Inventory. It's also a good idea to keep your Weapons and Armor in good repair; if the durability of an item falls to zero, that item becomes useless and cannot be wielded until it is repaired.

Armor with six Sockets—you could do a lot with that!

EXPANSION WEAPONS & ARMOR

Diablo II: Lord of Destruction features many new Weapons and Armor, especially in the area of magically enhanced items of this sort. This includes new Weapons specific to some of the Character Classes, as well as Elite and Crafted Weapons. Crafted weapons are created using the Horadric Cube (see table in this guide's *Appendix*). Elite (Hell mode) weapons are discussed in *Chapter 4: The Lists.*

One of the other key expansion set additions is the increased use of Sockets in both Armor and Weapons. Armor can now have sockets; in fact, as many as *six* sockets! Weapons that previously had just one or two sockets now may sometimes have one more. These extra sockets (and the addition of sockets for Armor) greatly increase the number of unique attributes you can add to your items. Factor in the addition of Jewels and Runes, and the possibilities are mind-boggling!

The following discusses the Weapons and Armor that have been added to the vast *Diablo II* arsenal with the addition of the expansion set.

Class Specific Items

Most of these new items are specific to certain Character Classes (like Claw-class weapons for the Assassin), so we have listed them as such.

ASSASSIN

Katar

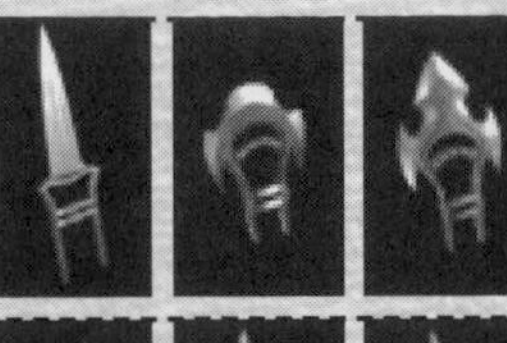

Claw

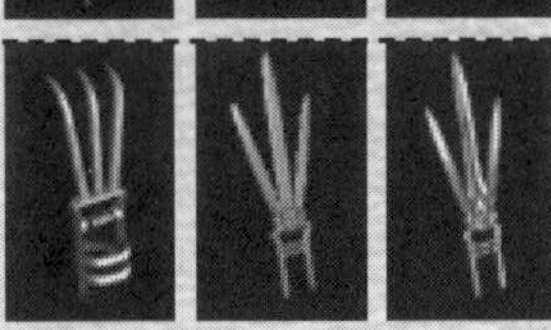

BARBARIAN

Primal Helms (such as Jawbone Visor)

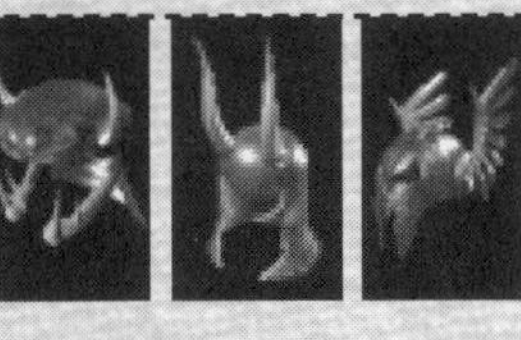

AMAZON

New Javelins and Spears

DRUID

Animal Helms (such as a Wolf Head or Ram's Head)

NECROMANCER

Totems (such as Shrunken Heads and Fetish Trophies)

SORCERESS

Orbs and Globes

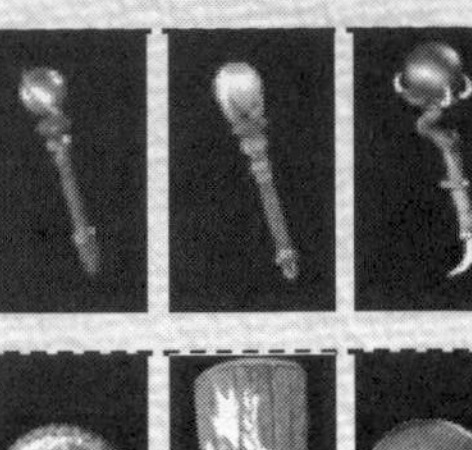

PALADIN

New Shields

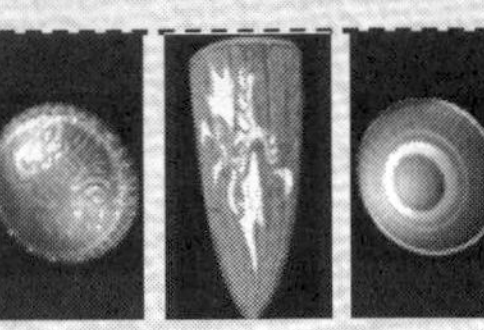

MAGICAL WEAPONS & ARMOR

Magical Weapons and Armor are handled the same way in the expansion set as they are in *Diablo II*, although there a great many additions (which are covered in this guide). Basically, a series of Prefixes and Suffixes (each with sets of attributes) determines what a Weapon or piece of Armor will ultimately become. For example, if you pick up a weapon that's the Cobalt Sword of The Titan, the Prefix is 'Cobalt' and the Suffix is 'of The Titan.' Both combine to give an added cold attack and increased strength. In this way, literally hundreds of thousands of unique Magical Weapons and Armor can be created in any *Diablo II* Realm game. The expansion set has added greatly to the richness of this already spectacularly complex formula by adding even more modifiers. For a complete list of the Magic Prefixes and Suffixes, see the *Appendix* in the back of this guide.

THE BELT

The Belt is critical to your success because it enables you to store potions and/or scrolls for quick and easy access. You are automatically given four slots to hold items, but if you wear a larger Belt or Sash, you will have more space available. The number keys 1, 2, 3, and 4 activate the potion or scroll in the corresponding Belt slot. If you are using a larger belt with slots above, the potion or scroll that was above will automatically slide down into the location you just selected.

A larger Belt opens up more slots, making a greater number of potions and scrolls readily available.

Simply pressing one of the four number keys (1-4) quickly and automatically uses potions and scrolls without having to worry about moving your mouse to double-click on an item—it also frees up precious space in your Inventory. You can place Scrolls, Mana Potions, Health Potions, Antidote Potions, Rejuvenation Potions, and Stamina Potions on your Belt in any spot. Throwing Potions are the only exception to this rule; these cannot be placed in your Belt and must be equipped in your hand to use instead.

Scrolls

There are two kinds of standard Scrolls in the *Diablo II* Realm, Town Portal Scrolls and Identify Item Scrolls. Both varieties can be purchased individually or in books called Tomes. For the purposes of saving space in your Inventory, picking up a Tome is very wise—you can save 18 Inventory slots by filling a Tome with 20 scrolls. Here's a little more insight into each of the two scrolls:

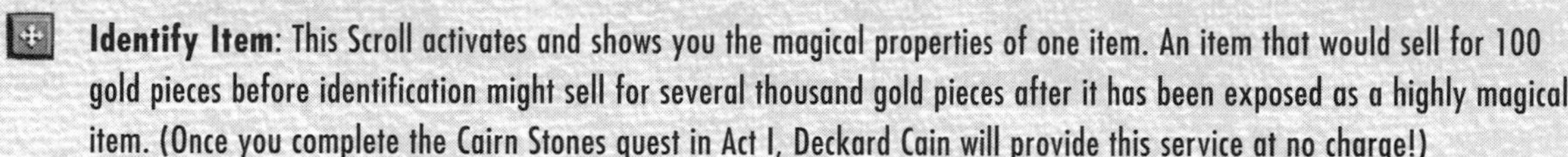

- **Identify Item**: This Scroll activates and shows you the magical properties of one item. An item that would sell for 100 gold pieces before identification might sell for several thousand gold pieces after it has been exposed as a highly magical item. (Once you complete the Cairn Stones quest in Act I, Deckard Cain will provide this service at no charge!)
- **Town Portal**: When activated, a Town Portal Scroll opens a doorway back to the town of the current Act. The importance of this Scroll cannot be understated; not only does it provide a quick and easy way to get back to town for dumping loot or selling items you've acquired during your conquests, but it also allows you to immediately escape dangerous situations. In *Chapter 3: The Quests*, we sometimes suggest that you open a Town Portal before you face a particularly tough enemy. Doing this in advance will save you the trouble of executing the command in the heat of action if your situation becomes desperate.

TIP

Oftentimes it's a good strategy for party members to open several Town Portals, one or two screens apart. This allows you to run and escape from difficult situations even if one of the Town Portals is surrounded by enemies.

Potions

Potions are literally the lifeblood of your character in *Diablo II*. The two most important potions are Healing potions and Mana potions, which as their names imply, replenish your Health and Mana respectively. There are, however, other potions in the game that are worth looking into, because you'll more than likely find the need to use them all from time to time. Here's a list of the potions and what they do:

- **Healing**: These potions replenish your Health, and come in five varieties—Minor, Light, Healing, Greater, and Super Healing. Each of these potions does more healing than its predecessor. The variety of Healing potion you can buy in the game is dependant on the Act your character is in.

WARNING

The effects of a Healing potion take time to improve your health, so don't wait too long to use one; it may not respond quickly enough to replenish your health in time to stave off an enemy's attack.

- **Mana**: Mana potions replenish the Mana energy that courses through each character's body. Even though Mana is regenerated by characters on their own, it's occasionally necessary to augment the natural Mana replenishment with this potion. These potions also come in five varieties of increasing strength—Minor, Light, Mana, Greater, and Super Mana. Remember, you cannot purchase Mana potions in town—you must find these in your journeys or rely on certain magical techniques for obtaining them.
- **Antidote**: This potion cures poison instantly. However, you may want to stock up on these potions if you're facing a great number of poison-spewing enemies—they only cure poison, they don't protect against it.
- **Rejuvenation**: This potion instantly refills about one-third of both your Mana and Health simultaneously!
- **Full Rejuvenation**: This potion instantly tops off both your Mana and Health. This can be a huge benefit at higher levels when you have lots of Mana and Health points and are taking large hits of damage at once.

TIP

If you need of Rejuvenation Potions, they can be created by placing three Mana potions and three Health potions in the Horadric Cube and Transmuting them.

- **Stamina**: Simply put, this potion restores your stamina instantly. It is essential when you must engage in excessive running.
- **Thawing**: There's nothing worse than getting frozen in a tough battle. If this happens, you can use a Thawing potion to instantly take the deep-freeze off your character and return to battle!
- **Oil**: This potion must be thrown and causes an explosion and resulting fire that damages enemies heavily.
- **Exploding Potion**: This throwing potion causes an explosion that does damage within a small radius. It's most effective when thrown into a tight group of enemies.
- **Rancid Gas Potion**: This throwing potion causes poison damage on any enemy near it when it detonates.
- **Choking Gas Potion**: This is a more damaging version of the Rancid Gas Potion.
- **Strangling Gas Potion**: This is the 'big-daddy' of the Gas Potions, and deals a large area of poison damage that lasts a considerable amount of time.

ETHEREAL ITEMS

Any type of armor or weapon, even one with magical properties, can be Ethereal. These expansion set items appear translucent in the Inventory, and when equipped, they appear translucent on the character wielding them. Their ethereal nature gives them an improved fundamental ability. However, they have decreased durability and cannot be repaired (although they do not lose durability on Hirelings). You can place Zod Runes (Indestructible) in some Ethereal Items to prevent them from being destroyed. Magic, Rare, and Unique Items can be Ethereal, but you cannot get Ethereal Items when Imbuing.

RUNES

Runes are a great new addition to the expansion set. These scripted tablets can be inserted into Socketed items to give them special powers (much like Gems or Jewels). The fascinating thing about Runes is that if they are placed in a specific order into an item, they produce extra benefits! Check out the *Appendix* of this guide for a complete list of Runes, as well as the Rune Word combinations and their abilities.

NOTE

Runes must be inserted in the correct order to make Rune combinations work.

CHARMS

Also new to the expansion set, Charms are magical items that (once identified) you need only carry in your Inventory to enjoy their benefits. These are covered in detail in *Chapter 4: The Lists.*

Charms are great, but you can quickly fill up your Inventory with them.

SHRINES

Throughout the *Diablo II* Realm, you will find Shrines and Wells to aid you. They are randomly placed, so if you come across a Resist Fire Shrine, don't automatically assume that you'll be facing monsters that attack with fire! Here's a breakdown of the Shrines you'll encounter along with their recharge status (whether they'll reset and recharge after they've been used once):

REFILL SHRINE (RECHARGES)

Refills both your Mana and Health.

HEALTH SHRINE (RECHARGES)

Refills your Health only.

ARMOR SHRINE (RECHARGES)

Boosts your Armor by 100%.

COMBAT SHRINE (RECHARGES)

Increases both your likelihood to hit and maximum damage by 200%.

RESIST FIRE SHRINE (RECHARGES)

Increases your resistance to fire by 75%.

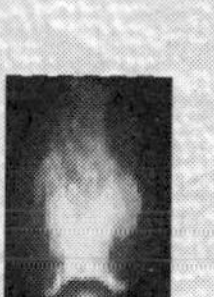

MANA SHRINE (RECHARGES)

Completely restores your Mana.

MANA RECHARGE SHRINE (RECHARGES)

Increases the rate at which your Mana refills by 50%.

RESIST COLD SHRINE (RECHARGES)

Provides 75% more resistance to cold.

RESIST POISON SHRINE (RECHARGES)

Provides 75% greater resistance to poison.

RESIST LIGHTNING SHRINE (RECHARGES)

Provides 75% more resistance to lightning.

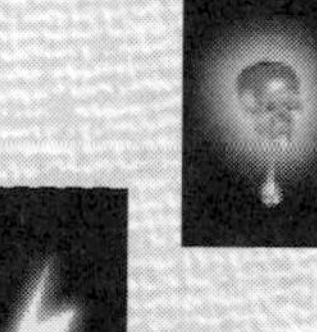

SKILL SHRINE (RECHARGES)

A very powerful Shrine, this one provides +2 to all skills you have already developed.

RECHARGE SHRINE (RECHARGES)

Recharges your Mana at a rate that's 400% faster than normal.

STAMINA SHRINE (RECHARGES)

Provides unlimited Stamina while active.

EXPERIENCE SHRINE (DOES NOT RECHARGE)

Gives 50% more experience per kill. This is a critical Shrine. If you find one, activate it and then go pick a few fights to get your Experience up quickly.

MONSTER SHRINE (DOES NOT RECHARGE)

When you touch this Shrine, the nearest enemy becomes a Unique monster!

POISON SHRINE (DOES NOT RECHARGE)

This Shrine is a double-edged sword—it will poison you when you touch it, but it will also give up 5-10 Gas potions.

FIRE SHRINE (DOES NOT RECHARGE)

Numerous firebolts erupt in a ring of death and damage anything nearby—including monsters, you, and your allies.

EXPLODING SHRINE (DOES NOT RECHARGE)

Like the Poison Shrine, this one also causes explosions when touched, but will also release several Exploding Potions.

GEM SHRINE (DOES NOT RECHARGE)

Upgrades one Gem from the player's Inventory and drops it on the ground. If there is no Gem to upgrade, it gives a random chipped Gem.

EVIL URNS

Although not Shrines per se, Evil Urns are similar devices in Act V that can potentially give you something worthwhile, but more often than not they'll spew forth a Unique Monster! Use them at your own risk.

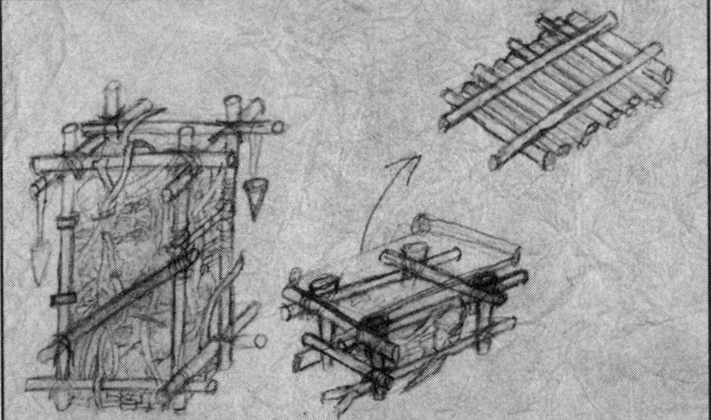

HARDCORE

Hardcore mode is for players who like to live on the edge. You have only one life in this mode, and if you die, you are completely dead; there's no resurrecting a Hardcore character. With this in mind, your Hardcore character should always have plenty of Health or, better yet, Rejuvenation potions handy, and you should stick to attacks that keep you out of harm's way. Also, avoid games with heavy lag or people you do not trust! Just to become a Hardcore character involves a great challenge because you must first complete *Diablo II or Diablo II: Lord of Destruction* on the Normal difficulty setting. Once you have accomplished this enormous task, you'll be given the option to create a Hardcore character.

Notice the checkbox for making your new character an elite Hardcore variety.

As an added bonus, you will also get a special title for your Hardcore character based on how many Acts of the Expanded game you've completed. For completing five Acts you get Conqueror as a prefix; for 10 Acts you get Destroyer, and for 15 Acts you get Guardian. Considering the challenges involved in finishing *Diablo II* or the expansion set on the Hell difficulty level, a title like Guardian will be well earned!

NOTE

Although death in Hardcore mode is permanent, you can allow another player to retrieve your items and gold by 'looting' your body. The main catch is that this player must be in the game when you die. You must also allow looting before you die! Keep in mind that being able to loot your body might be an incentive for someone to kill you, as well.

DIFFICULTY LEVELS

There are actually two difficulty levels above the Normal skill level (which this book was written on); they are Nightmare and Hell. As you might expect, there are some important things to know about these higher levels of play, so Eric Dodds, Carlos Guerrero, and Geoff Fraizer of Blizzard Entertainment have agreed to impart their vast knowledge of how to compete in these two upper difficulty levels of the game. Here's what they have to say…

- It's best to hang out in Act IV for a while, cleaning it out a few times before you move on to the next difficulty level—Expansion, Act V. This will help to make your character(s) more 'buff.'
- You get the most experience from monsters no more than five levels lower than your own level.
- Melee classes have trouble hitting monsters that are too much above their own level. Do not begin Nightmare level until your character has reached at least level 30; hold off on Hell until level 50. In general, if you find yourself having difficulty hitting monsters, go back to a previous difficulty level for a while.
- The monsters in Normal - Act V go up to level 42, so you should optimally leave Normal difficulty somewhere between levels 30 and 40.
- The monsters in Nightmare – Act V go up to level 70, so you should optimally leave Nightmare difficulty somewhere between levels 50 and 70.
- You can move on to the next Act earlier, but since the experience loss for death is higher in each successive difficulty level, you want to make sure you are ready to advance to the next difficulty level. Take your time and build your levels.
- You can hang out in a difficulty level longer than it would normally be valuable for you to do so by playing in games with several players, thus upping the experience reward for killing monsters. It should also be noted, however, that the monsters also become more difficult when there are more players in the game.
- In the higher difficulty levels you can find exceptional items (better versions of the items found in normal difficulty). These are the items you want to imbue or socket as quest rewards on higher difficulty levels.

Hell difficulty can be, well... Hell.

Chapter 2

THE CHARACTERS

CHARACTER DEVELOPMENT

One of the great things about the *Diablo II* games is the fact that there are 210 distinct skills (30 for each of the seven characters). How these skills are developed and used makes character skill development an important, if not critical, part of the *Diablo II* experience. The choices you make when selecting and enhancing skills can create dramatically different characters with only a few different selections. For example, a Necromancer that puts all of his skill points into Raise Skeletons, Skeleton Mages, and Skeleton Mastery will be very different (and therefore require different strategies) than a Necromancer who specializes in Curses & Poison and Bone Skills. The same rule applies to all character classes—a Druid that spends his points in Summoning will not use the same strategies as a Druid that focuses on Shape-Shifting or Elemental skills.

In the entire course of a single-player game you are likely to get in the neighborhood of about 35 skill points (plus about 4-7 more points in Act V) to distribute. This may sound like a lot, but when you consider that any one skill can take *all* of those skill points, you will obviously be able to make practical use of only a few skills in a single game. This means that the *Diablo II* realm is almost infinitely replayable, even as a single-player game. The permutation of skill combinations is huge, and as such we suggest that you choose the skills you think will benefit you most, then build them up and experiment with their use. This chapter contains detailed information about each of the skills for the seven character classes. In addition to mere descriptions of the skills, we've provided strategies for how to use and combine each one to your advantage.

Wherever relevant, we've also included information about the skills as they pertain to multiplayer or single-player action, or indeed, certain locations within the *Diablo II* Realm. You'll notice with the original five character classes that we also point out skills that changed between the original *Diablo II* and the release of the expansion set.

THE ORIGINAL FIVE DIABLO II CHARACTERS

The original *Diablo II* environment allowed you to embark on your quest using one of five character classes: Barbarian, Sorceress, Necromancer, Amazon, or Paladin. With *Diablo II: Lord of Destruction*, two new characters (the Druid and the Assassin) have been added to the mix. This section recaps the original five characters' skill trees and includes some of the subtle adjustments that have been made to the skills since our first *Diablo II Official Strategy Guide* was published.

As you might expect, each of the original character classes has its own strengths and weaknesses, but to further their innate abilities are the three skill sets that each character can improve upon. Each set of skills can be enhanced as the character matures and gains experience within *Diablo II* and the expansion set. Many expert players prefer to fully develop only one skill line, with the other skill lines partially developed or even ignored. This extreme customizability leaves the door open for significant variation between character's abilities throughout the game.

What follows is a skill-by-skill breakdown for the original five *Diablo II* character classes.

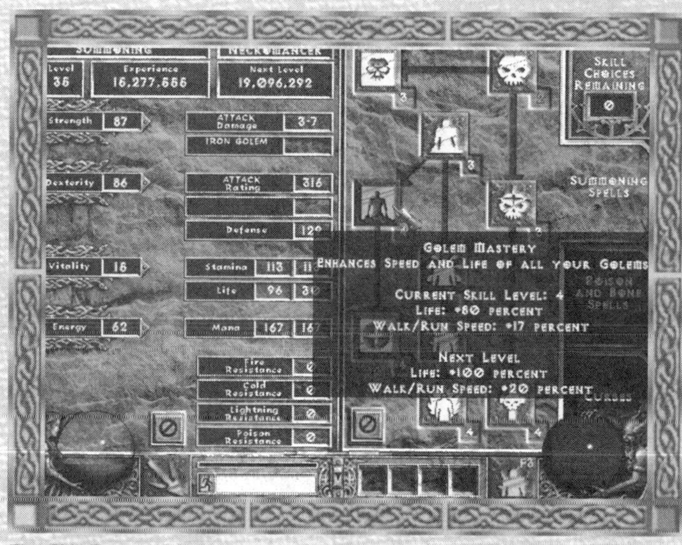

The Skill Tree screens show you at what level your skills are, as well as what the next skill level offers you.

ALTERED SKILL

Many skills have been altered within each Character Class for the expansion set. To make it easier to spot skills that have changed as you read this chapter, we have reversed-out the image of their icons. Refer to the ALTERED SKILL boxes to find out exactly what's new with each of these modified skills.

Icon for Unchanged Skill

Icon for Altered Skill

THE NECROMANCER

The Necromancer is a dark spell-caster whose incantations are geared toward the raising of the dead and the summoning and control of various creatures for his purposes. Although his goals are often aligned with those of the forces of light, some believe that these ends cannot justify his foul means. Long hours of study in dank mausoleums have made his skin pale and corpselike, while his figure has more in common with a skeleton than a man. Some shun him for his peculiar looks and ways, but none doubts the power of the Necromancer, which is the stuff of nightmares.

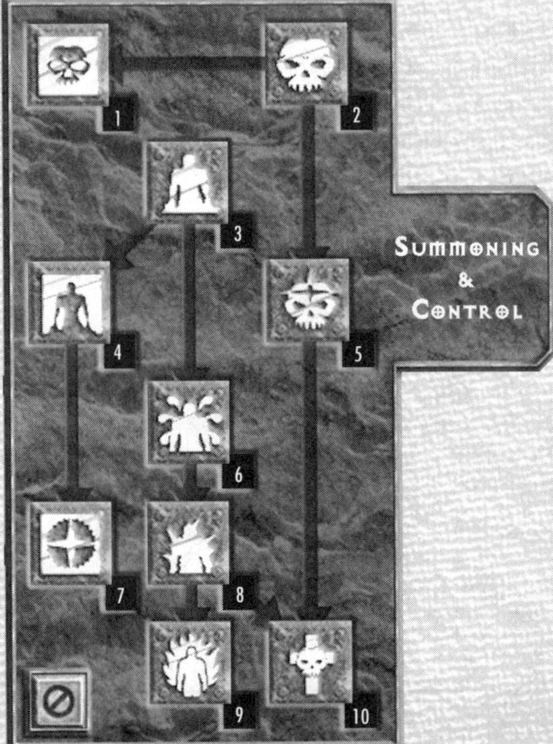

THE NECROMANCER SKILLS

There are three skill sets that the Necromancer can develop as he moves forward in the *Diablo II* Universe. As with the other characters, the skills you choose to develop substantially affect the Necromancer's abilities throughout the game. The three skill sets are Curses, Poison & Bone, and Summoning & Control. There is good reason to invest at least some skill points in each of the skill areas, but ultimately you'll have to make a decision as to which kinds of abilities you want your Necromancer to have. Should he have a powerful Golem, or should Skeletons do his bidding? Read on to find out the pros and cons of each skill.

SUMMONING & CONTROL

1. Skeleton Mastery
2. Raise Skeleton
3. Clay Golem
4. Golem Mastery
5. Raise Skeletal Mage
6. Blood Golem
7. Summon Resist
8. Iron Golem
9. Fire Golem
10. Revive

POISON & BONE

1. Teeth
2. Bone Armor
3. Poison Dagger
4. Corpse Explosion
5. Bone Wall
6. Poison Explosion
7. Bone Spear
8. Bone Prison
9. Poison Nova
10. Bone Spirit

CURSES

1. Amplify Damage
2. Dim Vision
3. Weaken
4. Iron Maiden
5. Terror
6. Confuse
7. Life Tap
8. Attract
9. Decrepify
10. Lower Resist

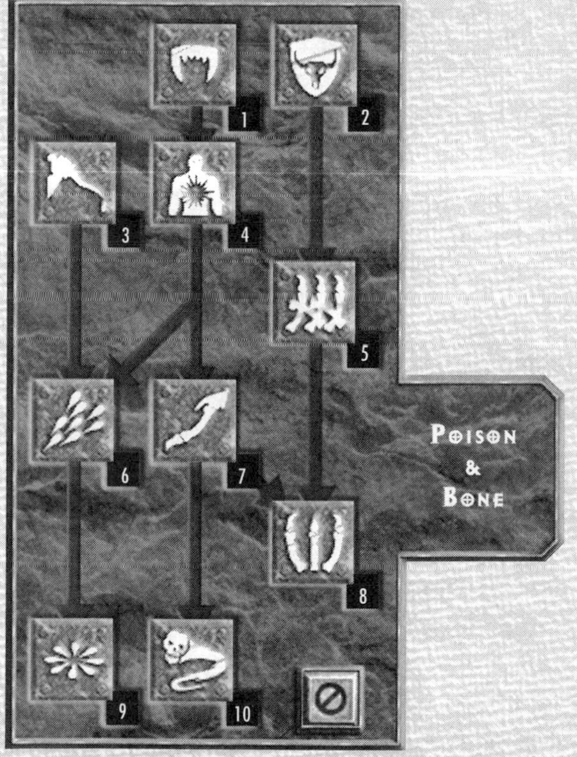

POISON AND BONE

The Poison and Bone skill set incorporates various magical attacks that are associated with, quite literally, poison and bone. These skills/spells serve a variety of purposes—including defense (Bone Armor), attack (Teeth), trap (Bone Prison), and Corpse Explosion, which is a powerful skill that does damage to nearby enemies according to how many hit points the corpse had (before its death).

Teeth

Level: 1	Prerequisites: None

This fires multiple magic teeth from another realm. As you add points to this skill, Teeth increases the number of 'teeth' that are released and the amount of damage that each tooth does. The advantage of Teeth is that it inflicts 'blow through' damage—it goes through the first target and will then hit another target (or targets) behind the first. For these reasons, Teeth is best used against rooms full of enemies, especially at higher skill levels where the amount of damage it inflicts is substantial.

Teeth is a magical missile-type skill that is useful early on for the Necromancer.

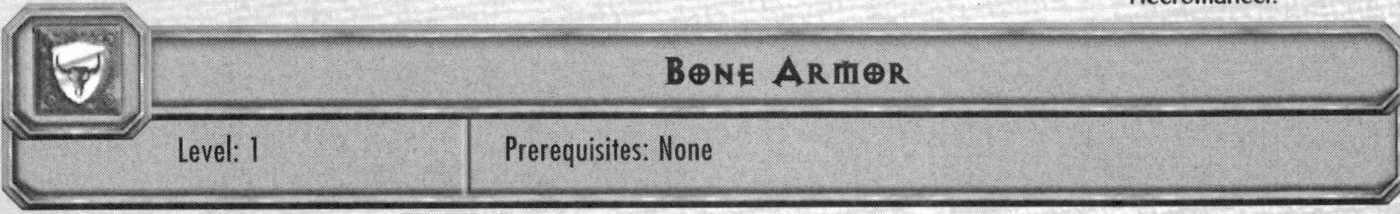

Bone Armor

Level: 1	Prerequisites: None

Invoking this skill creates a protective shield of rotating bone that absorbs the damage enemies inflict on your character. As you put skill points into Bone Armor, you begin to see significant gains in the amount of damage this skill can absorb, making it a valuable tool when fighting with groups of enemies. Bone Armor is especially important if you choose not to use a lot of summoning to aid in your quest through *Diablo II*.

TIP

If you're going to be using Bone Armor for melee combat, assign a hot-key to it so you can recast it frequently. This skill effectively absorbs the enemy's attack damage, but it won't last long against the toughest monsters or large groups of foes.

Poison Dagger

Level: 6	Prerequisites: None

With a weapon of the dagger class in hand, the use of this spell poisons the target you hit. The bonus of this is that you will not only do damage to the enemy with the dagger attack, but the poison continues to work and do damage for a certain number of seconds (depending on skill level). After you've put five or six skill points into Poison Dagger, it can become a 'fire and forget' type of weapon—you need only walk up to the enemy, hit them once with the Poison Dagger, then move away and let the Poison do its work. The more skill points you invest in Poison Dagger, the longer the poison lasts and, more importantly, the greater damage it does. The Mana cost for Poison Dagger is almost insignificant. So as long as you have a dagger handy (which is mandatory for this skill), you'll be able to inflict plenty of damage on your enemies after landing only one hit.

NOTE

Poison Dagger is only for hand-to-hand (melee) combat, and does not have an effect with a dagger that is thrown.

Corpse Explosion

Level: 6	Prerequisites: Teeth

This skill gives you the ability to turn an enemy corpse into a bomb! Once an enemy is dead, you need only target the spell and the enemy's body violently explodes, damaging (or killing) all nearby enemies. As you put skill points into Corpse Explosion, the radius of the explosion increases, thus making it an excellent area of effect weapon. An exploding corpse does damage equal to between 60-100% of its hit points (before it died), making this skill one of the most powerful in the Necromancer's arsenal!

Corpse Explosion is one the most important skills for the Necromancer because it does damage that's linked to the hit points of the corpse it explodes.

Corpse Explosion is often used when the Necromancer comes up against a large group of enemies. The Necromancer may kill just one of the enemies, and then invoke the Corpse Explosion either killing or heavily damaging any nearby enemies. It's so powerful that Blizzard QA has deemed this Necromancer skill a 'must.'

TIP

Multiplayer Tip: Corpse Explosion is particularly effective in large multiplayer games, because the enemies become more powerful when there are more players in a game. Since Corpse Explosion does damage according to the hit points of the monster corpse it's used on, it becomes considerably more powerful in these situations.

Bone Wall

Level: 12	Prerequisites: Bone Armor

This skill creates a barrier of bone that shoots up as a length of wall. The 'bone wall' that's created by this skill prevents any enemies from passing through it, although the walls only last for just over 45 seconds and the number of hit points they have is limited by the amount of skill points that you have put into the skill. For example, a level 1 Bone Wall has under 20 hit points, so an enemy from Act III isn't going to take more than a few seconds to break through the wall and come after you! Because Bone Wall doesn't actively harm the enemy, it has limited use, so you shouldn't put too many of your valuable skill points into it.

Bone Wall can give you a chance to get away from a persistent enemy by creating a physical barrier.

TIP

Bone Wall is best used as a temporary measure to buy time if you have a large group of enemies following you. For example, if you enter a room full of monsters and your health is low, you may want to back out and throw up several Bone Walls to slow the enemy down while you retreat.

Poison Explosion

Level: 18 | Prerequisites: Poison Dagger, Corpse Explosion

This skill is basically a Corpse Explosion that also does poison damage. It's a very powerful spell and does a whopping amount of damage to nearby enemies. The bonus of Poison is that it continues to do damage over time—not only when it first hits, but as long as the enemy remains poisoned, as well. There's a reason why this skill is not accessible until your character is at level 18, and it's because Poison Explosion is a 'must have' skill that will go a long way to helping you complete the game.

Like Corpse Explosion, Poison Explosion is best used against tightly grouped packs of enemies. When the corpse explodes, it deals heaps of poison damage to every nearby enemy with every passing second. Poison Explosion is also highly effective when used on a Corpse that's in a small room or narrow corridor; in short, it's similar to hurling a strangling or choking gas potion into a confined area.

Bone Spear

Level: 18 | Prerequisites: Corpse Explosion

Bone Spear summons a bone missile of magic that flies forth from the Necromancer's hands and inflicts a solid amount of damage on the enemy it hits. The real advantage to Bone Spear is that it will pass through the enemy at which it is aimed, and then proceed to damage any enemy that it strikes behind your target. This makes Bone Spear very handy for both one-on-one ranged fights, as well as attacking a group of enemies.

TIP

Bone Spear is a great weapon to use in an underground passage or any area where you're fighting many enemies in a narrow corridor. When in such a situation, your Bone Spear will blow through the targeted enemy and continue on, damaging all enemies behind it!

Bone Prison

Level: 24 | Prerequisites: Bone Wall, Bone Spear

When invoked, this unique skill raises a ring of bone around the target. This ring is designed to prevent the target from getting at you (or moving anywhere for that matter), but it will also prevent *you* from getting to the enemy, which can make it difficult to take them out. The Bone Prison is best used to trap an enemy just long enough for you to escape (if running is your choice). Basically, Bone Prison is not unlike Bone Wall except that it forms a circle around the enemy rather than forming a wall.

Poison Nova

Level: 30 | Prerequisites: Poison Explosion

This skill sends a ring of poison that explodes outward 360 degrees from the Necromancer. It's a very powerful spell that poisons all nearby enemies when invoked. As skill points are added to it, the Poison Nova inflicts a considerable amount of damage per second to any enemy in its wake. Poison Nova is another skill that deserves serious consideration for any Necromancer because it enables you to begin inflicting any nearby enemies with poison damage at any time. Unfortunately, the Poison Nova has a fairly high Mana cost so you can't really use it as a staple skill, but it comes in handy whenever you need to attack several enemies at once. It can also be used to replace Poison Explosion if necessary, and it doesn't require a corpse for you to use it!

Poison Nova is a skill that can single-handedly take out large groups of enemies. The power of poison should not be overlooked.

Bone Spirit

Level: 30 | Prerequisites: Bone Spear

Bone Spirit releases a spirit (in the form of a shimmering ball) that tracks the target (or finds one), hunts it down, and hits it. It is essentially a high-power seeking missile that will inflict massive damage to any enemy. This skill isn't available until you have reached the lofty heights of Level 30, and although it's tempting to pour points into it, the fact that it can only be used against a single enemy makes it a very specialized skill that isn't particularly effective against groups of enemies. It does increase dramatically in damage at a fast pace, however, and outstrips Bone Spear in damage potential with the investment of a few skill points. Ultimately, it's probably better to pour your skill points into Bone Spear if you're going to be fighting large groups of monsters without the help of friends or summoned creatures.

CURSES

The Curses are a set of skills that affect the enemy hoards in various ways. As a rule, Curses are used in conjunction with other attacks, such as skeletons or golems. In multiplayer games, Curses work to the benefit of the entire party, not just the Necromancer using them. For example, an Amplify Damage curse invoked on a group of tough monsters will literally make it twice as easy for your group to take out those enemies.

Amplify Damage

Level: 1	Prerequisites: None

Amplify Damage is a valuable skill because it increases the amount of non-magical damage the cursed unit receives. No matter the level of Amplify Damage, it always increases the damage taken by 100%. This means that every hit you or one of your minions lands on a cursed unit does the damage of two hits! As skill points are added to Amplify Damage, the duration and the effect radius increase substantially.

Amplify Damage is a very important skill. Even at level 1, it can make a huge difference in **Diablo II**.

Assign a hot-key to Amplify Damage so you can switch to it at a moment's notice. When you employ this skill on a group of enemies within its radius, they are all cursed, taking twice the damage they normally would from each hit your Necromancer or his skeletons/golems land. Because the Mana cost for this skill is small, it's an absolute must-have for all Necromancers.

Dim Vision

Level: 6	Prerequisites: None

Dim vision reduces the sight radius of the targeted enemy down to one yard. This literally means that they can barely see past their own noses. If you have the ability to launch a ranged attack (with Teeth or with Skeleton Mages), you can sit back and take the cursed enemies out without them ever seeing you! Dim Vision is also often used to blind enemies that rely on ranged attacks (such as Dark Archers) so that they cannot fire their weapons at you or your party.

NOTE

If you must escape, Dim Vision can also provide the cloak of cover you need to get past a particularly difficult enemy, whether you're underpowered or simply too injured to continue the fight. Casting Dim Vision on a tough enemy blankets them in darkness and gives you a chance to get away before the curse wears off.

Weaken

Level: 6 | Prerequisites: Amplify Damage

Weaken reduces the amount of damage the cursed unit can do to you or your minions. When it is used on an enemy (or group of enemies), it reduces the enemy's attack by one third. This skill is best used in a defensive situation where you are surrounded by a great number of enemies and are taking hits from multiple sides. By using Weaken in this crisis, you can reduce the damage you take while you hack through the enemy group.

Iron Maiden

Level: 12 | Prerequisites: Amplify Damage

This skill forces the cursed monster to take the damage that it inflicts through its attacks on others. Although Iron Maiden has a fixed radius (4.6 yards) that doesn't change with the addition of skill points, it can still affect multiple enemies with one use if those enemies are nearby your Necromancer. Iron Maiden is a great skill for quickly shortening the life of the enemies it affects because each and every time they land a hit on you, a party member, or your minions, they take that much damage back on themselves! In this regard, it truly will hurt them more than it hurts you when they land a blow!

Terror

Level: 12 | Prerequisites: Weaken

Terror makes the cursed monsters run away in fear. Although the radius of this skill never changes with the addition of skill points, the duration of the curse extends by one second for each skill point. More than likely, a skill like Terror is not something you'll be using frequently, but when you're in a tight spot and need to force a group of enemies away quickly, this curse will do the job.

NOTE

Terror does not work on Unique monsters or Bosses, so don't waste any time attempting to get a powerful monster to run away from you—use your Mana for offensive skills instead.

Confuse

Level: 18 | Prerequisites: Dim Vision

Confuse affects the enemy by essentially driving them insane and causing them to attack nearby monsters (or you and your team members) randomly. It's important to remember that these attacks are random, and can mean that an enemy that wasn't attacking you before it was cursed may now turn its anger toward your character (in multiplayer). Still, this is a highly effective curse when used in a group of enemies because it will cause them to drop whatever they were doing (most likely chasing you), and attack each other. The chaos that ensues greatly reduces their collective hit points—they may even kill each other.

Confuse makes monsters attack nearby creatures at random, but that includes you (if you're nearby)!

Life Tap

Level: 18	Prerequisites: Iron Maiden

This curse is an effective way to replenish your Life. When you curse an enemy with Life Tap, they give up the Life they lose to *you* with every hit you land on them! The amount of Life that you'll steal back from the enemy is always 50% of the attack that you land, so the harder you hit, the more Life points drain to your character. Obviously, this is a skill that can change your fortunes quickly if you're running low on Life, but it can also be of great benefit to your fellow party members (in multiplayer) who can also heal from this curse.

NOTE

When one of your minions (skeletons or golems) hits the enemy, they don't return 50% of the enemy's health to you, but they do take that health for themselves, thus giving you a way to heal your minions.

Attract

Level: 24	Prerequisites: Confuse

This skill is a highly effective tool for wearing down or eliminating one particularly tough monster. When Attract is used on an enemy, it becomes a target for other enemy forces, and is therefore attacked as aggressively as you would be. It should be noted, however, that Attract makes the target one of equal interest to the enemies; not greater interest. Therefore, when you use Attract on a particular enemy, the other enemies will attack whoever they are closer to—you (or your party), or the enemy that you've cursed. Still, if you can use this curse and then run away quickly, the enemies will go after the cursed creature and leave you alone.

Decrepify

Level: 24	Prerequisites: Terror

Decrepify is a curse that slows down the enemies it affects. This is one of the few skills in the game that slows enemies down without using cold or freezing to accomplish this end. As skill points are added to Decrepify, both the duration of action and the area of effect of this curse are improved. When used in multiplayer action, this skill is a powerful tool that slows down enemies long enough for your ranged-weapon party members (or Skeletal Mages) to get in a flurry of shots before the enemy can approach your position.

Aside from cold spells, Decrepify is the only skill that slows the enemies.

Lower Resist

Level: 30	Prerequisites: Life Tap, Decrepify

Many of the Necromancer's skills (as well as other character's skills) rely on magic to get the job done. At certain points in the game, however, you'll run into enemies that have a substantial resistance to magic, thus making some of your skills like Teeth and Bone missiles considerably less effective. When Lower Resist is used, the cursed enemies have a reduced resistance to magical attacks, making them easier to deal with. Likewise, other resistances (such as fire) are also lowered, making other skills and minions (such as Fire Golems) more effective. As you add skill points to Lower Resist you'll greatly improve the radius of effect, duration, and even the percentage that the resistance is lowered. Even in its lowest form, Lower Resist takes greater than 50% of the enemy's resistance away!

Summoning and Control

The Necromancer, as his name would imply, has the ability to raise the dead and employ them to do his bidding. The Necromancer's power extends not only over the dead, but also over the elements, which means that he is also capable of summoning Golems from the ground beneath his feet, calling up the fires of Hell, or even creating a Golem that steals Life for your cause.

NOTE

It should be noted that all Skeletons, Golems, and Raised Dead that the Necromancer summons (or controls) will contribute experience to the Necromancer who created them. In short, experience points for whatever the Necromancer's minions kill pour into the Necromancer's experience pool, which often makes leveling up easier in multiplayer games.

Skeleton Mastery

Level: 1	Prerequisites: Raise Skeleton

Skeleton Mastery is a very important skill if you have any intention of using Skeletons to help your Necromancer make it through the game. It's a very good idea to put at least a few points into Skeleton Mastery because it dramatically improves the effectiveness of the Skeletons fighting for you (including Skeleton Mages). With each point you invest in Skeleton Mastery, you increase your minion's hit points and the damage they inflict; however, in higher levels your Skeletons may have a hard time keeping up with the enemies they'll face.

TIP

It's okay to use Skeletons early in the game, but once you get into Act III, your Skeletons will begin to have a harder time defeating the enemies and you'll find yourself creating replacement Skeletons very frequently. In the testing department at Blizzard, the testers tend not to rely on Skeletons in higher levels, instead choosing to augment their Skeleton minions with a Golem.

Raise Skeleton

Level: 1 | Prerequisites: None

As the name implies, this skill raises a skeletal warrior that will fight to the death for your Necromancer. Using this skill, the Necromancer can create a small army of Skeletons that will follow him and fight any enemy that gets in their path. When combined with Skeleton Mastery, the Skeletons created using this skill can become very powerful, and indeed they can do the lion's share of the killing for the Necromancer in the first two Acts.

Because one more Skeleton can be raised with every new skill point you put into Raise Skeleton, the temptation is to put in as many points as you can so that you can create a large army of Skeletons to fight for your cause. The problems with this strategy are twofold. First, it's difficult to manage all those skeletons, especially in a tight environment such as an underground cavern. Many Skeletons get lost or won't be able to quickly follow the Necromancer through the narrow corridors. Secondly, as you progress through the game (into Act III and beyond), you'll find that the relatively weak Skeletons get destroyed quickly by the tougher enemies, and it becomes a challenge to find dead bodies with which to resurrect new Skeletons.

For the above reasons, it's usually best to put just a few points into Skeletons but even more into Skeleton Mastery. This tactic provides you with stronger Skeletons and still allows you to put points into the Curses and other Summoning skills, such as the Golems.

Clay Golem

Level: 6 | Prerequisites: None

This skill raises a Golem from the earth to fight for the Necromancer, but unlike the Raise Skeleton skill, you can raise only *one* Clay Golem at a time. One of the great advantages to Clay Golems is that they heal themselves automatically. After a bloody battle, you can sit back and wait while your Golem recovers or simply create another Golem. A level 1 Golem has an impressive 100 hit points, but a level 20 Clay Golem has over 750 hit points and can do over 35 points of damage with a single hit—and that's without any points in Golem Mastery! For this reason, it's better to move from your Skeletons to a Golem (along with Golem Mastery) as you move to higher levels.

Clay Golems are tough and can do more than just inflict damage to enemies; they can also act as decoys at higher levels.

NOTE

The important thing to remember about Golems over Skeletons is that they do not require an enemy corpse in order for the Necromancer to raise them. In certain situations this can be important because there are not always dead enemies nearby for the Necromancer to raise, making a Golem (which can be created out of thin air) very handy indeed.

Golem Mastery

Level: 12 | Prerequisites: Clay Golem

Boiled down, Golem Mastery can best be described as a skill that increases the health and speed of Golems. Indeed, if you're going to be using Golems to help you as you wind your way through *Diablo II*, it will certainly pay to have put some skill points into this area. Some Blizzard employees are fond of putting all of their skill points into Golems and Golem Mastery, thus creating a sort of super-sidekick that can fight with the toughest of enemies. By the time you have put five points into Golem Mastery, you've doubled your golem's hit points, so it's well worth the investment.

Raise Skeletal Mage

Level: 12 | Prerequisites: Raise Skeleton

This skill is similar to Raise Skeleton, except that (as the name implies) it raises a Skeleton Mage to fight for your Necromancer. A Skeleton Mage is a skeleton with a ranged attack (shoots over a distance) and can be one of four classes: Fire, Cold, Poison, or Lightning. Each of these has advantages and disadvantages, but unfortunately you can't choose which kind of Skeleton Mage will appear when you raise it. If you have only one Skeleton Mage, however, you can keep raising one after another until you get the kind you want; the only cost of doing this is Mana, along with enemy bodies from which to raise these Mages.

Skeletal Mages give the Necromancer a minion that can use ranged attacks. In combination with Skeletons, Skeletal Mages provide a great one-two punch.

A Skeleton Mage with poison does poison damage to the enemy, whereas each of the other three classes does damage according to their class. For example, a cold Skeleton Mage shoots blasts of cold at the enemies, and each blast of cold has a chance of freezing the enemy, or even breaking the enemy into chunks of ice! Skeleton Mages are great to have in conjunction with regular Skeletons because they add the ability to attack from afar, rounding out your Necromancer's party.

 TIP

A common tactic at Blizzard QA is to put skill points into Skeletons, Skeleton Mages, and Skeleton Mastery so that you can have several Skeletons for melee combat and a pair of Skeleton Mages to stand back and fire from afar. This combination works very well, especially when enough points have been put into Skeleton Mastery, which improves the abilities of **both** the Skeleton Mages and the Skeletons.

Blood Golem

Level: 18	Prerequisites: Clay Golem

Blood Golem raises a golem that's connected to you in health. This means that when the Blood Golem hits an enemy, he'll steal Life from the enemy and it will be reflected in *your* health globe (your health will go up). The Blood Golem may sound like it presents a win-win situation that steals health with its attacks, but there's a downside as well. When the Blood Golem takes a hit, you'll take a hit with it! The key is that the Blood Golem usually steals more health than he loses for you by taking hits. The exception to this occurs when the Blood Golem is surrounded by a large group of enemies and is taking hits fast and furiously while only dishing out a small amount of punishment. When this happens, you'll wish your Blood Golem was somewhere else. Fortunately, it can be if you simply re-create a new Blood Golem as you're running away from the action.

 NOTE

You can have only **one** golem active at a time, meaning you can't have an Iron Golem and a Blood Golem working in tandem. For this reason, it's best not to split your skill points between two kinds of golems. Choose which type you want to use and stick with it; put points into other golems only if it means opening up your skill tree.

Summon Resist

Level: 24	Prerequisites: Golem Mastery

Summon Resist is a unique skill that increases the elemental resistance for all of your summoned creatures. This means that any Golems, Raised Dead, or Skeletons that you have in your party benefit from increased resistance to fire, cold, lightning, and poison attacks. If you are going to progress through the game while using summoned creatures, then it's well worth putting at least one point toward Summon Resist—even at level 1, it dramatically increases your resistance to any elemental attacks. As you progress into Acts III and IV, having some resistance to elemental magic attacks is a great asset to your summoned creatures.

Iron Golem

Level: 24	Prerequisites: Blood Golem

This skill raises a golem from a metal item that you throw onto the ground (or that's already lying on the ground). The cool part about Iron Golem is that it takes on the properties of whatever item you create it from! Therefore, if you create an Iron Golem out of a set of chain mail armor, you'll end up with a golem that has a very high amount of hit points and defense rating. On the other hand, if you create an Iron Golem out of a sword that has ice damage on top of its normal damage, then the Iron Golem also has those attack properties. This is an incredibly creative way to create special golems with unique skills, and it gives you a great motivation to hang on to unique weapons and armor that might otherwise not hold your interest.

 TIP

If you find a great weapon early in the game that you can't use (or don't want to use), it may be worth putting it in your personal Stash so that you can use it later to create a powerful Iron Golem!

Fire Golem

Level: 30 | Prerequisites: Iron Golem

This skill creates a golem of fire that draws strength from fire attacks. This kind of golem becomes more valuable later in the game when you must deal with more fire-related attacks (as you get closer to Diablo). With Fire Golems, the more skill points you put into them, the more damage they absorb from fire attacks. It should also be noted, however, that they become more expensive with every skill point you invest.

Fire Golems are excellent against enemies that use fire against you (like those you'll find in Hell).

Revive

Level: 30 | Prerequisites: Raise Skeletal Mage, Iron Golem

This skill literally resurrects a dead monster to fight for your Necromancer. These resurrected enemies are not like Skeletons or Golems, however, and they won't follow you as religiously as the other creatures you summon. Revived creatures will fight for you, but they are only a shadow of what they were before they died, meaning that at lower skill levels they have only about 10% of the original number of hit points they had when they were living. However, if you put enough skill points into Revive, you can create revived monsters that are actually *more* powerful than their living counterparts (level 10 and up). Revived monsters last for only 180 seconds (three minutes) after you create them, so unlike other summoned creatures they cannot serve you indefinitely.

There are two other important aspects of Revive to remember. First, Skeleton Mastery points go toward improving revived monsters. Secondly, although you can resurrect tough enemies, you cannot bring Bosses back to life to fight for your cause.

 NOTE

Remember that as you invest skill points into Revive, the Mana cost of reviving goes **down** (which is a good thing), and the hit points and number of monsters you can revive goes **up** (which is also good).

THE AMAZON

This powerful woman warrior belongs to nomadic bands of fighters that roam the area near the South Sea. The Amazon is accustomed to fighting to defend her own, and her lifestyle has made her fiercely independent and able to endure severe hardships in her quest for survival. The Amazon is highly skilled in bowmanship, but is also adept in the use of spears and various throwing weapons. Despite the Amazon's skills at ranged fighting, she is still very dangerous in hand-to-hand combat, and can fend for herself impressively.

THE AMAZON SKILLS

There are three skill sets that the Amazon can develop as she climbs in experience the *Diablo II* universe. Which skills are developed ultimately affect her abilities as the quest toward victory progresses. The three skill sets are Bow & Crossbow, Passive & Magic, and Javelin & Spear. The Amazon's large list of passive skills makes her a tempting character; this is because passive skills, once you put skill points into them, are always 'on'. By putting skill points into passive skills as well as active skills, you will get more mileage out of your skill points. However, there are advantages and disadvantages to every skill choice you make.

Javelin & Spear

1. Jab
2. Power Strike
3. Poison Javelin
4. Impale
5. Lightning Bolt
6. Charged Strike
7. Plague Javelin
8. Fend
9. Lightning Strike
10. Lightning Fury

Passive & Magic

1. Inner Sight
2. Critical Strike
3. Dodge
4. Slow Missiles
5. Avoid
6. Penetrate
7. Decoy
8. Evade
9. Valkyrie
10. Pierce

Bow & Crossbow

1. Magic Arrow
2. Fire Arrow
3. Cold Arrow
4. Multiple Shot
5. Exploding Arrow
6. Ice Arrow
7. Guided Arrow
8. Strafe
9. Immolation Arrow
10. Freezing Arrow

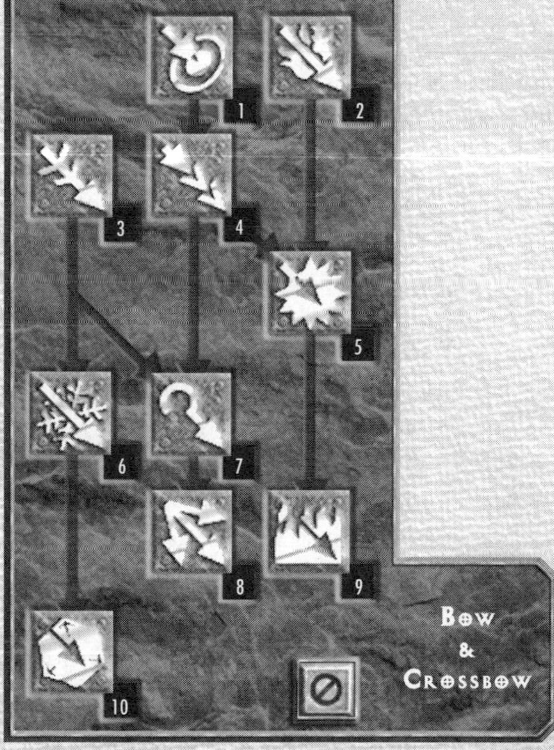

BOW & CROSSBOW

These are all ranged weapons, meaning they are fired from a distance and keep the Amazon away from the enemy. Seven of the skills in this skill group are specific weapons, such as the Cold Arrow, the Immolation Arrow, and the Magic Arrow. The other three skills—Strafe, Multiple Shot, and Guided Arrow—are modifiers of existing arrow weapons (either from a Crossbow or from a Bow). These don't offer up new distinct missile weapons, but rather they make your existing missile weapon better. For example, Multiple Shot sends out several (more when skill points are applied to it) arrows for every *one* arrow you fire. How you apply your points in the Bow and Crossbow category greatly affects how you fight through the game, so choose to suit your style.

Magic Arrow

Level: 1	Prerequisites: None

The Magic Arrow skill shoots an arrow created entirely from Mana, meaning you do not need to have any arrows in your quiver to fire. This is a very important skill, especially early in the game when you may find yourself running out of arrows, and will help you to extricate yourself from many sticky situations. It can be used as an emergency backup or used to save conventional arrows whenever you have an excess supply of Mana or Mana potions. This arrow's damage is the same as a normal arrow. As skill points are added to it, the damage it causes goes up while its Mana cost actually goes *down*. At level 12, the Magic Arrow's cost goes down to ZERO, making it an entirely free weapon.

Although Magic Arrows aren't guided, they never miss their target. Consequently, it is an excellent skill to have if your Dexterity rating is low.

NOTE

The Magic Arrow skill is best paired with Critical Strike. This is because the Magic Arrow never misses and Critical Strike will often double the damage of the hit. Use a high-powered Bow or Crossbow (which adds to the damage of the Magic Arrow) and you'll have a weapon that can take you through the entire game!

Fire Arrow

Level: 1	Prerequisites: None

When active, Fire Arrow modifies one of your arrows by adding fire to it (you'll need arrows or bolts to make this work). When it hits, the Fire Arrow causes both normal and fire damage, making it much more effective than using a plain arrow. As with all skills, the more skill points you put into Fire Arrow, the more effective it ultimately becomes—especially when combined with Critical Strike.

NOTE

The Fire Arrow can be used as a kind of "advanced scout" when fired into the darkness of a dungeon. Each Fire Arrow is its own light source, lighting up the area around it as it flies through the air. In this way, it can be a great way to get a peek at what's coming before it emerges from the darkness.

The Fire Arrow gives the Amazon a ranged attack that provides both normal and fire damage.

Cold Arrow

Level: 6	Prerequisites: None

When active, this skill produces an icy blue arrow that smacks its target with a blast of cold, slowing it down for a period of time (depending on the number of skill points invested). The more skill points, the greater the chance that it will actually freeze and shatter the enemy into bits of ice (which subsequently melt). The Cold Arrow is a powerful ranged weapon because it usually turns its target blue (makes them cold) when it hits, slowing the enemy down considerably. This is an important tool when you're trying to keep your distance from an enemy, so that you don't have to get into melee combat. One tactic that works well is to hit each enemy in a group with a Cold Arrow, causing them all to move slowly, then pick them off one at a time while they plod toward you. Like the Fire Arrow, the Cold Arrow is also its own light source, which means that you can use it to see into the dark when you're exploring dingy dungeons.

Multiple Shot

Level: 6	Prerequisites: Magic Arrow

Multiple Shot magically splits one arrow into multiple arrows at a Mana cost to your character. As you put more skill points into this skill, you'll produce more arrows with every shot. The arrows eventually form a 120-degree arc that fans out from your position when you fire. As you might expect, this can be a highly effective weapon when used against groups of enemies, especially those in wide open spaces. When you combine Multiple Shot with Critical Strike, a high level of Dexterity, and a magical bow/crossbow of some sort, this skill can become your bread and butter for dealing with the enemy hoards you will frequently face.

ALTERED SKILL

Multiple Shot has been changed in the expansion set so that it always does 75% of the total damage, instead of full damage. It also can hit each target only once. In other words, if there are five targets, it may hit them all, but each one only once.

Ice Arrow

Level: 18	Prerequisites: Cold Arrow

The Ice Arrow differs from the Cold Arrow in a specific way—rather than slowing the enemy with cold, it completely freezes the opponent for a time. Indeed, Ice Arrow causes some cold damage while stopping the target in its tracks. The duration of the freeze depends on the number of skill points you've poured into this skill. Once an opponent is frozen, the likelihood that they'll get smashed into chunks of ice on the next hit is reasonably good. For this reason two hits with Ice Arrow often send even the strongest enemies tumbling to the ground as melting hunks of ice. The Ice Arrow can be used in conjunction with the Valkyrie skill, allowing you to stand back and freeze opponents while the Valkyrie hacks them to pieces.

Ice Arrow will freeze enemies in their place—sometimes it will even smash them to bits!

TIP

The Ice Arrow can be a very effective weapon when fighting enemies that can be respawned after they die. This is because an enemy that is turned to ice and then smashed **cannot** be resurrected from death, making your job of clearing out monsters considerably easier.

Guided Arrow

Level: 18	Prerequisites: Cold Arrow, Multiple Shot

The Guided Arrow is the ultimate tracking arrow because it can literally make 90-degree turns to find its target. In fact, you don't even need to specify a target with the guided arrow; once you fire it, it makes the necessary turns and adjustments to hit the nearest enemy (assuming that there is an enemy nearby). A great way to use this skill is to hide in a corner of a room or at an intersection of a dungeon where the arrow can fly in multiple directions, then fire randomly. The Guided Arrows will fly toward the enemies and hit them even if they are in other rooms. Guided Arrow is best used when getting close to the enemy is something you absolutely don't want to do!

Exploding Arrow

Level: 12	Prerequisites: Fire Arrow, Multiple Shot

This arrow explodes, causing fire damage around the area of impact. It does damage to enemies near the foe you've targeted, making it a great weapon for dealing with crowds of bad guys. The higher the skill level, the more damage the arrow inflicts. As you might also expect, it lights up the area it explodes in, thus making it yet another way to cast some light down a dark corridor or light up a darkened room.

TIP

When firing an Exploding Arrow into a group of enemies, always aim at the enemy in the center of the group.

Strafe

Level: 24	Prerequisites: Guided Arrow

Strafe is a unique skill that fires a missile at each of the targets near your location. As you pour skill points into Strafe, the number of enemies that will be hit by a single shot increases. It's not uncommon to level Strafe up to eight missiles—if eight enemies were onscreen, each of them would take a hit by activating this skill. As with Multiple Shot, this is an important skill for fighting against several enemies, but it's particularly effective when you're fighting in large open areas where foes are approaching you from all sides. Most importantly, this skill works with any missile class weapon, including arrows, bolts, spears, and javelins!

ALTERED SKILL

Strafe has been altered significantly. It now starts at −40% damage at level 1 (instead of +10%), which substantially affects its power. That said, it's still a valuable skill, especially if you invest a few points into it.

Immolation Arrow

Level: 24	Prerequisites: Exploding Arrow

This arrow creates an area on the ground that ignites and burns for a set amount of time, depending on the level of the skill. Although Immolation Arrow causes an area of fire around the impact point, it also does fire damage when it hits its target. This is an excellent skill to use on groups of tightly packed enemies or through narrow doorways where the enemies try to file through and attack you. As you add skill points to Immolation Arrow, the explosion damage (initial hit damage), the fire damage, and the duration of the burning all increase dramatically with only a one-point-per-level increase in Mana cost. Immolation Arrow is a *must* for the Amazon, and best of all, the fire it creates will not hurt you or any members in your party (in single *or* multiplayer).

The Immolation Arrow is like an arrow with a fire bomb on its tip!

Freezing Arrow

Level: 30	Prerequisites: Ice Arrow

This skill launches an arrow with a cold damage area of effect that not only damages, but also often freezes the enemies it hits—even enemies that are nearby! The result is a very powerful skill that can literally turn the enemy into chunks of ice with a single hit. At the very least, it freezes the enemies and slows them so that subsequent hits can do enough damage to finish them off.

NOTE

Although Freezing Arrow becomes very expensive (Mana-wise) as you put skill points into it, its attack value and area of effect damage make it an absolutely invaluable tool later in the game when you meet up with multiple powerful and dangerous enemies. If you're going to follow the Bow and Crossbow skill tree, you should strive to put a few points into Freezing Arrow.

PASSIVE & MAGIC

The Passive & Magic skills are the most important of the three skill trees for the Amazon. The passive skills of Dodge, Avoid, and Evade are critical to your survival in higher levels. They give your character a chance to avoid being hit every time an enemy attacks, while the Valkyrie gives you a partner in battle that not only fights to the death, but also heals her own wounds over time. How you choose to use your skills in this skill tree greatly affects how you do battle and how effective your other skills are.

Inner Sight

Level: 1	Prerequisites: None

This skill places a small light source on all monsters within a radius, which appears as little 'sparkles' dancing above their heads. Because it illuminates the enemies to some degree, this skill allows the Amazon to see dangers in dark places, and can be very useful in dungeons and underground passages. Adding a small amount of light radius to an enemy is a handy feature, but the real benefit of Inner Sight is that it dramatically lowers the enemy's defense rating, making it considerably easier for you to damage them. Essentially, Inner Sight makes the enemy easier to see in dark places and decreases their armor class, which makes your life a heck of a lot easier.

TIP

Multiplayer Tip: It's great to have an Amazon in the group with a couple of skill points invested in Inner Sight because every member of the party benefits from the enemy's substantially reduced defense. In short, it's a great way to make a little Mana go a long, long way with your party.

Critical Strike

Level: 1	Prerequisites: None

Critical strike creates a chance that you will do double physical damage when you attack an enemy with either ranged or thrust attacks. As you add points to this skill, the chances that you'll do double damage go up. In fact, by the time Critical Strike is at level 10, you have a better than 50% chance of getting a double-damage hit (with every weapon you use). Critical Strike is a passive skill. You need never worry about activating it because it is always on. This allows you to concentrate on fighting, knowing that many of your hits carry substantially more weight.

NOTE

Because of its passive nature and its ability to double the damage of almost every hit you land (at higher levels), Critical Strike is one of the most important skills an Amazon can learn. Successful Amazons nearly always have some investment in this skill.

Dodge

Level: 6 | Prerequisites: None

This skill affects the chance that the Amazon moves out of the way of a hand-to-hand enemy attack. Dodge works only when the Amazon is not moving, but it may make the difference between life and death for your character when you're in a heavy duty fight. If an enemy swings at you and a hit is imminent, your Dodge skill kicks in and you'll still have a chance to step out of the way of that attack. The more points you put into Dodge, the harder it is for the enemy to hit you; if you put points into Dodge up to level 10, the enemy has less than a 50% chance of hitting you.

Dodge automatically gives the Amazon a greater chance of dodging out of the way when an enemy attacks in hand-to-hand combat.

NOTE

You'll know that you dodged an enemy attack when you see your Amazon jump aside as she makes a 'yip' sound.

Slow Missiles

Level: 12 | Prerequisites: Inner Sight

This is an active skill that, when used, slows nearby enemies' missiles by one third. This skill comes in very handy when you're facing groups of enemies that are firing projectile weapons because it gives you time to step out of the way of oncoming attacks. As you pour skill points into Slow Missiles, the length of time that the skill is active increases substantially—by level 9 you can get more than a minute's worth of effect. The Slow Missiles skill is best used when you're in open areas and multiple enemies are firing ranged weapons at you. In conjunction with Avoid, this skill makes it very difficult for enemies to damage you with ranged attacks.

Avoid

Level: 12 | Prerequisites: Dodge

Avoid is similar to Dodge, except that it works for ranged attacks. This means that if an enemy throws or shoots a ranged weapon at you, and it is going to hit you, Avoid increases your chances of stepping out of the way of the enemy attack. As you might expect, having points in both Avoid and Dodge (as well as Evade) will help to make the Amazon a very difficult target for your opponents to hit.

TIP

When you get into Acts III and IV and of **Diablo II** (and Act V of the expansion set) the enemy packs a much harder punch, making every chance you have to avoid one of their hits very important. For this reason, anyone using the Amazon should have at least one point in each of Dodge, Avoid, and Evade.

Penetrate

Level: 18	Prerequisites: Critical Strike

Penetrate gives your Amazon an increased Attack Rating with her ranged attacks. This skill is very powerful because your attacks (such as arrow or spear attacks) carry an increased Attack Rating between 40-325%, depending on how many skill points have been added to it. If you have chosen to follow the Javelin and Spear skill tree, then putting points into the passive Penetrate skill is critical. The development of this passive skill along with Critical Strike is an awesome combination. If you develop these two skills, then you'll not only have the chance of your ranged weapons doing double damage with Critical Strike, but you'll also be able to increase the Attack Rating *on top* of that with Penetrate.

TIP

Many Blizzard QA testers use a combination of Penetrate, Critical Strike, and Evade/Avoid/Dodge to enable their characters to dispatch any foe in the game.

Decoy

Level: 24	Prerequisites: Slow Missiles

This skill creates a duplicate copy of your Amazon. Although the decoy that's created does not fight in your stead, it *will* draw fire from enemies, as it appears to be you! Even in multiplayer the Decoy that's created when you use this skill looks like you to your enemies, making it an effective tool in both single player, cooperative multiplayer, and player vs. player. Ultimately, the Decoy is best used when you get into a situation where you're being overwhelmed by enemies; invoking the Decoy at this point will be useful in distracting enemies while you attack them from your position. The downside to the Decoy is that it does not last very long (10 seconds for a level 1 Decoy). However, as you add points to this skill you may access the Decoy for as much as a minute and a half at a time.

Decoy is a great way to get an enemy off your back because the Decoy places another equally attractive target beside you for your foes to attack.

Evade

Level: 24	Prerequisites: Avoid

Evade is a particularly valuable skill because it gives your Amazon a chance to escape any attack while moving. This differs from Avoid and Dodge. Those skills apply only when your character is standing still, whereas Evade works when your character is *on the run*. For this reason you can see why combining Evade, Avoid, and Dodge can make it very difficult for enemies to land a hit. Evade is highly effective once you get to level 5 because it provides a 50% chance that the enemy does not land its attack. At level 18, Evade gives a chance for your character to avoid area-of-effect spells/attacks, which means that in some instances clouds of poison or areas of burning ground can be negotiated without taking a hit!

Valkyrie

Level: 30 | Prerequisites: Decoy, Evade

This is one of the Amazon's most powerful skills. Indeed, the Valkyrie is a very formidable ally to have fighting by your side. When invoked, this skill summons a magical Valkyrie warrior to fight for your cause. Even a level 1 Valkyrie has over 350 hit points and packs a substantial punch as an offensive force. As you pour points into the Valkyrie, she gains a great deal of strength. For example, a level 5 Valkyrie has over 650 hit points and also has 100% modifiers on attack, defense, and damage bonuses!

The Valkyrie is perhaps the Amazon's best skill. When created, the Valkyrie is very tough and fights fiercely in your name.

NOTE

A high-level Valkyrie, a Decoy, and a quality mercenary hired in town can give you a fair-sized company to help battle through the later Acts of the **Diablo II** universe.

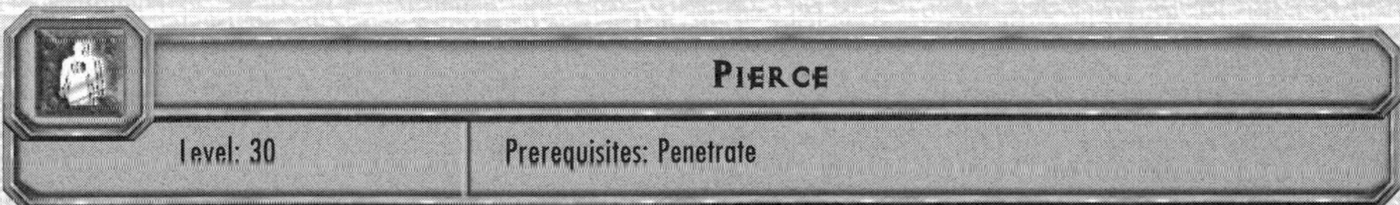

Pierce

Level: 30 | Prerequisites: Penetrate

This passive skill gives the Amazon a chance that any ranged weapon you use, be it a spear or an arrow, after hitting its target will then continue through toward the next target. As with Penetrate, this skill is important if you choose to fight the enemy from a distance at all times. Pierce, however, requires 15 skill points before it reaches a 40% chance of passing through an enemy, so it's not always a worthwhile use of your skill points just to slightly improve your chance of piercing an enemy.

 JAVELIN & SPEAR 

This group of skills enhances the abilities of the Javelin and Spear class of weapons. Each skill in this tree in some way improves upon the Javelin/Spear attacks, or more specifically, they improve upon weapons that use a thrusting or throwing attack. The higher level skills such as Fend and Lightning Fury provide an excellent power punch, while skills like Power Strike and Plague Javelin help to provide a backbone of skills that will serve you well as your Amazon progresses through the *Diablo II* universe.

Jab

Level: 1	Prerequisites: None

Jab delivers multiple hits in a single attack, and is essential if you choose to follow this arm of the skill tree. By perforating the enemy multiple times within the span of a normal attack, you can sometimes finish the creature off in one fell swoop, rather than attempting to hit it multiple times. The downside to the Jab skill is that each successive hit is slightly less powerful, and not every jab is guaranteed to hit. However, as you add points to Jab, it quickly becomes more effective in terms of Attack Rating and the amount of damage it inflicts on the enemy.

ALTERED SKILL

For the expansion set, Jab is now affected by weapon speed, so try to get weapons with a very fast attack speed. The damage inflicted on the enemy when using Jab is actually lower in the first few levels of this skill. Indeed, it's not until you reach level 5 Jab that you start to see an increase in the damage modifier (meaning that you must put skill points into Jab for it to be most effective).

Power Strike

Level: 6	Prerequisites: Jab

The Power Strike is a straight-forward skill that simply adds lightning damage to an attack. Adding a different type of damage to an attack is always good because it improves both the damage done and the attack strength for thrusting attacks. Although Power Strike has a Mana cost, it is nominal and relatively insignificant compared to the benefit supplied by the spell. This skill is best used when fighting small groups or single enemies because the lightning damage affects only a single targeted enemy.

Poison Javelin

Level: 6	Prerequisites: None

A Poison Javelin is best used in areas where there are plenty of enemies.

In short, poison is a great way to damage a group of monsters in a short period of time, so it stands to reason that if you can combine poison with a javelin attack you can create some serious carnage. Poison Javelin increases the damage done to an enemy (over and above the normal damage your attacks inflict), but it also poisons the target and any nearby targets. The poison then continues to damage the enemy as long as it lasts; the duration of the poison effect increases with every skill point used for this ability.

TIP

Poison Javelin leaves a trail of poison clouds in the area behind it as it flies through the air. For this reason you can use a Javelin throw to block a narrow hallway or valley so that any enemy passing through it becomes poisoned. This technique can be very effective, but timing is important since the poison cloud lasts only a few seconds.

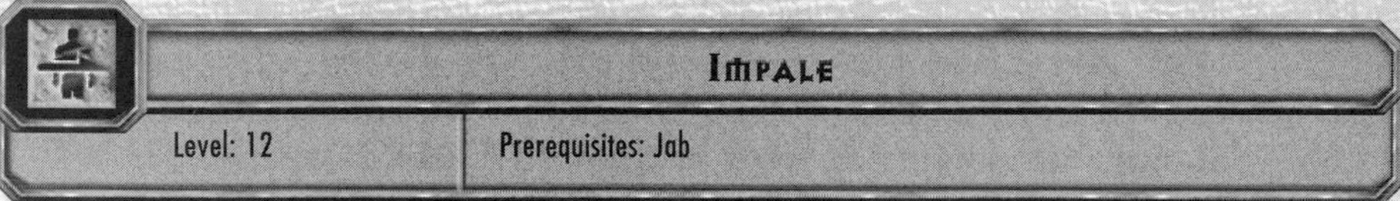

Impale

Level: 12	Prerequisites: Jab

This skill is a more powerful single attack that inflicts a much greater amount of damage on the enemy you're attacking—especially at the higher levels. As you put more points into Impale the Attack Rating goes up considerably, but with a higher cost on the durability of the Javelin you're using. Despite this increased strain on the durability of the particular weapon you are holding, this skill is well worth the Mana cost. As with Power Strike, Impale is best used against small groups or single enemies because it can affect only one foe at a time.

ALTERED SKILL

As with several other skills in the expansion set, Impale has been altered so that weapon speed dictates how fast the attacks occur.

Lightning Bolt

Level: 12	Prerequisites: Poison Javelin

Lightning Bolt turns the Javelin you are throwing into a lightning bolt that does a large amount of damage to the enemy it hits. As Lightning Bolt increases in level, it causes a huge amount of damage, and the Mana cost associated with this skill at those higher levels won't break your Mana bank (so to speak). Due to the nature of lightning, the bolt that's created is an excellent source of light. As with other similar weapons, you can use the Lightning Bolt to illuminate unexplored or darkened areas, such as caves and tombs. If you're lucky, it may even hit an unsuspecting enemy!

Charged Strike

Level: 18 | Prerequisites: Power Strike, Lighting Bolt

This skill provides a lightning attack that also releases charged bolts that move away from your position, doing damage to whatever enemies they encounter. These bolts are not guided, so there's no guarantee that they'll hit any enemy; however, when you're in close combat and fighting against a group of enemies, using Charged Strike can inflict the kind of damage that makes your job much easier. The first few levels of this skill see a substantial increase in the effectiveness of Charged Strike, so if you choose to put one point into it, you should be prepared to add at least a few more to make it effective in the later Acts of *Diablo II*.

Charged Strike packs an electrical punch that wreaks havoc on enemies.

Plague Javelin

Level: 18 | Prerequisites: Lightning Bolt

This weapon is very similar to Poison Javelin, but it also creates an expanding cloud of poison around the target it hits. The explosion of poison, however, is not the only benefit of Plague Javelin. Indeed, Plague Javelin's duration changes dramatically with every skill point added to it. In fact, you get one extra second of duration for every skill point, and when you factor in the damage per second, this skill quickly becomes worthwhile. Like the Poison Javelin, this skill leaves a trail of poison that can be used as a deadly barrier in crowded areas or narrow passageways, but the Plague Javelin also inflicts an area of damage when it impacts the enemy. This explosion of poison means that firing a Plague Javelin into a group of enemies will leave *all* of them poisoned as their final breaths leave their wracked bodies.

ALTERED SKILL

Plague Javelin now has a cool-down timer between castings, so it can't be used consecutively. Fortunately, the cool-down time is relatively short.

Fend

Level: 24 | Prerequisites: Impale

This skill is for hand-to-hand combat only and is very effective when you are surrounded by a group of foul creatures. Fend attacks multiple targets quickly, hitting *every* adjacent enemy! With a few skill points in Fend you can take down a feverish group of enemies in a few hits, because each time you strike, each adjacent enemy takes a hit. As skill points are added to Fend, it becomes increasingly effective as both the Attack and Damage modifiers increase dramatically.

 TIP

Assign a hot key to the Fend skill so you can use it if you suddenly become surrounded by a group of enemies. A few uses of Fend can thin out the enemy ranks very quickly and, at the very least, open up a pathway for your escape.

Lightning Strike

Level: 30	Prerequisites: Charged Strike

This skill turns your Javelin into a lightning bolt as soon as it makes contact with the enemy. When you hit your foe, Lightning Strike releases chain lightning that travels from enemy to enemy within range. This skill is very similar to Lightning Fury, except that it's not nearly as powerful and requires you to be adjacent to the enemy in order to start the chain of lightning. This is an excellent skill to master if you enjoy getting into melee combat with your Amazon, but if you prefer to fight from afar, put your points into Lightning Fury.

 NOTE

It's important to note that with both Lightning Strike and Lightning Fury the initial hit is **weaker** than the chain lightning hits that follow. It's not uncommon for the enemy you hit first to remain standing while those behind him fall at the hands of the sparks. For this reason it isn't always the best idea to hit the toughest enemy first when using these skills.

Lightning Fury

Level: 30	Prerequisites: Plague Javelin

Lightning Fury is a skill that turns your Javelin into a chained lightning bolt as soon as it leaves your hands. The result is a single thrown Javelin that can take down or seriously injure an entire group of enemies, depending on the level of the skill and the strength of your enemies. This is a ranged skill and is best used that way, although you can certainly use it in melee combat if necessary. Ideally, you'll want to stay out of harm's way, fire Lightning Strike at the 'lead' enemy, and then sit back and watch the tentacles of electricity rip through the enemy ranks. Lightning Fury can be used in the same way a grenade is lobbed into an enemy area. If you fire a Lightning Fury at an enemy who's the first of many behind him, the resulting chain lightning will rip through every enemy within range and possibly even clear out the room for you!

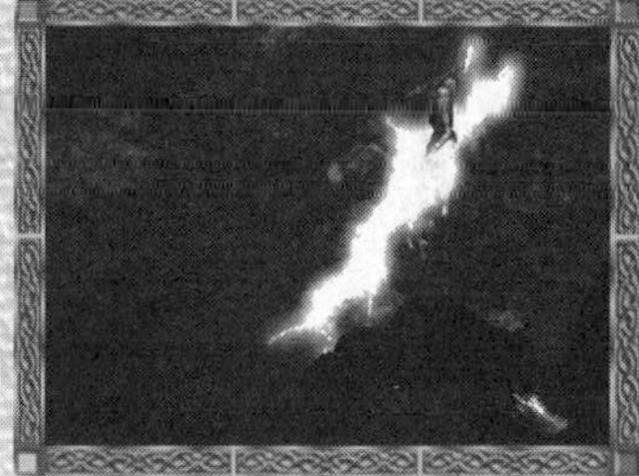

There's a reason that Lightning Fury is a Level 30 skill—it's powerful!

 TIP

A nifty trick with Lightning Fury is to bounce it off a wall when attacking enemies. This can be effective because the lightning attacks that spread out after the bounce are more powerful than the original attack.

THE PALADIN

The Paladin is a battle-ready warrior for whom faith is a shield; he fights for what he believes to be right. Furthermore, his steadfastness gives him powers to do goo upon friends, and wreak cruel justice upon foes. There are those w call the Paladin an overwrought zealot, but others recognize in him the strength and goodness of the Light. The Paladin is a crusading believer in all that is good, just, and holy. He stands tall and intimidates with a deep, commanding voice that sounds appropriat coming from either the pulpit or the battlefield.

THE PALADIN SKILLS

There are three skill sets that the Paladin can develop as he progresses in the *Diablo II* realm. As with the other characters, which skills are developed in each area ultimately affect the Paladin's abilities in the game. The three skill sets are Combat, Offensive Auras, and Defensive Auras.

Defensive Auras

1. Prayer
2. Resist Fire
3. Defiance
4. Resist Cold
5. Cleansing
6. Resist Lightning
7. Vigor
8. Meditation
9. Redemption
10. Salvation

Offensive Auras

1. Might
2. Holy Fire
3. Thorns
4. Blessed Aim
5. Concentration
6. Holy Freeze
7. Holy Shock
8. Sanctuary
9. Fanaticism
10. Conviction

Combat

1. Sacrifice
2. Smite
3. Holy Bolt
4. Zeal
5. Charge
6. Vengeance
7. Blessed Hammer
8. Conversion
9. Holy Shield
10. Fist of the Heavens

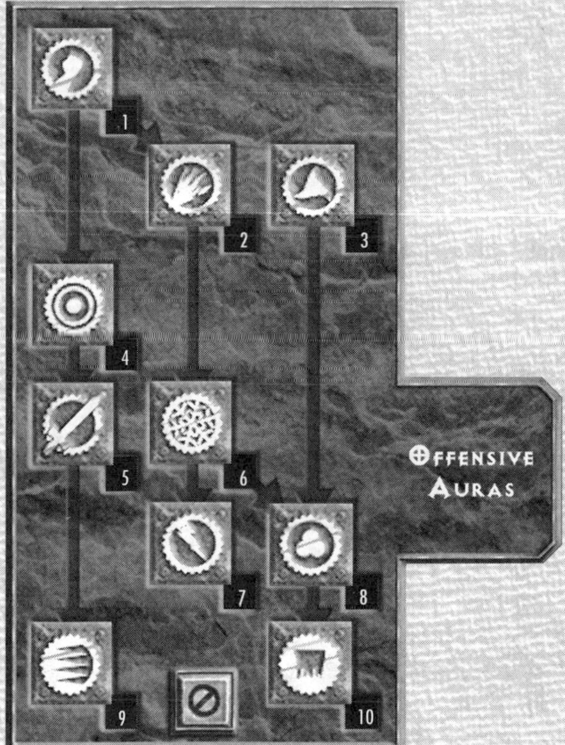

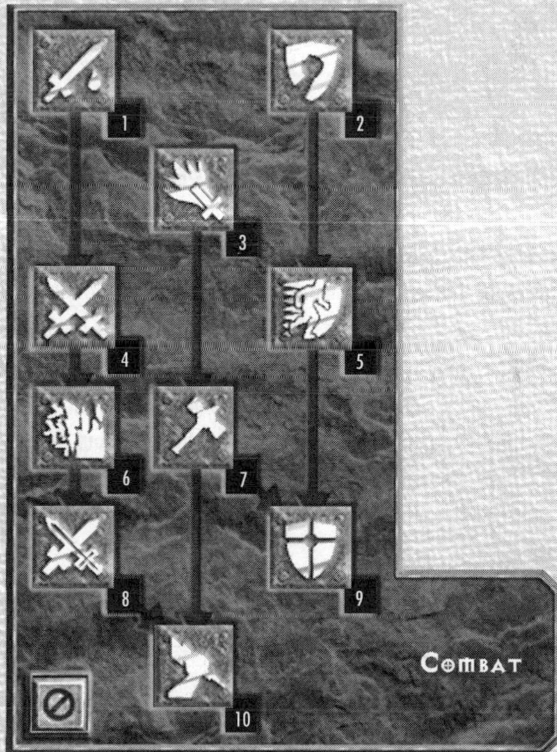

COMBAT

As the name implies, this set of skills aids the Paladin in his ability to engage in combat against the evil forces he will face. From multi-faceted attacks such as Smite (which not only damages, but also knocks back and stuns), to melee enhancing skills like Zeal, this line contains important skills that the Paladin must use in order to be successful.

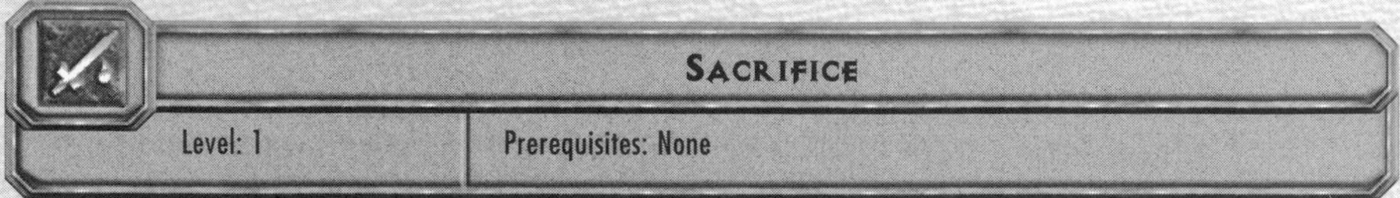

Sacrifice

Level: 1 | Prerequisites: None

This is an odd skill because it gives you the ability to do more damage to the enemy by improving your Attack Rating; but it does so at the cost of 8% to your health. The upside of Sacrifice is that it greatly increases the damage you do, and the cost is always only 8% of your Life, regardless of your level of Sacrifice. Still, the cost of draining some of your own Life in order to do damage must always be weighed against the benefits of having a more powerful attack.

If you have a Life-stealing weapon (which replenishes lost Life with every hit), then Sacrifice becomes a very practical and powerful skill. However, if you do not have such a weapon or item, it would behoove you to keep Health potions on hand at all times if you're going to use this skill.

Smite

Level: 1 | Prerequisites: None

Smite is best described as a shield bash. When this skill is used, it knocks back and damages the enemy. The real benefit, however, is in its ability to stun the enemy. When you Smite an enemy, they become stunned for a short time (increasing as more skill points are spent on this skill), and during this time they cannot move, attack, cast spells or use abilities. By the time Smite reaches level 15, you're doing a crushing amount of damage (225% more) and the enemy is being stunned for a full three seconds, which means that you can continue to hit them without fear of retaliation.

Smite not only knocks the enemy back, but it also stuns them and does damage, as well.

TIP

You can take even a tough enemy out by simply continually using Smite on them. Every time you use Smite, the enemy is knocked back, stunning them for a brief period of time. If you Smite them repeatedly, you can push them back against a wall and simply continue to Smite them or trade a sword attack with a Smite attack until they are dead. Using this technique prevents your foe from fighting back as they are perpetually stunned.

Holy Bolt

Level: 6 | Prerequisites: None

Holy Bolt is a powerful bolt of divine energy that damages undead monsters, often to the point of destroying them in one shot. Although this skill is effective *only* against the undead as an attack, you can still use it any time to heal members of your party by shooting them with it! Holy Bolt is unique because it can be used as both a weapon and an instrument of healing. For this reason, it's worth having a skill point or two invested in it.

ALTERED SKILL

Holy Bolt has been 'beefed up' for the expansion set, making it more effective and generally more desirable to use.

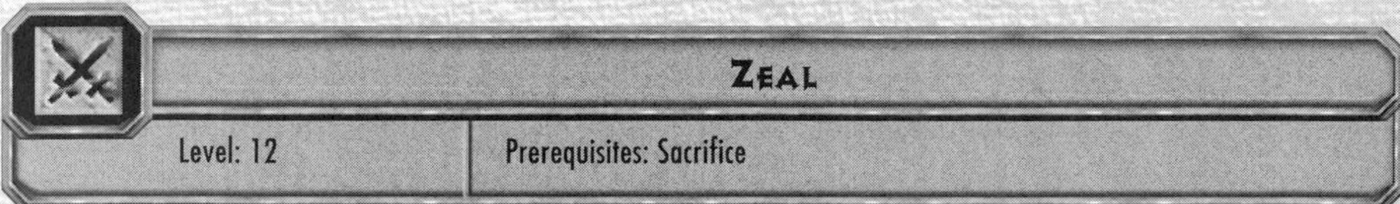

Zeal

Level: 12 | Prerequisites: Sacrifice

This skill is extremely effective when you are surrounded because it enables you to quickly strike multiple adjacent enemies with one attack. As you add points to this skill, you'll be able to land more hits with a more powerful attack, making this a valuable tool when fighting with a group of enemies in close quarters. Zeal can also be used to make a weapon with a very slow attack speed, such as a spear, much faster, providing the massive damage that a slow weapon offers at a vastly improved rate of speed.

NOTE

Zeal also works effectively against one enemy. If you have a level 3 Zeal that has four hits, it will hit a single enemy four consecutive times without hesitation. This is a great way to take enemies out in one attack.

ALTERED SKILL

For the **Diablo II: Lord of Destruction**, Zeal is limited to five hits, but is now more likely to land a hit when used.

Charge

Level: 12 | Prerequisites: Smite

This is a skill that's related to Smite since it uses a shield bash to hit the enemy. Charge, however, also substantially increases the amount of damage the smash does and closes ground on the enemy by making your Paladin run up to the enemy and then hit it with a hard shield smash. The enemy is not stunned as with Smite, but the attack is often powerful enough to take an enemy out in one or two Charges. This is a good skill to use to close distance on an enemy quickly and surprise them.

Vengeance

Level: 18 | Prerequisites: Zeal

Vengeance is a unique skill that not only does standard damage, but also adds fire, lightning, and cold damage to the attack. This is an important skill because it not only deals a wicked blow to an enemy that has no resistances, but it also affects monsters that have specific resistances. For example, if an enemy has resistance to fire, then the Vengeance attack still hits them with standard attack, cold attack, and electrical attack. This is a skill well worth employing at any time, and when a few skill points have been invested in it, the enemies you hit are slowed by cold for several seconds as well.

Blessed Hammer

Level: 18 | Prerequisites: Holy Bolt

The Blessed Hammer creates a spinning mallet that spirals outward, damaging any enemies it encounters, while doing double damage to undead creatures. This is not a targeted weapon, but when it hits an undead creature it will do a heap of damage, often killing the undead in one hit. As skill points are added to Blessed Hammer it gains a great deal of attack strength, but since its Mana cost also increases and it can be difficult to use in close quarters, it is not a skill in which points should be heavily invested.

Conversion

Level: 24 | Prerequisites: Vengeance

This skill gives a chance that you'll convert a monster to fight for your Paladin, but only for a short period of time. The duration of this effect is extended when more skill points are invested in the skill, along with the chance of a successful conversion. This skill works with your normal melee weapon attack, with the enemy being damaged by each hit. However, there's a chance that your attack will also convert the enemy to your side; if this happens, a small symbol appears over the head of the enemy and they become your ally for the prescribed amount of time.

Conversion temporarily makes your enemy an ally.

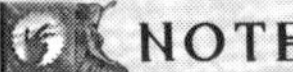

NOTE

Although you **can** convert multiple enemies to fight for you at the same time, you must convert them one at a time. Hence, you won't ever be able to achieve the numbers of followers that the Necromancer summons with Revive.

Holy Shield

Level: 24 | Prerequisites: Charge, Blessed Hammer

Holy Shield magically enhances your shield to absorb damage while increasing your chance to block an enemy's attack. The drawback is that it takes a whopping 35 Mana, and in the first few levels doesn't provide a huge benefit to your Paladin. However, once Holy Shield reaches level 10, it becomes a substantial defensive skill that lasts for a full two minutes and gives almost a 200% defensive improvement.

ALTERED SKILL

Holy Shield now also adds to Smite damage.

Fist of the Heavens

Level: 30 | Prerequisites: Blessed Hammer, Conversion

This is a skill that not only does a substantial amount of damage with a lightning bolt, but also releases Holy Bolts after the initial hit. These Holy Bolts then go about doing their own damage to any nearby undead, or, if you have party members nearby, the Holy Bolts will heal them! This is a high-level skill that carries a steep Mana cost (although this has been leveled off in the expansion set), but you'll be able to take some tough enemies down in one or two shots once you've invested 10+ skill points into it. Fist of Heavens is a must-have when fighting against any group of undead because of the radiating Holy Bolts that extend from the initial lightning strike area.

ALTERED SKILL

Fist of the Heavens has had several changes for the expansion set, not the least of which is an added cool-down period. The power of Fist of Heavens has been increased substantially and the Mana cost, while still high, now levels off as you invest skill points.

OFFENSIVE AURAS

This set of skills is aimed at improving existing combat skills, but also provides some unique attributes that wreak havoc with the enemies. For example, Holy Fire will periodically hit any nearby enemies with a blast of fire, while Thorns returns damage to the monster inflicting it on you! Where the Offensive Auras really shine, however, is in multiplayer action. A multiplayer team without a Paladin versed in these skills will be at a considerable disadvantage.

Might

Level: 1	Prerequisites: None

This aura increases the amount of damage caused by your character and friendly units. Might, like all auras, is best used when it can help an entire party rather just your Paladin; however, it is still a very powerful aura by itself. Indeed, at level 7 it is already doubling the attack value of any hits you land on an enemy monster.

TIP

Activate Might when playing in a tight group during a fight with tough monsters in Multiplayer. This aura will increase your offensive power (as a group) enough to alter the outcome of a close battle in your favor.

Holy Fire

Level: 6	Prerequisites: Might

This aura is a very powerful skill that, when active, periodically blasts unfriendly units with a hit of fire! The amount of damage that it does on the nearby enemies varies within a range for the level of the skill. By putting more skill points into Holy Fire, you not only increase the amount of damage that you inflict on nearby enemies, but also increase the radius of effect. A great way to use this skill is to run into an area with a large group of enemies, drink down a stamina potion, then simply run around and avoid the enemies while the Holy Fire hits them every few seconds. This technique comes in very handy when your armor is damaged or you are near death, but still need to kill off a group of enemies.

When active, this skill launches a fire attack on all nearby enemies.

NOTE

Once you reach Act III, Holy Fire will not be effective enough to use consistently—the damage it inflicts may not take out the tougher enemies you'll face.

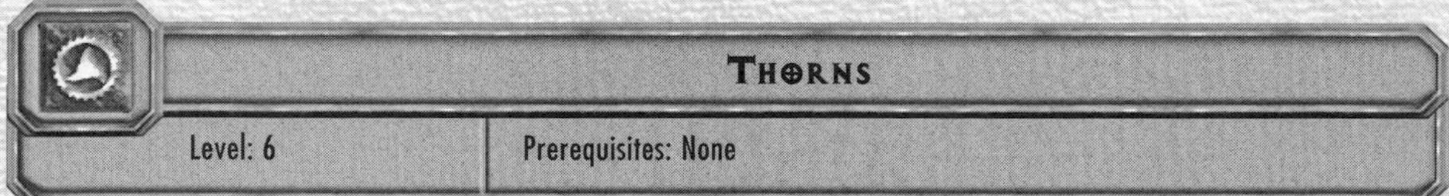

Thorns

Level: 6 | Prerequisites: None

This is (in the opinion of many Blizzard employees) the most powerful aura the Paladin has at his disposal. This aura returns damage to any enemy that inflicts damage on you or any ally that is within the radius of its effect. The key to this skill is just how much damage is returned! Indeed, if an enemy hits you and inflicts 10 points of damage, and you have Thorns at level 1, the enemy takes a 250% hit, or 25 points, back! Marvel at the numbers: Thorns at level 10 returns over 600% damage to the enemy! The one downside to Thorns is that it is effective only with melee attacks and does not apply to damage inflicted by ranged weapons or magical effects.

NOTE

Having Thorns active at higher levels can be enough for enemies to kill themselves with one successful hit against you. For example, at level 10, if an enemy hits with a 10-point attack, it takes a 61-point hit in return.

Blessed Aim

Level: 12 | Prerequisites: Might

This aura increases your Attack Rating, while doing the same for all nearby allies. The bonus to your Attack Rating increases as you add points to Blessed Aim, and the radius of effect is also improved. Although it can be effective in the single-player game, Blessed Aim is one of the auras that's more important during multiplayer action where it can help to improve the Attack Rating of the entire group.

Concentration

Level: 18 | Prerequisites: Blessed Aim

Concentration gives you a chance that your attack will not be interrupted, and adds to the damage your attacks do. This is an important aura because when you're in a pitched battle, taking many hits from multiple sides, your attacks will get interrupted and you'll find it hard to land a blow on an enemy. Concentration increases the chance that your attacks will follow through even if you're being interrupted by an enemy attack. As skill points are added to Concentration, your chance of being interrupted decreases. Use this skill in tense situations where you need your attacks to find purchase on enemy flesh!

Holy Freeze

Level: 18 | Prerequisites: Holy Fire

Holy Freeze acts somewhat like Holy Fire—it affects units within its radius every few seconds. However, instead of inflicting cold damage, it merely slows the enemies down. As with all auras, this is a very valuable skill to use in a group situation because it will freeze all nearby enemies, making them slower and ultimately more manageable for other party members to destroy. Also, Holy Freeze is an attack powered by the faith of the Paladin and not elemental magic, so resistances against cold do not protect enemies from this spell.

Holy Shock

Level: 24 | Prerequisites: Holy Freeze

Holy Shock hits unfriendly units with a spark of electricity every few seconds. The amount of damage that this aura inflicts on the nearby enemies varies within a range for the level of the skill, but the addition of skill points increases the amount of damage that you deal on nearby enemies, as well as the radius of effect. You can clear an area filled with a large group of enemies by drinking a stamina potion and then running around while avoiding the enemies as Holy Shock hits them every few seconds. This technique is especially useful when your armor is damaged, your weapon has broken or you are near death but you still need to kill off a group of enemies.

This skill periodically hits nearby monsters with an electrical spark!

Sanctuary

Level: 24 | Prerequisites: Thorns, Holy Freeze

Sanctuary is a special aura that essentially prevents undead monsters from reaching the Paladin. It does substantial damage to the undead and, as a rule, destroys them before they have a chance to get close enough to cause you damage. This aura is especially useful in places like the Graveyard or the Tombs where the undead thrive. As you add points to Sanctuary, both the damage inflicted on the undead and the radius of effect increases dramatically. However, because many of the tougher monsters you face in *Diablo II: Lord of Destruction* are not undead, it's not advisable to put all of your eggs into this one basket.

Fanaticism

Level: 30	Prerequisites: Concentration

Fanaticism boosts the attack rate and power for the Paladin and nearby party members (within a radius of 7.3 yards). This aura moderately increases these attack factors, but after level 2 the amount that the rating increases may not be worth the cost of a skill point to you. This is an excellent aura to use in multiplayer when your party wants to quickly hack through a large group of enemies; the increase in Attack Rating allows your party members (and yourself) to strike quicker, do more damage, and prevent the enemy from attacking.

Conviction

Level: 30	Prerequisites: Sanctuary

Conviction is an aura that reduces the armor class and maximum resistances of enemies that come within its radius of effect. For example, an enemy within six yards of a Paladin with level 1 Conviction active has its defense rating lowered by 49%, and its maximum resistances reduced by 26%. Because this affects any enemies within the radius, it can benefit other party members in multiplayer if they are fighting close to your position.

ALTERED SKILL

Conviction has been improved to lower elemental resistances of the enemies even more than before. It should also be noted that it is possible to have an enemy's elemental resistance reduced below zero in certain cases when using Conviction!

DEFENSIVE AURAS

This set of skills is aimed at improving existing defensive combat skills. For the Paladin, the Defensive Auras are of great importance in multiplayer games because of their ability to protect/affect other party members. Again, as with the Offensive Auras, the Defensive Auras are great in single-player action, but really shine when they can be applied to a team.

Prayer

Level: 1	Prerequisites: None

This is one of the Paladin's most powerful skills because it has the ability to heal you and your nearby allies passively, simply by being readied. When it heals you or a member of your party, Prayer takes Mana from your reserve, but only when it heals; otherwise it is simply 'on' passively waiting for your health to fall below optimum. When used in a multiplayer party, Prayer is incredibly important, especially at higher levels, because it can heal everyone in the party simultaneously.

NOTE

In multiplayer, the Paladin can simply stay behind other party members and leave the Prayer skill active in order to heal everyone as they take hits. This skill underscores the importance of having a Paladin in a multiplayer party.

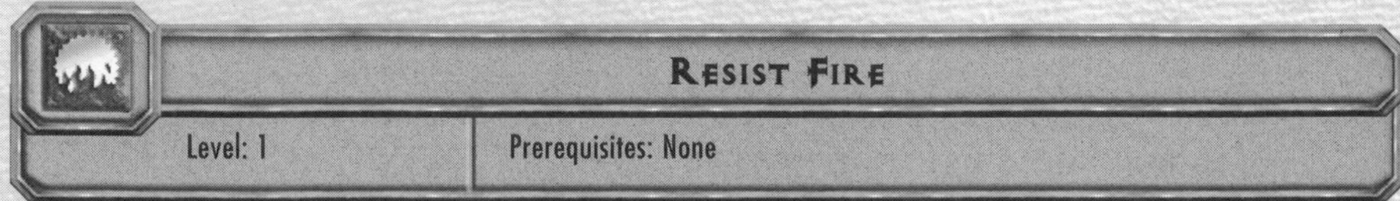

Resist Fire

Level: 1 | Prerequisites: None

This skill increases your resistance to fire, along with any friendly units within the radius of the aura. Once again, this is a great way to protect yourself and your party members in a multiplayer game when you're up against enemies that deal out fire-based damage. Note that this skill doesn't require the expenditure of Mana, so it can be left on indefinitely.

Defiance

Level: 6 | Prerequisites: None

Defiance boosts your defensive rating substantially when active. It also does the same for party members in the same amount (between 70 and 230%, depending on skill level), making it an excellent tool for multiplayer games. As you add points to Defiance, you'll increase the radius of this aura's effect, as well as the amount of defensive boost it affords you and the other allies under its influence.

Resist Cold

Level: 6 | Prerequisites: None

This skill increases your resistance to cold, along with that of any friendly units within the radius of the aura. Use this aura to help protect yourself and your party members in a multiplayer game when you're up against any enemies that attack with cold. Note that this skill doesn't require the expenditure of Mana, so it can be left on indefinitely to provide constant protection.

Cleansing

Level: 12 | Prerequisites: Prayer

Cleansing reduces the amount of time that poison will affect you or any members of your party within the aura's radius of effect. This aura is important in places like the Tombs or the Spider Cave where you're likely to face several enemies that can infect you with a dose of poison. Because poison can be so devastating, especially to a party if they all get poisoned, this aura is a huge asset in multiplayer games.

Resist Lightning

Level: 12 | Prerequisites: None

As with the Resist Fire and Resist Cold auras, Resist Lightning affords you and the nearby members of your party some level of protection from lightning attacks. Of course, when more skill points are added to Resist Lightning, you'll acquire increased radius and resistance ratings, making this a powerful aura when you're taking electrical damage from enemies.

Vigor

Level: 18	Prerequisites: Cleansing, Defiance

This aura boosts the stamina regeneration rate of you and your allies so you are able to more quickly recover from running. Stamina recovery is only one part of the benefits of this aura, however, because it also increases your maximum stamina and walk/run speed! As an added bonus, any nearby allies also feel the effect of Vigor (depending on how many skill points have been added to this skill). Vigor is best used in situations where you and/or your party members need to be nimble, moving quickly to hit the enemy before running away.

Vigor is a skill that boosts the stamina regeneration rate for both you and nearby allies.

Meditation

Level: 24	Prerequisites: Cleansing

This aura increases the Mana recovery rate for your Paladin and nearby party members. In the first level, Meditation speeds up Mana recovery by 60%; however, when you've put 20 skill points into this aura, you can get a Mana regeneration rate that's 300% faster than normal! In a group of Sorceresses and Necromancers, this ability to regenerate Mana quickly is a highly prized skill.

Redemption

Level: 30	Prerequisites: Vigor

Redemption is one of the most powerful skills in the game. When it is left on, this aura reclaims the bodies of fallen enemies and turns them into Mana and Health for your Paladin! Not only is this a fantastic way to restore Mana, but it also works to permanently remove dead monster corpses that could otherwise be resurrected by certain enemies. Redemption is a powerful aura and should be used whenever there is a lack of Mana or you need to eliminate fallen enemies from the battlefield.

Salvation

Level: 30	Prerequisites: None

This aura protects you and any nearby allies from all enemy elemental damage—including cold, fire, and electrical damage. Each skill point you add to Salvation grants a small bonus to the amount of damage that is diverted from these attacks. Paladins engaged in multiplayer battles enjoy the dramatic increase in the radius of effect for Salvation. By the time you've invested 10 skill points into this aura, you'll have an effective protection radius of nearly 20 yards, which means that your party member can stray farther from you and still be protected under the effects of this aura.

THE SORCERESS

One of the rebellious women who have wrested the secrets of magic use from the male-dominated Mage-Clans of the East, the Sorceress is an expert in mystical creation *ex nihilo*. Although she lacks hand-to-hand combat skills, she does have fierce combative magics for both offense and defense.

Both solitary and reclusive, the Sorceress acts based on motives and ethics that often seem fickle and even spiteful. In reality, she understands the struggle between Order and Chaos all too clearly, and uses this to balance and fit into her role as a warrior in the battles of *Diablo II*.

THE SORCERESS SKILLS

The three skill sets that the Sorceress can develop are Fire, Lightning, and Cold. As with the other characters, the skills that are developed in each area ultimately affect the abilities the Sorceress ends up mastering in *Diablo II*.

The Sorceress is the master of magic. So if you're looking for some bone-crushing melee combat, the Sorceress is probably not your best choice. However, if you want visually impressive and extremely powerful magic, this is the character for you.

COLD

1. Ice Bolt
2. Frozen Armor
3. Frost Nova
4. Ice Blast
5. Shiver Armor
6. Glacial Spike
7. Blizzard
8. Chilling Armor
9. Frozen Orb
10. Cold Mastery

LIGHTNING

1. Charged Bolt
2. Static Field
3. Telekinesis
4. Nova
5. Lightning
6. Chain Lightning
7. Teleport
8. Thunder Storm
9. Energy Shield
10. Lightning Mastery

FIRE

1. Fire Bolt
2. Warmth
3. Inferno
4. Blaze
5. Fire Ball
6. Fire Wall
7. Enchant
8. Meteor
9. Fire Mastery
10. Hydra

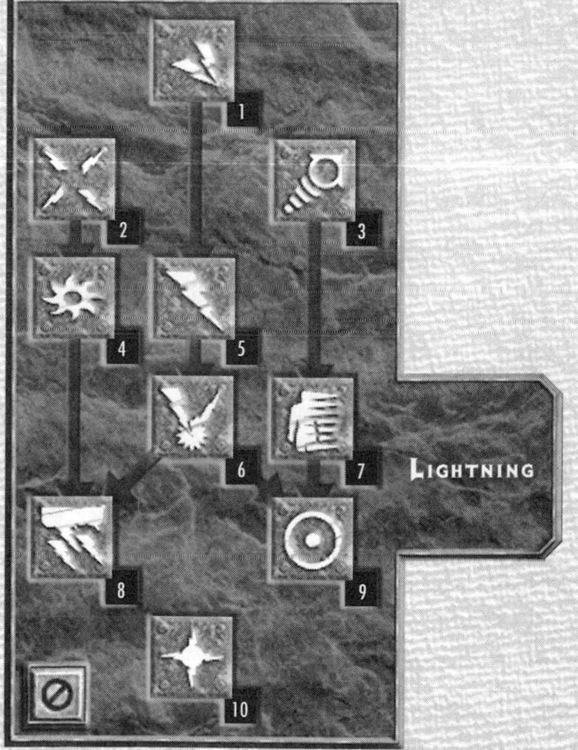

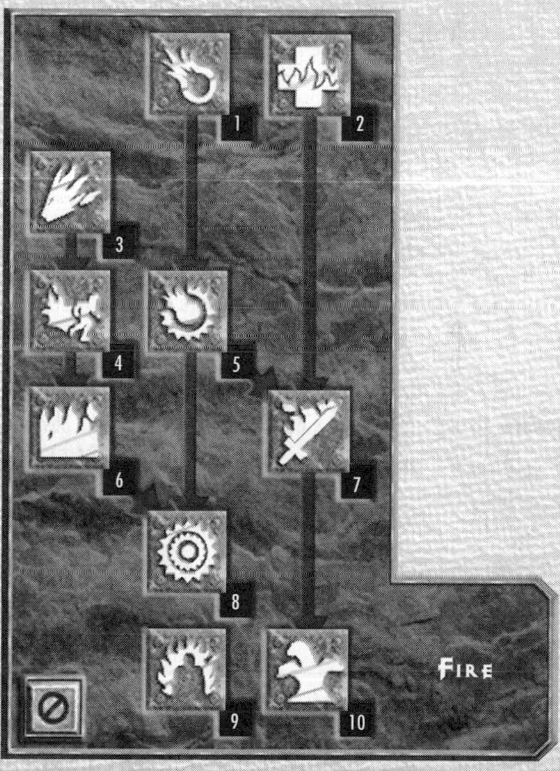

FIRE

These spells give the Sorceress command over the powerful realm of fire, and include the very effective spells Fire Wall and Blaze. In addition she has Meteor, which can instantly eliminate almost any tightly grouped pack of enemies. While all of the fire spells are worthwhile, perhaps the most important is Warmth. This ability helps to improve the Mana recharge rate for the Sorceress, which is the lifeblood of this spell-caster.

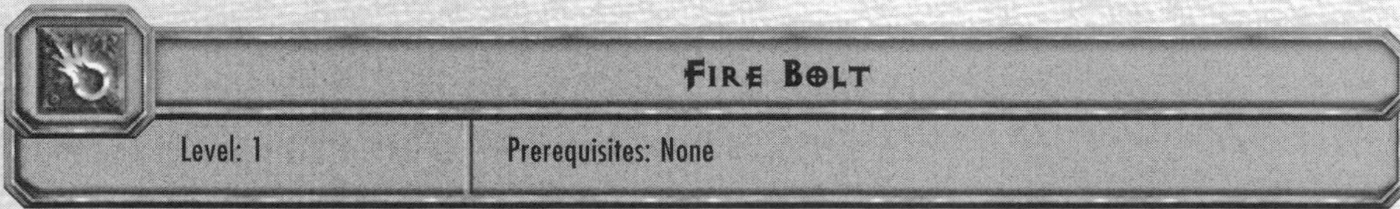

Fire Bolt shoots a stream of flames that causes fire damage to a single enemy. The Sorceress starts the game with a staff that grants this skill. Fire Bolt increases in power as you put skill points into it, but its Mana cost stays the same at 2.5 points.

Although Fire Bolt uses little Mana, it can hit only one enemy and its damage is limited. This means that there are other skills in the Fire skill tree that you will want to explore, especially when you are fighting larger groups of tougher monsters.

This is the bread-and-butter spell for the Sorceress that can be effectively used throughout much of the game.

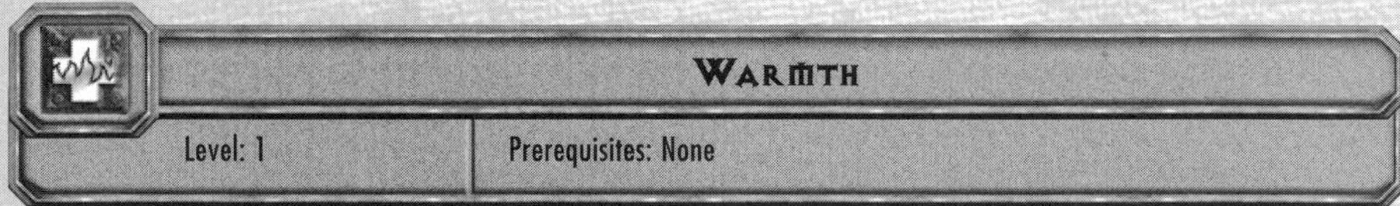

Warmth is a passive skill that increases the Mana recovery rate of the Sorceress. It is imperative that you add points to this skill because the Sorceress requires plenty of Mana to cast her spells.

Warmth increases the Mana recharge rate by a percentage. When you reach level 9 of Warmth, you'll see a recharge rate that is greater than double the standard recharge rate, which obviously makes this one of the most important skills in the game. You should put as many points into Warmth as you can afford because, as the game progresses, you'll (as a Sorceress) rely more heavily on magic.

TIP

Don't wait to put points into Warmth. The benefits of having at least five points in this skill will hold you in good stead from the very first Act.

Inferno

Level: 6	Prerequisites: None

Inferno resembles a flame-thrower that follows the direction that you move your mouse (the front of the Sorceress). The more points that you put into Inferno, the greater the range of the flame and the more damage it causes.

After adding just a few skill points to Inferno, you can increase the damage points *per second* to around 37-47! This kind of power can cut a path through a line of enemies very quickly. This is a great spell to employ when you are backed into a corner and surrounded by multiple enemies.

Blaze

Level: 12	Prerequisites: Inferno

Blaze leaves a wall of fire wherever the Sorceress goes. This wall of fire inflicts a significant amount of damage every second the enemy is inside it, so there are a couple of important uses for this spell.

Perhaps the coolest spell in the game, Blaze leaves a trail of highly damaging flames behind the Sorceress as she moves.

First, you can use Blaze to enclose a group of enemies by running around them in a circle. This forces the enemies to pass over the deadly fire to get at you or, at least, keeps them trapped while you get away or prepare another spell. Secondly, use Blaze when you're running away from a group of enemies. As you flee, the enemies often chase you and get trapped in the fire that you leave behind. Since Blaze causes a large amount of damage every second, most enemies succumb in short order.

Fire Ball

Level: 12	Prerequisites: Fire Bolt

This spell is like a Fire Bolt with a wide area of effect. Fire Ball shoots an orb of flame that causes fire damage around the impact point, thus damaging anything within the area.

A ranged spell, Fire Ball is great to use against groups of enemies that are even a short distance away. If you get too close, however, it may prove difficult to invoke the spell with enemies swinging at you.

Enchant

Level: 18	Prerequisites: Warmth, Fire Ball

Enchant magically enhances a weapon with fire damage and increases the Attack Rating. This spell is a necessity during hand-to-hand combat. If you don't take part in a lot of melee combat, it's best to stick with one level of Enchant rather than sinking several points into it.

On the other hand, if you plan to use Enchant on a regular basis, it's definitely worth adding skill points. Invest 20 skill points into Enchant, and you'll be able to imbue a weapon with impressive fire damage for nearly 10 minutes.

TIP

In multiplayer, you can use Enchant to add fire damage to the weapons of your party members.

Fire Wall

Level: 18	Prerequisites: Blaze

This is a classic spell from the original *Diablo*. Fire Wall creates a barrier of flame that inflicts a huge amount of damage on any enemies that venture into it. You can use this spell for many purposes, including creating a defensive 'grid' of Fire Walls that the enemy must traverse in order to reach your position.

Fire Wall is a powerful spell that lasts longer and grows wider with each level it attains. It's highly recommended that any Sorceress put as many points into Fire Wall as possible. Note that at level 10 Fire Wall causes 250 points of damage *per second*!

Fire Wall is similar to Blaze, except that it inflicts considerably more damage. When choosing which Fire skill to develop, put this one at the top of the list.

ALTERED SKILL

In **Diablo II** you could cast Fire Wall multiple times in rows so that every square inch of a room was left burning, thus killing anything inside. In the expansion set, however, a cool-down period has been added to Fire Wall, but not to worry—additional damage has also been added to this skill.

Meteor

Level: 24	Prerequisites: Fire Ball, Fire Wall

This spell summons a meteor to drop from the sky a short time after it is invoked, causing massive fire damage and leaving a wide area of scattered flames. It can be used on enemies in other rooms, on groups, or anywhere you have a line of sight. Meteor often takes the targeted monsters with it, and is often used to clear out rooms or areas where the Sorceress would not want to venture without a preliminary Meteor strike.

ALTERED SKILL

Meteor has been given a cool-down time so that it cannot be cast in quick succession.

Fire Mastery

Level: 30	Prerequisites: Meteor

Fire Mastery is of critical importance because it increases the amount of damage caused by all Sorceress fire spells. Putting just two extra skill points into Fire Mastery boosts the damage bonus from 22% to 54%. When you factor that into spells like Fire Wall and Meteor, it means you'll be able to inflict massive damage on the enemy!

Hydra

Level: 30	Prerequisites: Enchant

A sure favorite among those who play as the Sorceress, the Hydra spell creates a multi-headed beast of flame that shoots fire bolts at nearby enemies. It's great to use when you must defend an area from advancing enemies while simultaneously healing your character, dealing with inventory, or simply avoiding combat. Hydras act as sentinels that stand guard and attack any enemy that comes within their range. Although the damage they do is not substantial, a grid of five or six Hydras in a crossfire can handle most enemies.

The Hydra makes a great defensive sentinel.

ALTERED SKILL

Hydra has been given a cool-down time so that it cannot be cast in quick succession.

LIGHTNING

These spells allow the Sorceress to use lightning to destroy her enemies. They also enable her to use the energy of lightning to engage in telekenesis and teleporting. Like Fire and Cold, Lightning is an important form of elemental damage, so develop this skill tree in at least a limited way to take advantage of the damage it deals.

Charged Bolt

Level: 1	Prerequisites: None

This spell fires multiple, randomly moving bolts of electricity toward the target. Each bolt does a small amount of electrical damage when it hits an enemy, with more bolts (which do more damage) being released at higher levels. At level 20 you unleash an impressive 22 bolts, but the amount of damage that each bolt does is not substantial enough to make the kind of impact that's necessary later in the game. For this reason, Charged Bolt is best used early on—avoid spending skill points on it after the first Act.

TIP

Since Charged Bolt is a relatively inexpensive spell in terms of Mana, it can be used to 'search out' areas you cannot yet see. Sometimes it's a good idea to send a few Charged Bolts into a room or area that's off-screen, thus doing some preliminary damage to any enemies that might be lurking ahead.

Static Field

Level: 6	Prerequisites: None

Static Field is very powerful as an initial way to greet any group of enemies because it causes each target in a radius around your Sorceress to lose one third of its current hit points. This is especially helpful when you're in a group and are fighting a powerful enemy with a large number of hit points, because two hits with a Static Field will chop that foe's hit points in half. Each successive hit of Static Field causes the target to lose one-third of its current hit points, making it easy to damage your opponent, but less effective for ultimately killing them with this spell alone.

This is an incredibly powerful spell because it reduces the enemy's hit points by one-third, no matter how strong your adversary!

TIP

If you are so inclined, you **can** kill enemies with Static Field, but it takes numerous castings to get the enemy's health low enough. It's much better to use the spell a few times and then simply attack the enemy with your staff or wand when it is weakened, rather than wasting precious Mana.

Telekinesis

Level: 6	Prerequisites: None

This skill allows the Sorceress to pick up items, open doors and crates, and attack monsters and players from a distance. The primary use for Telekinesis is for opening crates or stashes from afar to avoid taking any hits or damage from a trap. Telekinesis is also very useful in combat—it is comparable to how the Paladin uses Smite. When cast on an enemy, it shoves the enemy back, does damage to it, and stuns it for a short period of time!

TIP

Telekinesis can be used to pick up objects on the other side of a grating or blocked passage, or to grab a valuable item before it can be reached by anyone else. Also, you can use this spell to activate a town portal from a distance—**very** effective when there is a pack of monsters between you and your only way out.

Nova

Level: 12	Prerequisites: Static Field

Nova is an awesome spell that generates an electrical shockwave that spreads out in all directions around your Sorceress, causing substantial lightning damage to all targets within its range. It's a superb choice for the first two Acts of *Diablo II*, but it can't compete with the higher-level monsters and their resistance to elemental damage later in the game. For this reason, Nova is well worth investing in, but is not the only spell you want to develop.

Lightning

Level: 12	Prerequisites: Charged Bolt

Lightning sends out a bolt of pure electrical energy that goes right through all targets, inflicting a healthy dose of damage to each one. As you approach level 20 in this skill, the amount of damage being done is huge, and because it passes through one enemy and onto the next, it offers an excellent means for attacking groups of enemies that are stacked in tight hallways or narrow canyons.

 TIP

Whenever the enemies are stacked two or three deep, you should use Lightning to blow through them with raw electrical power. This is a spell that deserves its own hot-key for easy access.

Chain Lightning

Level: 18	Prerequisites: Lightning

Chain Lightning sends out a streak of lightning that bounces and jumps through several targets, doing damage to everything it hits along the way. As skill points are added to Chain Lightning, both the amount of damage and the number of hits grows. For example, when this spell is at level 10, it branches out 11 times! Remember that it even bounces off of walls, so put it to good use when you're in a cramped dungeon!

Chain Lightning is a great spell for taking out large numbers of enemies in a wide area of occupation.

Teleport

Level: 18	Prerequisites: Telekinesis

Teleport instantly moves the Sorceress to the area you've targeted with your mouse. It's a very powerful spell that can get you out of trouble or transport you over vast expanses in the blink of an eye, but it is not without its limitations. For example, you cannot teleport to any area that you would not otherwise be able to walk to, which in areas like the Lost City leaves some ridges off-limits. Still, when you're in a pickle and are taking a beating from some pesky monsters, you can often simply teleport to high ground or to the other side of a wall to get your Sorceress out of trouble.

Thunder Storm

Level: 24 | Prerequisites: Nova, Chain Lightning

This skill creates a thunderstorm that will periodically hit a nearby enemy with a bolt of lightning. It is much more powerful and effective when you've been able to put a few skill points into it. The level 1 Thunder Storm has a minimum damage of 1, whereas level 2 has a minimum damage of 11, so just one skill point makes a 1100% difference!

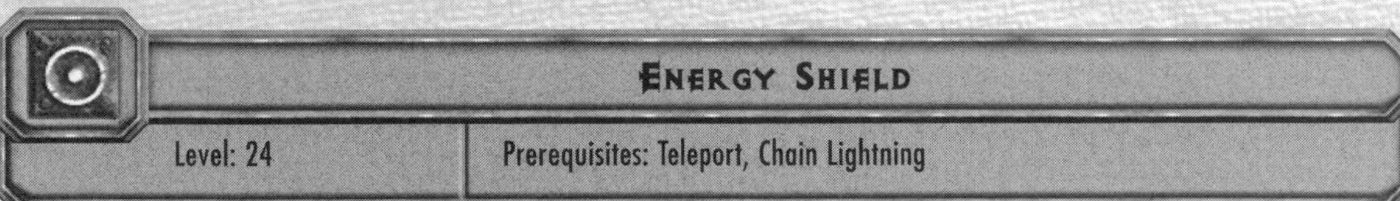

Energy Shield

Level: 24 | Prerequisites: Teleport, Chain Lightning

Energy Shield creates a defensive shelter that's based on your Mana supply. This shield absorbs some physical and all magic damage through Mana instead of hit points, thus extending your life considerably in hairy situations. You can add to your lifespan by using the Energy Shield and then drinking both Life and Mana potions to keep your Life and Energy Shield topped off. Use this spell only when you have plenty of Mana or are in desperate need of extra 'Life' since your Mana will drain quickly as you take hits, leaving you with no way to employ other skills.

Lightning Mastery

Level: 30 | Prerequisites: None

Lightning Mastery is a passive skill that reduces the Mana cost of lightning spells with each point that you put into the mastery. If you are going to develop the Lightning skill tree, it is imperative that you invest skill points in Lightning Mastery because it can ultimately save you hundreds, or even thousands, of Mana points over the course of an entire game.

COLD

This skill tree gives the Sorceress control over the realm of cold and ice. Cold is an important element because it naturally slows enemies, but more than that it can sometimes freeze enemies and shatter them into tiny shards of ice that melt away. An enemy that's been destroyed in this manner cannot be resurrected. Like the other elemental damage spells, Cold is an important skill tree to invest in, even if it's in just a limited way.

Ice Bolt

Level: 1 | Prerequisites: None

This is a base-level spell that not only inflicts cold damage on the target, but also slows the enemy for a period of time. How much damage is inflicted and how long the enemy is slowed depends on how many skill points you've put into this spell. Invest at least one skill point here because the slowing of enemies can be an important ability later in the game, and of course Ice Bolt is a prerequisite for learning Ice Blast and Glacial Spike.

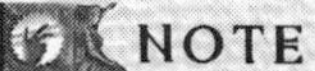

NOTE

Slowing your enemies with cold is something that shouldn't be underestimated. This is an excellent spell to have hot-keyed in the first two Acts of **Diablo II** because it can delay a tough enemy long enough for you to take them out or run away.

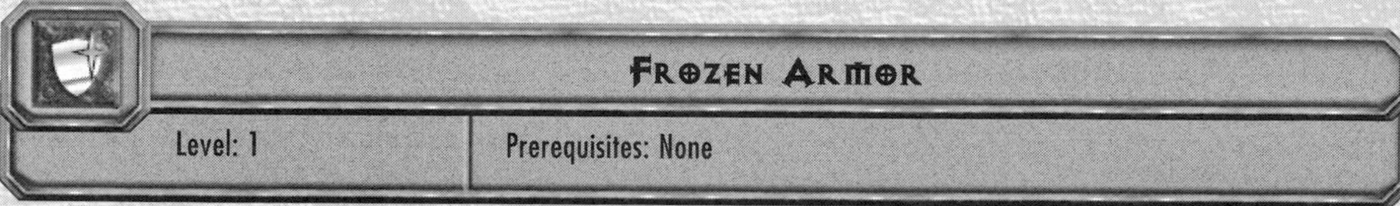

Frozen Armor

Level: 1 | Prerequisites: None

Frozen Armor is a long-lasting defensive spell that improves your Defensive Rating, while freezing any enemy attacker that lands a hit on your character. The duration of Frozen Armor (two minutes at level 1, and almost six minutes at level 20) is the real bonus because you can simply invoke it and move on. It's most effective when your Sorceress is involved in a great deal of melee fighting.

Frost Nova

Level: 6 | Prerequisites: None

Frost Nova generates an icy shockwave that spreads out in all directions around your Sorceress, freezing all targets it hits as it travels outward from your position. For this reason, the Frost Nova is an excellent skill to use when you are in an area that's tightly packed with enemies. By putting just two extra skill points into Frost Nova, you can double the length of time that it slows enemies with cold and nearly *doubles* the damage it does. Put at least three skill points into Frost Nova for best use in Acts I and II.

The Frost Nova freezes anything it hits.

Ice Blast

Level: 6 | Prerequisites: Ice Bolt

This spell creates a bolt of ice that freezes and damages the enemy target. In short, it's a more powerful version of the Ice Bolt. Its unique quality is that it doesn't just slow the enemies, it freezes them for a short time while dealing significant damage. The amount of damage climbs quickly with just a few skill points invested. Augmenting Ice Blast to level 3 gives you the power to freeze enemies for five seconds and still do over 20 points of damage for a relatively small Mana cost.

NOTE

Remember that a frozen enemy can sometimes be smashed by taking another Ice Blast or by taking a hit from a melee weapon. One bonus of freezing and then smashing your enemies into ice shards is that their destroyed bodies cannot be resurrected.

Shiver Armor

Level: 12	Prerequisites: Ice Blast, Frozen Armor

This is an armor that not only causes damage to the enemy when they hit you, but also hits them with a cold blast that slows them for four seconds. The 'offensive' nature of Shiver Armor masks the fact that it also increases your Defense Rating when active, making it a 'three-in-one' tool that can hit, protect, and slow your enemies all at once. Shiver Armor is effective at level 1, so you don't necessarily have to put a lot of skill points into it for it to be effective. Obviously, this is a spell that's best used when your Sorceress is involved in melee combat situations.

Glacial Spike

Level: 18	Prerequisites: Ice Blast

Glacial Spike is one of the most powerful cold spells in the game because it freezes an entire group of monsters rather than just one. Its damage is so substantial that enemies often simply smash into a hundred shards of ices and melt away after they take a single hit. Glacial Spike is a must-have skill that becomes considerably more powerful with just a few skill points. Use it against any group of enemies and watch them all freeze or shatter with just a few shots. Unfortunately, the radius of effect (2.6 yards) for Glacial Spike does not change when more skill points are added, but this is offset by the increased attack value and length of cold effect that the enemy must endure with each successive skill level.

Glacial Spike severely punishes any group of enemies it hits. Those that aren't destroyed will be slowed by the cold.

Blizzard

Level: 24	Prerequisites: Frost Nova, Glacial Spike

Blizzard creates a massive hailstorm that damages all enemies caught beneath its fury with a cascade of icy mayhem. More skill points in this spell means a longer duration of effect and more damage done from each ice shard that falls from the sky. Needless to say, this is a show-stopper when you're facing a large group of tightly-packed enemies. Blizzard also works well indoors, and is probably best used in rooms full of enemies trapped within an enclosed area.

Blizzard is the most visually impressive of the cold skills, but along with the great eye-candy, it also packs a massive punch.

ALTERED SKILL

Blizzard has been given a cool-down time so that it cannot be cast in quick succession. As with the other skills that have been modified in this manner, Blizzard's punch has been increased to help compensate for the delay period.

CHILLING ARMOR

Level: 24	Prerequisites: Shiver Armor

Chilling Armor is another multipurpose spell that both attacks and defends. It offers you an armor bonus while also launching an Ice Bolt at any enemies that hit you, thus damaging and slowing your attacker. This spell is most useful when you're alone facing three or four enemies at once.

FROZEN ORB

Level: 30	Prerequisites: Blizzard

Frozen Orb is a very powerful spell that serves multiple purposes. When cast, it sends out a large orb of ice that flies out in a straight line while spinning out Ice Bolts in all directions. This is a great weapon for a narrow hallway where there's a lineup of enemies, but it's also of great use in places such as a Carver camp because the bolts fly everywhere. It is an impressive display when you can eliminate the Shaman in a Carver Camp with the Frozen Orb (preventing him from resurrecting his minions) while the Ice Bolts literally carve up the Carvers.

ALTERED SKILL

Not to sound like a broken record, but Frozen Orb now has a delay period so that you cannot cast it again and again without hesitation. Like Blizzard and Frost Nova, however, it now also has more power to help compensate for the cool-down period.

COLD MASTERY

Level: 30	Prerequisites: None

While Cold Mastery doesn't reduce the Mana cost of your Cold spells, it does lower your enemy's resistance to cold-based damage by a percentage. Just two extra skill points doubles the effectiveness of any of your damaging cold spells, so it's well worth the investment. Being able to freeze, shatter, or slow opponents with cold damage can be the difference between life and death for your character, so if you plan to use Cold-based skills, Cold Mastery is critical (of course, you can't actually put points in it until you're near the end of Act IV).

THE BARBARIAN

The Barbarian is usually a member of any of several tribes living on the fringes of civilization. These tribes refuse the influence of those they see as soft and weak, and the Barbarian is no different. Ceaseless clan warfare and the constant struggle to survive in the hostile wilderness are reflected in the Barbarian's sturdy and powerful frame.

Perhaps lacking the sophistication of the other characters, the Barbarian has an acute awareness of his surroundings. Because of his shamanistic belief in the animal powers with which he identifies, the Barbarian is sometimes associated with stories of lycanthropy. In fact, he believes he can call upon totemic animal spirits to infuse him with supernormal strengths and abilities, but these abilities only work to improve his already superb battle tactics.

THE BARBARIAN SKILLS

The Barbarian is a pure fighter, and most of his skills augment these core abilities. His three skill sets are Combat Skills, Combat Masteries, and Warcries. As with the other characters, the skills that are developed in each area ultimately affect the abilities of the Barbarian as he progresses through the *Diablo II* universe.

Out of the Masteries, the higher level weapons that the Barbarian is likely to find are swords. Therefore, if you're looking to create an uber-Barbarian, it is usually prudent to put points into Sword Mastery.

Warcries

1. Howl
2. Find Potion
3. Taunt
4. Shout
5. Find Item
6. Battlecry
7. Battle Orders
8. Grim Ward
9. Warcry
10. Battle Command

Combat Masteries

1. Sword Mastery
2. Axe Mastery
3. Mace Mastery
4. Pole Arm Mastery
5. Throwing Mastery
6. Spear Mastery
7. Increased Stamina
8. Iron Skin
9. Increased Speed
10. Natural Resistance

Combat Skills

1. Bash
2. Leap
3. Double Swing
4. Stun
5. Double Throw
6. Leap Attack
7. Concentrate
8. Frenzy
9. Whirlwind
10. Berserk

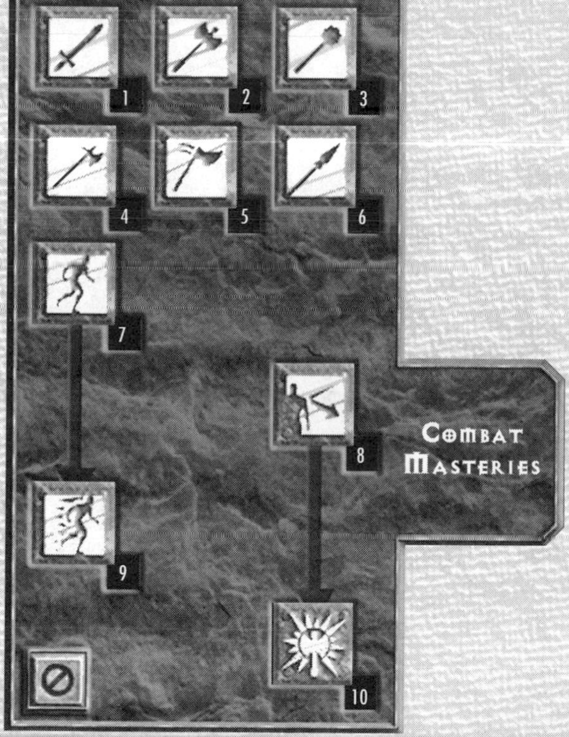

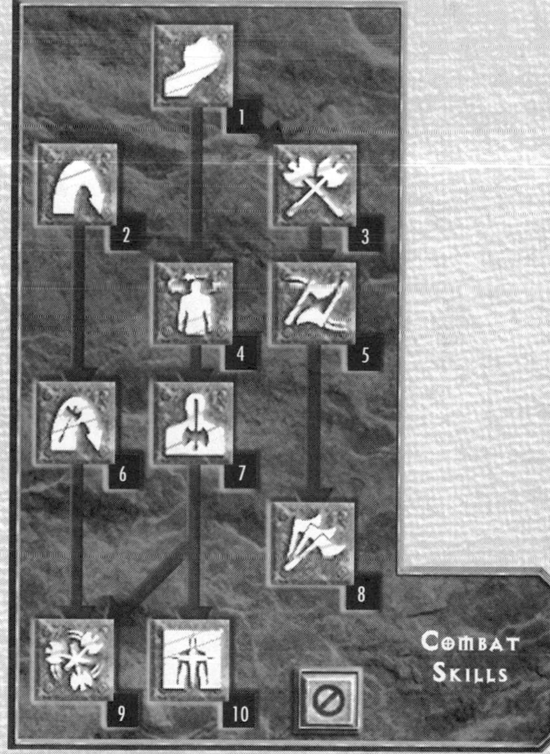

COMBAT SKILLS

This skill tree is the main attack skill tree of the Barbarian, and includes the critical skills of Bash and Leap Attack. Although the Barbarian's Masteries are very important, he'd be hard-pressed to succeed without having at least a few of the skills in the Combat skill tree.

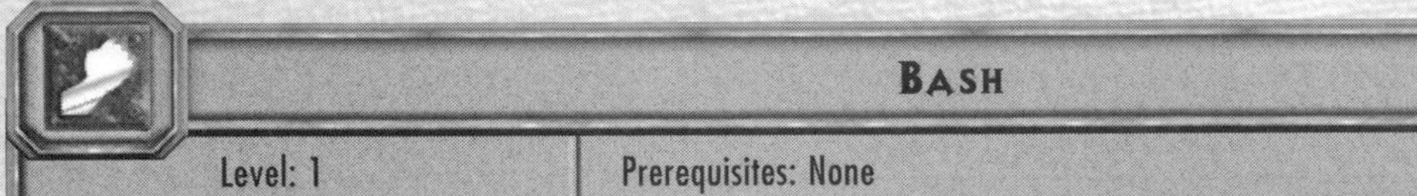

Bash

Level: 1	Prerequisites: None

This skill delivers a powerful smashing blow that knocks the target back, stuns it, and inflicts a substantial amount of damage. Bash not only adds additional damage, it also increases the damage and attack modifiers, thus giving you a powerful hit that knocks back the enemy and stuns it for a brief time. Bash is a skill that is great to use against monsters that are exceptionally tough, because it will get them out of your way while providing a brief period of time for you to attack again, run, or switch skills.

Bash is a Level 1 skill, but you can use it for effect throughout the entire game.

Leap

Level: 6	Prerequisites: None

Perhaps the Barbarian's most versatile and important skill, Leap enables the Barbarian to jump over obstacles. Leap not only moves you around the map nicely, but it enables you to do things that other players cannot do. For example, you can leap over rivers or cut corners over areas that the other party members or monsters must walk around. With the Leap skill, you can access places you otherwise couldn't, such as in the Arcane Sanctuary, or use it to escape a scary situation from which you normally couldn't run.

Of course, to get the kind of distance that will *really* make a difference, you must put six or seven points into this skill. As an added bonus, when you land after performing a Leap there's a small amount of 'knock-back' that occurs against enemies. Although this doesn't damage the enemies, it gives you a cushion of space when you land.

NOTE

In multiplayer action, you can often use Leap to reach an item before a party member. This is just one of the advantages of being a Barbarian.

Double Swing

Level: 6 | Prerequisites: Bash

This skill provides a quick double attack that enables you use weapons held in both hands in the space of a single attack. For example, if you have an axe in one hand and a sword in the other, Double Swing quickly swings both weapons and causes damage with both. However, this isn't the only benefit of this skill. It also provides a bonus to your Attack Rating that makes each attack a little better.

Oftentimes, it's a good idea to make Double Swing your standard attack for your left mouse button. Therefore, each time you attack, you're performing a Double Swing and getting the Attack Rating modifier. This will enable you to cause more damage faster, plus it's a great technique to use throughout the game.

The drawback to using Double Swing is that it costs two Mana points each time it's used. This skill is best used when you have a Mana recharge item or if you have additional Mana potions to maintain your reserve.

ALTERED SKILL

Double Swing has been altered for the expansion set so that it's now affected by weapon speed. That is to say, if you put two slow-attack-speed weapons in your hands and use Double Swing, it will be slower than if you're carrying very fast weapons.

Stun

Level: 12 | Prerequisites: Bash

This skill not only stuns the enemy that you're attacking, it also increases the Attack Rating for that attack. Similar to skills like Bash and Smite, Stun is great for keeping an enemy stunned and unable to retaliate against your attacks.

If you consistently use Stun against an enemy, the enemy won't be able to respond to your attacks because it will be perpetually stunned until its death. When you put a few skill points into Stun, the duration of the stun increases so that you can have more time in-between attacks. This provides more time to choose how to finish off the enemy, attack another enemy, or run if you need to.

Double Throw

Level: 12 | Prerequisites: Double Swing

Like Double Swing, Double Throw simply allows you to quickly throw two weapons (one from each hand). In addition, it increases the Attack Rating of each thrown weapon. The importance of the Attack Rating increase cannot be overstated. After adding just a few skill points to Double Throw, the attack improves by 50%!

NOTE

The only downside to Double Throw is that you must have weapons that you can throw. When fighting lots of enemies, you need plenty of throwing weapons at your disposal. If not, you'll run out of weapons and be left without a weapon with which to fight.

Leap Attack

Level: 18	Prerequisites: Leap

This is a skill that allows you to leap onto a target and then immediately attack. The Leap Attack is very powerful because you cannot be hit *while* you're in the act of leaping. After adding just a few skill points, you can leap about 10 yards and increase the damage inflicted by nearly 200%. Many Blizzard employees use Leap Attack to jump in and out of melee fighting so as to avoid taking hits while still causing substantial damage.

This is arguably the Barbarian's best skill. You can use it for attacks or for getting around!

Leap Attack is also useful because you can leap further at level 1 than with the standard Leap skill at the same level, and can use it to leap from place to place, regardless of the presence of enemies. For example, there are enemies in the Arcane Sanctuary on nearby platforms that attack you. In this case, you can simply Leap Attack over and take out the enemies rather than looking for the proper teleporter usually required to transport you to the action.

Concentrate

Level: 18	Prerequisites: Stun

With this skill, your attack can be uninterrupted, which can be critical for the Barbarian. When surrounded by enemies, having your attack interrupted by being hit is a common occurrence. However, when using Concentrate, your attack will finish, regardless of any damage you take.

Concentrate is also a handy skill because it improves your Attack and Defense Rating while you're attacking the enemy. It's nice to have at least one point in this skill just in case you get surrounded by a pack of creatures.

ALTERED SKILL

For **Diablo II: Lord of Destruction**, Concentrate has been buffed up so that it increases your Defense Rating. It's now much harder to be interrupted (when you're attacking), making this skill much more valuable.

Frenzy

Level: 24	Prerequisites: Double Throw

When this skill is invoked, a successful hit increases the attack speed and velocity for each successive hit. After placing a few skill points into it, the duration of action is long enough that you can deliver several consecutive, faster, and more powerful hits because Frenzy also increases your Attack Rating.

This skill is considerably more powerful after adding six or seven skill points to it, but even then it's most effective against enemies that require several hits to kill. For example, if you use Frenzy on an enemy that requires only one or two hits to kill, then the cumulative effects of Frenzy will be lost. Therefore, Frenzy is best used against tougher enemies that require several hits to take down and is not as useful against run-of-the-mill fodder.

ALTERED SKILL

Like Double Swing, Frenzy is now affected by weapon speed. The slower your weapons, the slower it performs.

Whirlwind

Level: 30 | Prerequisites: Leap Attack, Concentrate

As the folks at Blizzard like to say, "Think Tasmanian Devil." With this skill, your Barbarian's weapons actually go into a 'whirlwind' and hack away at anything in their path. It's important to note that in the first few levels it actually penalizes you by decreasing the damage it causes. However, after you get past level 3, Whirlwind not only increases the damage you inflict (substantially), but it also increases the Attack Rating.

A great tactic for Whirlwind is to click on an area behind a group of enemies and have your Barbarian clear a path as he chops them into little pieces.

ALTERED SKILL

Whirlwind, like Frenzy and Double Swing, is also affected by weapon speed now.

Whirlwind is a skill that's been likened to watching the Tasmanian Devil of cartoon fame.

Berserk

Level: 30 | Prerequisites: Concentrate

This is a powerful skill that makes your Barbarian go berserk. You attack with both a greater Attack Rating and Magical Damage Rating. You must remember that when you put points into this skill and receive the huge attack bonuses, its duration actually goes *down* rather than up. This is because the effect of the skill is so great that any duration longer than 1.5 seconds at higher levels would make the skill too powerful.

ALTERED SKILL

Berserk now does more damage and also inflicts magical damage.

COMBAT MASTERIES

A Barbarian who's mastered the six arts (mace, axe, sword, pole arm, throwing, and spear) is a force to be reckoned with. Unfortunately, putting many points into all of the Masteries is not feasible, so the best thing to do is choose a Mastery and run with it. Oftentimes, gamers wait and hold onto skill points until they pick up a weapon that they like, and then put the skill points into the area that matches that weapon.

Masteries

Level: All Masteries available at Level 1	Prerequisites: None

This set of skills adds to the damage inflicted by the class of weapons that you've put the skill points into. The masteries include Sword, Axe, Mace, Pole-Arm, Throwing, and Spear. When points are added to these skills, the damage inflicted by the improved weapon class increases dramatically. For example, if you want to use swords throughout the game, then Sword Mastery is the skill to put your skill points into.

The player who puts points into the Masteries will always be more successful than the player that puts their points into other Barbarian skills exclusively. The reason why Masteries are so powerful is that they dramatically improve the performance of groups of weapons. Therefore, no matter which weapon in that class you're using, you always have the benefit of the Mastery.

If a Barbarian invests heavily in Axe Mastery, the benefits of the Mastery are always there, no matter which axe he uses as he passes through the game. No casting is required to utilize Masteries. You only need the kind of weapon that benefits from the Mastery into which you've put your points.

TIP

Derek Simmons, Senior QA Analyst at Blizzard, suggests that you save skill points that you have earmarked for Masteries until you find a weapon that you'll want to keep and use throughout the game. Usually around Act II, you will have found a few desirable weapons, and one is probably a favorite. When you've decided on the class of weapon you are going to keep, you can put your points into that Mastery so that you can best use the great weapon you've found!

Increased Stamina

Level: 12	Prerequisites: None

While this skill simply improves your stamina, just a few points give you a stamina bonus of 60%! The catch is whether or not you're the kind of player that needs to have increased stamina. For example, if you rarely run, then there isn't much need to put skill points into this skill. Likewise, if you occasionally run but often find yourself with Stamina Potions that you don't use, then it's probably not a good idea to waste a point in Increased Stamina.

However, if you constantly run to move, attack, or get away from the enemy, then having a higher level of Stamina will be important to you. Obviously, you'll want to invest a skill point or two into Increased Stamina to lower your dependence on resting or collecting and drinking Stamina Potions.

Iron Skin

Level: 18	Prerequisites: None

Iron Skin is a skill that improves your overall Defense Rating. With a few points added to it, this skill becomes very powerful—the Barbarian often has a high Defense Rating since his strength allows him to wear massive armor.

Iron Skin modifies the overall Defense Rating by a percentage. So, if you put in eight skill points, your Barbarian's Defense Rating doubles, which is an impressive boost to a very important statistic. For example, if your Barbarian has a Defense Rating of 200, and you've put eight skill points into Iron Skin, then your Barbarian improves his Defense Rating to 400!

Increased Speed

Level: 24	Prerequisites: Increased Stamina

This skill increases the speed at which the Barbarian walks and runs. Having the ability to walk and run faster has major implications in *Diablo II*. If you can walk faster, then you don't have to rely on Run to escape from certain enemies, thus sparing your Stamina. Likewise, if you can run faster, you can escape from fast enemies that you would not have been able to previously elude. Even in the first couple of levels, it's well worth adding a point or two into this skill if you can spare them.

Having increased speed can make running away from, or catching up to, enemies much easier.

Natural Resistance

Level: 30	Prerequisites: Iron Skin

In the higher levels of *Diablo II: Lord of Destruction*, one of the main dangers to your character comes from magical attacks (fire, cold, poison, and electrical). Natural Resistance is a skill that increases your resistance to these attacks, thus making your life considerably easier at higher levels.

The benefit you receive from putting skill points into this skill may seem small; however, even a 20% protection from a magical attack can mean the difference between life and death.

Warcries

The skills in this area are great tools for the Barbarian at any time. However, many of them, like Taunt and Battle Command, really shine when used in a multiplayer team situation.

Battle Command, for example, gives each party member who's close to you an extra skill point in every skill they have for a brief period of time. The first skill in this set is Howl, which forces the enemies to run away from your position. This skill is handy whether you're in the Blood Moor of Act I or in the deepest recesses of Hell.

Howl

Level: 1	Prerequisites: None

This skill frightens monsters into retreating from your position. Howl works within a specific radius around your character, which you can see when Howl is used. Upon using this skill, enemies run for a set distance or a set amount of time, depending on how many skill points have been put into Howl. This skill works just as well in Act IV as it does in Act I, so it's valuable to use at any time during the game.

Howl is a very handy skill that will send your enemies running!

 TIP

You can use Howl to make a group of enemies more manageable. For example, if a group of enemies runs at you, you can invoke Howl and send the first row of enemies away, leaving only those that weren't affected to fight you. This can reduce the number of enemies you have to face at once, thus making your task easier.

Find Potion

Level: 1	Prerequisites: None

With this skill, there's a chance that you may find a potion on a dead body. The potion you find is generated randomly, but the most common are Health Potions or Mana Potions.

As a rule, this skill doesn't need more than one or two skill points added to it. Even with a 15% chance of getting a Health Potion, this usually creates enough potions that your Barbarian won't have to worry about buying potions in town. This is a great skill for multiplayer action as well, because you can search the bodies of the dead and turn up Health Potions for your party members that may be in need of healing.

Taunt

Level: 6	Prerequisites: Howl

This skill taunts a monster to approach and fight. Although this may not seem like a skill you'd use often (because enemies come to you anyway), there are uses for this skill that will help your Barbarian in single and multiplayer mode.

In single-player combat, you can use Taunt to bring ranged-weapon enemies directly to you rather than having to run them down yourself. Also, you can bring enemies out of a room where they may be lurking (for example, when you want to pull minions away from their controller, such as the Countess in the Tower). Lastly, you can use Taunt in multiplayer mode to pull an enemy off a party member that's taking a beating, thus sparing them from death in certain situations.

NOTE

It should be noted that Taunt also decreases the Attack and Defense Rating of the enemy, so it has value beyond simply drawing enemies toward you.

Shout

Level: 6 | Prerequisites: Howl

Shout is a skill that dramatically increases the Defense Rating of your Barbarian and any allies. Even a level 1, Shout adds 100% to your defense bonus for 16 seconds. When playing multiplayer, this skill attaches to any ally that's close enough to you, so they will also enjoy the greatly enhanced Defense Rating. This skill is excellent to use just before you move into a heavy melee battle.

Find Item

Level: 12 | Prerequisites: Find Potion

Like Find Potion, this skill increases the chance to find an item. The item you find is randomly generated, but it could range from gold to weapons and everything in-between.

Using Find Item is a great way to gain wealth for the Barbarian. Simply use Find Item to scour every corpse you come across, and then sell the results of your searches in town.

Battle Cry

Level: 18 | Prerequisites: Taunt

Battle Cry reduces the Defense Rating of enemies within the radius of effect of this skill. The result is a dramatic reduction in the enemy's ability to cause damage and defend itself; and an enemy that can't defend itself or fight back well is exactly what you want in melee combat.

This skill is best used when fighting in tight quarters or against several enemies that are in close proximity. The duration of this skill is the most important part of Battlecry, especially when you're facing tough monsters that may take more than a minute to kill. To increase the duration of this skill, just add more skill points.

Battle Orders

Level: 24 | Prerequisites: Shout

This skill is especially powerful in multiplayer situations because it gives you *and* your party boosts in Life, Stamina, and Mana for a relatively small Mana cost. The downside to Battle Orders is that it costs one-third of your hit points to invoke! You should only use Battle Orders when it can benefit your party in multiplayer, or when you have a Life-stealing piece of equipment to compensate for the Life lost as you attack.

Since the Barbarian can use Find Potion to scrounge up healing potions, you may want to use the extra potions you find to counteract the Life lost when you use this skill. On the upside, the benefits this skill bestows on you and your party are very worthwhile, and the more points you put into this skill the longer the effects last.

Grim Ward

Level: 24	Prerequisites: Find Item

This skill turns a fallen enemy into a gruesome totem that frightens away enemies and prevents them from coming near the area where the ward stands. When you use Grim Ward, the enemies will not pass the area near the ward until it disappears, thus giving you extra time to regroup or create a town portal. It is especially effective when you need to run from enemies and there are bodies in your path.

Warcry

Level: 30	Prerequisites: Battle Cry, Battle Orders

This is a powerful and useful skill that damages and stuns nearby monsters. The amount of damage and the length of the stun effect are limited by the number of skill points in the skill. However, even at level 1, Warcry packs a substantial punch.

The stun effect from Warcry should provide ample time to prepare another attack while the enemy recovers. Although it costs 17 Mana points to cast Warcry, this skill is worth the price in certain situations. Use Warcry to slow down the pace of a frenzied battle by stunning or killing all the enemies near you.

Battle Command

Level: 30	Prerequisites: Battle Orders

This is a very powerful and important skill for use with a party in multiplayer games. Battle Command increases the level of *all* of your skills (and those of nearby allies) by one level! This means that each party member that was within the radius of your Battle Command when it was cast has an additional level of each skill they have, regardless of the type of character they are.

In a tough battle against formidable opponents, this skill can turn the tide in your party's favor. As you add skill points to Battle Command, you receive only one benefit: time. The more points you add, the longer the duration of this skill's effect. Having the ability to fight for 30 seconds with a higher skill level for a party of six players amounts to a huge advantage.

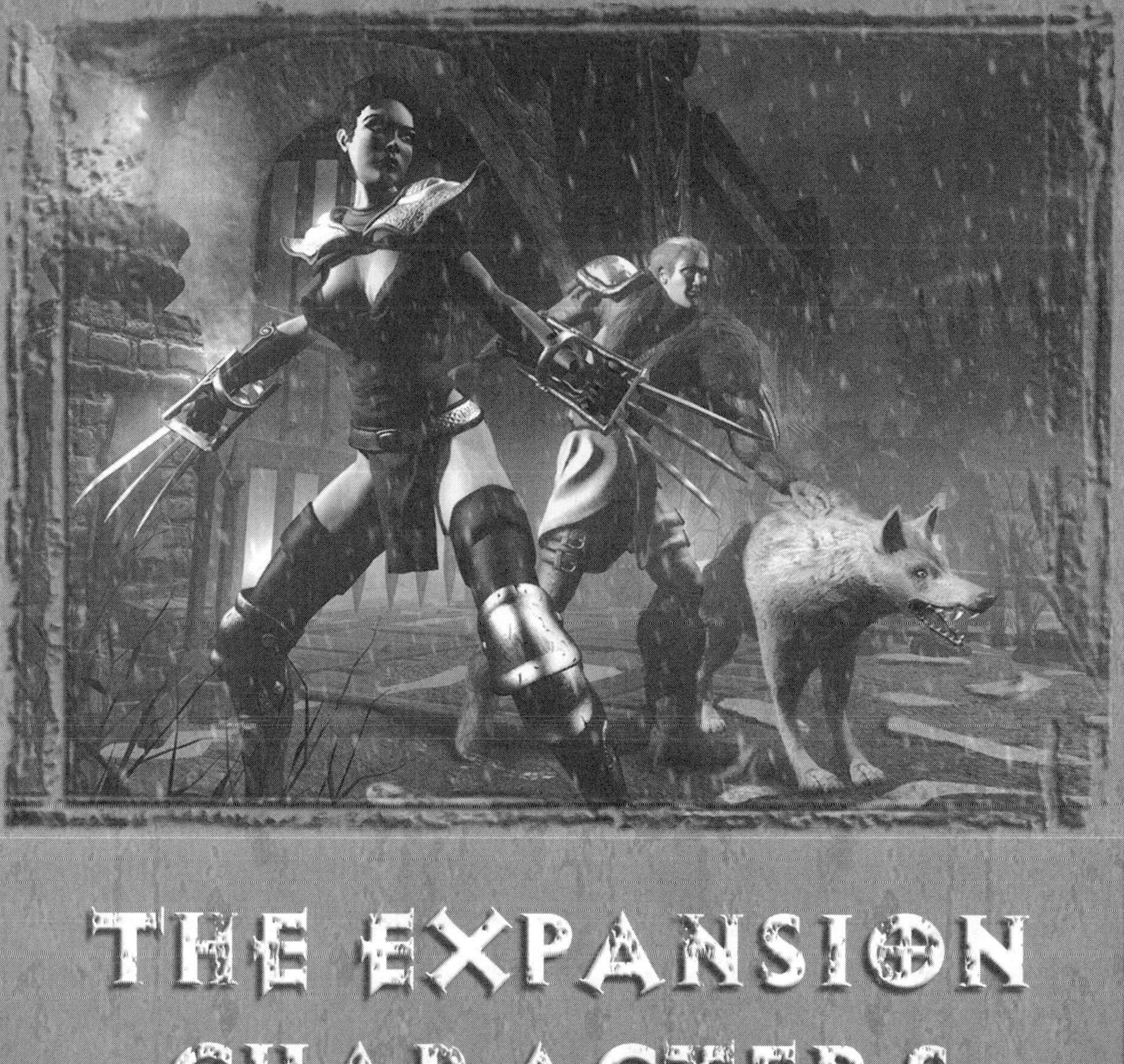

THE EXPANSION CHARACTERS

- THE ASSASSIN
- THE DRUID

THE ASSASSIN

Assassins are those who are only rumor. They are whispers in the night, faint noises in the woods just beyond your vision. They are trained in the art of killing with stealth and skill, and as such do not employ the magical arts directly, but rather use enchanted items that mimic elemental powers. As the folks at Blizzard put it, "to further avoid potential corruption, they focus on the natural abilities of the mortal body—powers of the mind and unarmed combat." The Assassin's skills are broken up into Martial Arts, Shadow Disciplines, and Traps. It is especially important to employ all skill areas to be successful with the Assassin, but when the skills are combined properly, she is a formidable force in the fight against eternal evil.

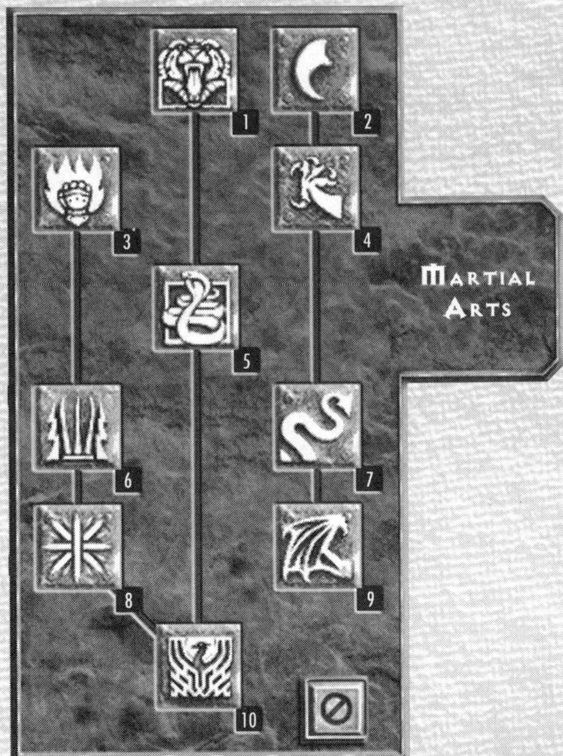

THE ASSASSIN SKILLS

The Assassin's three skill trees (Martial Arts, Traps, and Shadow Disciplines) complement each other much like the skills of the other characters. The key elements of the Assassin skills are the combination of the Charge-up Skills and Finishing Moves in the Martial Arts tree, and the awesome power of the Traps skill tree, which provides many ways to trick your enemies into an early grave. Lastly, the Shadow Disciplines provide the finishing touches that make the Assassin a formidable character. From Claw Mastery to summoning a Shadow Warrior to fight at the Assassin's side, the Shadow Disciplines are a valuable asset to sink skill points into.

Martial Arts

1. Tiger Strike
2. Dragon Talon
3. Fists of Fire
4. Dragon Claw
5. Cobra Strike
6. Claws of Thunder
7. Dragon Tail
8. Blades of Ice
9. Dragon Flight
10. Phoenix Strike

Shadow Disciplines

1. Claw Mastery
2. Psychic Hammer
3. Burst of Speed
4. Weapon Block
5. Cloak of Shadows
6. Fade
7. Shadow Warrior
8. Mind Blast
9. Venom
10. Shadow Master

Traps

1. Fire Blast
2. Shock Web
3. Blade Sentinel
4. Charged Bolt Sentry
5. Wake of Fire
6. Blade Fury
7. Lightning Sentry
8. Wake of Inferno
9. Death Sentry
10. Blade Shield

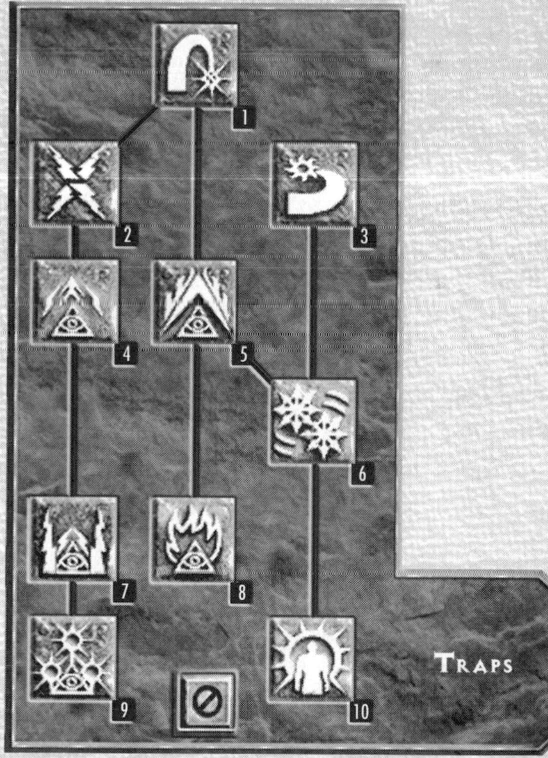

NOTE

Many of the Assassin's skills change their incremental increase after 8 skill points and 16 skill points—including Fist of Fire, Claws of Thunder, Blades of Ice, Phoenix Strike, Psychic Hammer, Mind Blast, Venom, Fire Blast, Shock Web, Blade Sentinel, Charged Bolt Sentry, Wake of Fire, Blade Fury, Lightning Sentry, Wake of Inferno, Death Sentry, and Blade Shield. All these skills increase their incremental damage at these skill point levels. Note that the incremental damage numbers mentioned for these skills in this chapter refer to incremental changes prior to these skill point levels.

MARTIAL ARTS

The Martial Arts are a combination of attacks and moves that can be divided into two categories—Charge-up Skills and Finishing Moves. These are unique to the expansion set and can be used in combination to unleash devastating amounts of damage on the enemy. As the Assassin uses a Charge-up Skill, she accumulates charges that circle around her body. She can continue to charge-up with several skills, then she can use a Finishing Move to unleash all of the charged-up power from her previous attacks.

TIP

There are two types of Martial Arts skills: the Charge-up Skills and the Finishing Moves. Each of the Assassin's skills can be charged-up three times. When you hit with either a normal move or a Finishing Move, the charged-up energy/attack is transferred onto the enemy!

A great way to use these moves is to set your left mouse button to a single Charge-up Skill or a series of them, and use your right mouse button for Finishing Moves. This enables you to charge-up with the left button, moving from skill to skill until you have six or more Charge-up Skills active, and then end with a Finishing Move by clicking the right mouse button!

Tiger Strike

Level: 1	Prerequisites: None

This is a Charge-up Skill that adds whopping amounts of damage with each new charge. The Tiger Strike is best suited for fighting really tough monsters or groups of enemies, rather than individual mid-range monsters. In fact, it's so effective that the enemy you're fighting is often dead before you get to the really juicy three-charge limit where a Finishing Move can come into play. Tiger Strike can help considerably when battling formidable foes like Andariel or Duriel because you'll be able to amass a full set of three charges, then use a powerful Finishing Move.

Tiger Strike has an initial effect of adding 40% to the Attack Rating and 100% extra damage for each Charge-up (up to 300%). With each successive skill level, the Attack Rating goes up 10%; the Charge-up damage increases 20% for the first charge, 40% for the second, and 60% for the third. As you can see, it quickly becomes a very powerful attack with just a few skill points.

Dragon Talon

Level: 1	Prerequisites: None

Dragon Talon is a Finishing Move that knocks the enemy back while unleashing any Charged-up Skills. It starts out with one kick (in level 1), but later (at level 12) you will be doing as many as three consecutive kicks with each attack. It should be noted that your Charged-up Skills are discharged only on the first kick of Dragon Talon, and not on subsequent kicks.

Dragon Talon's knock-back ability is excellent for keeping tough, melee-fighting enemies away from you. Although adding Charged-up Skills makes it much more powerful, Dragon Talon is a great skill on its own. Initially, it adds 40% to your Attack Rating. Each additional skill point provides 7% more damage and a 12% boost to your Attack Rating.

Dragon Talon is an excellent early Finishing Move.

Fists of Fire

Level: 6	Prerequisites: None

Fists of Fire is a Charge-up Skill that adds fire with every charge, which is applied differently throughout the three charge-ups. After the first charge, it adds fire damage to your attack; after the second charge, it summons a fire attack over a radius; and after the third charge, it burns over time (2.5 seconds). Although 2.5 seconds doesn't seem like a long time, it's surprising how many enemies will be damaged by this after-burn while rushing up to attack you.

The initial effect of Fists of Fire adds 50% to your Attack Rating, then it adds 6-10 fire damage with the first charge, a ranged burn of two yards on the second charge, and a burn that lasts for 2.5 seconds on the final charge. Each additional skill point placed into Fists of Fire adds an extra 10% to your Attack Rating and increases fire damage by five. Naturally, using a Charge-up Skill like this with a Finishing Move like Dragon Tail is an awesome combination, especially against fire-sensitive enemies.

 NOTE

You must be using Claws to enable Fists of Fire.

Dragon Claw

Level: 6	Prerequisites: Dragon Talon

Dragon Claw is a Finishing Move that uses two claw-class weapons. This skill is much like the Barbarian's Double Swing, since it allows the Assassin to swing her claw-class weapons twice in quick succession. Of course, this makes for a devastating attack even without the modifiers that come with it, but when you factor in an additional 50% to your Attack Rating and 50% more damage when you use it as a Finishing Move, it gets even better. Dragon Claw adds 10% to your Attack Rating and 5% to Damage with each skill point you invest in it.

Cobra Strike

Level: 12	Prerequisites: Tiger Strike

Cobra Strike is a Charge-up Skill that adds Mana and Life stealing to the Finishing Moves. The importance of this skill to the Assassin cannot be understated because it's one of the few reliable ways for her to replenish her Mana and Life supply while actively fighting. The first hit adds 60% to the Attack Rating and steals 40% Life from the enemy you attack. The second attack adds a steal of 40% Mana. The third one doubles the steals to 80% Life and Mana (a significant amount).

If you need Mana and Life steal, Cobra Strike is the Assassin's first choice skill.

Try combining Cobra Strike with a Finishing Move like Dragon Flight to teleport and strike your enemy from a short distance away. Your Attack Rating increases 15% with each skill point you put into Cobra Strike, while the first and second charges go up 5%, and the third charge gets a 10% boost. After investing few skill points in this skill, you can steal more than 100% of an enemy's health!

Claws of Thunder

Level 18	Prerequisites: Fists of Fire

Claws of Thunder is a Charge-up Skill that adds lightning damage with each successive attack and requires the Assassin to have claw-class weapons readied. When discharged by a Finishing Move, the first charge inflicts lightning damage on the enemy, the second charge sends out a Nova from the enemy you hit, while the third charge sends Charged Bolts out from your target! This attack is very valuable when fighting a large group of monsters as it can instantly destroy a throng of foes.

Claws of Thunder gives you an improved Attack Rating that's 80% above normal, and does 1-80 points of lightning damage of its own. The first charge does 1-80 lightning damage, the second does 1-20 Nova damage, and the third charge does 1-40 Charged Bolt damage.

When you invest additional points into the skill, the damage for the first charge adds 10 points of lightning damage, the second increases the maximum lightning damage of the Nova by seven, and the third charge boosts the maximum lightning damage of the Charged Bolts by 11.

Dragon Tail

Level: 18	Prerequisites: Dragon Claw

Dragon Tail is a powerful Finishing Move that knocks back your enemy with an explosive kick and does fire damage. Much like the Dragon Talon (only more powerful), the Dragon Tail is best used against enemies that you want to push back so that they can't hit you. When fighting a Boss monster, use a Charge-up Skill on the minions, then unleash the Dragon Tail on the Boss.

This skill inflicts 50% of fire damage and has a range of four yards in the first level. With each subsequent skill point, Dragon Tail dishes out an extra 10% of fire damage. This is the Finishing Move of choice once you reach level 18.

This is a cool Finishing Move both because of the knockback and the fire damage.

Blades of Ice

Level: 24	Prerequisites: Claws of Thunder

Blades of Ice is a Charge-up Skill that accumulates cold damage with each successive hit. It's a key skill whenever you're in a situation where the Assassin is getting overwhelmed by enemies. The first charge does cold damage on the enemy, the second causes cold damage to an area, and the third is capable of freezing enemies (always a good thing). It should be noted that you must have claw-class weapons readied to use Blades of Ice, but don't let that stop you from chilling out the enemy with a full charge and a Finishing Move like Dragon Claw.

This skill increases Attack Rating by 70%. The first charge does 15-35 points of cold damage, the second adds a radius of 3.3 yards, and the third charge freezes for four seconds. When you place additional points into the skill, cold damage is increased by eight points, freeze duration is extended by 0.4 seconds, and Attack Rating gets a 10% boost.

Dragon Flight

Level: 24	Prerequisites: Dragon Tail

Dragon Flight is a Finishing Move that teleports you beside your enemy so you can kick them and finish them off. This comes in very handy when you're trying to hit a Boss that's behind some minions, or if you need to skip over an obstacle.

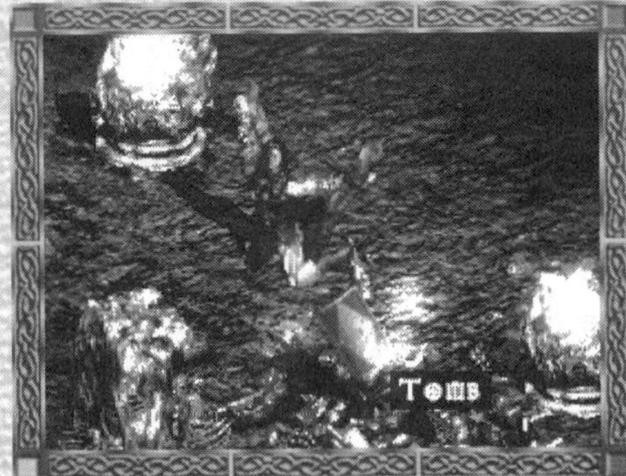

Teleporting to your enemy to deliver a Finishing Move is what Dragon Flight is all about.

Dragon Flight is useful when fighting against an enemy that lays fire down in front of you, enabling you to leap over the blaze without taking any damage. One caveat to the Dragon Flight skill is that it has a cool-down period, so you can't use it in quick succession. Still, despite this limitation, it's a very powerful skill that merits at least a few skill points once your Assassin reaches Level 24. Your Attack Rating increases 100% when you teleport to hit the enemy, and it goes up another 20% with each skill point added. Initially, Dragon Flight enhances kick damage by 100%, increasing by 25% with every additional skill point.

 NOTE

You must be able to target the enemy in order to teleport to him/her. In other words, you cannot use this skill if your opponent is off your screen.

Phoenix Strike

Level: 30	Prerequisites: Cobra Strike, Blades of Ice

Phoenix Strike is a Charge-up Skill that adds elemental attacks to your Finishing Moves! The first charge drops a meteor, the second summons chain lightning, and the last throws piles of ice out in radiating rivulets. Needless to say, you'll want to put a point or two into this skill once you reach Level 30. Depending on what kind of result you want (elementally speaking), you can use your Finishing Move after the particular Charge-up that provides the desired result. If you want to drop a Meteor, then use the Finishing Move after the first Charge-up. However, if you prefer to put the big freeze on your enemies, then wait and use the Finishing Move after you've charged-up to level 3.

Initially, this skill provides a 70% increase to Attack Rating, 20-40 points of Meteor damage for the first charge, 1-40 points of Chain Lightning damage for the second charge, and 16-32 points of damage of Chaos Ice Bolt damage for the third charge. With every additional point into the skill, the Attack Rating increases by 15%, Meteor damage increases by six points, Chain Lightning's maximum damage is boosted by 11 points, and Chaos Ice Bolt damage improves by four points.

SHADOW DISCIPLINES

This set of skills adds to the mystery and power of the Assassin. The Shadow Disciplines don't make the attacks, they make the attacks better. They don't hide the Assassin, they make her harder to see. They can also cause poison damage and summon a Shadow Warrior to fight at the Assassin's side. In short, the Shadow Disciplines are a set of very important skills that augment the Assassin's other skill sets, while still providing a great set of unique and devastating abilities.

Claw Mastery

Level: 1	Prerequisites: None

Claw weapons are a new weapon class that the Assassin uses to achieve her goals. A claw class weapon can be worn on each hand so that the enemy can be attacked with a dual swing. This skill improves the Assassin's use of these weapons in much the same way that Sword Mastery or Axe Mastery improves the Barbarian's ability to handle those weapons. If you want to fully appreciate the Assassin experience and use some of the great Charge-Up and Finishing Moves that involve the use of claw-class weapons, then you'll need to put some points into Claw Mastery.

Claw Mastery is a key skill if you're planning on using any claw-class weapons.

The first point you put into Claw Mastery gives you a 35% jolt to damage and increases your Attack Rating by 30%. Every point you put into this skill thereafter will increase damage by 4% and your Attack Rating by 10%. If you pour six or eight points into Claw Mastery and have some magic Claws, you'll be a force to be reckoned with.

Psychic Hammer

Level: 1 | Prerequisites: None

This is a psychic blast that knocks back and damages enemies. You can directly target monsters, such as a Shaman, even if other monsters (like minions) stand between you and your target. This facet of the Psychic Hammer makes it an important skill, especially early in the game (Act I) when you're facing a Fallen or Carver Shaman. Not only does Psychic Hammer knock back the target, but it also does 2-5 extra points of damage, with one more base point of damage for every point you add to it.

 TIP

Because Psychic Hammer knocks back the target, it also enables you to put some space between yourself and a particularly nasty monster.

Burst of Speed

Level: 6 | Prerequisites: Claw Mastery

As its name implies, Burst of Speed allows you to move more quickly than usual. Not only does it increase your walking speed, it also increases your *attacking* speed, allowing you to inflict more damage in a shorter period of time. Burst of Speed is an excellent skill to combine with claw-class weapons and Claw Mastery to create a powerful and fast attack that will prevent the enemy from swinging back at you. This skill lasts a remarkable two minutes with just one skill point, which is usually more than enough time to get you through perilous situations. One skill point into Burst of Speed gives you a 21% increase to your Attack speed and a 23% boost to your walk/run speed. With each successive point, you'll add to your speed, as well as an extra 12 seconds of effect.

Additional points in this skill will improve Attack Speed and walk/run speed. It will initially add 6% to both categories, but the increment will grow smaller as you add points.

Weapon Block

Level: 12 | Prerequisites: Claw Mastery

This skill provides a chance to block an enemy attack (it's passive), but only when you're using dual claw-class weapons. If you're using Weapon Block while you've got claws in each hand, you'll stand a good chance to block any enemy's attack. In other words, you don't have to feel any loss because you're not carrying a shield when you have two claw-class weapons active. Think of Weapon Block as a magical shield that protects you even though you've chosen to have offensive weapons in your hands.

Initially, Weapon Block gives a 26% chance to block, but you get an extra percent with every point you put into it. This skill is well worth the investment if you don't have the Vitality or the armor to withstand many hits. Weapon Block will initially increase your chance to block by 6%, but the increment will grow smaller as you add points.

Cloak of Shadows

Level: 12	Prerequisites: Psychic Hammer

Cloak of Shadows casts a shadow to blind nearby enemies, thus making it impossible for them to target you. When you use this skill, your own light radius will drop dramatically; however, any enemy that was on your screen, but had not yet spotted you, will not see you for the duration of the skill's effect—unless you are hit, which immediately terminates the effect. There are many practical applications to this skill, not the least of which is simply to blind a group of nasty monsters so that you can pass without having to face off against them in mortal combat.

Cloak of Shadows also enables you to fight enemies in a given area one at a time, rather than battling a rushing mob that spots you simultaneously—a prime example is the dilemma of fighting Fetishes in the Flayer Jungle.

By blinding the enemy, you can move about with impunity.

Don't use Cloak of Shadows until the enemies that you want to blind are on the screen (in plain view to you). This isn't a skill to use ahead of time; rather, it's a skill that you can use to get yourself out of dangerous situations when you enter an area with a plethora of enemies.

The initial Cloak of Shadows skill has a range of 20 yards, lasts for eight seconds, and lowers monsters' defense by 21%. It is also important to note, however, that you will also reduce your own defense when this skill is in effect.

TIP

Use Cloak of Shadows in tandem with the Traps skill tree for an awesome combination. When a group of enemies is approaching you, use the Cloak of Shadows to blind them, then lay down a selection of your most devastating traps while they're unable to target you. This technique is affectionately referred to as the "Cloak 'em and Smoke 'em" method.

Fade

Level: 18	Prerequisites: Burst of Speed

Fade raises all of your resistances for a brief period of time, and also lowers the duration of any curses that might be affecting you. This is a crucial skill if you have limited resistances to elemental damage when entering areas like the Arcane Sanctuary or the Maggot Lair. Initially, Fade reduces Curse duration by 47% and resists all elements 19% more effectively. It lasts two minutes and increases in increments of 12 seconds with each skill point you add (the resistances go up, as well).

Additional skill points will increase the ability to reduce curse duration and resist all. Reduce curse duration will initially improve by 6%, but will increase in smaller increments thereafter. The ability to resist all will get an 8% boost, but will also grow in smaller increments as you invest more points.

NOTE

If you've chosen not to have armor or items that provide you with a lot of elemental protection, you'll most certainly run into some serious problems as you get into Act III and beyond. Fortunately for the Assassin, Fade helps to bridge that gap if you're otherwise without the resistances you need.

Shadow Warrior

Level: 18	Prerequisites: Cloak of Shadows

Shadow Warrior summons a mercenary cloaked in darkness to fight at your Assassin's side. The catch is that she uses whatever attacks you have readied—if you're using Fists of Fire and Cobra Strike, she will too. The Shadow Warrior also performs normal attacks, which act as a Finishing Move and will release anything that she's charged-up in her battles. This battle companion has a finite amount of life, and will eventually be returned to the ethereal plane from which she came—but in the meantime, she can dish out major damage on your behalf! With every successive skill point you put into Shadow Warrior, you'll get 14.5 more health points (in the Shadow Warrior's life bar). Her Attack Rating increases 15% and her Defense increases 12%. Therefore, putting more points into Shadow Warrior quickly builds up a powerful ally in battle.

Having a clone of yourself to fight is very handy, indeed.

Mind Blast

Level: 24 | Prerequisites: Cloak of Shadows

Mind Blast is literally a surge of mental energy that not only damages and stuns enemies, but also converts many of them to fight for your cause! The power and convenience of this skill is obvious—if you can hit a group of enemies with a Mind Blast (that has a few skill points in it), then you'll have a good chance of immediately turning two or three of them to fight for your cause. Having the enemy fight for you is great, but Mind Blast also initially does between 10 and 20 points of damage on the enemies (not a lot, but still significant).

Use Mind Blast when you want to turn your enemies to fight on your side.

Initially, the skill lasts 6-10 seconds doing 10-20 points of damage with a 21% chance to convert. With additional points, damage is increased by two and the chance to convert increases by 3%, but the chance to convert increment will grow smaller.

 WARNING

Perhaps the most satisfying aspect of Mind Blast is that you get the sense that the skill is ensuring that the monsters you fight do the work for you. Don't get too cocky, however, because the conversion only lasts for a limited time and there's no guarantee that any number of enemies will be converted when Mind Blast is used.

Venom

Level: 30 | Prerequisites: Fade

Venom is a powerful skill that adds poison damage to your attacks, regardless of the weapon you're using. This is certainly a high-level skill—it starts out doing 37-78 points of damage over two seconds (in addition to the damage your regular attack gives you). As you put more points into this skill, the Attack Strength and duration become even greater. If you're not into using Fade or Burst of Speed very often (see Warning below), then Venom is a powerful substitute.

With additional points, the skill will improve Damage by 12 points and extend the duration of the effect in four-second increments.

 WARNING

You cannot use Venom, Fade, or Burst of Speed simultaneously. You can use only one of the three at any given time.

Shadow Master

Level: 30	Prerequisites: Shadow Warrior

In short, Shadow Master is a more powerful Shadow Warrior. However, that's somewhat of an oversimplification of this deadly ally who's available once you've reached Level 30. The Shadow Master fights beside you, not unlike the Shadow Warrior, but she has access to *all* of your Assassin's skills, not just the ones you have active. This makes her an excellent companion that can do anything you can do—except summon her own Shadow Warrior/Master. Sink some points into this skill when it becomes an option. The Shadow Master will not only help you to rack up experience, she'll also keep tough enemies distracted while you unleash your own Assassin skills.

Shadow Master starts at 188 Life. Placing additional points will give 28 to Life, 15% to Attack Rating, and 16% resist all, but the increment for this last category will grow smaller as you add points.

TRAPS

Traps are a very unique and innovative set of skills; they can be placed anywhere and will activate when the enemy approaches. They complement the Assassin's stealth abilities and her ability to lure enemies into areas where her traps exist. Traps are a very powerful set of skills, and are not to be taken lightly. When used judiciously, they can make the difference between victory and defeat—and are quite fun to use, too.

TIP

One key tip for using the Trap skill set is to also put some points into Shadow Warrior. As Rob Foote, tester at Blizzard says, "The Shadow Warrior is a 'Trapassin's' best friend." When you summon a Shadow Warrior and hotkey a trap skill to your right mouse button, the Shadow Warrior will cast the same trap. Twice the traps, twice the carnage!

Fire Blast

Level: 1	Prerequisites: None

The Fire Blast trap throws a surge of fire at the enemy that inflicts plenty of damage, including area of effect damage. This is a simple trap that's best suited for lower levels. At higher levels, the damage doesn't have quite the same effect, but is still a very effective and useful trap. Fire Blast is not only effective in straight-up combat, but it's also great when an enemy is in a hard-to-reach area where fighting the monster directly would put you at risk. Because Fire Blast is a ranged weapon that also does area of effect damage, you can throw a Fire Blast trap and let it do the work for you! Initially, Fire Blast has a 4.6-yard blast radius and it does 3-4 points of fire damage. Each additional skill point will increase damage by two.

Fire Blast is a good skill for groups of enemies because it does damage over an area.

Shock Web

Level: 6	Prerequisites: Fire Blast

When deployed, Shock Web sends out a web of lightning toward approaching enemies. Although this trap is less effective in open areas, it's excellent in a tight spaces like the Claw Viper Temple and Maggot Lair. Basically, any time an enemy is forced to walk through the Shock Web area of effect, this skill is doing the job. A skill point invested in Shock Web throws six spikes that do 5-6 damage over 3.6 seconds. Each skill point you add will improve damage by one and increase the number of spikes. This can become a very effective skill with just a few points when used in the proper environment.

 NOTE

Shock Web is not as effective in large open areas because it doesn't cover enough ground to successfully hit all of the enemies approaching you (usually attacks come from every direction).

Blade Sentinel

Level: 6	Prerequisites: None

Blade Sentinel sets a spinning blade that patrols between you and a target point. This is an excellent trap for narrow areas, such as doorways in places like the Claw Viper Temple where streams of enemies come through a single doorway. In those situations, a Blade Sentinel cuts back and forth, causing major damage in a short period of time. Initially, this skill inflicts 6-10 points of damage with each pass of the blade and lasts four seconds. Each skill point into Blade Sentinel increases damage by three. It also has a cool-down time so that it cannot be used in quick succession.

 TIP

Another key use for Blade Sentinel is to place it in a doorway when you're trying to run away from a group of monsters. Using this technique can stem the tide of nasty creatures long enough for you to regroup, heal, use a Town Portal, or whatever you need to do to fix what ails your character.

Charged Bolt Sentry

Level: 12	Prerequisites: Shock Web

The Charged Bolt Sentry is a powerful lightning damage dispenser. When enemies get close, powerful charged bolts are released in waves. Although the bolts do a substantial amount of damage, they do not reliably hit enemies as they fan out from their source. Often the Charged Bolt Sentry is most effective when you drop it inside a doorway to a new area that's crowded with enemies. Initially, it releases five waves of five bolts, causing 1-7 points of damage each. Additional points in this skill will improve damage by 1.5.

Charged Bolt Sentry does a lot of damage, but it's not guaranteed to hit.

NOTE

As you add points to the Charged Bolt Sentry, each bolt inflicts an increasing amount of damage.

Wake of Fire

Level: 12	Prerequisites: Fire Blast

This trap lets loose waves of fire when triggered. Although it hits enemies more reliably than the Charged Bolt Sentry, it doesn't do as much damage. The Wake of Fire releases five waves, causing 5-10 points of damage per wave. Additional points in the skill will increase damage by two. Like the Charged Bolt Sentry, it's a good choice for a doorway to a crowded area you've just opened up, or even in a doorway or area behind you to protect your flank.

Blade Fury

Level: 18	Prerequisites: Blade Sentinel, Wake of Fire

Blade Fury is a skill that enables you to throw several spinning blades that will bounce off enemies and do extra damage with each hit. Each blade does 8-10 points of damage. Additional points in the skill will increase damage by three. The minimum damage they do (eight points) is substantial, making Blade Fury an excellent skill for both defense or as an offensive weapon in combination with other traps and Cloak of Shadows.

Lightning Sentry

Level: 24	Prerequisites: Charged Bolt

The Lightning Sentry shoots lightning at nearby enemies in streams that can do whopping amounts of damage. The key to this skill is that it can do 10-20 points of damage with each of the 10 blasts of lightning that streams out of it. This means that any one given lightning bolt could either devastate an enemy completely or not even harm them at all (if they have lightning resistance). Still, with 10 bolts and the possibility of up to 20 points of damage per bolt, it's usually a very effective trap to use. With each skill point that you put into Lightning Sentry, you get five more points of potential damage with every lightning strike!

Lightning Sentry is a powerful trap that'll take out all but the toughest enemies.

Wake of Inferno

Level: 24	Prerequisites: Wake of Fire

Wake of Inferno is basically an Inferno spell in a trap that spews fire at any enemy wandering too close. At level 1, this trap does 8-21 points of damage per second and shoots 10 times after it's created. Every subsequent skill point that you put into it adds eight points of damage per second, quickly making this a formidable weapon against most enemies that lack adequate fire resistance.

Death Sentry

Level: 30	Prerequisites: Lightning Sentry

The Death Sentry is a very cool trap that detonates nearby enemy corpses when an opponent gets close. If you've ever played the Necromancer and enjoyed the Corpse Explosion skill, the Death Sentry is essentially a portable corpse exploder that allows your Assassin to engage in the same heinous corpse-exploding activities. Whenever you are near a pile of corpses, lay down a Death Sentry and it will detonate corpses whenever an enemy wanders near. The Death Sentry can be used effectively on the fly, as well—when fighting a group of monsters, drop a Death Sentry as soon as one of them is felled to detonate enemy corpses as they appear. Initially, this skill inflicts 40-80% damage of the corpses original Life over a radius of 3.3 yards. This radius of effect increases by 0.3 with each additional skill point. Death Sentry also deals 20-30 points of lightning damage initially, which increases in increments of four with each skill point.

Blade Shield

Level: 30	Prerequisites: Blade Fury

When this skill is activated, blades circle your Assassin and damage any enemies that get too close. Invest in Blade Shield if you're putting a lot of points into the Martial Arts skill tree and are planning to do plenty of hand-to-hand combat. It inflicts 1-30 points of damage over 20 seconds, ensuring that enemies won't last long if they continue to pursue you—Blade Sentry will land several consecutive hits on them if they persist. As you put points into Blade Shield, the damage increases and the duration of action goes up in four-second increments.

Blade Sheild is a great offensive or defensive weapon, doing damage to enemies when they get too close.

 TIP

Put at least one skill point into Blade Shield (once you're at level 30) if you plan to engage in a lot of hand-to-hand combat.

The Assassin Revealed

This section contains a series of strategies and hints specific to the Assassin. Of course, with 30 skills and literally thousands of skill combinations, it's impossible to show every effective tactic; however, these are some tried and true strategies for making the most of your time as an Assassin. Thanks go out to Carlos Guerrero, Jeanette Clausen, Robert Foote, Ron Frybarger, Chris Van Der Westhuizen, Ted Barken, Michael Backus, and especially Dean Lee and Jason Hutchins from Blizzard QA for their expert help with these strategies.

 NOTE

Here's how the points break down for an Assassin (played from the beginning of the game through Act V):

Total Skill Points (50 Levels and 5 Acts): **54**

Total Stat Points (50 Levels and 5 Acts): **255**

ASSASSIN SKILL COMBINATION

Here's a breakdown of an effective skill combination and point dispersal that will direct your Assassin along certain successful paths. This section also includes an alternate skill combination.

SKILL POINT SPREAD

- 10 points into area of attack Traps, such as Wake of Fire
- 10 points into Claw Mastery
- 1 point into Shadow Warrior
- 10 point into Cloak of Shadows
- 10 points into Blade Shield
- 2–3 points into Cobra Strike (which you don't need if you have a Life/Mana stealing weapon)
- 2–3 points into Dragon Claw
- 2 points into Weapons Block
- 1 point into Dragon Flight

STATS POINT SPREAD

- 35% into Strength
- 30% into Dexterity
- 20% into Mana
- 15% into Vitality

FIGHTING SEVERAL ENEMIES AT ONCE

1. Use Wake of Fire to lay down some area of effect damage.
2. Use Cloak of Shadows to amplify the damage of Wake of Fire, as well as blind the enemies.
3. Stay out of the fray until after the third wave of fire from the sentry.
4. Jump in and clean up the mess with Cobra Strike and Dragon Claw. You should be able to earn back your Mana with three uses of Cobra Strike.

Fighting a large group of enemies is made easier with skills like Wake of FIre Sentry.

Fighting Bosses (Super Unique Monsters)

1. Cast Shadow Warrior so the Boss can focus on her.
2. Lay down some Wake of Fire sentry.
3. Keep your skill button on Cobra Strike so that your Shadow Warrior can replenish her own Vitality and Mana from the Boss. Keep tossing in traps or, if you're daring, jump into the mix with Cobra Strike/Tiger Strike/Dragon Claw/Wake of Fire.

Using Charge-Up Skills and Finishing Moves is key to dealing with Bosses.

Blizzard Tips

These tips come straight from the Blizzard QA team, with special input from Dean Lee, Carlos Guerrero, and Jason Hutchins. The tactics listed here specifically apply to the combination we've shown in this section, but are also great tips for all-round Assassin gameplay.

- **Cold Damage:** Your Martial Arts skills will be much more effective if you can slow the enemies down (especially Bosses) because it will allow you rack up more charges. Get yourself a claw/katar with cold damage or, if you can't find one, buy a socketed claw/katar and put a sapphire in it.
- **Attack Speed:** Get items that will help you increase your attack speed and give you "fast hit recovery" so you can lay down your Martial Arts moves with great efficiency and effectiveness.
- **Point Distribution:** For the first two or three Acts, put more points into Wake of Fire sentry; the enemies in the first three Acts are fairly susceptible to fire attacks. However, as you get closer to Act IV, put more points into Claw Mastery since most of those monsters have high fire resistance.
- **Mid-Game Assassin Strategy:** If you're approaching some heavy duty monster types, throw up a couple of Inferno sentry traps within the midst of the enemy, then start raining grenades. When you're done, only pieces of monsters remain.
- **Late-Game Assassin Strategy:** The Shadow Master/Rogue duo is an extremely effective support force for your Assassin. While your Rogue is raining death from long distance, your Shadow Master is engaging enemies by using a variety of deadly Assassin skills. This leaves you free to drop a few Lightning Sentry/Wake of Inferno traps among the offending monsters and then rain grenades on them. Your small force will obliterate most opposition in no time.

- **Best Hireling for the Assassin:** The best hireling to have for an Assassin is the Act I Rogue. She is one of the few hirelings available that can do ranged attack damage and gets significantly more powerful as she advances with you throughout the game. Always try to equip her with good armor and a great bow, and she will take care of the rest.
- **Weapon Block:** Always put some points into Weapon Block. This will come in handy later on in the game when you're surrounded by hordes of monsters. It could even mean the difference between life and death.
- **Claw Mastery:** Claw Mastery is extremely important if your Assassin plans to specialize in Martial Arts.
- **Cobra Strike**: If you run out of Mana and/or health potions, the Cobra Strike skill can be used instead. If you're careful enough, you won't have any need for potions, saving you several trips back to town.

ALTERNATE COMBINATION

SKILL POINT SPREAD

- 20 points in Shadow Warrior/Master
- 2 points in Burst of Speed
- 10 points in Claw Mastery
- 20 points in Mind Blast
- 1 point in COS/Tiger Strike/Cobra Strike/Dragon Claw

STATS POINT SPREAD

- 30% into Strength
- 20% into Dexterity
- 20% into Vitality
- 25% into Mana
- 5% discretionary points

THE DRUID

The Druid is the master of the natural world and, as such, is able to change his form into that of an animal. His powers for transmogrification into animal form include the Werebear and Werewolf, both of which are powerful and formidable creatures. The Druid is also the master of Elemental and Primal magic, which gives him control over elemental forces such as fire and wind, but also allows him to utilize a myriad of plants and animals to secure himself when faced with mortal danger. Many a Druid has been saved by a Life-giving vine that sucks the health out of corpses while a giant cave bear stands at his side to defend him.

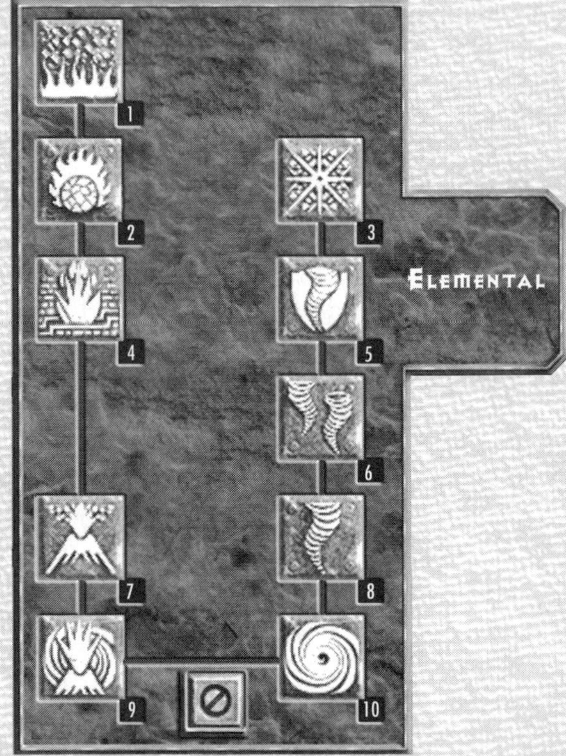

THE DRUID SKILLS

There are three branches to the Druid skill tree: Elemental, Shape Shifting, and Summoning. Each skill tree contains unique skills that can be developed in tandem with skills from other areas, or by themselves. As with the five original character classes, how you place points into the Druid skills will dramatically affect how he behaves in the game.

Elemental

1. Firestorm
2. Molten Boulder
3. Arctic Blast
4. Fissure
5. Cyclone Armor
6. Twister
7. Volcano
8. Tornado
9. Armageddon
10. Hurricane

Shape Shifting

1. Werewolf
2. Lycanthropy
3. Werebear
4. Feral Rage
5. Maul
6. Rabies
7. Fire Claws
8. Hunger
9. Shock Wave
10. Fury

Summoning

1. Raven
2. Poison Creeper
3. Oak Sage
4. Summon Spirit Wolf
5. Carrion Vine
6. Heart of Wolverine
7. Summon Dire Wolf
8. Solar Creeper
9. Spirit of Barbs
10. Summon Grizzly

ELEMENTAL

The Elemental tree includes skills that summon the forces of the elements to bear for the Druid. Wind in the form of Hurricanes, Twisters, and Tornadoes complement skills that utilize the power of fire, cold, and even the volcanic might that lies within the earth itself. These skills give deadly magical attributes to the natural elements that surround the Druid, and can be brought to punish those that would stand in his way.

Firestorm

Level: 1 | Prerequisites: None

This is, quite literally, a firestorm that shoots out onto your enemies when invoked. This skill is similar to the fire attack that Diablo uses at the end of Act IV— powerful and especially useful in the first two Acts. The charges of fire that Firestorm releases will travel through enemies, also striking foes that aren't directly in front of your Druid. Putting a few points into this skill is important not only because you'll use this skill, but also because it's a prerequisite for other skills, such as Molten Boulder. Firestorm initially does 3-7 points of damage per second, but ramps up (damage-wise) with every skill point you drop into it. It also has a cool-down time so that it cannot be used in quick succession.

The Druid's Elemental Skills are truly forces to be reckoned with.

Molten Boulder

Level: 6 | Prerequisites: Firestorm

A boulder of flaming hot magma that both damages and knocks back your opponents. The first hit of Molten Boulder always knocks back the enemy, unless it's impossible (if they're backed up against a wall). If the enemy can't be knocked back or if the Molten Boulder hits some scenery (like a tree), then the Molten Boulder explodes. Skills that both knock back and damage enemies are excellent against larger monsters that excel in melee combat. Molten Boulder keeps enemies away from you, destroying some in the process. This skill does 11-16 points of fire damage at level 1 (which includes a small radius of area of effect damage). Damage increases with every skill point you spend. It also has a cool-down time so that it cannot be used in quick succession.

Arctic Blast

Level: 6 | Prerequisites: None

The Arctic Blast skill sends a jet of icy air out that freezes enemies in their tracks. Many *Diablo II* players are partial to cold attacks because they not only damage the enemy, but also slow them down and possibly even shatter them. This eliminates them permanently with no chance for resurrection; their corpses cannot be used for nefarious activities (such as Corpse Explosion). For this reason Artic Blast is very effective against Shamans and Unravelers. This skill does a surprising 8-15 points of cold damage per second over a 5.3-yard radius. It's important to note that this is not a radius effect. Rather, it's a straight line that affects all units in the area of the line (for four seconds). As you put points into Arctic Blast, the damage and range increases and the duration is extended by 0.6 seconds per point.

NOTE

Arctic Blast can also be very effective against groups of enemies because it sprays out, much like the Sorceress' Inferno skill (with cold instead of fire).

Fissure

Level: 12	Prerequisites: Molten Boulder

Fissure opens volcanic vents below your opponents and causes damage. This skill is best used in open areas where you are free to move around and coax your enemies into the area of Fissure's effect. Of course, Fissure can be used anywhere, but ideally you'll want to lay it down directly below your enemies or where they're heading. For example, if you're in an enclosed area like the Catacombs or Jail, drop it in a room where a group of enemies must cross the Fissures as they approach you. This attack does an impressive 15-25 points of damage per second (over 3.2 seconds); damage increases as you add skill points. It also has a cool-down time so that it cannot be used in quick succession.

Fissure literally opens up the ground beneath your opponents.

NOTE

The Fissures that open up are random, so being able to move around freely to coax monsters into the area of effect of this skill is very important. It's very useful in Act II because the large, open expanses of desert allow you to maneuver easily.

Cyclone Armor

Level: 12	Prerequisites: Arctic Blast

Cyclone Armor is a protective barrier created by swirling winds that shield you from the elemental damage of Fire, Cold, or Electricity. If you find yourself in an area where you're taking an excessive amount of elemental damage or you don't have much elemental resistance, Cyclone Armor will bail you out nicely. At level 1 this skill absorbs 40 points of elemental damage, and with each successive point you put into it, you'll endure an additional 12 points of elemental damage. This skill is useful in any circumstance, but is absolutely critical if you're short on amulets, armor, or rings that provide resistances.

Twister

Level: 18 | Prerequisites: Cyclone Armor

This skill is somewhat like Charged Bolt. It randomly sends out three small whirlwinds of destruction that not only damage, but also stun your enemies. Although you can't guarantee a hit with it, it's almost always worthwhile when used in a crowded area. Twister's ability to stun is (on its own) a valuable skill, and the combination of a stun and damage attack combined is extra attractive in areas where you might otherwise be overwhelmed by a large group of enemies. Upon triggering Twister, several of those enemies will be stunned for 0.4 seconds initially, preventing them from hitting you or your party members. Twisters do 6-8 damage at level 1, ramping up with each point you put into this skill.

Volcano allows you to summon the awesome power that lies below the Earth's crust and send it forth unto your enemies.

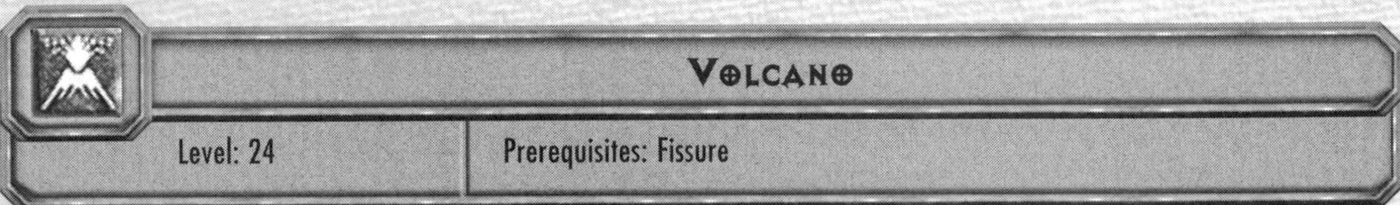

Volcano

Level: 24 | Prerequisites: Fissure

Volcano is a Vesuvius that rises up from the ground and throws liquid hot magma on your enemies. A crack opens in the ground and fire pours out, doing splash damage on everything around it. Although Volcano has a cool-down period that prevents more than two Volcanoes from being active at one time, it lasts a fairly long time and dishes out plenty of damage. This is an excellent skill in a hallway or long room where the majority of enemies are coming at you from the other side. Put a Volcano between you and the enemies as they rush you to deliver plenty of damage while you switch to another skill to augment the Volcano's damage. Initially, Volcano does 15-20 points of fire damage, ramping up quickly with each point put into this skill.

Tornado

Level: 24 | Prerequisites: Twister

Tornado is similar to Twister, but instead of several swirling storms of destruction, there's only one, and it's larger and much more powerful. Another benefit of this skill is that it's not affected by your enemy's resistances to elemental damage, making it an ability that's virtually guaranteed to do 25-35 damage when it hits. Like Twister, Tornado is not guaranteed to hit the enemy, but again, it's powerful enough that it's worth taking that chance, especially in enclosed areas. Also, it can blow through enemies, doing damage to monsters in succession. The effectiveness of a skill like Tornado is greatly diminished in wide-open spaces where you're being attacked from all sides by hordes of enemies. It also has a cool-down time so that it cannot be used in quick succession.

NOTE

Because wind skills aren't reduced by elemental resistances, their damage is very effective against all enemies. The damage is physical; Twister is, as well. This skill provides +8 damage per skill point spent.

Armageddon

Level: 30 | Prerequisites: Volcano, Hurricane

This is a meteor shower that rains down fiery death on your enemies. The great thing about Armageddon is that it follows the caster around, rather than just affecting one area. Therefore, if a group of enemies is following you or persists on attacking you while you're using this skill, they'll likely get pummeled. Use it when you're attacking a heavy-duty monster with minions; you can invoke the skill so that it damages any minions that get close while you concentrate on the big boy(s). Initial fire damage is 25-75, increasing with every point you invest in this skill. It also has a cool-down time so that it cannot be used in quick succession.

Hurricane

Level: 30 | Prerequisites: Tornado

Like Armageddon, Hurricane is centered on the character that invokes it. This skill is the big daddy of windstorms, and will considerably damage any enemy within its realm of effect. Hurricane does 25-50 damage at first level. Hurricane is a very effective skill to use at any time; the key is simply getting to level 30 so that you can learn it!

Shape Shifting

The Shape Shifting skills allow the Druid to convert himself into one of two creatures, and once he is in these other forms, do incredible amounts of inhuman damage to his enemies. While in these altered states, any weaponry the Druid wields adds its power and abilities to the attacks that come naturally to the beast.

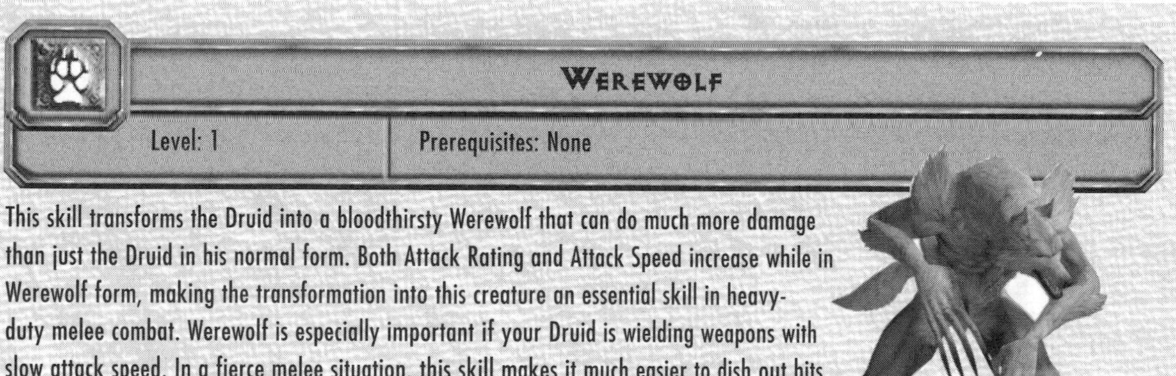

Werewolf

Level: 1 | Prerequisites: None

This skill transforms the Druid into a bloodthirsty Werewolf that can do much more damage than just the Druid in his normal form. Both Attack Rating and Attack Speed increase while in Werewolf form, making the transformation into this creature an essential skill in heavy-duty melee combat. Werewolf is especially important if your Druid is wielding weapons with slow attack speed. In a fierce melee situation, this skill makes it much easier to dish out hits on the enemy in a timely fashion. It also has a cool-down time so that it cannot be used in quick succession.

NOTE

The speed growth is exponential, not linear, so the speed modifier is most noticeable with speed enhancing items. With no speed enhancing items, your attack in Werewolf form is nearly the same speed as in human form.

The first level of Werewolf gives a 50% boost to your Attack Rating and adds 20% to your Attack Speed, but the actual duration of the skill is relatively short. To gain more time in Werewolf form, put a few points into Lycanthropy. Werewolf initially gives +25% to Life and adds 25% to stamina that remains constant.

Becoming a Werewolf instantly increases both your Attack Strength and Attack Speed, but you'll need to put points into Lycanthropy to really make it sing.

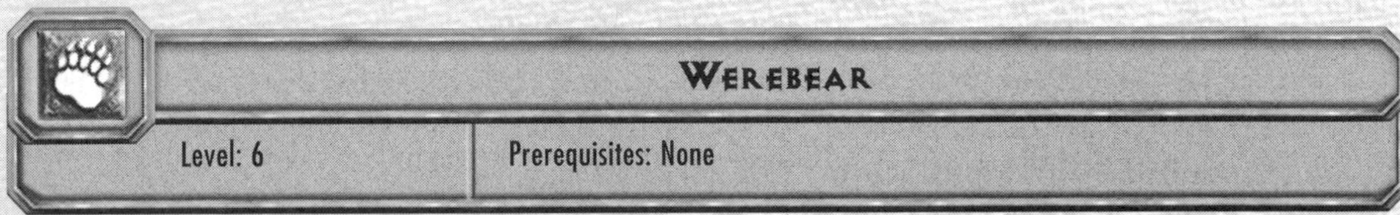

Werebear

Level: 6	Prerequisites: None

Like Werewolf, this skill changes the Druid into another form—a giant bear that walks on its hind legs. When compared to a Werewolf, the Werebear form affords you more Defense and its attacks do more damage, but the attack speed is a bit slower, so there's an obvious trade-off. The Werebear is best used for fighting against smaller groups of stronger monsters, where connecting with several attacks in a short period of time isn't as important as landing fewer, more powerful blows. At level 1, Werebear adds 120% to Life and 50% to Damage, making you one tough customer in a flash. This skill's Life enhancement remains constant when assigning additional points to it. However, the 50% Damage and 25% Defense bonus do increase per skill level. It also has a cool-down time so that it cannot be used in quick succession.

NOTE

The choice of whether to take the Werebear over the Werewolf is a straightforward choice of defense & power over speed & accuracy. Although both are excellent, the Werebear is the way to go if you want crushing power. Likewise, if you want a swifter attack speed, stick with the Werewolf. Either way, it's probably best to choose one or the other rather than dividing your points between the two.

Lycanthropy

Level: 1	Prerequisites: Werewolf

The Lycanthropy skill is passive (which is great because it doesn't actively eat away at your Mana) and improves the length of time the Druid will remain in the form of a Werewolf or Werebear. Therefore, if you are planning on spending time in another form, it's mandatory that you pour points into Lycanthropy. As an example, just one point in Lycanthropy adds 20% to his Life as a Werebear and increases the duration of Werewolf/Werebear by 40 seconds! Every subsequent point added to this skill adds 5% to your Life and 20 extra seconds in Werebear/Werewolf form. In the case of Werebear and Werewolf, when it comes to Lycanthropy, you can't have one without the other.

 TIP

Put some points into Lycanthropy when using the Werebear or Werewolf forms—it'll pay off immediately.

Feral Rage

Level: 12	Prerequisites: Werewolf

Feral Rage steals Life from enemies when the Druid is in Werewolf form. Basically, it sends the Werewolf into a frenzied rage that steals Life, does damage, increases run/walk speed, and even acts as a Charge-up skill. At level 1, this skill steals only 2%-6% of Life, but it increases your run/walk speed 19%-31%, increases damage by 50%, and boosts your Attack Rating by 20%. Feral Rage initially lasts a surprisingly long 20 seconds! In short, there's a lot going on with this skill, including a Charge-up feature that gives you more benefits with each consecutive hit. It doesn't allow for a Finishing Move like the Assassin's Charge-up skills, but the Charge-up does do extra damage/Life-steal with each consecutive hit (up to three hits), making it even more valuable. Feral Rage improves per skill point spent.

Maul

Level: 12	Prerequisites: Werebear

Maul is a skill that's used when in Werebear form, and it acts in a similar fashion to Feral Rage in terms of being a Charge-up skill. Maul allows the Druid to attack his opponents relentlessly and boosts the Attack Rating and damage, but instead of stealing Life, Maul stuns the opponent. At level 1, Maul lasts 20 seconds, increases the Attack Rating by 20%, boosts damage 25%-75%, and stuns the opponent for 1.7-2.8 seconds. This is a great skill to use against tough enemies because every time you connect with a hit, you'll stun them, too. This prevents them from fighting back and, thus, hitting you. If the Werebear form is your form of choice, then Maul is a skill that you'll want to invest in once you're at level 12. Stun length, damage, and Attack Rating increase for every additional point spent on this skill.

NOTE

The Feral Rage and Maul skills also add their "Charge up" to other melee attacks and skills. For instance, you can have Maul assigned to one mouse button and Attack assigned to the other. When you are "Charged up" your Attack Rating and damage for your Attack skill will also be increased.

Rabies

Level: 18	Prerequisites: Feral Rage

The Rabies skill will inflict poison (disease) on opponents when the Druid is in Werewolf form. At level 1, this skill increases the Attack Rating by 50% and delivers 18-43 points of poison damage over four seconds. However, because Rabies is a disease, it does not act exactly like normal poison damage. When an enemy has taken a hit after you've invoked Rabies, they'll turn green and will suffer the effects of the hit. During the four seconds that they're affected, they can also pass the disease along to any enemies that get too close to them! A clever tactic for using Rabies in tight, crowded rooms is to hit one enemy with it, then move back to a doorway so that your enemies must crowd around and touch one another. Several monsters will likely become infected and will take damage even before you meet them face to face! This skill provides +13 poison damage and 17% to Attack Rating per skill point spent.

Rabies will ready your Werewolf/Werebear for a vicious confrontation.

NOTE

The Rabies skill is very useful in Act III when you're facing those pesky Fetishes!

Fire Claws

Level: 18	Prerequisites: Feral Rage, Maul

This skill adds fire to your attacks when in either Werebear or Werewolf form. With one point of invested in Fire Claws, you get an additional 15-20 points of fire damage with a 50% bonus to your Attack Rating. With every subsequent point you put into it, you get a 15% boost to the Attack Rating and another six points of fire damage. Fire Claws is effective when fighting anything without resistance to fire.

Hunger

Level: 24	Prerequisites: Fire Claws

Hunger steals Life and Mana from enemies when the Druid is in changed form. The trade-off is that it reduces damage by 75%. Consequently, you don't use it for attacking per se, but just strictly to steal Life. Fortunately, it does an *excellent* job at this, taking a whopping 72% of your opponents' Life and Mana while also boosting your Attack Rating. Hunger is a fantastic tool for replenishing the Druid's Life and Mana in key situations when a trip back to town is either impractical or impossible. This occurs in Act V when you're facing the Ancients in the Rite of Passage Quest. If you leave via Town Portal, the Ancients regenerate back to their pristine state, making it essential to replenish your levels on the fly. This skill adds 18% to both Life and Mana steal, as well as a +10% bonus to Attack Rating per skill point spent.

Shock Wave

Level: 24	Prerequisites: Maul

In Werebear form, Shock Wave enables the Druid to send a powerful force to stun—and damage—his enemies. Initial damage of 10-20 goes up by three points with every additional skill point added. This is a powerful skill that has many useful purposes. First, it can be used to stun nearby monsters so that you can move about and kill them without fear of their attacks (using a normal sword attack in combination with frequent Shock Waves). Secondly, it can be used to stun nearby enemies that are pummeling your character so that you can flee the area and save your skin. Lastly, it can be used repeatedly as an offensive weapon, but because the damage it does is limited and the Mana cost is substantial, this is an impractical alternative for most Druids.

The Shock Wave skill is great for both stunning and damaging nearby enemies—plus it looks great!

NOTE

Shock Wave's stun length increases per skill point spent, starting at 1.6 seconds and increasing by 0.6 per point.

Fury

Level: 30	Prerequisites: Rabies

Fury allows the Druid to land multiple attacks at once when in Werewolf form. It starts with two consecutive attacks (eventually mustering up to five in a row), each inflicting 100% damage and increasing the Attack Rating by 50%. The great thing about Fury is that it's a handy skill whether you're fighting a single opponent or groups of them. When fighting a solitary foe, you'll do a huge amount of damage quickly on that one enemy; with a group of monsters, you'll hit them all (depending on the level of the skill). Like the Paladin's Zeal, Fury has a five-hit cap on it, but it's still a valuable skill in any situation. Fury increases Attack Rating by 7% and damage by 17% per skill point spent.

SUMMONING

This line of skills enables the Druid to summon aid from the plant, spirit, and animal kingdoms in his quest against evil. Summoning skills provide invaluable means to protect against Health and Mana loss, and create a formidable force of creatures to fight in your stead. Several of these skills are invaluable to the Druid for success through Act V and beyond. Neglect this skill tree at your own peril.

TIP

Adding points to Spirit Wolf boosts the Attack Rating and Defense Rating of Summon Dire Wolf and Summon Bear. Putting points into Dire Wolf adds to the Life of Spirit Wolf and Bear. Points in Summon Bear increases the damage of Spirit Wolf and Dire Wolf. What this means is that you must put points into all three of these skills to get the full benefit out of them, even if you're really only using one.

The Wolf/Bear Connection

The Spirit Wolf, the Dire Wolf, and the Grizzly all have interconnected passive bonuses. The Spirit Wolf adds a passive bonus to wolves and bears that increases the Attack and Defense Ratings by 50% at level 1. The Dire Wolf has a passive bonus that gives 50% more Life to wolves and bears, and the Grizzly has a passive bonus that that increases wolf and bear damage by 25% at level 1. Therefore, you must put points into all three of these skills to make them work for each other, empowering formidable minions as a Druid.

Raven

Level: 1	Prerequisites: None

This skill summons a Raven to attack your enemies from the air. As an added bonus, multiple Ravens can be summoned at once (up to a total of five) and all peck away at the enemies together. Perhaps the best part about the Ravens is that they do damage with every hit, and they *cannot* take damage from enemies! As described by the Blizzard Crew, they're 'Attacks waiting to happen' because they continue to attack until they're done. At level 1, you get one Raven that will attack 12 times and do 2-4 points of damage with each hit—guaranteeing 12 hits. With each skill point you put into Raven, you get one more point of damage, one more hit, and one more Raven (up to five). After five points, you can have a murder of Ravens that follow you around and peck at the enemies as they show up on your screen. Because the Druid does not have a natural ranged attack, the Raven can serve this purpose, attacking enemies on the edge of the Druid's vision. This skill adds +1 to damage and +1 to hits per skill point spent.

The Raven is a friend if you're a Druid, and five of them are a murderous group of friends that fight at your side.

NOTE

While not an impact skill, the Raven is a skill that can change the course of a game subtly by chipping away at your enemies, thus making it easier for you to kill them yourself.

Poison Creeper

Level: 1	Prerequisites: None

This skill summons a creeping vine that weaves its way through the ground, poisoning all it contacts. Once summoned, the Poison Creeper follows your Druid around wherever he goes and poisons all enemies it contacts. At the first level, the Poison Creeper has a life of 15 and does 4-6 poison damage over four seconds. With every point you put into this skill, you'll add three to its life and 2.5 to the amount of poison damage it will do, so putting a few points into this skill will benefit its abilities greatly. Poison Creeper is a skill that's used like the Raven, that is to say it's an adjunct to your other attacks and skills rather than being a primary means of attack. It eats away at your enemy's health (and sometimes does them in), making it much easier for you (or your minions) to dispose of them once you fight them face to face.

Summon Spirit Wolf

Level: 6	Prerequisites: Raven

Summon Spirit Wolf brings a Spirit Wolf to your side to fight with you and for you. The Spirit Wolves have the ability to teleport, making them very effective for getting across bridged areas or areas that have only one narrow pathway as access, such as the area early in Act V. You can have a maximum of five Spirit Wolves summoned at any one time, but unlike the Ravens they have a set amount of life, and can be killed by enemies even before they do any killing for you! At level 1, each Spirit Wolf has 35 Life and does 2-5 damage with each hit. Each successive skill point into Summon Spirit Wolf provides an additional 1-2 damage, +15% to Attack Rating and Defense, and an extra wolf (up to a limit of five). Use this skill in combination with the Oak Sage when dealing with several enemies at once.

Spirit Wolves and Dire Wolves are valuable to have fighting at your side, although they will not save you against a powerful boss.

NOTE

Of course, all of the Druid's minions can teleport in a manner of speaking—they will teleport forward out of necessity to catch up with your Druid. However, the Spirit Wolves can teleport offensively as well, moving across rivers or chasms with their teleport skill specifically to attack an enemy.

Oak Sage

Level: 6	Prerequisites: None

Oak Sage is a spirit that increases the Life of your Druid and his minions. The spirits are much like the Paladin's Auras, except that they have a set amount of life and can be attacked and ultimately killed by enemies. The benefit of Oak Sage is that it (at level 1) adds 50% to the Life of your Druid and his minions, and has a life of 30 points of its own. The key to using this skill successfully is to keep an eye on it and invoke it again after enemies kill it. It's easy to get distracted while the Oak Sage spirit is being pummeled. Once it is killed, you lose its huge health bonus for you and your minions. Every point into Oak Sage gives the spirit nine more Life and add 5% to the Life aura.

NOTE

Hot-key Oak Sage so that you can instantly re-summon it whenever it is destroyed by enemies.

Carrion Vine

Level: 12	Prerequisites: Poison Creeper

The Carrion Vine is a creeping vine that consumes enemy corpses and returns some Life to your health globe. It's an important skill for the Druid because it not only consumes corpses and replenishes Life for him, but it also gets rid of corpses that might otherwise be resurrected or used by skills such as Corpse Explosion. Keep a Carrion Vine slithering around at all times to ensure that you don't go through an entire belt of healing potions in one area. At level 1, the Carrion Vine has a life of 47, making it much harder for the enemy to kill than the Poison Creeper vine. It also takes 4% of the corpse's total health and returns it to you. As you add points to this skill, the Carrion Vine acquires more Life, and increases the amount (percent) of Life that it heals.

NOTE

Don't worry about any corpses going to waste—the Carrion Vine consumes corpses only if you need some Life.

Heart of Wolverine

Level: 18	Prerequisites: Oak Sage

This spirit adds to the Attack Rating and Damage of your party when active. Heart of Wolverine is an important skill, especially when you're out on your own and don't have a Paladin using Concentration (or Blessed Aim) nearby. At level 1, this skill adds 20% to the damage you inflict and 25% to the Attack Rating of you and any of your minions within 20 yards. As you add points to this skill, you'll get increases in both the Attack Rating and Damage. Again, in the absence of a nearby Paladin party-member, Heart of Wolverine makes you and your minions (such as Dire Wolves) much more powerful.

Summon Dire Wolf

Level: 18	Prerequisites: Oak Sage, Summon Spirit Wolf

This maniacal wolf consumes opponents' corpses, increasing the damage it does. Dire Wolves are bigger and meaner than Spirit Wolves, and as such you can have no more than three of them at one time. Still, their ability to chow down on corpses and increase their Attack Strength makes them valuable, especially when used in conjunction with an Oak Sage. At level 1, the Dire Wolf has 57 hit points and does 8-13 points of damage. Every subsequent point added to this skill gives more damage, more life, and an extra wolf, up to a limit of three. These wolves are excellent to have around along with a murder of Ravens and an Oak Sage spirit.

Solar Creeper

Level: 24	Prerequisites: Carrion Vine

The Solar Creeper is a vine that eats enemy corpses in order to replenish your Mana. It's basically a Carrion Vine that steals Mana rather than Health. That said, the Solar Creeper is also a lot tougher than the Carrion Vine in terms of how many hits it can take from enemies. The Solar Creeper is useful only if you're actively using skills that require a great deal of Mana, like the skills in the Elemental Skill Tree. Put a point into Solar Creeper for those times when Mana runs low or is stolen from you (like in the Arcane Sanctuary of Act II). At level 1, the Solar Creeper has 82 health points (so it can take a fair bit of damage), and it returns 2% of the corpse's Mana to you. Each point you put into Solar Creeper increases its Life by 16 points, slowly increasing in Mana recovery.

NOTE

Both the Carrion Vine and the Solar Creeper can be used, if, for nothing else, to prevent bodies from being resurrected, plundered (by Barbarians looking for items or potions), or exploded (with Corpse Explosion).

Summon Grizzly

Level: 30	Prerequisites: Summon Dire Wolf

This skill summons a vicious Grizzly Bear to fight alongside the Druid. The Grizzly is a very powerful companion that can take enemies down with a single swipe. Interestingly, the Grizzly's hit points do not go up as you add points to this skill, but you can passively raise the Grizzly's hit points with the passive hit point bonus that you get from Dire Wolf (see sidebar). Once you reach Level 30 and can access the Grizzly, you'll find it to be a valuable asset to have this beast fighting at your side. When the Grizzly nears death, simply re-create it (you can have only one going at a time), and be sure to use Oak Sage to help preserve your ferocious ally as long as possible. The Grizzly does 37-75 damage at level 1 and increases in damage dramatically per skill point spent.

The Grizzly is so powerful, it's too bad that you can have only one at a time!

Spirit of Barbs

Level: 30	Prerequisites: Heart of Wolverine

Somewhat like the Paladin's Thorns, this spirit reflects damage done to you back on the enemy. At Level 1, this skill will return 50% damage to the enemy that hit you. It also has a range of 20 yards that will also include your minions. Although Spirit of Barbs doesn't return as much damage as Thorns, a soloing Druid can use this and two other skills simultaneously, where a Paladin can have only Thorns and *one* other skill active. This is definitely a very important skill in later Acts and higher difficulty settings. With every point you put into Spirit of Barbs, you'll get an extra 10% damage returned to the enemy, as well as 21 more points of Life for the Spirit.

The Druid Revealed

This section contains a series of strategies and hints that are specific to the Druid. As with the Assassin, with 30 skills and thousands of skill combinations, it's impossible to show every effective tactic; however, these are some tested tactics for making the most of your time as a Druid. Thanks go out to Carlos Guerrero, Roger Eberhart, Robert Foote, Ron Frybarger, Matt Lee, Michael Backus, and especially Dean Lee and Jason Hutchins from Blizzard QA for their expert help with these strategies.

NOTE

Here's how the points break down for a Druid played from the beginning of the game through Act V:

Total Skill Points (50 levels and 5 acts): **54 points**

Total Stat Points (50 levels and 5 acts): **255 points**

Druid Skill Combinations

With thanks and kudos to Dean Lee and Jason Hutchins at Blizzard QA, here's a breakdown of an effective skill combination and point dispersal that will direct your Druid along certain successful paths. This section also includes a pair of alternate skill combinations.

Skill Point Spread (Balanced Druid)

This allocation creates a Druid who's reasonably well-balanced and able to effectively handle many different situations.

- 5 Points into Lyncanthropy
- 5 Points into Werewolf
- 4 Points into Raven
- 2 Points into Hunger
- 1 Point into Shockwave
- 4 Points into Spirit Wolf
- 2 Points into Feral Rage
- 5 Points into Oak Sage
- 4 Points into Carrion Vine
- 5 Points into Arctic Blast
- 5 Points into Cyclone Armor

All extra points can be put into other areas of your choice.

STATS POINT SPREAD

- 35% points into Strength
- 25% points into Dexterity
- 10% points into Mana
- 30% points into Vitality

ALTERNATE DRUID

SKILL POINT SPREAD (WOLF DRUID)

This allocation creates a Druid who's heavy in the Summoning tree that focuses on being a Wolf most of the time.

- 10 Points into Lyncanthropy
- 10 Points into Werewolf
- 4 Points into Raven
- 10 Points into Spirit Wolf
- 10 Points into Feral Rage

All extra points can be put into other areas of your choice.

STATS POINT SPREAD

- 35% points into Strength
- 30% points into Dexterity
- 10% points into Mana
- 25% points into Vitality

FIGHTING SEVERAL ENEMIES AT ONCE

1. Use Shock Wave or Arctic Blast to lay down some area of effect damage.
2. Use Oak Sage to give your minions and yourself more health.
3. Keep a murder of Ravens and a pack of Dire Wolves (or Spirit Wolves) on hand, and use a Poison Creeper Vine.

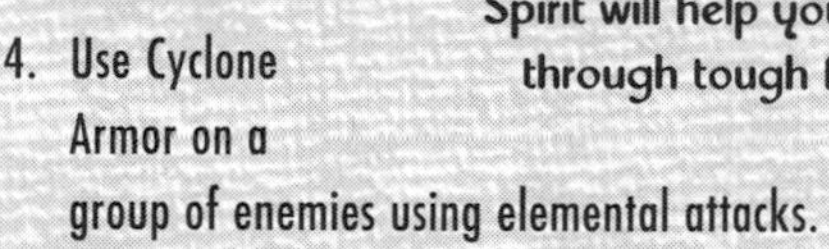

Having a Bear, Spirit or Dire Wolves, a Vine, and a Spirit will help you to get through tough fights.

4. Use Cyclone Armor on a group of enemies using elemental attacks.
5. A strategically placed Volcano and use of Twister can effectively eliminate a large group of enemies. Try to stay away from the fight as much as possible.

FIGHTING BOSSES (SUPER UNIQUE MONSTERS)

1. Use the Grizzly Bear so the Boss focuses on it instead of you. If the Grizzly's not available, use Dire Wolves or Spirit Wolves.
2. Use Shock Wave to stun the monster.
3. When fighting Bosses/Uniques surrounded by normal monsters, always place the Volcano directly under the Boss. This will ensure that he is interrupted constantly and takes massive damage.

You'll have to use some tricks to fight the Bosses that stand in your way of completing some quests.

Another Take on the Druid - The Tank

(From Jason Hutchins, Assistant QA Manager)

You can make a Druid that has over 900 hit points by the time he is at level 30. Here's how you do it:

1. Alternate between assigning five points to Vitality and then five points to Strength at each skill level. The goal here is to have your Vitality and Strength within five points of each other until you reach level 20. By this time, you will begin to really need some points in Dexterity to improve your Attack Rating.

2. I would suggest being very frugal with your points in Energy. My level 34 Druid needs only about 40 Energy to recast all of his pets and change forms.

3. The skills that you want to focus on are Lycanthropy and Werebear. Put one Skill Point into Werewolf so that the points that you are spending on Lycanthropy are not 'wasted' while you wait to qualify for Werebear.

4. Even though Werebear and Werewolf are both melee skills, remember that your attacks are still determined by the weapons that you wield, so make sure you have high-damage weapons! Your best friend here is the maul; Druids have a "fast attack rate" when using a maul. The Werewolf form is even faster with the maul, but the Werebear really shines when using it.

5. The skills Maul and Hunger when in Werebear form are devastating. You will find that you can kill most creatures in one hit. This makes up for the Werebear's slow attack speed.

6. One of the most important skills that affects your hit points is the summoning skill, Oak Sage. This skill increases the health of you and your minions and party members, making it a great mid-game skill. However, it becomes more important for you to have the bonus Attack Rating granted by "Spirit of Wolverine" by the middle Act IV and early into Act V.

7. By the time you reach level 30, you will be ready to learn Spirit of Barbs. This skill grants you, your pets, and your party members a skill similar to the Paladin's Thorns Aura. If you have a lot of hit points, you will be well served by this pet. Even the deadly monsters in Act V, regardless of the armor you wear, become a lot less terrifying!

NOTE

Do not put any points into the Elemental skills when creating a tank!

Chapter 3

THE QUESTS

THE QUESTS

The quest strategy supplied here is compiled from our two previous *Diablo II* guides. They are meant as skeletal walkthroughs to help you find your way and complete each of the quests (although it is not always necessary to complete them in order, you will if you follow this guide). Because of the distances that you must travel in the *Diablo II* universe, the unpredictable nature of many of the maps, and the randomness of monsters, items, and shrines, it would be impossible to provide a detailed walk-through for every possible permutation and combination of gameplay situations. Instead, this section features the high points of your adventures and ensures you're going in the right direction as journey from Act I through V—and beyond, when you replay them at higher skill levels.

ACT I
THE SIGHTLESS EYE

ROGUE ENCAMPMENT

The non-player characters or NPCs in the Rogue Encampment play important roles in your efforts to complete Act I. Here is a list that points out each character's role in terms of buying, selling, identifying, and repairing items. Knowing just who to go to can save time when you're in a rush to buy a particular item or heal your aching wounds. Keep in mind that any NPC who sells items will also buy any type of saleable item from you.

WARRIV

A caravan master who is involved in the first two acts and helps to advance *Diablo II*'s story. He stands near Your Private Stash in the Rogue Encampment.

CHARSI

A blacksmith who repairs, buys, and sells Weapons, Armor, and Arrows/Bolts. Charsi seems to have an affinity for Barbarians.

AKARA

Not only is Akara important for some of the quests, she also fully replenishes your Health and Mana when you talk to her. This spiritual guide of the Rogues buys and sells Scrolls, Tomes, Potions, Wands, Staffs, and Scepters.

KASHYA

The leader of the Rogues is willing to hire some of her warriors out to aid you in your quests.

DECKARD CAIN

Your guide from the original *Diablo*, he is available to assist you after you complete the Cairn Stones quest. Apart from sagely advice and information, Cain will identify items free of charge for the rest of the game.

GHEED

A slick salesman who deals in Armor, Weapons, Magic Items, and Keys. You can also Gamble on his unidentified magical wares and possibly gain Rare, Unique, or even Set Piece items.

Mercenaries

Mercenary names and attributes are randomly assigned at the beginning of the game, so it's not possible for this book to list which of the mercenaries will match up with a particular set of stats. Therefore, we supply the important information about the range of abilities a group of mercenaries will have so that you can decide whether it's worth shelling out the gold for their services or not. The mercenaries in the Rogue Encampment can be hired from Kasha, and will have attributes that are within the following ranges:

Level: 3-10 **Life:** 30-60

Gold (cost): 150-490 **Defense:** 15-45

Damage: 1-3 or 2-4 **Special Attack:** None/Cold Arrow/Fire Arrow

Quest 1: Den of Evil

As you would expect from the first quest of the game, this one begins near the Rogue Encampment in the Blood Moor and is meant to help you cut your teeth and get a feel for your character. Before you begin this quest, move around the Blood Moor and fight until you gain a level. This will earn you a skill point and some more attribute points to improve your character. Akara will now give this speech to begin your first quest:

AKARA

"There is a place of great evil in the wilderness. Rashya's rogue scouts have informed me that a cave nearby is filled with shadowy creatures and horrors from beyond the grave.

I fear that these creatures are massing for an attack against our encampment. If you are sincere about helping us, find the dark labyrinth and destroy the foul beasts. May the Great Eye watch over you."

Move through the Blood Moor and keep an eye out for a cavern entrance. When you discover the entrance, you can descend into the Den of Evil.

Descend into the Den of Evil—look for a cave entrance somewhere in the Blood Moor.

The Den of Evil is a one-level cavern that must be cleared of all monsters.

The Den of Evil consists of only one level, and the completion of the quest requires you to clear it of all monsters. The Quest log (which can be accessed by pressing the letter 'Q') will inform you of your progress. Toward the end of the quest, it will tell you just how many enemies remain for you to destroy.

As you work your way through the Den of Evil, you will meet one Unique monster by the name of Corpse Fire whose special attack (Spectral Hit) does massive damage. When all of the enemies have been defeated, you will have completed the quest. At this point, you can visit Akara who will give you a rare extra Skill Point to put into one of your character's skills.

You will meet one Unique monster in the Den of Evil.

When the quest is complete, the sun will shine into the Den of Evil.

QUEST II: SISTERS' BURIAL GROUNDS

This quest is triggered by either talking to Kashya after completing the Den of Evil quest or by stumbling across the Cemetery. When it's over, Kashya will then offer you the option to hire Rogue mercenaries from her.

"My Rogue scouts have reported an abomination in the Monastery graveyard! Apparently, Andarial is not content on taking only our living. Blood Raven, one of our finest captains in the battle against Diablo at Tristram, was also one of the first to be corrupted by Andariel. Now you'll find her in the Monastery graveyard raising our dead as zombies! We cannot abide this defilement! If you are truly our ally you will help us destroy her."

KASHYA

You must cross the Cold Plains to reach the Burial Grounds.

The battle to kill Blood Raven occurs in the Burial Grounds, located off the Cold Plains. Fight your way through the Cold Plains, gaining experience and money along the way—an extra level of experience never hurts when facing an adversary like Blood Raven.

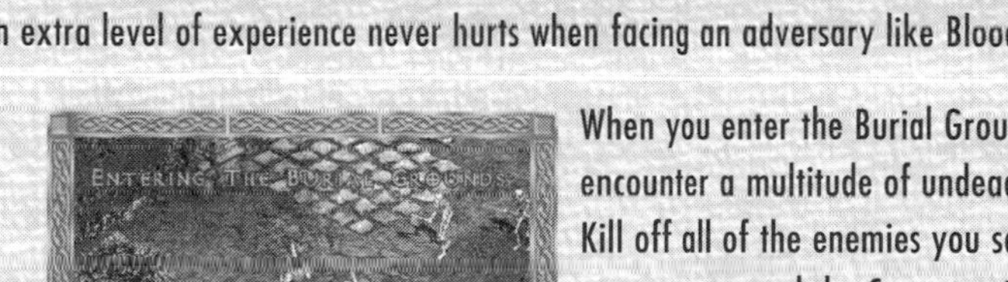

There will be plenty of undead to deal with as you approach the Cemetery.

When you enter the Burial Grounds you'll encounter a multitude of undead monsters. Kill off all of the enemies you see and work your way toward the Cemetery in the central area.

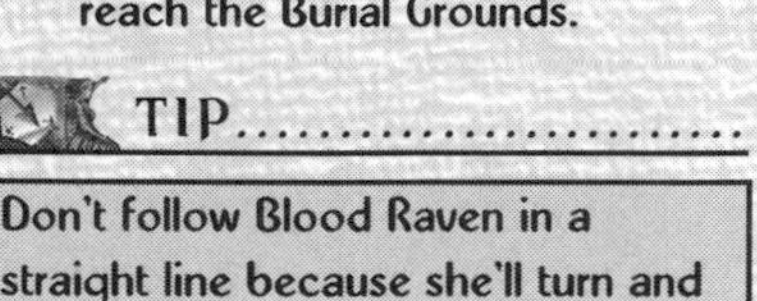

TIP

Don't follow Blood Raven in a straight line because she'll turn and shoot quickly, and most certainly hit you if you're right behind her.

Blood Raven will put up a good fight!

Eventually you'll see Blood Raven. She's fast and raises new zombies straight out of the ground to fight for her cause! Blood Raven fights with a bow and likes to run away if she takes any hits. Because she's so fast, you'll need to run to catch up to her. It's also important to remember that Blood Raven does fire damage with fire arrows, so she's one tough customer.

If you're a character class that can fight hand-to-hand battles, it's best to pin Blood Raven in a corner to fight her; otherwise, she'll repeatedly run away, and then fire arrows at you when she stops. Her 'run and shoot' approach can result in you taking a lot of damage without hitting her much.

When Blood Raven dies, she'll often drop a magic item or two!

When Blood Raven is dead, descend into the Crypt and Mausoleum—there's some great loot and cool items in these areas. Both the Crypt and Mausoleum are designed to raise your character's level and give them wealth, so it could hurt you not to explore these areas.

The Mausoleum and Crypt are not cakewalks, however, so expect to see a couple Unique monsters (which are random) and plenty of other beasts when you venture to these areas.

The Crypt and Mausoleum are both worth exploring to boost your experience and wealth.

TIP

When using an Amazon against Blood Raven, attack by throwing javelins. This is a wise tactic because it provides your best chance to do a lot of damage from a distance. As a Necromancer, Amplify Damage is a key spell to use on her. When you're a Barbarian, Bash can knock Blood Raven off her rhythm.

QUEST III: THE CAIRN STONES

Your character should be between level 6 and 8 to approach The Cairn Stones quest. This quest is enabled either by completing the Blood Raven quest or discovering the Tree of Inifuss. Once the quest is enabled, you must talk to Akara, at which time she'll tell you to get the scroll from the Tree of Inifuss (unless you've already been there).

AKARA

"It is clear that we are facing an Evil difficult to comprehend, let alone combat. There is only one Horadrim Sage, schooled in the most arcane history and lore, who could help us... his name is Deckard Cain. You must travel to Tristram. I pray that he still lives."

The Tree of Inifuss is in the Dark Wood. To get there, you must enter the Stony Field and find the Underground Passageway.

You will face plenty of enemies in the Underground Passageway, so be ready to fight. When you exit, you'll be in the Dark Wood. Here, you must explore and attempt to find the Tree of Inifuss. Once again, your task is seriously challenged by a host of monsters.

When you reach the Tree of Inifuss, you must fight a Unique Gargantuan Beast that is extremely strong and fast, as well as his minions. Once they are disposed of, you can click on the tree to get the Bark Scroll, then use a Town Portal or Waypoint to get back to the Rogue Encampment for Akara's help in deciphering your new-found artifact. Once the Scroll has been deciphered, you'll be able to visit the Cairn Stones and open the Portal to Tristram.

A Unique Gargantuan Beast, Treehead Woodfist, guards the Tree of Inifuss.

A fight against Rakanishu and his minions awaits you at the Cairn Stones. Once he's dead, touch the stones in the order written on the scroll by right-clicking its image in your inventory to open a red portal that transports you to Tristram.

The Cairn Stones are in the Stony Field. They're guarded by Rakanishu, a Unique monster that's Lightning Enchanted and returns damage to you every time you hit him.

When the stones are touched in the correct order, a portal to Tristram opens.

Tristram is swarming with enemies. Release Deckard Cain from his prison in the middle of Tristram to open a Portal back to the Rogue Encampment.

TIP

You can run to Tristram, hit the cage Cain is in, then run out quickly and get out; but if you do this, you will miss a lot of monsters and you won't get Wirt's Leg—a key element of a most interesting Horadric Cube Recipe (see the recipe list in Chapter 1: The Basics).

Releasing Cain will satisfy this quest, but there's more to do in Tristram than releasing Cain.

After Cain is released you can fight Griswold—a Unique monster who's cursed. Griswold puts up a tough fight, but he's relatively slow—a ranged attack should take him out fairly easily.

Griswold is cursed and will fight you to the death.

In the far (left) side of Tristram you'll see Wirt. Pick up his leg, which can at the very least be used as a weapon and may even take you someplace cool (see Horadric Cube Recipes)! When you take Wirt's leg, his corpse will spew out gold he bilked you out of in the first game like a slot machine giving up a jackpot!

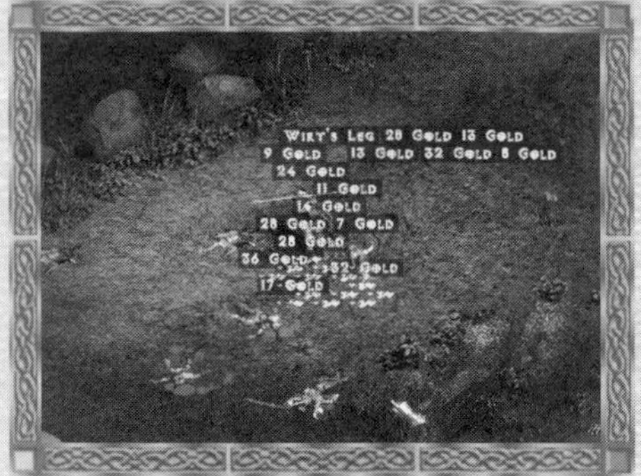

Take Wirt's leg and collect all of the money he dishes out.

Return to the Rogue Encampment and Deckard Cain will thank you. From this point forward he'll identify items for free.

QUEST IV: THE FORGOTTEN TOWER

Finding the Moldy Tome in the Stony Field activates this quest. Your character should be between levels 6-9 to undertake this quest. When you read the Tome you'll learn this:

TOME

"...And so it came to pass that the Countess, who once bathed in the rejuvenating blood of a hundred virgins, was burned alive. And her castle in which so many cruel deeds took place fell rapidly to ruin. Rising over the buried dungeons in that god-forsaken wilderness, a solitary tower, like some monument to Evil, is all that remains.

The Countess's fortune was believed to be divided among the clergy, although some say that more remains unfound, still buried alongside the rotting skulls that bear mute witness to the inhumanity of the human creature."

The Forgotten Tower is in the Black Marsh, which can be reached by traveling through the Dark Wood. Needless to say, there will be all kinds of monsters getting in your way as you move through these areas, so keep a Town Portal scroll on hand at all times, and remember to activate any waypoints you come across on your travels.

You must find this book in the Stony Field to activate the Forgotten Tower quest.

As you travel through the Dark Wood and the Black Marsh, you'll face a lot of opposition, so be prepared to fight.

When you reach the Forgotten Tower you'll soon realize that the tower has been razed and the real adventure lies underground. Enter and be prepared to hack through five levels before you reach the Countess (the boss for this quest). Each level of the Forgotten Tower has at least one Unique monster or Champion group that you must face. These monsters are generated randomly so we can't tell you for sure what you'll face, but it's safe to say that these five Tower levels will keep you busy.

There are a few things you need to know about the Countess before you meet her. First, she's Fire Enchanted, so she's capable of dealing fire damage. Specifically, the Countess likes to conjure up Fire Walls in your way, so be prepared to do some fancy footwork to avoid the flames.

Formidable minions also guard the Countess, and it's important to take them out first or you'll never be able to successfully fight her. The Barbarian's Taunt skill is excellent for this situation because the Countess won't leave the room she's in, allowing you to use Taunt to pull her minions out one at a time and kill them individually. After her servants are out of the way, move in and fight the Countess one-on-one.

You may face a group of Champions or a Unique monster on every level of the Forgotten Tower.

The Countess is a formidable foe.

Once the Countess has been defeated, you'll discover all the riches to be had!

TIP

The Fire Walls used by the Countess are to be reckoned with. If you have an item that reduces the effect of an enemy's magic or some fire resistance, you can endure the flames without taking much damage.

QUEST V: TOOLS OF THE TRADE

This quest is enabled after completing the Forgotten Tower quest and having a conversation with Charsi. Upon completion, Charsi will imbue one of your items with magical properties, making this a significant accomplishment in your on-going adventure. To begin this quest you should be around level 10 before you talk to Charsi.

"When I fled the Monastery, I left behind my Horadric Malus, an enchanted smithing hammer. If you can retrieve it for me, I will use its magic to strengthen your equipment."

CHARSI

You must now visit the Outer Cloister (be sure to hit the Waypoint marker there). Follow this path to get there: move from the Dark Wood to the Black Marsh to the Tamoe Highlands to the Monastery. This is a long and arduous journey that will require you to be victorious in many battles.

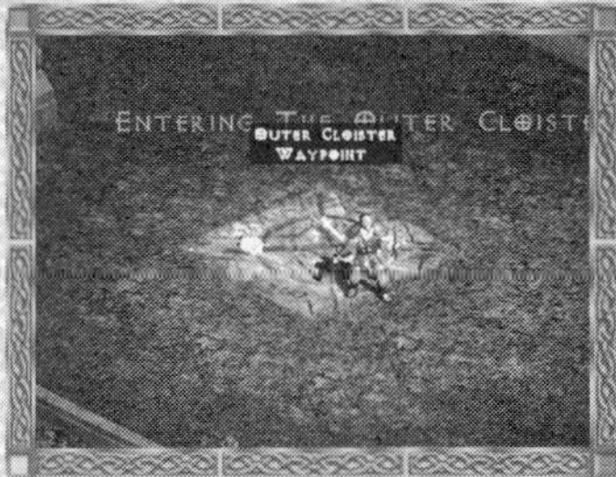

You'll fight many battles as you approach the Outer Cloister.

TIP

In Multiplayer, every player that is in the party of the character that returns the Malus to Charsi gets the reward, so make sure you are grouped before completing the quest!!

Eventually, you'll work your way into the Barracks. As you fight through, you'll notice a small image on your map that looks like a hammer—this is where the Malus (and The Smith) are located.

The Barracks will provide lots of monsters for you to fight before you actually meet up with The Smith.

The Smith is a Unique monster that's extra strong and fast. There's a Devilkin and his minions in with The Smith, as well, so take them out before you go toe to toe with this beast.

When you've finished off The Smith, grab the Malus and return it to Charsi; she'll imbue something for you. Charsi can imbue any non-magical, non-thrown, non-socketed, non-jewelry item, making it a rare item in the process by granting it 3-5 magical attributes. Many players hold off on imbuing an item until they find a particular weapon or piece of armor that's especially good. They then journey back to Charsi to get their rare item.

The Smith is a powerful enemy, but you should be able to handle him if you take his minions out first. Keeping your distance and using ranged attacks is always a good idea.

You get only once chance to imbue an item, so choose carefully.

TIP

There are two important things to know about Charsi imbuing items. First, she does this only **once** in the game, so choose your item carefully. Secondly, if you imbue things like gloves or belts (items not normally chosen to be imbued), you can often acquire good attributes such as increased statistics or health regeneration.

QUEST VI: SISTERS TO THE SLAUGHTER

This is the last quest of Act I, and is given to you by Deckard Cain. When you face this quest, your character should be between level 12 and 16. After you've completed the five other quests of Act I, talk to Cain in the Rogue Encampment and he'll give you the quest while passing along some words of wisdom.

CAIN

"It is certain that we face the demon queen Andariel, who has corrupted the rogue sisterhood and defiled their ancestral monastery. This does not bode well for us, my friend.

Ancient Horadric texts record that Andariel and the other lesser evils once overthrew the three prime evils—Diablo, Mephisto, and Baal—banishing them from Hell to our world.

Here, they caused mankind untold anguish and suffering before they were finally bound within the Soulstones.

Andariel's presence here could mean that the forces of Hell are once again aligned behind Diablo and his brothers. If this is true, then I fear for us all. You must kill her before the Monastery becomes a permanent outpost of Hell and the way east lost forever."

To reach your destination, you must travel to the Barracks, down three levels of the Jail, onward to the Inner Cloister, then to the Cathedral, and finally into the Catacombs. Your battles in the Jail will be difficult. Often you'll take damage from enemies behind bars—you cannot immediately reach them, but they can still use ranged weapons against you.

After passing through the three Jail levels, you'll find yourself in the Inner Cloister. You'll face a Unique Spike Fiend by the name of Flame Spike the Crawler unless you're playing in the expansion set (this creature was removed from *Lord of Destruction)*. Eliminate the creature if necessary and then proceed to the Cathedral.

Fight your way through the Cathedral to the Catacombs entrance, then descend and get ready for a rough ride. There are plenty of randomly generated Unique and Champion monsters to face in the Catacombs, so be sure to hit the Waypoint marker on level 2—you'll probably need to use it.

There's a small room in the Catacombs level 4. Clear it and the surrounding area, then open the double doors to face Andariel. Andariel is tough, scary, and a vicious opponent. In addition to her other attacks, she throws out a lot of poison, so anything you have that can give you poison resistance will help considerably. Some items have Poison Resistance, and the Paladin's Cleansing Aura is excellent—it will help everyone in your party in Multiplayer.

The Catacombs are full of Unique and Champion monsters.

Andariel is a ferocious creature, but you can defeat her!

ACT II
THE SECRET OF THE VIZJEREI

LUT GHOLEIN

As in the Rogue Encampment, the NPCs in Lut Gohlein play important roles in your efforts to complete Act II. This list gives a brief description of each character's role in this Act.

WARRIV

After providing your transportation from the Rogue Encampment, he sets up trade routes in Lut Gholein.

LYSANDER

This addled alchemist buys and sells Potions, Keys, and various other items.

FARA

A former Paladin, she automatically replenishes your Health and Mana when you deal with her. Fara also repairs and sells Armor and Weapons, both mundane and Magical.

DECKARD CAIN

Coming with you from the Rogue encampment, he continues to provide sagely advice as well as identifying items for you.

ATMA

The owner of the public house, she is looking for a hero to avenge her murdered husband and son. Atma gives you the Radament's Lair quest.

GEGLASH

The town drunk who offers a few laughs and some cryptic information on the current state of affairs.

DROGNAN

This aged sorcerer buys and sells Staffs, Scepters, Wands, Scrolls, Tomes, and Health Potions.

GRIEZ

In charge of guarding the city, he also hires out his well-trained Mercenaries.

ELZIX

His days as a renowned bandit behind him, he buys and sells Weapons and Armor. He is also willing to let you Gamble on his unidentified Magical items.

JERHYN

The troubled young leader of Lut Gholein.

KAELAN

A Guard of the Palace.

MESHIF

The captain of a ship that will be your eventual transport to the next Act.

Mercenaries

As in the Rogue Encampment, mercenary names and attributes are randomly assigned in Lut Gohlein. Therefore, we supply the important information about the range of abilities a group of mercenaries will have so that you can decide whether it's worthwhile to hire them or not. The mercenaries in Lut Gohlein can be hired from Griez, and will have attributes that are within the following ranges:

Level: 9-17 **Life:** 120-180

Gold (cost): 300-700 **Defense:** 25-60

Damage: 2-6 or 3-8 **Special Attack:** None/Jab Attack/Poison Resistance (ability)

Quest I: Radament's Lair

Since Atma has a personal stake in Radament being destroyed, she is the one who assigns you this quest. Your character should be between level 16 and 18 by the time you reach this quest. She provides you the following valuable information:

"In the sewers below our city, there lurks a horrid creature that hungers for human flesh. The creature has killed many, including my son and my husband. If you destroy it, I will reward you. Please be careful though, that beast has taken enough from us already. The sewer entrance is through the trap door just up the street."

ATMA

Once you enter the Sewers, you must pass through several levels before you reach the area where Radament is located. Be sure to hit the Waypoint marker on Level 2 of the Sewers in case you die. This will make your journey back much quicker. There are plenty of new enemies in the Sewers; you'll typically face Burning Archers and Burning Dead, so ready an item that gives you fire resistance.

The trap door to the sewers below Lut Gohlien is easy to find.

The Sewers teem with new and ferocious enemies.

Radament can resurrect his minions after you kill them.

When Radament dies, you can get the Horadric Scroll and take it to Cain.

When you reach Radament, you'll have a tough fight indeed. Radament can poison you, and he's also magic resistant, which can make life hard for the Sorceress. He's also surrounded by his minions, which he can resurrect after you've killed them. Using cold based or freezing attacks is an excellent way to deal with Radament because if you can shatter one of his servants, it's gone forever and cannot be resurrected. Likewise, when the Necromancer uses Raise Skeleton on a fallen minion, it means that it can no longer work in Radament's favor.

When Radament is dead, pick up the Book of Skill that he drops and read it to get an extra skill point! Then, search for the Horadric Scroll in a nearby chest. Take this Scroll to Cain and you'll receive an important new quest.

QUEST II: THE HORADRIC STAFF

Once you have delivered the Horadric Scroll to Cain, he will send you on a quest for the Horadric Staff. He also reveals some important details when describing your quest.

CAIN

"Ahh... The lost Horadric Scroll! What a fortunate turn of events...

As the last living Horadrim, I **alone** have knowledge of its meaning. Now, to read the Horadric runes it bears... Hmmm...

The Horadric Mages, after binding Baal within Tal Rasha, magically sealed off his Burial Chamber from the mortal realm. Those same Mages also crafted fearsome Horadric Staves and imbued them with the special power to open the Chamber's hidden door.

After nearly losing one to the thievery of a rogue sorcerer, they divided all the Horadric Staves into two parts—wooden shaft and metal headpiece—hiding them separately to safeguard them.

The Horadrim foresaw our current plight and designed the hiding places to reveal themselves to worthy heroes like you.

Collect both parts of a Horadric Staff and unite them using a Horadric Cube. Then, you may enter Tal Rasha's Burial Chamber."

This quest is the longest and most involved you've undertaken thus far in *Diablo II*. The three items you need to obtain are the Horadric Cube, the Horadric Shaft, and the Viper Amulet (top of the Horadric Staff). The first piece you need to find is the Horadric Cube, which is somewhere on level 3 in the Halls of the Dead, located in the Dry Hills.

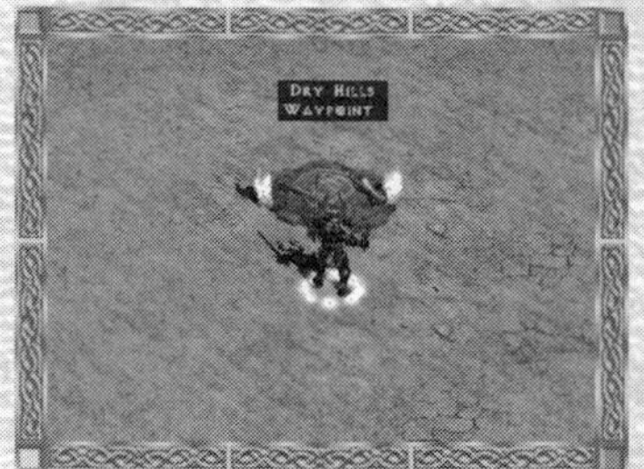

You must venture through the Dry Hills to reach the Halls of the Dead.

When you get to level 3 of the Halls of the Dead you'll find a Unique Sabre Cat guarding the Horadric Cube, along with a bevy of other monsters that would like nothing better than to destroy you. Once these enemies have been dealt with, pick up the Horadric Cube and put it in your Inventory.

Monsters that do not like uninvited guests guard the Horadric Cube.

TIP

The Horadric Cube is a special item that you'll want to keep throughout the game. The Cube can be used to 'transmute' objects and create new ones. Check out Chaper 1: The Basics to learn more about the Horadric Cube, including a list of recipes!

The next item you'll need is the Horadric Shaft, which you'll find on level 3 in the Sand Maggot Lair, located in the Far Oasis. The Shaft is guarded by a Unique monster called Cold Worm the Devourer.

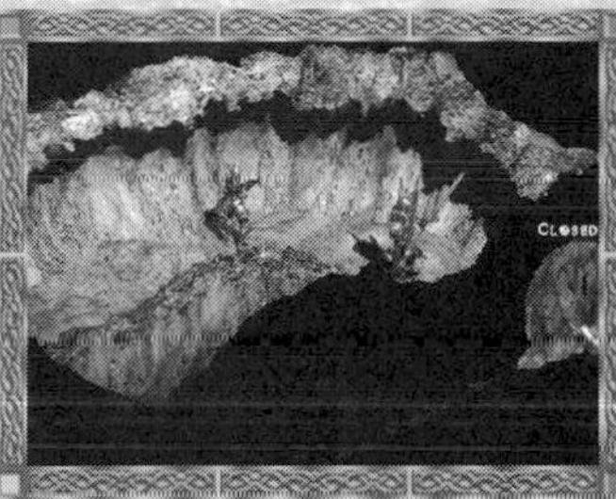

Next, you'll need to enter the Sand Maggot Lair in the Far Oasis.

Cold Worm the Devourer will be only part of the enemy equation in your quest to obtain the Horadric Shaft, so be prepared to fight long and hard, and carry potions and Town Portal Scrolls with you. Be warned that bringing a mercenary on this quest can often be more of a nuisance than a help—the corridors are so narrow that your companion will often just get in your way!

Cold Worm the Devourer will put up a fight for the Horadric Shaft.

The final item you must acquire to complete this quest is the Viper Amulet. You'll find it on level 2 of the Claw Viper Temple in the Valley of the

You must find your way through the Valley of the Snakes to the Claw Viper Temple.

You must face Fang Skin before acquiring the Viper Amulet.

Snakes, which is past the Lost City, and then beyond the Far Oasis.

You'll meet a host of enemies in the Claw Viper Temple, and when you come to the Viper Amulet you must fight a Unique monster named Fang Skin. This beast is extremely fast and presents a challenging battle. Take along Plenty of Thawing potions and some Cold resistance would be a good idea, too. Once the last piece of the quest is in your Inventory, head back to Lut Gohlein and visit Deckard Cain to have him identify both parts of the Staff. Then, follow his directions carefully to restore it to usefulness.

QUEST III: TAINTED SUN

If you finish the Horadric Staff quest, then the Tainted Sun quest is already complete. If you haven't accomplished this yet, then Tainted Sun is a stand-alone quest. You are tasked with your new quest when you enter the Lost City. The sun goes out and you must find the Viper Temple to destroy the evil altar (thus releasing the Viper Amulet) to undo the evil that has blackened the day.

This quest overlaps with the Horadric Staff quest. If you are attempting The Tainted Sun quest first, then go to the Lost City to trigger it.

QUEST IV: THE ARCANE SANCTUARY

Drognan in Lut Gohlein gives you the quest to seek out the Arcane Sanctuary. After you kill Radament, Jheryn will give you the Seven Tombs quest. Drognan will activate the Arcane Sanctuary quest, which will allow you to enter the palace. You'll proceed through the Harem to the Palace Cellar, where you'll find the Arcane Sanctuary. When accepting this quest from Drognan, he gives you some advice.

"I've been researching the old records, trying to find the location of Tal Rasha's Tomb. Though I haven't found the Tomb itself, I may have a good lead for you.

The great Vizjerei Summoner, Horazon, built his Arcane Sanctuary somewhere around here. He was a powerful spellcaster and kept demons as slaves within the Sanctuary. He kept a close eye on great events, too—such as the imprisonment of Baal within Tal Rasha's Tomb.

If you could find Horazon's Sanctuary, I'm sure that it would hold some clue as to the Tomb's location. Though I doubt Horazon is still alive, you must proceed with caution. There's no telling what could be waiting inside.

When I spoke of this with Lord Jerhyn, he asked that I send you to him. Perhaps he knows of a secret entrance or the like."

DROGAN

In Lut Gohlein, go to the Palace and request entrance. Once inside, descend to Harem level 1, then further to level 2. Of course, the Harem is not easy; you'll have enemies to fight the whole way, so be prepared.

The Harem is not a walk in the park—there will be many battles to be fought.

After the Harem you'll descend through three levels of Palace Cellar, eventually finding the entrance to the Arcane Sanctuary. Fire Eye, a Unique Sand Raider, guards this passage. Destroy this monster to finish the quest, then enter the Arcane Sanctuary.

Take out Fire Eye to clear the way to the Arcane Sanctuary.

Enter the Arcane Sanctuary and start working your way through it. Be absolutely sure to hit the Waypoint in the middle of the Sanctuary because it's entirely possible that you'll die in this area and will need to get back quickly.

Be sure to hit this Waypoint in the Arcane Sanctuary.

TIP

When moving in the Arcane Sanctuary, the Barbarian and the Sorceress have definite advantages over the other character classes. The Barbarian's Leap is very effective for bypassing teleporters to get from one ledge to another, while the Teleport Skill of the Sorceress achieves the same ends.

QUEST V: THE SUMMONER

This quest is activated when you meet the Summoner in the Arcane Sanctuary. During this encounter, he'll taunt you with a tortured laugh.

The Summoner is impersonating Horazon. He is located near the end of one of the Arcane Sanctuary's four branching paths, and he is protected by a host of deadly beasts. When you find him, you must destroy him. Resistance to cold is important when fighting the Summoner because he uses Ice Blast. The Paladin's Resist Cold aura is very useful in this situation, and will not only help the Paladin, but also any party members (in Multiplayer), as well. As a rule, it's best to use ranged weapons against the Summoner rather than getting into hand-to-hand combat because he packs a substantial punch.

The Summoner is tough, but he must be taken out if you are to proceed.

QUEST VI: THE SEVEN TOMBS

Jerhyn gives this quest. He tells you that you need to search for Diablo himself, and that the search will take you to Tal Rasha's Tomb. Here, you must find the chamber with the Circle of Seven Symbols, place the Horadric Staff into receptacle in its center, and kill Duriel. Thus begins the quest for the Seven Tombs. Jerhyn has some advice to give during this exchange.

JERHYN

"I have heard of your many deeds of skill and bravery. I feel I can trust you with something I have been hesitant to speak of...

Drognan and I have concluded that the Dark Wanderer who passed through here recently was Diablo, himself! Drognan believes that Diablo is searching the desert for the secret tomb where the great Horadrim, Tal Rasha, keeps Baal imprisoned.

You must find Diablo and put an end to the terrible evil that has fallen upon our city! Drognan is wise and is sure to have some helpful advice for you as to how Tal Rasha's tomb may be found.

It may take you quite some time to find The Tomb. May you be **ready** when you do."

Take the portal to the Canyon of the Magi. When you arrive, touch the Waypoint marker in case you need to go back. Tal Rasha's tomb is located along the perimeter of this desert area. Distinguish the real tomb from the six "false" tombs by matching the symbol shown in your Quest screen to the symbol on the pillars at the temple's entrance.

Match the Symbols to locate the Tomb of Tal Rasha.

Once inside the chamber, place the staff in the Horadric Orifice; this will blow a hole in the wall and open a doorway to the tomb of Tal Rasha. You must then kill Duriel.

Placing the staff in the Orifice will open a passage to the Tomb of Tal Rasha.

Duriel is a powerful foe with plenty of hit points, so prepare for a long battle.

When fighting Duriel, it helps to have something that reduces freeze/cold duration, because Duriel will use this magic on you. It is important to note, however, that his chilling field is a Demonic power and not an Elemental magic, so resistances to cold are ineffective in staving off this attack. Keep Duriel at a distance and you'll fair much better than if you engage him in close combat. Duriel closes fast and has a powerful melee attack that will do both stun and knock back. He also has a huge amount of hit points, so you'll have to pound away to take him out.

 TIP

Create a Town Portal as soon as you enter Tal Rasha's Tomb. Once the fighting begins, you may not have time to do this and get out alive and a Town Portal is your only means of excape from Duriel's lair!

The one exception for the ranged-weapon advice is the Barbarian. His powerful abilities in Melee attack make it best for him to go toe-to-toe and use Double Swing with two weapons against Duriel. Once Duriel's dead, click on Tyrael the Angel to free him. Tyrael delivers a speech and a portal to Jerhyn opens (near palace steps). Back in Lut Gohlein, go to Meshif and head east.

ACT III
THE INFERNAL GATE

KURAST DOCKTOWN

As in the Rogue Encampment and Lut Gohlein, the NPCs in Kurast Docktown play important roles in your efforts to complete Act III. This list gives a brief description of each character's role in this act.

MESHIF

His ship stands ready to take a full cargo and you back to Lut Gohlein, should you wish to return.

DECKARD CAIN

He continues to offer guidance and his skills as a master of identification during your continuing journeys here.

ORMUS

An enigmatic figure, he automatically replenishes your Health and Mana when you talk with him. He also buys and sells Masks, Scepters, Wands, Staffs, Scrolls, and Tomes.

ALKOR

Living in a small hut, this secluded fellow buys and sells Potions while inviting the wayward adventurer to Gamble on his unknown magical treasures.

HRATLI

An enchanter by trade, he buys, sells, and repairs Armor and Weapons of many kinds.

ASHEARA

Leader of the Iron Wolves, she will gladly sell you the services of her magic-wielding Mercenaries.

NATALYA

A shadowy woman who offers advice cloaked in mysteries.

MERCENARIES

As in the other two towns, mercenary names and attributes are randomly assigned, so again only the important information about the range of abilities a group of mercenaries has is included. The mercenaries in Kurast Docktown can be hired from Asheara, and will have attributes that are within the following ranges:

Level: 15-26 **Life:** 240-400

Gold (cost): 600-1285 **Defense:** 80-150

Damage: 3-8 or 4-10 **Special Attack:** None/Cold Spells/Fire Spells/Lightning Spells/Fast Cast

QUEST I: THE GOLDEN BIRD

This quest starts when you meet the first Unique monster after leaving Kurast Docktown. It doesn't matter where; it's simply the first one you find. Destroy it and you receive the Jade Figurine as your treasure. This item must be given to Meshif. In exchange, he will present you with the Golden Bird. You can now go to Alkor. He will take the Golden bird. Finally, leave Alkor and return for your reward. Do this and you'll get a potion of life that adds a permanent +20 to your Life!

Defeat the first Unique monster you meet outside of the Rurast Docktown to begin this quest.

QUEST II: BLADE OF THE OLD RELIGION

Find the Pygmy village in the Flayer Jungle. Hratli will then give you the quest to find an enchanted dagger called the Gidbinn. You must kill a Unique Pygmy in the village and return the blade to Ormus. Hralti gives you the quest and shares some advice.

"As I told you before, I placed an enchantment upon the dockside in order to keep the demons at bay. But lately, the enchantment seems to be weakening. If memory serves me correctly, there is a holy Skatsimi blade that could revitalize the enchantment. The blade is called Gidbinn. Find it, and our sanctuary here will remain safe."

HRALTI

You must kill the Pygmy to get the Gidbinn.

Venture into the Flayer Jungle and move around until you find the Pygmy Village. This area can be confusing to find your way around. Just remember that you're entering a new area when you see two pillars.

You'll find the Gidbinn in the Pygmy Village. You must kill the Pygmy with the Gidbinn in his hand. To take the Pygmy out, remember that he will always charge you, so you don't have to worry about chasing him down—even if he runs away briefly.

Use a Town Portal to go back to Kurast Docktown and talk to Ormus. He will give you a rare magical ring that's random in nature, but always useful. As an additional reward, Asheara will make the hiring of her Iron Wolf mercenaries free!

QUEST III: KHALIM'S WILL

Deckard Cain gives this huge, over-arching quest to you. He adds some words of wisdom and a stern reminder as to your true purpose in Kurast for good measure.

CAIN

"Never forget that your ultimate purpose here in Kurast is to destroy Mephisto. The ancient Horadrim imprisoned the Lord of Hatred inside the Guardian Tower that is located within the Temple City of Travincal.

Know this, friend—the only way to gain entry to Mephisto's prison is to destroy the artifact known as the Compelling Orb. Mephisto used this device to control the Zakarum Priests and their followers. The Orb can only be destroyed with an ancient flail imbued with the spirit of the one incorruptible priest.

Soon after his imprisonment, Mephisto worked his evil corruption on the Zakarum priesthood. All were turned to his dark ways, save one—Khalim, the Que-Hegan of the High Council.

Mephisto directed the other Council priests to slay and dismember Khalim and then scatter his remains across the Kingdom. The Priest Sankekur succeeded Khalim as Que-Hegan, eventually becoming the embodiment of Mephisto here on the mortal plane.

The corrupted High Council fashioned an Orb to control the rest of the Zakarum faithful and used their powers to hide the lair of their master from mortals.

Your task is to collect the scattered relics of Khalim—his Heart, his Brain, and his Eye. Then, using the Horadric Cube, transmute Khalim's Flail with his relics. Once this is accomplished, you must destroy the Compelling Orb with Khalim's Will to open the way into the corrupt sanctum of Mephisto."

In this quest you must find three body parts and a Flail. You will find the first body part, the Eye, in the Spider Cavern, which is located in the Spider Forest. Be sure not to confuse the Spider Cavern with the Arachnid Lair.

You must journey to the Spider Cavern, which will require you to move through the Spider Forest and fight the creatures that stand in your way.

A Unique monster called Sszark the Burning, a Fire Spinner, guards the first body part. When you've defeated Sszark (fire resistance is helpful when fighting him), you'll be able to open a chest that contains the Eye and some other valuables; take them.

After you defeat Sszark the Burning, you can get the Eye of Khalim.

You must destroy Endugu in the Flayer Dungeon to get at the Brain of Khalim.

The Heart of Khalim is on level 2 of the Sewers.

The next piece to collect is the Brain of Khalim. It's located on the third level of the Flayer Dungeon and is guarded by Witch Doctor Endugu (a Flayer Shaman). Once you defeat him, the Brain is yours for the taking.

The third piece of the body, the Heart, is in level 2 of the Sewers. There are two entrances in Upper Kurast and two in the Bazaar. Once in the Sewer, you'll find a lever that opens level 2. Within this small area is a chest containing the Heart.

TIP

The Flayer Dungeon is located near the Pygmy Village.

The last thing you need to find is the Flail. It is held in Travincal by one of the members of the High Council, whom you have to kill. You must put the body parts and the Flail into the Horadric Cube, and then transmute them into a very powerful Flail called Khalim's Will.

When fighting the High Council, hire an Iron Wolf Mercenary, if you don't already have one.

You must get the Flail by fighting the High Council in Travincal.

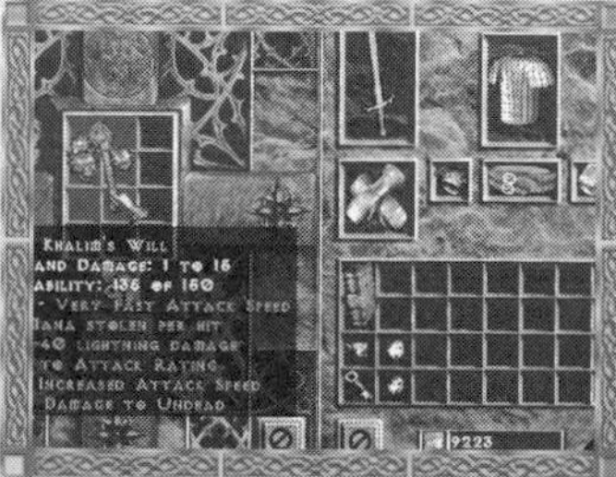

Put the body parts and the Flail into the Horadric Cube, and then transmute them into Khalim's Will.

QUEST IV: LAM ESEN'S TOME

This quest asks you to find the Book in a particular area of the city, then return it to Alkor, who impatiently gives you directions.

"It pains me to waste time with you, so I'll get right to the point. There is a very special book, which you must find for me. It was written long ago by a sage known as Lam Esen, who studied Skatsimi magic and the effects of the Prime Evils on the mortal world. The Black Book was lost when the Children of Zakarum took over this land. Now, you must reclaim it without delay! Its knowledge may aid us in this dark time ahead."

ALKOR

Descend into a ruined temple from one of the three locations.

In Upper Kurast, the Bazaar, and the Causeway there are staircases, which when clicked on descend into temples below the surface. One of these is a ruined temple, and this is where you need to go.

You must fight the Battlemaid Sarina to get Lam Esen's Tome.

In the ruined temple you find Lam Esen's Tome, which is guarded by the Unique monster Battlemaid Sarina, a Flesh Hunter. Defeat her to get the book, then give it to Alkor to earn five attribute points.

QUEST V: THE BLACKENED TEMPLE

This quest is given by Ormus. You must find the Temple City of Travincal, kill the evil High Council there, and smash the Compelling Orb with Khalim's Will. Ormus congratulates you, then presents you with this new challenge.

ORMUS

"You have done well, my friend. Your courage and valor are an inspiration to us all. But now the time has come to face those responsible for the evil that has stifled our land. You must destroy the High Council of Zakarum! Long ago, these elders were charged with the stewardship of Mephisto, the Lord of Hatred, who was imprisoned within the Guardian Tower. Through the generations, these pious men slowly fell more and more under the sway of Mephisto's malevolent power and the Council became an evil mockery of its former glory.

It is Mephisto's Hatred that has corrupted Zakarum and turned its devout followers into paranoid fanatics. That is why you must travel to the Temple City of Travincal and slay the Council. Once they are gone, Mephisto's hold over this land and its people will be broken!"

The three council members are Unique monsters with minions, which will make them more than a handful to battle. Once you take them out, you'll end up inside the Travincal area and find a Compelling Orb. Smash this Orb to open the doorway to the Durance of Hate.

NOTE

This quest is related to the Khalim's Will quest.

The council members are in the Temple City of Travincal.

Locate the Compelling Orb and smash it with Khalim's Will.

QUEST VI: THE GUARDIAN

This quest is given by Ormus after you smash the Compelling Orb in the previous quest. You must find the Tower and entrance, then race through to confront Mephisto and kill him. Ormus explains the critical nature of your quest.

"Diablo and Baal have surely found the Temple City by now. They seek to free their brother, Mephisto, who was imprisoned by the Horadrim in the Temple's Guardian Tower. You must reach him before his brothers do and prevent them from releasing Hatred upon the world."

ORMUS

While in the Durance of Hate, you should hit the Waypoint on level 2 for an easy way to return here should you die or need to flee. If you don't, you'll regret it later.

The Durance of Hate is guarded well.

Mephisto is well guarded by Blood Lords and Council Members.

When you reach Mephisto, you'll see that he has many Blood Lords and Council Members defending him. Meteors, Firewalls, and other destructive forces will be flying at you as you try to take him down. Obviously, fire resistance is is helpful when you're dealing with his minions, but Lightning resistance is vital when dueling with Mephisto.

Mephisto also inflicts poison, launches charged bolts, and fires lightning bolts. In short, he's your worst nightmare. In order to be successful you must first kill all of Mephisto's minions, then go after him. Upon his defeat, Mephisto drops his Soulstone and a rare or unique item!

Take out Mephisto's minions first or you'll never bring him down.

ACT IV
THE HARROWING

PANDEMONIUM FORTRESS

The Pandemonium Fortress is the last of the encampments that you will find in *Diablo II* before moving on to Expansion Act V, and there are just four NPCs to interact with. There are also no mercenaries for you to hire here, which adds to the pressure you're no doubt feeling as the game reaches its climax.

DECKARD CAIN

Following you to the very edge of Hell, his dedication to your quest, as well as his continued help in identifying items, is well appreciated.

TYRAEL

The Archangel who fought Diablo and Baal and the crafter of the runeblade Azurewrath. What else needs to be said?

JAMELLA

This Warrior of Light who outfits those making assaults upon Hell will buy and sell Weapons, Armor, Scrolls, and Potions. She will also allow you to test your hand against the fates by Gambling on the unknown items in her stock.

HALBU

Brother in arms to Jamella, he buys, sells, and repairs Weapons and Armor.

QUEST I: THE FALLEN ANGEL

Tyreal charges you with seeking out and destroying the Unique monster that harbors the spirit of the fallen Angel Izual. Tyrael describes the perilous situation.

TYRAEL

"There is a dark, tortured soul who was trapped within this forsaken realm long ago. He was called Izual by mortal men, and in ages past he was my most trusted Lieutenant. Yet against my wishes he led an ill-fated assault upon the fiery Hellforge itself.

Despite his valor and strength, Izual was captured by the Prime Evils and twisted by their perverse power. They forced him to betray his own kind and give up Heaven's most guarded secrets. He became a corrupt shadow of his former self; a fallen angel trusted neither by Heaven nor Hell.

For his transgressions, Izual's spirit was bound within the form of a terrible creature, which was summoned from the Abyss. His maddened spirit has resided within that tortured husk for many ages now.

It seems to me that he has suffered long enough. I implore you, hero, find Izual and release him from his cruel imprisonment. Put an end to his guilt and suffering."

Search the Plains of Despair until you come across the wandering Izual.

In this quest you must kill Izual in the Plains of Despair. Izual is randomly wandering the area, so you must first search for him.

Izual has a Frost Nova attack and a sword, so cold resistance will help. It's also a good idea to fight him from afar so that you don't feel the wrath of his sword. When Izual has been destroyed you get two skill points to allocate as you see fit.

As you would expect this late in the game, you'll have your hands full during your battle against Izual.

QUEST II: THE HELLFORGE

Cain tells you, "The time has come for you to destroy Mephisto's Soulstone!" and sends you to the Hellforge to do the job. If you didn't take the Soulstone earlier, he'll give it to you anyway (saying he picked it up for you).

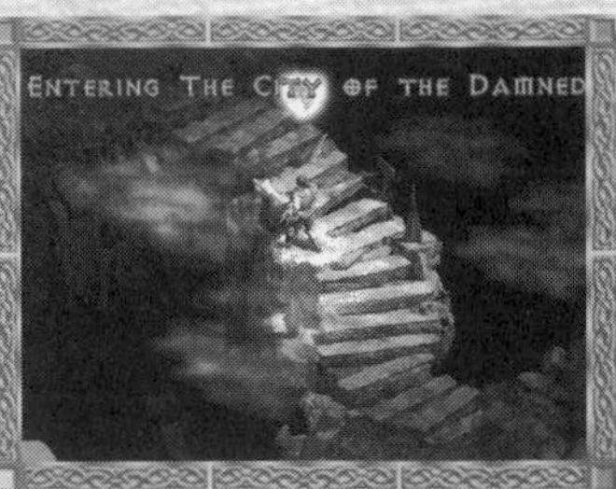

To reach the Hellforge, you must cross the Plains of Despair and enter the City of the Dammed.

To reach the Hellforge, cross the Plains of Despair. When you arrive in the City of the Dammed, descend the large staircase. Make sure to activate the nearby Waypoint!

Descend this staircase to get to the Hellforge.

At the bottom of the staircase, go into the River of Flame. About halfway through, you'll enter the Hellforge. This is where you will meet Hephasto, the Smith's big brother. You must not only kill him, but all the other monsters, as well—this is no small task.

In the Hellforge you'll face off against Hephasto.

When Hephasto dies, you pick up the Hellforge Hammer. This will be used to destroy the Soulstone on the Hellforge. Equip the Hellforge Hammer, then click on the forge. The Soulstone will leave your Inventory and arrive on the Hellforge. Smash the stone and you'll get a large number of high-quality Gems (just in time to throw them into your socketed items/weapons). Take a Town Portal back to the Pandemonium Fortress and prepare for the final quest.

The Soulstone will be destroyed on the Hellforge, and you will get some high-quality Gems for your efforts.

QUEST III: TERROR'S END

Tyrael gives you the final quest where you must find and kill Diablo. He also has some important things to say before you begin this enormous task.

"The time has come to hunt down and destroy Diablo himself. But beware, the Lord of Terror is not to be underestimated. He single-handedly destroyed the town of Tristram and corrupted the last noble hero who tried to stop him. This time, you must defeat him for good. Only by destroying the Soulstone, which he carries, will his spirit be banished forever. Good luck. Though this be our darkest hour, it may yet be your greatest moment!"

TYRAEL

At the end of the River of the Flame there's a Waypoint. You need to activate it because you'll most certainly be coming back.

You must open five seals in Diablo's lair to trigger his appearance. Move around the Chaos Sanctum and hit the five seals to open them. Unfortunately, three of these seals will randomly spawn a Unique monster:

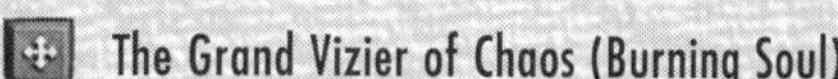

- The Grand Vizier of Chaos (Burning Soul)
- Lord De Seis (Oblivion Knight)
- The Infector of Souls (Venom Lord)

The Waypoint is important because this is the toughest part of the game, and it's likely that you'll be working your way back.

This is one of the seals you must open to make Diablo appear.

When you've broken all five seals, Diablo shows up and you must defeat him to complete the game. He has numerous attacks, including his awesome Flame Circle that acts as a Fire Nova, a special Bone Cage spell that will imprison you, the snaking Fire Serpent, and his Lightning Inferno that projects a devastating stream of red death. On top of this he has a powerful melee attack and a charge that deals massive damage. He's the toughest enemy in the game, as he should be.

NOTE

The River of Flame Waypoint is the last event you will keep in a saved game (until you defeat Diablo). The five seals must be opened in the same session as your victory over Diablo, so schedule some time for this epic battle!

KILLING DIABLO

If there is more than one character in his lair (including minions or mercenaries) and you try to run from Diablo, he will try and imprison you in the Bone Cage. You are then at the mercy of any of his potent spells and death is a mere heartbeat away. Therefore, in a multiplayer situation, you're better off standing and fighting.

The following are strategies for destroying the final boss as each of the character classes.

TIP

Don't be afraid to go out and try to build up your levels more before you face Diablo, and be sure to take LOTS of Mana and Health potions when you do take him on. There's no magic way to destroy the Lord of Terror, but you can flee toward one of the opened seals for a momentary respite to recharge Mana and Health or prepare your next attack—Diablo will not follow you that far. Use Town Portal often; if you open one up ahead of time, expect Diablo to create a Bone Prison around it! Finally, build up your fire and lightning resistances as these are his main forms of magical attack.

BARBARIAN

Go toe-to-toe with Diablo, but run when he is about to launch the Lightning Inferno (Diablo makes a certain gesture when this is about to happen), then go back and fight. Also use your Leap Attack because you can't be hit when you're actively Leaping. Make sure you are stocked with healing or, better yet, Rejuvenation potions.

NECROMANCER

Use a Golem to distract, then curse Diablo with Amplify Damage. The lesser Necromancer minions are largely wasted on Diablo, so only use a Golem to distract him and then attack him with anything you've got. If you are using Poison or Bone spells, be sure you bring along plenty of Mana or Rejuvenation potions.

SORCERESS

Use the Meteor skill plus Static Field to knock down his hit points quickly. Remember, the Static Field skill takes the enemy's hit points down by 1/3 every time you use it. In Diablo's case, that's a LOT of hit points. Be sure to keep a good supply of Mana or Rejuvenation potions at your fingertips.

PALADIN

The Paladin should use Thorns for the same reason the Sorceress uses Static Field. Every time Diablo hits the Paladin, the damage will be returned (many times over if Thorns has skill points in it). Make sure to keep a full belt of Health and Rejuvenation potions as well.

AMAZON

The Amazon needs to put some points into the Decoy skill to keep Diablo distracted. If she's using a bow, then fire the Immolation Arrow with a Long War Bow or Heavy Crossbow. Her battle strategy can be summed up quite simply—hit and run! Points into the passive skills such as Dodge, Evade, and Critical Strike are also crucial to secure victory. Having Health, Mana, Rejuvenation, and even Stamina potions are all good ideas.

NOTE

If your character dies while battling Diablo, then the Lord of Terror will be restored to full health once you resume battle.

ACT V QUESTS

HARROGATH

NON-PLAYER CHARACTERS

The non-player characters or NPCs of Harrogath and Act V play important roles in both your efforts to complete the Act, as well as the advancement of the story. Here is a list that points out each character's role in terms of buying, selling, identifying, and repairing items. Knowing just who to go to can save time when you're in a rush to buy a particular item or heal your aching wounds. Don't forget that any NPC who sells you an item will also buy any saleable item from you.

NIHLATHAK

Nihlathak seems untrusting of your motives, but will take your gold in trade for items or on a Gamble.

ANYA

After rescuing Anya in one of the quests, she becomes the person you see if you want to Gamble.

DECKARD CAIN

He is still the same down to earth guy, ready to give advice and identify items when you need it most.

QUAL-KEHK

Qual-Kehk is the man to see if you're looking for Hirelings in Act V.

LARZUK

Larzuk is the blacksmith who will repair your armor and weapons, and sell you anything you need to replace your old or damaged goods.

MALAH

Malah is the person you see to be healed and replenished, much like Akara in Act I and Fara in Act II.

QUEST I: SIEGE ON HARROGATH

This is the first quest of Act V, and although it's not an easy one (it is, after all, 80% into the game), it's still not too complex in its structure. Your goal is to work your way over a vast expanse of terrain, kill Shenk the Overseer, then return to Harrogath.

LARZUK

"If you're here to defeat Baal... you must prove it! As we speak, Harrogath is under siege by Baal's demons. Catapults rain death just outside the town walls. Baal himself travels up the sacred mountain, having left in charge here one of his most vicious generals, Shenk the Overseer. A ruthless taskmaster, he lashes his own minions into suicidal frenzies on the battlefield. If you wish to prove yourself to us, destroy the monster, Shenk, that commands those infernal catapults outside Harrogath. If you manage to do this, return to me."

After talking to Larzuk in Harrogath, you can venture forth into the Bloody Foothills in an effort to find Shenk the Overseer. You'll find this area filled with Death Maulers, Enslaved, Catapults, and Fanatic Enslaved. About halfway through, you'll come across a Super Unique Monster called Dac Farren—a Demon that's Cold Enchanted. Having some resistance to cold will be important, but it's also probably a good idea to have some Thawing potions handy.

It will pay to have some Thawing potions ready when you meet Dac Farren.

You'll not only face the enemies as you move up through the Bloody Foothills, but you must also deal with the Catapults along the way as well. The Catapults can fire at you from as far away as three screens, and will shoot balls of Poison, Cold, and even Lightning. The only way to avoid these attacks is to keep moving. Of course, it can be difficult to avoid getting bogged down with the congestion of enemies, so it's important to keep your resistances to elemental damage up.

Shenk is a tough customer, but if you made it this far you can deal with him. Use a Town Portal if you get into trouble.

You can only truly get rid of a Catapult by destroying it.

When the quest is complete, Larzuk will Socket one of your items!

Eventually, you'll face Shenk the Overseer (who is Extra Strong). He is surrounded by minions and is, himself, a powerful foe. Defeat Shenk, then return to Harrogath where Larzuk will reward you by Socketing one of your items!

QUEST 2: RESCUE ON MOUNT ARREAT

You must now rescue some Barbarians who have been imprisoned in the Frigid Highlands. Qual-Kehk needs your help to free these brave warriors. In return, you'll be able to hire them as your comrades in arms.

"My concerns have turned to my men taken prisoner on the battlefield by Baal's demons. I hate to think what's happened to them. As you journey up the mountain, keep your eyes open for my soldiers and bring them back to me if you can."

QUAL-KEHK

Your goal in this quest is to patrol the Frigid Highlands and rescue 15 of Qual-Kehk's men (Barbarians). This is a treacherous area because it's swarming with many different enemies, including Enslaved, Catapults, and Demon Imps that teleport from the ground up to Crush Beasts and Barricaded Towers.

The Demon Imps can be hard to handle.

You must fight several Super Unique Monsters along the way, including Thresh Socket (Cursed), Eyeback the Unleashed (Extra Strong, Extra Fast), and Sharptooth Slayer (Extra Fast). All of these enemies come with their own minions, and each is difficult to destroy, especially with all of the other activity that will be going on. For this reason, it's a good idea to destroy Catapults and Evil Demon Huts as you move through the area. You'll find the Barbarians in crude enclosures. You must simply open the door and a Town Portal will appear that they will use to return to Harrogath.

Evil Demon Huts continually spawn Demon Imps. Destroying them will make your life easier if you plan on hanging around the area.

WARNING

Imprisoned Barbarians can die, so don't release them until the area is relatively clear.

Look for the Waypoint in the Frigid Highlands.

Once the Barbarians have been released and at least 11 of them are back in Harrogath, you can return to town and talk to Qual-Kehk to claim your reward—the privilege to hire Barbarians from him.

Eyeback the Unleashed is scary, but you are scarier!

To get some extra goodies, you can venture into Abaddon, where you'll fight tough enemies, but gain lots of experience and wealth.

QUEST 3: PRISON OF ICE

Anya is missing, and Malah implores you to go and find her. You must work your way through the area of the Frozen River to find Anya. There are suspicions that Nihlathak is at the root of Anya's disappearance, but you must find her first to be sure.

MALAH

"There is a matter which I hesitate to share, but I believe you are the only one who can help me now. Anya, the young alchemist and daughter to one of our slain Elders, has been missing for some time. She is a strong, crafty woman with a spirit like no other. One night, just before your arrival, I overheard her and Nihlathak arguing about her father's death. The next morning she was gone. Nihlathak has his own talk as to where she went and why. Don't believe him! I fear he is at the root of her disappearance. Please, if you can, search for Anya and bring her back to us. She'll know what to do about Nihlathak."

You must fight some Unique Monsters in the Arreat Plateau while looking for the entrance to the Crystalline Passage.

You must first work your way through the Arreat Plateau, fighting every inch of the way against various Unique Monsters. You're looking for the entrance to the Crystalline Passage, which will be located on an icy cliff somewhere along the edge of the Arreat Plateau.

Enter the Crystalline Passage when you discover its location.

Inside the Crystalline Passage, you'll face Frozen Creepers, Stygian Harlots, Moon Lords, and even some Champions. Your goal is to find the entrance to the Frozen River that lies below. This is where Anya is being kept.

You may have to face a Champion like this Berserker Moon Lord in the Crystalline Passage.

When you find the entrance to the Frozen River, bravely enter.

The Frozen River is vast, and you'll have to fight many enemies to explore it all, including Rot Walkers, Abominables, Blood Temptresses, and the usual bevy of Super Unique Monsters. You'll also come across some Evil Urns. These devices can potentially give you something worthwhile, but more often than not they'll spew forth a Unique Monster! Use them at your own risk.

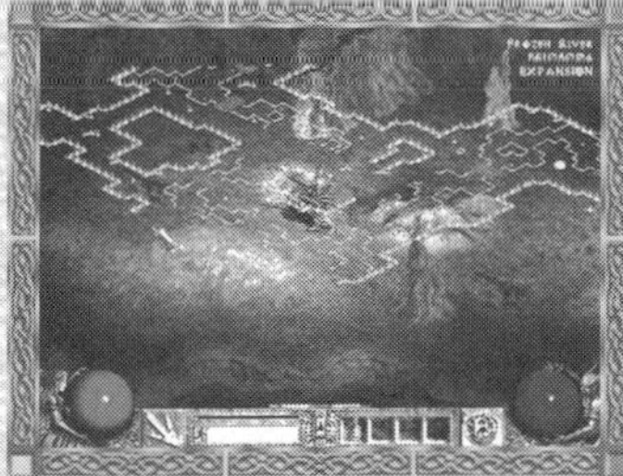
The dungeon is as vast as it is dangerous.

If you open an Evil Urn, be prepared to face enemies like Devil Vex the Cold.

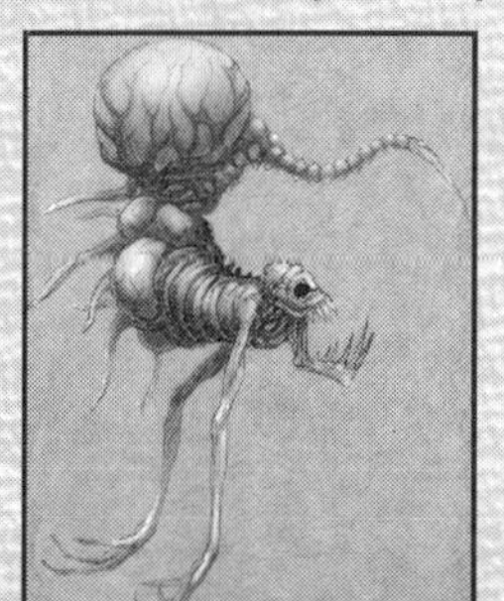

When you reach Anya you will confront Frozenstein. Defeat him, then return to town and get a potion to thaw Anya. Once you do this and return Anya to Harrogath, the quest is complete! As a reward, Anya gives you a Rare Class-specific item custom-made by Larzuk.

You must conquer Frozenstein before you can free Anya.

You'll need to take a trip back to Harrogath to get a potion that will thaw and free Anya.

QUEST 4: BETRAYAL OF HARROGATH

Nihlathak is revealed to be at the root of Harrogath's troubles. You must now find and destroy him to return the Relic of the Ancients to Harrogath. This will require you to travel through Nihlathak's Temple, the Halls of Anguish, and the Halls of Pain before you finally find him in the Halls of Vaught.

ANYA

"Nihlathak told me he struck a deal with Baal to protect Harrogath. In exchange for the demon's mercy, the misguided fool plans to give Baal the Relic of the Ancients, our most holy Totem! Doing so will allow Baal to enter Mount Arreat unchallenged by the Ancients. I tried to stop Nihlathak, but he imprisoned me in that icy tomb. Nihlathak must be stopped before he dooms the whole world. As much as I would love to strangle the life out of him, I'm afraid I haven't the strength. You must go to his lair through this portal I've opened, kill him, and then bring back the Relic of the Ancients. Stop Nihlathak from destroying what we have striven for eons to protect."

You'll fight your way through a mob of creatures after hopping through Anya's Portal. Defeat Pindleskin (Fire Enchanted) inside Nihlathak's Temple before proceeding into The Halls of Anguish. You'll face Prowling Dead and Defiled Warriors in this area as you search for the entrance to the Halls of Pain.

Pindleskin awaits when you begin this quest.

Enter the Halls of Pain when you find this entrance.

Find the Halls of Pain Waypoint, return to Harrogath to heal yourself and repair your armor and weapons, then continue. Keep working your way down through the Halls of Anguish and Pain until you find Nihlathak in the Halls of Vaught. You must vanquish this foe to complete the quest. Nihlathak likes to teleport, making him difficult to hit. He's also a Necromancer, so you can expect him to frequently use Corpse Explosion.

Anya will personalize an item in town as your reward for defeating Nihlathak.

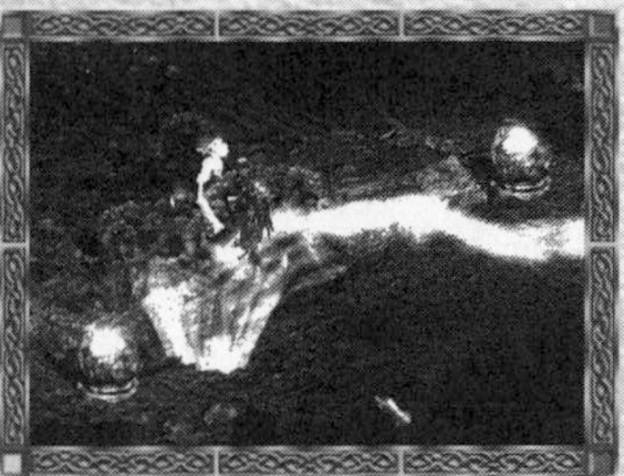

When you've defeated Nihlathak, you can return to town for your reward.

QUEST 5: RITE OF PASSAGE

You must now move up through the lands to reach the Arreat Summit, where you'll face the three Ancient Barbarians. This will truly be one of the toughest fights you've ever had to face, because you cannot leave the battle once it has begun. Stock up on potions and make sure you're in prime condition before you head out.

"Every time I hear of you, warrior, your deeds become more legendary. But take heed. You are approaching the very summit of Mount Arreat. I have never dared venture there. It is sacred—our most holy place. The legends say it is guarded by the Ancient Ones, who block the path of all who are unworthy. Your reputation here does not matter... It will be the Ancients who determine your worthiness. Good luck."

QUAL-KEHK

You must now move through the Glacial Trail into the Frozen Tundra where you'll face Demon Tricksters, Crush Beasts, Enslaved, Catapults, and the usual Barricaded Doors and Towers. Be sure to hit any Waypoints you find and keep yourself healthy as you climb toward the Arreat Summit, because once you begin to battle the Ancients, it won't be wise to leave—if you do, they'll reset.

Move through to the Frozen Tundra where you'll face more of these Crush Beasts, Enslaved, and Demon Tricksters.

When you get to the Ancients' Way entrance, move on in—you're almost to the Summit.

Continue to work your way through until you find the entrance to the Ancients' Way. If you want, you can enter the Icy Cellar as a side-quest, but this adventure is not necessary. Hit the Waypoint when you find it, and use the opportunity to return to Harrogath and heal up.

Hit the Waypoint when you come to it.

When you reach the Arreat Summit, you'll quickly find the Altar of the Heavens. This is the holy home to the three Barbarian Ancients—Talic the Defender, Madawc the Guardian, and Korlic the Protector.

BARBARIAN ANCIENTS

"We are the spirits of the Nephalem, the Ancient Ones. We have been chosen to guard sacred Mount Arreat, wherein the Worldstone rests. Few are worthy to stand in its presence; fewer still can comprehend its true purpose. Before you enter, you must defeat us."

These three Barbarians are tough, but if you use cold to slow them down and keep two away from you while you fight the third, you have a chance.

These three Ancients are very difficult to defeat because you cannot leave the area without having them reset to their original state. In other words, you *must* defeat them in a single grueling session without even using a Town Portal to return to Harrogath. These enemies are Barbarians, and as such use Barbarian Skills. Using cold to freeze them can help keep one or two of them away from you while you work on the third. One uses Whirlwind, one uses Leap Attack, and the other uses Double Throw along with Shout. Once you've managed to defeat these three, your quest is complete.

Once you've defeated the Barbarian Ancients, you'll have completed your quest!

DUNGEONS

There are several 'optional' Dungeons, like the Pit of Acheron, which you may choose to complete.

The experience you gain in these dungeons is ultimately worthwhile.

There are several Dungeons throughout this Act, including Abbadon, the Pit of Acheron, the Drifter Cavern, the Infernal Pit, and the Icy Cellar. All of these are in place as 'extra' areas you can go to build up experience and get some items and wealth. You don't even have to enter most of these Dungeons, but they are there nonetheless, and the experience you gain from them is invaluable when it comes time to face Baal.

QUEST 6: EVE OF DESTRUCTION

This is it, the final confrontation with Baal. You must make it through three levels of the Worldstone Keep, and then through the Throne of Destruction before you can face the Final Boss in the Worldstone Chamber.

BARBARIAN ANCIENTS

"You are a worthy hero! We augment your skill and grant you entry to the interior of Mount Arreat, wherein lies the Worldstone. Beware. You will not be alone. Baal, the Lord of Destruction, is already inside. The Archangel Tyrael has always been our benefactor, but even he cannot help us now. For Baal blocks Tyrael's spiritual presence from entering the chamber of the Worldstone. Only you, mortal, have the power to defeat Baal now. Baal threatens the Worldstone—and through it, the mortal realm, itself. You must stop him before he gains full control of the sacred stone. With it under his control, Baal could shatter the boundaries between this world and the Burning Hells, thus allowing the hordes of the Prime Evils to pour forth into the mortal realm like an unstoppable tide! If you are weak, the world as you know it could be lost forever. You must NOT fail!"

As you work your way from the Worldstone Keep Level 1 down to the Throne of Destruction, you will face a throng of enemies that include Greater Hell Spawn, Vile Witches, Fetid Defilers, Menace Worms, Death Lords, and Demon Sprites. Use Town Portals to return to Horrogath as many times as necessary to keep your supplies well stocked.

You'll face some tough monsters as you work your way through the levels of Worldstone Keep.

Once inside the Throne of Destruction, you'll find Baal sitting on his throne in front of the portal to the Worldstone Chamber. At this point Baal will summon five waves of minions, which, unfortunately, are considerable. Here's a list of the minions you'll face:

- Warped Shamans led by…
- Colenzo the Annihilator
- Death Mages and…
- Unravelers led by…
- Achmel the Cursed
- Council Members led by…
- Bartuc the Bloody
- Venom Lords led by…
- Ventar the Unholy
- Minions of Destruction led by…
- Lister the Tormentor

You must defeat many minions before you can face Baal.

Use a Town Portal to heal yourself up if things get too hairy.

When you've finally finished off the minions, you can follow Baal to the Worldstone Chamber. Baal will attack you with his Cold attack and his Nova. He'll also summon Festering Appendages to attack you while you battle him.

You must look to their names to know which is the real Baal and which is the clone. Of course, you could just destroy them both!

Ultimately, Baal will summon a clone of himself to fight you. Fighting the clone is a waste of time, but the two Baals will appear to be identical. The key to identifying the real Baal from the fake Baal lies in their names. The real Baal's name appears as BAAL, with the word DEMON just below. The fake or cloned Baal also has the word Demon under his name, but the the D and the B line up perfectly. The *real* Baal's name does *not* line up perfectly; instead, the word Demon is slightly off center to the right.

Battling Baal is no picnic.

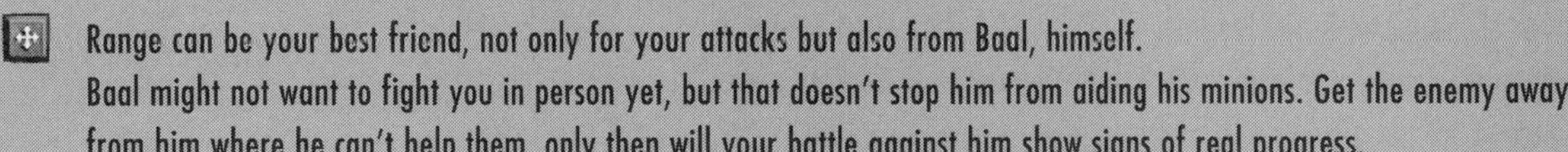

DEFEATING BAAL'S MINIONS

Thanks must go out to Michael Backus and the whole QA team for their insights on handling Baal, the Lord of Destruction. Here's what we suggest...

- If ever there was a bad guy with an ability you didn't like, get ready to face it here, because Baal is BAD!
- Range can be your best friend, not only for your attacks but also from Baal, himself. Baal might not want to fight you in person yet, but that doesn't stop him from aiding his minions. Get the enemy away from him where he can't help them, only then will your battle against him show signs of real progress.
- Don't attempt to take the minions on in one huge group—even when you are at your strongest. Use Guerrilla Tactics instead.
- Find a way to keep your Mana levels up without having to use potions all the time—for example, the Solar Creeper Vine for the Druid or the Cobra Strike Finishing Move for the Assassin.
- What's the best way to stop an enemy? Stop them cold in their tracks. If Baal can't attack as quickly, then you can attack him faster and more often. Slow him down with Cold attacks if you have them.
- Find a way to deal damage without having to click your mouse. Damage shields are vital. Pets, traps, and Hirelings are all there for a reason, so use them!

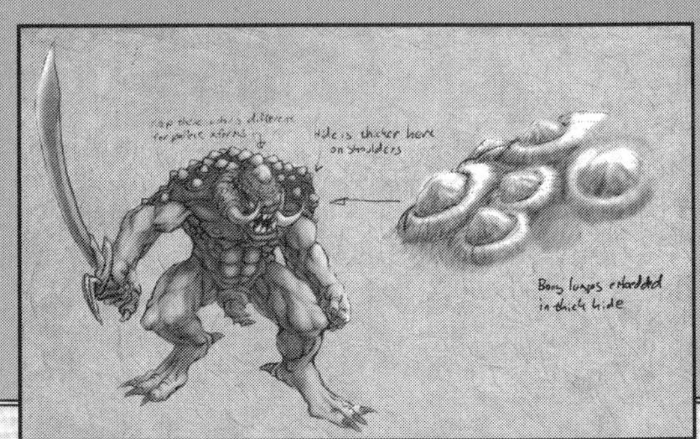

Chapter 4

THE LISTS

BESTIARY

This section of the book covers all of the enemy monsters you'll face in *Diablo II* and the expansion set, including the Standard monsters, the Unique monsters, and the Champion monsters. Every creature is examined thoroughly so that you can get a solid handle on just what to expect as you move through the game. For your convenience, much of the information is presented in table form, allowing you to glean just what you need quickly and then move on to playing the game.

DIABLO II MONSTERS

STANDARD MONSTERS

These are the Standard Monsters of *Diablo II*. You will encounter most, if not all, of them as you progress from the Blood Moor of Act I to Terror's End in Act IV. This is the section of the guide to use when you want to know more about a certain class of monster. Each creature has been listed and features a list of each variant, its resistances and special attacks, as well as which areas of the game you may encounter the beast.

Skeleton

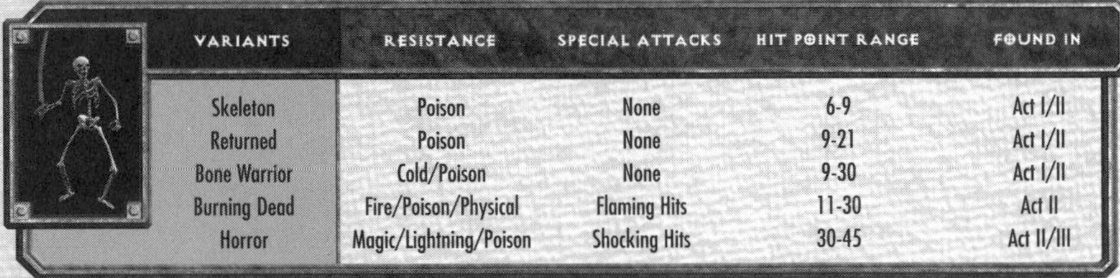

Variants	Resistance	Special Attacks	Hit Point Range	Found In
Skeleton	Poison	None	6-9	Act I/II
Returned	Poison	None	9-21	Act I/II
Bone Warrior	Cold/Poison	None	9-30	Act I/II
Burning Dead	Fire/Poison/Physical	Flaming Hits	11-30	Act II
Horror	Magic/Lightning/Poison	Shocking Hits	30-45	Act II/III

Zombie

Variants	Resistance	Special Attacks	Hit Point Range	Found In
Zombie	Poison	None	5-9	Act I
Hungry Dead	Poison	None	7-13	Act I
Ghoul	Poison	None	28-51	Act I
Drowned Carcass	Fire/Poison/Damage	None	47-85	Act III
Plague Bearer	Magic/Poison	Poison	39-69	Act II

Tainted

Variants	Resistance	Special Attacks	Hit Point Range	Found In
Afflicted	Lightning	Shoots Lightning Globe	28-40	Act I
Tainted	Lightning	Shoots Lightning Globe	26-37	Act I
Misshapen	Lightning	Shoots Lightning Globe	13-19	Act I
Disfigured	Lightning	Shoots Lightning Globe	20-28	Act II
Damned	Lightning	Shoots Lightning Globe	60-84	Act IV

Blood Hawk

Variants	Resistance	Special Attacks	Hit Point Range	Found In
Foul Crow	None	None	2-5	Act I
Blood Hawk	None	None	3-6	Act I
Black Raptor	Poison	None	7-15	Act II
Cloud Stalker	Fire/Lightning	None	8-18	Act III

Fallen

Variants	Resistance	Special Attacks	Hit Point Range	Found In
Fallen	None	None	1-3	Act I
Carver	None	None	3-7	Act I
Devilkin	None	None	3-9	Act I
Dark One	None	None	5-12	Act I
Warped One	All	None	10-25	Act III

Wendigo

Variants	Resistance	Special Attacks	Hit Point Range	Found In
Gargantuan Beast	None	None	9-15	Act I
Brute	None	None	18-29	Act I
Yeti	Cold	None	29-47	Act I
Crusher	Magic	None	57-92	Act II
Wailing Beast	Magic/Fire	None	54-87	Act III

Baboon Demon

Variants	Resistance	Special Attacks	Hit Point Range	Found In
Dune Beast	None	None	41-57	Act II
Jungle Hunter	None	None	45-63	Act III
Doom Ape	None	None	49-69	Act III
Temple Guard	None	None	53-75	Act III

Sand Raider

Variants	Resistance	Special Attacks	Hit Point Range	Found In
Sand Raider	None	Flaming Sword Hits	38-59	Act II
Marauder	None	Cold Charge	48-76	Act II
Invader	None	Flaming Sword Hits	51-80	Act II
Infidel	None	Cold Charge	61-96	Act III
Assailant	None	Flaming Sword Hits	72-113	Act III

Wraith

Variants	Resistance	Special Attacks	Hit Point Range	Found In
Ghost	Magic/Poison/Physical	Drains Mana	14-28	Act I
Wraith	Magic/Poison/Physical	Drains Mana	19-38	Act I
Specter	Poison/Physical	Drains Mana	34-69	Act II
Apparition	Poison/Physical	Drains Mana	36-72	Act II
Dark Shape	Poison/Physical	Drains Mana	41-82	Act III

Corrupt Rogue

Variants	Resistance	Special Attacks	Hit Point Range	Found In
Dark Hunter	None	None	4-7	Act I
Vile Hunter	None	None	8-13	Act I
Dark Stalker	None	None	12-20	Act I
Black Rogue	None	None	13-22	Act I
Flesh Hunter	Physical	None	26-43	Act III
Dark Spear Woman	None	None	6-9	Act I
Vile Lancer	None	None	11-16	Act I
Dark Lancer	None	None	16-24	Act I
Black Lancer	None	None	16-24	Act I
Flesh Lancer	None	None	34-52	Act III

Goatmen

Variants	Resistance	Special Attacks	Hit Point Range	Found In
Moon Clan	None	None	12-17	Act I
Night Clan	None	None	17-21	Act I
Blood Clan	None	None	19-23	Act I
Death Clan	Magic/Fire	None	26-32	Act I
Hell Clan	Fire	None	46-57	Act II

Fallen Shaman

Variants	Resistance	Special Attacks	Hit Point Range	Found In
Fallen Shaman	Fire	Raises Fallen/Fire	4-7	Act I
Carver Shaman	Fire	Raises Carver/Fire	9-15	Act I
Devilkin Shaman	Fire	Raises Devilkin/Fire	13-22	Act I
Dark Shaman	Fire	Raises Dark Ones/Fire	16-26	Act I
Warped Shaman	Fire/magic	Raises Warped Ones/Fire	32-45	Act III

Spire Fiend

Variants	Resistance	Special Attacks	Hit Point Range	Found In
Quill Rat	None	None	1-4	Act I
Spike Fiend	None	None	3-11	Act I
Thorn Beast	None	None	4-16	Act I
Razor Spine	None	None	4-17	Act I
Jungle Urchin	None	None	8-33	Act III

Sand Maggot

Variants	Resistance	Special Attacks	Hit Point Range	Found In
Sand Maggot	None	Lays Eggs/Spits Poison	47-59	Act II
Rock Worm	None	Lays Eggs/Spits Poison	50-62	Act II
Devourer	None	Lays Eggs/Spits Poison	56-69	Act II
Giant Lamprey	None	Lays Eggs/Spits Poison	61-75	Act III
Blood Maggot	None	Lays Eggs/Spits Poison	78-96	Act IV

Claw Viper

Variants	Resistance	Special Attacks	Hit Point Range	Found In
Tomb Viper	None	Freezing Charge Attack	16-26	Act II
Claw Viper	Cold	Freezing Charge Attack	21-34	Act II
Salamander	Cold	Freezing Charge Attack	25-41	Act II
Pit Viper	Cold/Poison	Freezing Charge Attack	27-45	Act II
Serpent Magus	Magic/Cold/Poison	Freezing Charge Attack	30-49	Act III

Sand Leaper

Variants	Resistance	Special Attacks	Hit Point Range	Found In
Sand Leaper	None	None	20-58	Act II
Cave Leaper	None	None	21-62	Act II
Tomb Creeper	Fire	None	23-69	Act II
Tree Lurker	Lightning/Fire	None	28-85	Act III
Cliff Lurker	Lightning/Fire/Physical	None	37-111	Act IV

Panther Woman

Variants	Resistance	Special Attacks	Hit Point Range	Found In
Huntress	None	None	17-29	Act II
Sabre Cat	None	None	18-31	Act II
Night Tiger	None	None	21-34	Act II
Hell Cat	None	None	23-38	Act II
Slinger	None	None	15-25	Act II
Spear Cat	None	None	17-29	Act II
Night Slinger	None	None	20-33	Act II
Hell Slinger	None	None	21-34	Act II

Swarm

Variants	Resistance	Special Attacks	Hit Point Range	Found In
Itchies	None	Drains Stamina	7-15	Act II
Itchies	Physical	Drains Stamina	7-15	Act II
Black Locust	Physical	Drains Stamina	8-16	Act II
Plague Bugs	Physical	Drains Stamina	9-19	Act II

Scarab Demon

Variants	Resistance	Special Attacks	Hit Point Range	Found In
Dung Soldier	None	Defend with Sparks	20-33	Act II
Death Beetle	None	Defend with Sparks	23-38	Act II
Scarab	None	Defend with Sparks	24-40	Act II
Steel Scarab	None	Defend with Sparks	27-44	Act II
Bone Scarab	None	Defend with Sparks	32-53	Act III

Mummy

Variants	Resistance	Special Attacks	Hit Point Range	Found In
Dried Corpse	Poison	Poison	19-44	Act II
Decayed	Poison	Poison	22-50	Act II
Embalmed	Poison	Poison	26-59	Act II
Preserved Dead	Poison	Poison	29-65	Act II/III
Cadaver	Poison	Poison	30-68	Act III

Greater Mummy

Variants	Resistance	Special Attacks	Hit Point Range	Found In
Hollow One	Poison	Poison Cloud/Unholy Bolt	62-75	Act II
Guardian	Poison	Poison Cloud/Unholy Bolt	69-85	Act II
Unraveller	Poison	Poison Cloud/Unholy Bolt	74-92	Act II
Horadrum Ancient	Poison	Poison Cloud/Unholy Bolt	82-120	Act II/III

Vulture Demon

Variants	Resistance	Special Attacks	Hit Point Range	Found In
Carrion Bird	None	None	20-32	Act II
Undead Scavenger	None	None	21-34	Act II
Hell Buzzard	None	None	26-43	Act III
Winged Nightmare	None	None	31-51	Act III

Mosquito Demon

Variants	Resistance	Special Attacks	Hit Point Range	Found In
Sucker	None	Drains Mana & Stamina	8-41	Act III
Feeder	None	Drains Mana & Stamina	9-45	Act III

Willowisp

Variants	Resistance	Special Attacks	Hit Point Range	Found In
Gloam	Lightning/Physical	Drains Mana	19-38	Act III
Swamp Ghost	Lightning/Physical	Drains Mana	21-41	Act III
Burning Soul	Lightning/Physical	Drains Mana	24-46	Act IV
Black Soul	Lightning/Physical	Drains Mana	25-50	Act IV

Evil Spiders

Variants	Resistance	Special Attacks	Hit Point Range	Found In
Arach	None	Spins Web	37-46	Act I
Poison Spinner	None	Spins Web	66-84	Act III
Flame Spider	None	Spins Web	69-88	Act III
Spider Magus	None	Spins Web	75-95	Act III

Thorned Hulk

Variants	Resistance	Special Attacks	Hit Point Range	Found In
Thorned Hulk	None	Stun	67-109	Act III
Bramble Hulk	None	Stun	70-114	Act III
Thrasher	None	Stun	73-119	Act III
Spike Fist	None	Stun	85-138	Act IV

Vampires

Variants	Resistance	Special Attacks	Hit Point Range	Found In
Banished	Cold/Physical	Steals Life/Cold/Fire	40-55	Act I
Ghoul Lord	Cold/Physical	Steals Life/Cold/Fire	61-84	Act II
Night Lord	Cold/Physical	Steals Life/Cold/Fire	64-88	Act III
Dark Lord	Cold/Physical	Steals Life/Cold/Fire	70-96	Act III
Blood Lord	Cold/Physical	Steals Life/Cold/Fire	76-105	Act III

Bat Demon

Variants	Resistance	Special Attacks	Hit Point Range	Found In
Desert Wing	None	Shocking Hit	14-48	Act II
Fiend	None	Shocking Hit	18-16	Act III
Gloom Bat	None	Shocking Hit	19-66	Act III
Blood Diver	None	Shocking Hit	21-72	Act III
Dark Familiar	None	Shocking Hit	24-84	Act IV

Fetish

Variants	Resistance	Special Attacks	Hit Point Range	Found In
Rat Man	None	Blow Darts	14-24	Act I
Fetish	None	Blow Darts	28-47	Act III
Flayer	None	Blow Darts	30-49	Act III
Soul Killer	None	Blow Darts	31-51	Act III
Stygian Doll	None	Blow Darts	32-53	Act III

Corrupt Archer

Variants	Resistance	Special Attacks	Hit Point Range	Found In
Dark Ranger	None	None	10-14	Act I
Vile Archer	None	None	12-17	Act I
Dark Archer	None	None	16-23	Act I
Black Archer	None	None	21-31	Act I
Flesh Archer	Physical	None	40-58	Act III

Skeleton Archer

Variants	Resistance	Special Attacks	Hit Point Range	Found In
Skeleton Archer	Poison	None	9-19	Act I
Corpse Archer	Poison	None	14-28	Act I
Bone Archer	Cold/Poison	None	14-28	Act I
Burning Dead Archer	Fire/Poison	Fire Arrows	21-42	Act II
Horror Archer	Lightning/Magic/Poison	Lightning Arrows	28-57	Act II

Sand Maggot Young

Variants	Resistance	Special Attacks	Hit Point Range	Found In
Sand Maggot Young	None	None	7-22	Act II
Rock Worm Young	None	None	8-23	Act II
Devourer Young	None	None	8-26	Act II
Giant Lamprey Young	None	None	9-28	Act III
Blood Maggot Young	None	None	12-36	Act IV

Blunderbore

Variants	Resistance	Special Attacks	Hit Point Range	Found In
Blunderbore	None	Knockback Attack	41-73	Act II
Gorbelly	None	Knockback Attack	45-81	Act II
Mauler	None	Knockback Attack	45-81	Act II
Urdar	All	Knockback Attack	62-111	Act IV

Zealot

Variants	Resistance	Special Attacks	Hit Point Range	Found In
Zakarumite	None	None	52-69	Act III
Faithful	None	None	57-75	Act III
Zealot	None	None	62-82	Act III

Frog

Variants	Resistance	Special Attacks	Hit Point Range	Found In
Swamp Dweller	None	Spits Fire Bolts	57-75	Act III
Bog Creature	None	Spits Fire Bolts	60-79	Act III
Slime Prince	None	Spits Fire Bolts	62-82	Act III

Cantor

Variants	Resistance	Special Attacks	Hit Point Range	Found In
Sexton	None	Lightning/Teleport/Blizzard	54-72	Act III
Cantor	None	Lightning/Teleport/Blizzard	60-79	Act III
Heirophant	None	Lightning/Teleport/Blizzard	65-86	Act III

Tentacle

Variants	Resistance	Special Attacks	Hit Point Range	Found In
Water Watcher	None	None	49-65	Act III
River Stalker	None	None	54-72	Act III
Stygian Watcher	None	None	60-79	Act III

Tentaclehead

Variants	Resistance	Special Attacks	Hit Point Range	Found In
Water Watcher	None	Spits Poison	49-65	Act III
River Stalker	None	Spits Poison	54-72	Act III
Stygian Watcher	None	Spits Poison	60-79	Act III

Skeleton Mage

Variants	Resistance	Special Attacks	Hit Point Range	Found In
Returned Mage	Poison	Posion	10-15	Act II
Bone Mage	Poison/Cold	Cold	12-16	Act II
Burning Dead Mage	Poison/Lightning	Lightning	14-20	Act II
Horror Mage	All	All	17-23	Act II

Fetish Shaman

Variants	Resistance	Special Attacks	Hit Point Range	Found In
Fetish Shaman	None	Raises Fetishes/Inferno	30-49	Act III
Flayer Shaman	None	Raises Flayers/Inferno	31-51	Act III
Soul Killer Shaman	None	Raises Soul Killers/Inferno	32-53	Act III

Finger Mage

Variants	Resistance	Special Attacks	Hit Point Range	Found In
Doom Caster	Fire/Lightning	Homing Missiles/Drains Mana	57-81	Act IV
Strangler	Fire/Lightning	Homing Missiles/Drains Mana	60-84	Act IV
Storm Caster	Fire/Lightning	Homing Missiles/Drains Mana	62-87	Act IV

Regurgitator

Variants	Resistance	Special Attacks	Hit Point Range	Found In
Corpulent	None	Eats and spits corpses	57-81	Act IV
Corpse Spitter	None	Eats and spits corpses	60-84	Act IV
Maw Fiend	None	Eats and spits corpses	62-87	Act IV

Undead Horror

Variants	Resistance	Special Attacks	Hit Point Range	Found In
Doom Knight	All	None	57-81	Act IV
Abyss Knight	All	All	60-84	Act IV
Oblivion Knight	All	Bone Spirit/Curses	62-87	Act IV

Megademon

Variants	Resistance	Special Attacks	Hit Point Range	Found In
Balrog	Fire	Inferno	57-81	Act IV
Pit Lord	Fire	Inferno	60-84	Act IV
Venom Lord	Fire/Poison	Inferno	62-87	Act IV

CHAMPIONS

Champion Monsters are randomly distributed throughout *Diablo II*, and appear in small packs. Champions are much tougher versions of Standard monsters. When these powerful monsters die, they usually give up a little more loot than Standard monsters do. Because you never know when you'll meet a pack of Champions, be ready for them at any time.

Champions and Uniques are random and can be found anywhere in the game, so be ready for them.

UNIQUE MONSTERS

Unique Monsters usually have two-word names, like 'Ooze Drool'. Occasionally this name is followed by an appellation, like 'the Hungry'. Uniques are randomly distributed throughout *Diablo II*, and they always appear with a small pack of Standard Monsters, labeled as 'minions'. Like Champions, they usually give up a little more loot than Standard monsters do.

SUPER UNIQUE MONSTERS

These are the preset 'boss' monsters that you'll face as you move through the quests of *Diablo II*. Each monster is listed below with their special abilities and the general locations where they appear in the game. Keep in mind that most of these monsters will appear with minions, making them extra difficult to defeat! For details about how to handle some of the trickier Super Unique Monsters, refer to *Chapter 3: The Quests*. The following table shows you exactly what each of the attributes means so that you can judge what you're up against when facing each of the bosses.

UNIQUE MONSTER ATTRIBUTES

Attribute	Effect
EXTRA STRONG	Min. Damage x3, Max. Damage x3, To Hit Plus 25%.
EXTRA FAST	Unique & Pack get Velocity Increase: Attack Rate x2 (Unique only).
MAGICAL RESISTANCE	Resist All 75% (Fire, Cold, & Lightning),
CURSE	50% hits, an Amplify Damage curse (MLVL/4) on attacker.
FIRE ENCHANTED	Fire Min. Damage + (Min. Damage), Fire Max. Damage + (Max. Damage), x2 To Hit, Fire Resist 75%.
COLD ENCHANTED	Cold Min. + (Min. Damage), Cold Max. +(Max. Damage), Cold Length +20, To Hit x2, Cold Resist 75%.
LIGHTNING ENCHANTED	Light Min. Damage + (Min. Damage), Light Max. Damage + (Max. Damage), To Hit x2, Light Resist 75%.
MANA BURN	Mana Min. Damage + (Min. Damage x4), Mana Max. Damage + (Max. Damage x4), To Hit x2, Magic Resist 75%.
SPECTRAL HIT	Fire, Light, & Cold Resist 20%; To Hit x2 (Random Fire, Cold, Light, Magic, & Poison do Element hit) + (Min. Damage) + (Max. Damage).
STONE SKIN	Damage Resist +80%, AC x3
MULTI - SHOT	Two more missiles of the same type are shot.
TELEPORT	(Health <33%) or (Ranged Monster & someone is close); Teleport if (Health <33%) add +25% of Max. Hit Points to Health.
AURA ENCHANTED	Might (at monster level 4), Holy Fire (at monster level 2), Thorns (at monster level 4), Holy Freeze (at monster level 2), Holy Shock (at monster level 2), Conviction (at monster level 4), Fanaticism (at monster level 4).
THIEVING	Monster steals potions out of the Belt (potions drop down to proper slot).
POISON STRIKE	Hit poisons target.
POISON CLOUD	Damages and poisons like Poison Javelin skill of the Amazon.
FIRE ARROW	Damages like Fire Arrow skill of the Amazon.

ANDARIEL

Special Attributes: Poison Strike, Poison Cloud

Found in: Act I, Monastery

BISHIBOSH (FALLEN SHAMAN)

Special Attributes: Magic Resistance, Fire Enchanted

Found in: Act I, The Cold Plains

BONEBREAK (SKELETON)

Special Attributes:	Extra Strong, Magic Resistant
Found in:	Act I, The Crypt

BLOOD RAVEN (CORRUPT ROGUE ARCHER)

Special Attributes:	Fire Arrow
Found in:	Act I, The Burial Grounds

COLDCROW (DARK RANGER)

Special Attributes:	Cold Enchanted
Found in:	Act I, The Cave

RAKANISHU (CARVER)

Special Attributes:	Lightning Enchanted, Extra Fast
Found in:	Act I, The Stony Field

TREEHEAD WOODFIST (BRUTE)

Special Attributes:	Extra Strong, Extra Fast
Found in:	Act I, The Dark Woods

GRISWOLD (CHARACTER FROM DIABLO)

Special Attributes:	Cursed
Found in:	Act I, Tristram

THE COUNTESS (DARK STALKER)

Special Attributes:	Fire Enchanted
Found in:	Act I, Forgotten Tower

PITSPAWN FOULDOG (TAINTED)

Special Attributes:	Cursed, Cold Enchanted
Found in:	Act I, Jail Level 2

FLAMESPIKE THE CRAWLER (RAZOR SPINE)

Special Attributes:	Cursed, Fire Enchanted
Found in:	Act I, Inner Cloister

BONE ASH (BURNING DEAD MAGE)

Special Attributes:	Extra Strong, Cold Enchanted, Magic Resistant
Found in:	Act I, Cathedral

THE SMITH (SPECIAL)

Special Attributes:	Extra Strong
Found in:	Act I, Barracks

CORPSEFIRE (ZOMBIE)

Special Attributes:	Spectral Hit
Found in:	Act I, The Den of Evil

RADAMENT (GREATER MUMMY)

Special Attributes:	Extra Fast
Found in:	Act II, The Sewers Level 3

BLOODWITCH THE WILD (HUNTRESS)

Special Attributes:	Extra Strong, Cursed
Found in:	Act II, Halls of the Dead Level 3

FANGSKIN (SALAMANDER)

Special Attributes:	Light Enchanted, Extra Fast
Found in:	Act II, Claw Viper Temple Level 2

BEETLEBURST (SAND WARRIOR)

Special Attributes:	Magic Resistant
Found in:	Act II, Far Oasis

COLDWORM THE BURROWER (SAND MAGGOT QUEEN)

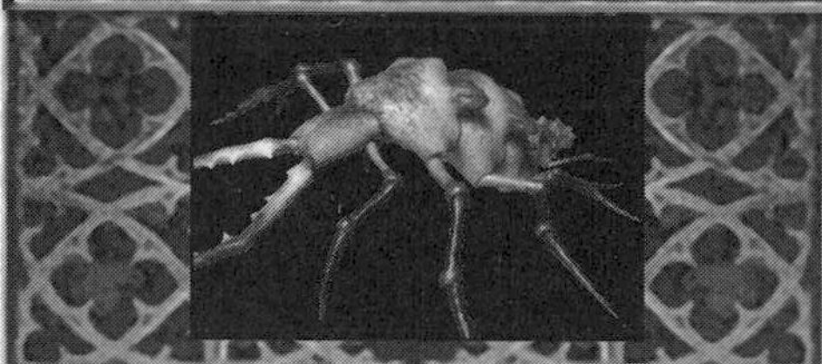

Special Attributes:	Cold Enchanted, Magic Resistant
Found in:	Act II, Maggot Lair Level 3

FIRE EYE (INVADER)

Special Attributes:	Fire Enchanted, Extra Fast
Found in:	Act II, Palace Cellar Level 3

DARK ELDER (PLAGUE BEARER)

Special Attributes:	Extra Fast, Magic Resistant
Found in:	Act II, Lost City

THE SUMMONER (SPECIAL)

Special Attributes:	Extra Strong, Extra Fast
Found in:	Act II, Arcane Sanctuary

ANCIENT KAA THE SOULLESS (UNRAVELER)

Special Attributes:	Magic Resistant, Extra Strong, Lightning Enchanted
Found in:	Act II, Tal Rasha's Tomb

CREEPING FEATURE (DECAYED)

Special Attributes:	Extra Strong, Cold Enchanted
Found in:	Act II, Stony Tomb Level 2

WITCH DOCTOR ENDUGU (SOUL KILLER SHAMAN)

Special Attributes:	Magic Resistant, Fire Enchanted
Found in:	Act III, Flayer Dungeon Level 3

STORMTREE (THRASHER)

Special Attributes:	Extra Fast, Lightning Enchanted
Found in:	Act III, Lower Kurast

BATTLEMAID SARINA (FLESH HUNTER)

Special Attributes:	Extra Fast, Spectral Hit
Found in:	Act III, Ruined Temple

Icehawk Riftwing (Gloom Bat)

Special Attributes:	Cold Enchanted, Teleportation
Found in:	Act III, Sewers Level 1

Sszark the Burning (Flame Spider)

Special Attributes:	Extra Strong, Cursed
Found in:	Act III, Spider Cavern

Ismail Vilehand (Council Member)

Special Attributes:	Extra Fast, Cursed
Found in:	Act III, Travincal

Geleb Flamefinger (Council Member)

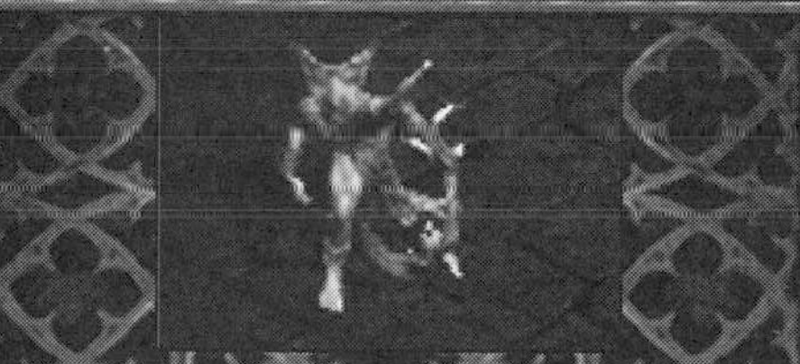

Special Attributes:	Extra Strong, Fire Enchanted
Found in:	Act II, Travincal

Toorc Icefist (Council Member)

Special Attributes:	Cold Enchanted, Stone Skin
Found in:	Act III, Travincal

WYLAND VOIDFINGER (COUNCIL MEMBER)

Special Attributes:	Mana Burn, Teleportation
Found in:	Act III, Durance of Hate Level 3

MAFFER DRAGONHAND (COUNCIL MEMBER)

Special Attributes:	Extra Fast, Extra Strong, Teleportation
Found in:	Act III, Durance of Hate Level 3

BREMM SPARKFIST (COUNCIL MEMBER)

Special Attributes:	Aura Enchanted, Lightning Enchanted
Found in:	Act III, Durance of Hate Level 3

INFECTOR OF SOULS (VENOM LORD)

Special Attributes:	Extra Fast, Spectral Hit
Found in:	Act IV, Chaos Sanctuary (seal)

HELPHASTO THE ARMORER (OVERLORD)

Special Attributes:	Aura Extra Strong, Cursed, Magic Resistant
Found in:	Act IV, River of Flame

GRAND VIZIER OF CHAOS (STORM CASTER)

Special Attributes:	Extra Fast, Thieving, Aura Enchanted
Found in:	Act IV, Chaos Sanctuary (seal)

LORD DE SEIS (OBLIVION KNIGHT)

Special Attributes:	Extra Fast, Aura, Thieving
Found in:	Act IV, Chaos Sanctuary (seal)

DIABLO

Special Attacks:	Lightning Inferno, Flame Circle, Cold Touch, Fire Wall, Firestorm, Bone Prison, Charge Attack
Found in:	Act IV, Chaos Sanctuary

(See p.154 for detailed strategy for defeating Diablo.)

EXPANSION MONSTERS

This section of the book covers all of the enemy monsters that appear in Act V of *Diablo II: Lord of Destruction*, as well as the Unique monsters (or bosses). Every creature is examined thoroughly so that you can get a solid handle on just what to expect as you move through the game. For your convenience, much of the information is presented in table form, allowing you to glean just what you need quickly, then move on.

STANDARD MONSTERS

These are the standard monsters of *Diablo II: Lord of Destruction*; that is to say, you'll see these critters in Act V. Although there's a chance that you won't see all the monsters in any one game, it's a safe bet that you'll come across most of them. This section tells you a little about each monster, shows you what the class of creature looks like, and then includes important statistics about each one. The 'Variant' column is merely the name of the creature within the category. The Resistance tells you if the monster is resistant to any elemental or magical attacks, or if it has increased resistance to physical damage. All of these monsters are seen only in Act V.

Baal's Minion Type

Variant	Resistances	Hit Point Range
Enslaved	None	805-1006
Ice Boar	None	855-1069
Slayer	None	830-1038
Fire Boar	None	868-1084
Hell Spawn	None	880-1100
Ice Spawn	None	880-1100
Greater Hell Spawn	None	880-1100
Greater Ice Spawn	None	880-1100

Demon Imp

Variant	Resistances	Hit Point Range
Demon Gremlin	None	274-451
Demon Imp	None	282-465
Demon Trickster	None	286-472
Demon Rascal	None	295-486
Demon Rogue	None	299-493

Reanimated Horde

Variant	Resistances	Hit Point Range
Reanimated Horde	Poison	498-747
Rot Walker	Poison	483-725
Prowling Dead	Poison	513-770
Unholy Corpse	Damage/Fire/Poison	528-792
Defiled Warrior	Magic/Poison	528-792

Siege Beast

Variant	Resistances	Hit Point Range
Siege Beast	None	1760
Crush Beast	None	1760
Blood Bringer	None	1760

Overseer

Variant	Resistances	Hit Point Range
Overseer	None	1660
Lasher	None	1685
Overlord	None	1735
Blood Boss	None	1760
Hell Whip	None	1760

Catapult

Catapults have no immunities and, thus, are their own group. They conjure up one of three kinds of elemental shots—Cold, Fire, or Poison—and lob them up to three screens away at you and your party as you move through an area. The only way to destroy a Catapult is to get close to it and take it out in person.

Putrid Defiler

Variant	Resistances	Hit Point Range
Putrid Defiler	Fire/Lightning/Cold/Poison	513-855
Retched Defiler	Fire/Lightning/Cold/Poison	528-880
Fetid Defiler	Fire/Lightning/Cold/Poison	528-880
Rancid Defiler	Fire/Lightning/Cold/Poison	528-880
Rank Defiler	Fire/Lightning/Cold/Poison	528-880

Succubus

Variant	Resistances	Hit Point Range
Succubus	None	409-654
Vile Temptress	None	421-674
Stygian Harlot	None	428-684
Hell Temptress	None	440-704
Blood Temptress	None	440-704

Stygian Fury

Variant	Resistances	Hit Point Range
Siren (Dominus)	None	409-654
Vile Witch	None	421-674
Stygian Fury	None	428-684
Blood Witch	None	440-704
Hell Witch	None	440-704

Abominable

VARIANT	RESISTANCES	HIT POINT RANGE
Snow Drifter	Magic/Cold	880-1056
Abominable	Cold	880-1056
Chilled Froth	Cold	880-1056
Frozen Abyss	Cold	880-1056

Suicide Minion

VARIANT	RESISTANCES	HIT POINT RANGE
Fanatic Enslaved	Fire	161-242
Berserker Slayer	Fire	166-249
Consumed Fire Boar	Fire	171-257
Consumed Ice Boar	Fire	174-260
Frenzied Hell Spawn	Fire	176-264
Frenzied Ice Spawn	Magic/Fire	176-264
Insane Hell Spawn	Magic/Fire	176-264
Insane Ice Spawn	Fire	176-264

Frozen Horror

VARIANT	RESISTANCES	HIT POINT RANGE
Frozen Creeper	Cold	1320-1760
Frozen Terror	Cold	1320-1760
Frozen Scourge	Cold	1320-1760
Frozen Horror	Cold	1320-1760
Frozen Scorch	Cold	1320-1760

Blood Lord

Variant	Resistances	Hit Point Range
Moon Lord	None	1245-1660
Night Lord	None	1283-1710
Blood Lord	None	1301-1735
Hell Lord	None	1320-1760
Death Lord	None	1320-1760

Death Mauler

Variant	Resistances	Hit Point Range
Death Mauler	None	531-654
Death Brawler	None	556-684
Death Slasher	None	572-704
Death Berserker	None	572-704
Death Brigadier	None	572-704

Pain Worm

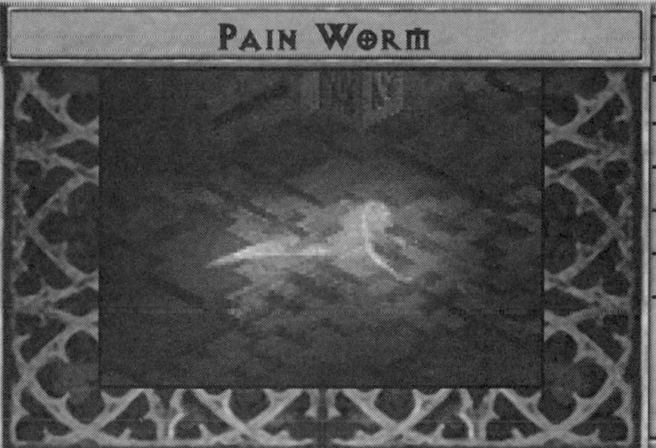

Variant	Resistances	Hit Point Range
Pain Worm	None	286-472
Torment Worm	None	291-479
Agony Worm	None	295-486
Menace Worm	None	299-493
Anguish Worm	None	299-493

ACT V CHAMPIONS

In *Diablo II*, Champions appeared with blue colored names. Now there are Fanatics, Ghostly, Berserkers, and Possessed. Each of these names gives these monsters (which are randomly generated) different bonuses. Not to worry, though—depending on which kind of Champion you're fighting you are eligible for other bonuses yourself. Here's what to expect from each of the Champion Classes.

Fanatics: Faster Speed, -30% to Armor Class.

Berserkers: Damage 4x, To Hit x4, Hit Points x1.5.

Ghostly: Half Speed, Approximately 1/5 chance for Cold Damage, Resist Damage 77%.

Possessed: Hit Points x12, Can't be cursed.

Champions: Minimum Damage x2, Maximum Damage x2, To Hit x2, Attack Rate +120%, Hit Points x6, Level Plus 4, Experience x3.

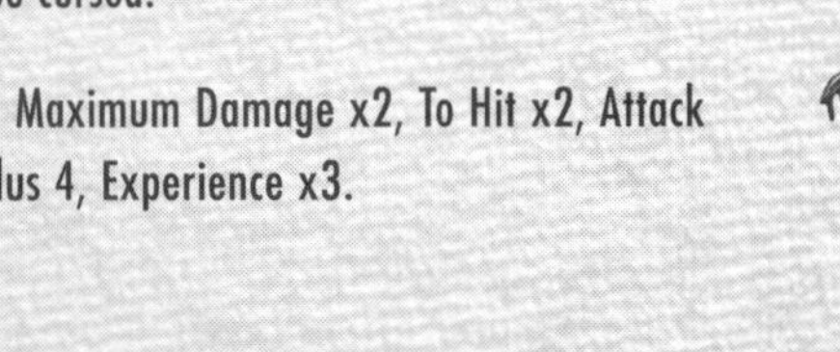

UNIQUE MONSTERS

Just like the Unique Monsters in Acts I-IV, the Uniques of the expansion set are randomly distributed throughout Act V, and they always appear with a small pack of Standard Monsters, which are labeled as 'Minions'. Like Champions, they usually give up a little more loot than Standard monsters do.

ACT V SUPER UNIQUE MONSTERS

These are the preset 'boss' monsters that you'll face as you move through Act V. Each monster is listed below with their special abilities and the general locations where they appear in the game. Keep in mind that most of these monsters will appear with minions, making them extra difficult to defeat! Below is a table that that shows you exactly what each of the attributes means so that you can judge what you're up against when facing each of the bosses.

DAC FARREN

Special Attributes:	Cold Enchanted
Found in:	Bloody Foothills (middle)

SHENK THE OVERSEER

Special Attributes:	Extra Strong
Found in:	Bloody Foothills (end)

ELDRITCH THE RECTIFIER

Special Attributes:	Extra Fast
Found in:	Frigid Highlands

THRESH SOCKET

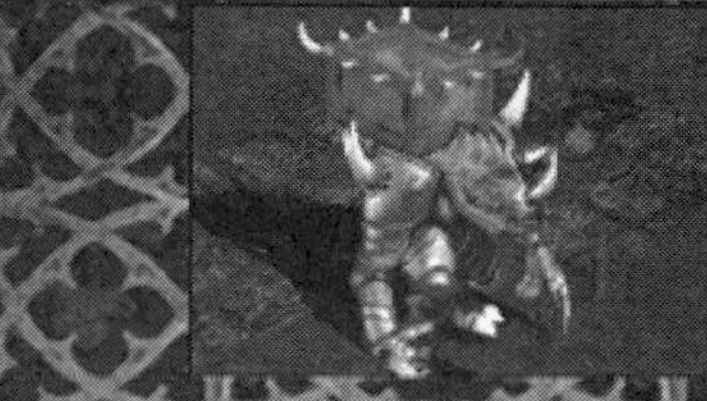

Special Attributes:	Cursed
Found in:	Frigid Highlands (middle)

EYEBACK THE UNLEASHED

Special Attributes:	Extra Strong, Extra Fast
Found in:	Frigid Highlands at entry to Arreat Plateau

SHARPTOOTH SLAYER

Special Attributes:	Extra Fast
Found in:	Arreat Plateau at entry to Crystalline Passage

FROZENSTEIN

Special Attributes:	Cold Enchanted, Mana Burn
Immunities:	Cold
Found in:	Frozen River (guarding Anya)

BONESAW BREAKER

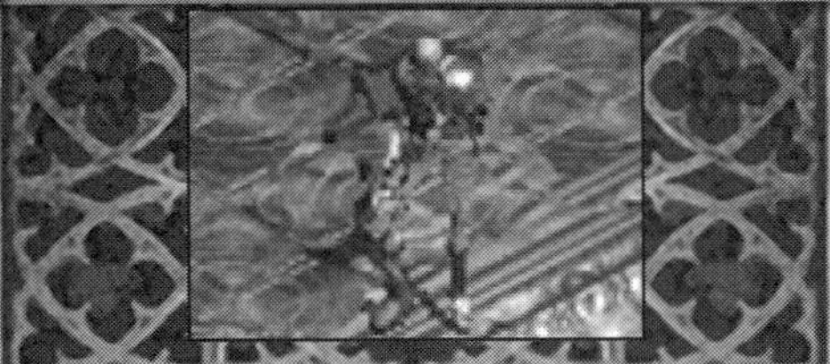

Special Attributes:	Undead, Extra Strong, Magic Resistant
Found in:	Glacial Trail

SNAPCHIP SHATTER

Special Attributes:	Extra Strong
Immunities:	Cold
Found in:	Icy Cellar

PINDLESKIN

Special Attributes:	Undead, Fire Enchanted
Found in:	Entrance to Nihlathak's Temple

NIHLATHAK

Special Attributes:	Teleport
Found in:	Halls of Vaught

TALIC

Special Attributes:	Whirlwind
Found in:	Arreat Summit

MADAWC

Special Attributes:	Shout, Double Throw
Found in:	Arreat Summit

KORLIC

Special Attributes:	Leap Attack
Found in:	Arreat Summit

ACT V FINALE MONSTERS

You face these monsters in the Throne of Destruction, leading up to the final showdown with Baal. On top of these Super Unique Monsters, you'll also face Demons, Unravelers, Council Members, Venom Lords, and Festering Appendages.

COLENZO THE ANNIHILATOR

Special Attributes:	Fire Enchanted
Immunities:	Fire
Found in:	Throne of Destruction

ACHMEL THE CURSED

Special Attributes:	None
Immunities:	Poison
Found in:	Throne of Destruction

BARTUC THE BLOODY

Special Attributes:	Lightning Enchanted
Found in:	Throne of Destruction

VENTAR THE UNHOLY

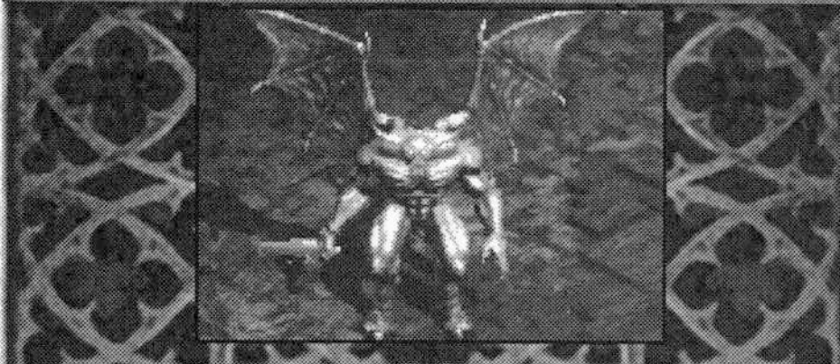

Special Attributes:	Extra Fast
Found in:	Throne of Destruction

LISTER THE TORMENTOR

Special Attributes:	Spectral Hit
Found in:	Throne of Destruction

BAAL (LORD OF DESTRUCTION)

Special Attacks:	Incineration Nova, Hoarfrost, Mana Rift, Destructive Strike, Festering Appendage, Vile Effigy
Special Attributes:	Duplication
Found in:	Worldstone Chamber

ITEM LISTS

This section covers the myriad of items found throughout the *Diablo II* Realm, including those specific to the expansion set—Jewels, Charms, Runes, and others.

CHARMS (EXPANSION SET ONLY)

Charms are unique items that you need only carry in your Inventory (once they're identified) to enjoy their benefits. Charms rely on a prefix/suffix randomization when created. The following tables cover the different varieties.

SMALL CHARMS MAGIC PREFIXES

	Bonus	Min	Max	Level Requirement
Stout	Defense	1	1	1
Stout	Defense	4	8	15
Burly	Defense	15	20	28
Stalwart	Defense	20	30	40
Red	Minimum Damage	1	1	16
Sanguinary	Minimum Damage	2	2	33
Bloody	Minimum Damage	3	3	50
Jagged	Max Damage	1	2	17
Forked	Max Damage	3	4	30
Serrated	Max Damage	5	6	45
Rugged	Stamina	4	8	1
Rugged	Stamina	9	16	15
Bronze	Attack Rating	2	4	1
Bronze	Attack Rating	6	12	15
Iron	Attack Rating	13	24	31
Steel	Attack Rating	25	36	49
'Fine	Attack Rating	10	20	21
Lizard's	Mana	1	2	12
Lizard's	Mana	3	7	12
Snake's	Mana	8	12	24
Serpent's	Mana	13	17	40
Shimmering	% Resist All	3	6	25
Azure	% Resist Cold	3	5	1
Lapis	% Resist Cold	6	7	10
Cobalt	% Resist Cold	8	9	20
Sapphire	% Resist Cold	10	12	32

	Bonus	Min	Max	Level Requirement
Russet	% Resist Fire	3	5	1
Garnet	% Resist Fire	6	7	10
Ruby	% Resist Fire	8	9	20
Crimson	% Resist Fire	10	12	32
Tangerine	% Resist Lightning	3	5	1
Ocher	% Resist Lightning	6	7	10
Coral	% Resist Lightning	8	9	20
Amber	% Resist Lightning	10	12	32
Beryl	% Resist Poison	3	5	1
Viridian	% Resist Poison	6	7	10
Jade	% Resist Poison	8	9	20
Emerald	% Resist Poison	10	12	32

[1] *Bonus 2: Max Damage Max 1 Min 3*

Small Charms Magic Suffixes

	Bonus	Min	Max	Level Requirement
of Craftsmanship	Max Damage	1	2	15
of Quality	Max Damage	3	4	28
of Maiming	Max Damage	5	6	43
of Dexterity	Dexterity	1	1	5
of Dexterity	Dexterity	2	2	16
of Balance	Fast Hit Recovery	5	5	29
of Greed	% More Gold	5	10	15
of Fortune	% Magic Find	2	2	18
of Good Luck	% Magic Find	3	4	33
of Life	Life	5	10	14
of Sustenance	Life	11	15	17
of Vita	Life	16	20	39
of Strength	Strength	1	1	5
of Strength	Strength	2	2	16
of Inertia	Fast Run Walk	3	3	27

Medium Charms Magic Prefixes

	Bonus	Min	Max	Level Requirement
Stout	Defense	2	3	1
Stout	Defense	4	6	10

continues on next page

	Bonus	Min	Max	Level Requirement
Stout	Defense	8	12	15
Burly	Defense	13	18	19
Burly	Defense	20	30	24
Stalwart	Defense	30	40	30
Stalwart	Defense	45	60	37
Red	Minimum Damage	1	2	8
Sanguinary	Minimum Damage	3	4	25
Bloody	Minimum Damage	5	7	47
Jagged	Max Damage	1	2	7
Jagged	Max Damage	3	4	15
Forked	Max Damage	5	7	22
Forked	Max Damage	8	9	32
Serrated	Max Damage	10	12	42
Rugged	Stamina	8	16	1
Rugged	Stamina	17	25	5
Rugged	Stamina	26	32	15
Bronze	Attack Rating	4	8	1
Bronze	Attack Rating	6	12	5
Bronze	Attack Rating	13	25	12
Iron	Attack Rating	26	38	18
Iron	Attack Rating	39	51	26
Steel	Attack Rating	52	64	36
Steel	Attack Rating	65	77	44
[1]Fine	Attack Rating	10	20	14
[2]Sharp	Attack Rating	21	48	21
Lucky	% Magic Find	1	1	1
Lucky	% Magic Find	2	2	1
Lucky	% Magic Find	3	4	1
Lizard's	Mana	2	4	1
Lizard's	Mana	5	7	6
Lizard's	Mana	8	12	12
Snake's	Mana	13	18	18
Snake's	Mana	19	23	25
Serpent's	Mana	24	29	33
Serpent's	Mana	30	34	41
Shimmering	% Resist All	3	6	12
Shimmering	% Resist All	7	13	26
Azure	% Cold Resist	5	10	1
Lapis	% Cold Resist	11	15	12
Cobalt	% Cold Resist	16	19	18
Sapphire	% Cold Resist	20	24	27

	Bonus	Min	Max	Level Requirement
Crimson	% Resist Fire	5	10	1
Russet	% Resist Fire	11	15	12
Garnet	% Resist Fire	16	19	18
Ruby	% Resist Fire	20	24	27
Tangerine	% Resist Lightning	5	10	1
Ocher	% Resist Lightning	11	15	12
Coral	% Resist Lightning	16	19	18
Amber	% Resist Lightning	20	24	27
Beryl	% Resist Poison	5	10	1
Viridian	% Resist Poison	11	15	12
Jade	% Resist Poison	16	19	18
Emerald	% Resist Poison	20	24	27

[1]*Bonus 2: Max Damage Max 1 Min 3*
[2]*Bonus 2: Max Damage Max 4 Min 6*

MEDIUM CHARMS MAGIC SUFFIXES

	Bonus	Min	Max	Level Requirement
of Craftsmanship	Max Damage	1	2	6
of Craftsmanship	Max Damage	3	4	13
of Quality	Max Damage	5	7	21
of Quality	Max Damage	8	9	30
of Maiming	Max Damage	10	12	40
of Dexterity	Dexterity	2	3	2
of Dexterity	Dexterity	4	5	13
of Balance	Faster Hit Recovery	8	8	14
of Greed	% More Gold	5	10	5
of Greed	% More Gold	11	22	15
of Life	Life	6	10	9
of Life	Life	11	15	9
of Sustenance	Life	16	20	19
of Sustenance	Life	21	25	34
of Vita	Life	26	30	50
of Vita	Life	31	35	66
of Strength	Strength	2	3	2
of Strength	Strength	4	5	13
of Inertia	Faster Run/Walk	5	5	18

LARGE CHARMS MAGIC PREFIXES

	Bonus	Min	Max	Level Requirement
Stout	Defense	3	5	1
Stout	Defense	6	9	5
Stout	Defense	10	12	9
Burly	Defense	13	15	12
Burly	Defense	16	22	16
Burly	Defense	23	30	20
Stalwart	Defense	33	40	24
Stalwart	Defense	44	50	29
Stalwart	Defense	60	100	34
Red	Minimum Damage	1	2	3
Red	Minimum Damage	3	4	12
Sanguinary	Minimum Damage	5	6	21
Sanguinary	Minimum Damage	7	8	32
Bloody	Minimum Damage	9	11	46
Jagged	Max Damage	1	2	2
Jagged	Max Damage	3	5	7
Jagged	Max Damage	6	8	12
Forked	Max Damage	9	11	18
Forked	Max Damage	12	14	24
Serrated	Max Damage	15	17	31
Serrated	Max Damage	18	20	39
Rugged	Stamina	12	24	1
Rugged	Stamina	25	36	5
Rugged	Stamina	37	50	15
Bronze	Attack Rating	6	12	1
Bronze	Attack Rating	13	27	5
Bronze	Attack Rating	28	42	9
Iron	Attack Rating	43	57	14
Iron	Attack Rating	58	72	18
Iron	Attack Rating	73	87	23
Steel	Attack Rating	88	102	29
Steel	Attack Rating	103	117	35
Steel	Attack Rating	118	132	41
[1]Fine	Attack Rating	10	20	11
[2]Fine	Attack Rating	21	48	16
[3]Sharp	Attack Rating	49	76	21
Lucky	% Magic Find	1	1	1
Lucky	% Magic Find	2	2	1
Lucky	% Magic Find	3	4	1
Lizard's	Mana	3	7	1
Lizard's	Mana	8	13	5

	Bonus	Min	Max	Level Requirement
Lizard's	Mana	14	20	9
Snake's	Mana	21	26	14
Snake's	Mana	27	33	18
Snake's	Mana	34	39	23
Serpent's	Mana	40	46	29
Serpent's	Mana	47	52	35
Serpent's	Mana	53	59	41
Shimmering	% Resist All	3	6	6
Shimmering	% Resist All	8	13	10
Shimmering	% Resist All	14	20	27
Azure	% Resist Cold	7	15	1
Lapis	% Resist Cold	16	22	7
Cobalt	% Resist Cold	23	29	15
Sapphire	% Resist Cold	30	36	22
Crimson	% Resist Fire	7	15	1
Russet	% Resist Fire	16	22	7
Garnet	% Resist Fire	23	29	15
Ruby	% Resist Fire	30	36	22
Tangerine	% Resist Lightning	7	15	1
Ocher	% Resist Lightning	16	22	7
Coral	% Resist Lightning	23	29	15
Amber	% Resist Lightning	30	36	22
Beryl	% Resist Poison	7	15	1
Viridian	% Resist Poison	16	22	7
Jade	% Resist Poison	23	29	15
Emerald	% Resist Poison	30	36	22
Fletcher's	Bow and Crossbow Skills	1	1	42
Acrobatic	Passive Skills	1	1	42
Harpoonist's	Javelin and Spear Skills	1	1	42
Burning	Fire Skills	1	1	42
Sparking	Lightning Skills	1	1	42
Chilling	Cold Skills	1	1	42
Hexing	Curse Spells	1	1	42
Fungal	Poison and Bone Spells	1	1	42
Graverobber's	Summoning Spells	1	1	42
Lion Branded	Combat Skills	1	1	42
Captain's	Offensive Auras	1	1	42
Preserver's	Defensive Auras	1	1	42
Sounding	Combat Skills	1	1	42
Fanatic	Combat Masteries	1	1	42
Expert's	Warcries	1	1	42

continues on next page

LARGE CHARMS MAGIC PREFIXES (CONTINUED)

	Bonus	Min	Max	Level Requirement
Trainer's	Summoning Spells	1	1	42
Spiritual	Shape Shifting Skills	1	1	42
Nature's	Elemental Skills	1	1	42
Entrapping	Traps	1	1	42
Mentalist's	Shadow Disciplines	1	1	42
Shogukusha's	Martial Arts	1	1	42

[1]Bonus 2: Max Damage Max 1 Min 3
[2]Bonus 2: Max Damage Max 4 Min 6
[3]Bonus 2: Max Damage Max 7 Min 10

LARGE CHARMS MAGIC SUFFIXES

	Bonus	Min	Max	Level Requirement
of Craftsmanship	Max Damage	1	2	1
of Craftsmanship	Max Damage	3	5	6
of Craftsmanship	Max Damage	6	8	11
of Quality	Max Damage	9	11	17
of Quality	Max Damage	12	14	22
of Maiming	Max Damage	15	17	29
of Maiming	Max Damage	18	20	37
of Dexterity	Dexterity	3	4	1
of Dexterity	Dexterity	5	6	10
of Balance	balance3	12	12	1
of Greed	% More Gold	5	10	1
of Greed	% More Gold	11	21	5
of Greed	% More Gold	22	33	14
of Life	Life	5	10	1
of Life	Life	11	15	6
of Life	Life	16	20	14
of Sustenance	Life	21	25	23
of Sustenance	Life	26	30	37
of Sustenance	Life	31	35	53
of Vita	Life	36	40	69
of Vita	Life	41	45	83
of Vita	Life	46	50	97
of Strength	Strength	3	4	1
of Strength	Strength	5	6	10
of Inertia	Fastest Run/Walk	7	7	15

GEMS

Gems may be inserted into socketed items to add powerful effects. Here's the table of Gem data for your reference.

GEM GRADES & EFFECTS

	Gems	Level	Weapons	Shields	Helms and Armor
Amethyst	Chipped	1	+40 to Attack Rating	+8 to Defense	+3 to Strength
	Flawed	5	+60 to Attack Rating	+12 to Defense	+4 to Strength
	Amethyst	12	+80 to Attack Rating	+18 to Defense	+5/6 to Strength
	Flawless	15	+100 to Attack Rating	+24 to Defense	+7/8 to Strength
	Perfect	18	+150 to Attack Rating	+30 to Defense	+9/10 to Strength
Topaz	Chipped	1	+1-8 Lightning Damage	12% Resist Lightning	7-9% Magic Item Find
	Flawed	5	+1-14 Lightning Damage	16% Resist Lightning	11-13% Magic Item Find
	Topaz	12	+1-22 Lightning Damage	22% Resist Lightning	14-17% Magic Item Find
	Flawless	15	+1-30 Lightning Damage	28% Resist Lightning	18-20% Magic Item Find
	Perfect	18	+1-40 Lightning Damage	40% Resist Lightning	21-25% Magic Item Find
Sapphire	Chipped	1	(1-3) Cold Damage	12% Resist Cold	+10 to To Mana
	Flawed	5	(3-5) Cold Damage	16% Resist Cold	+17 to To Mana
	Sapphire	12	(4-7) Cold Damage	22% Resist Cold	+24 to To Mana
	Flawless	15	(6-10) Cold Damage	28% Resist Cold	+31 to To Mana
	Perfect	18	(10-14) Cold Damage	40% Resist Cold	+38 to To Mana
Emerald	Chipped	1	+8 Poison Damage/3 sec	12% Resist Poison	+3 to Dexterity
	Flawed	5	+11 Poison Damage/3 sec	16% Resist Poison	+4 to Dexterity
	Emerald	12	+14 Poison Damage/3 sec	22% Resist Poison	+5/6 to Dexterity
	Flawless	15	+17 Poison Damage/3 sec	28% Resist Poison	+7/8 to Dexterity
	Perfect	18	+20 Poison Damage/3 sec	40% Resist Poison	+9/10 to Dexterity
Ruby	Chipped	1	(3-4) Fire Damage	12% Resist Fire	+10 to Life
	Flawed	5	(5-8) Fire Damage	16% Resist Fire	+17 to Life
	Ruby	12	(8-12) Fire Damage	22% Resist Fire	+24 to Life
	Flawless	15	(10-16) Fire Damage	28% Resist Fire	+31 to Life
	Perfect	18	(15-20) Fire Damage	40% Resist Fire	+38 to Life
Diamond	Chipped	1	125-129% Dmg. vs. Undead	5/6% Resist All	+20 to Attack Rating
	Flawed	5	130-135% Dmg. vs. Undead	7/8% Resist All	+40 to Attack Rating
	Diamond	12	136-145% Dmg. vs. Undead	9-11% Resist All	+60 to Attack Rating
	Flawless	15	146-155% Dmg. vs. Undead	12-15% Resist All	+80 to Attack Rating
	Perfect	18	156-170% Dmg. vs. Undead	16-20% Resist All	+100 to Attack Rating
Skull	Chipped	1	Steal 2% Life, 1% Mana	Attacker takes 4 Damage	Replenish Life +2, Mana Regin 8%
	Flawed	5	Steal 2% Life, 2% Mana	Attacker takes 8 Damage	Life +3, Mana 8%
	Skull	12	Steal 3% Life, 2% Mana	Attacker takes 12 Damage	Life +3, Mana 12%
	Flawless	15	Steal 3% Life, 3% Mana	Attacker takes 16 Damage	Life +4, Mana 12%
	Perfect	18	Steal 4% Life, 3% Mana	Attacker takes 20 Damage	Life +5, Mana 19%

SET ITEMS

Set items are among the coolest aspects of the *Diablo II* Realm. *Lord of Destruction* doubled the number of Sets, now bringing the total to 32 Sets out there and ready for your collection. Indeed, there's much more to be pieced together now, but that's not the most important change to Set Items. The expansion set also provides a bonus for having partial Sets. This means you must no longer piece together the *entire* Set to enjoy a bonus—you can now get *something* for having three of five Set pieces (only when playing the expansion).

NOTE

Numbers beside individual pieces in Sets refer to the level you must be at to use this item.

CIVERB'S VESTMENTS			
Partial Set	+15% Resist Fire		
Full Set	+300% Damage vs Undead	+25% Lightning Resist	+15% Resist Fire
Civerb's Ward	9	+15 Defense	+15% To Blocking
Civerb's Icon	9	Regenerate Mana +40%	Replenish Life +4
Civerb's Cudgel	9	+75 to Attack Rating	+17-23 to Maximum Damage

HSARUS' DEFENSE			
Partial Set	Attacker Takes Damage of 5		
Full Set	Attacker Takes Damage of 5	+5 to Maximum Damage	Cannot Be Frozen
Hsarus' Iron Heel	3	+25% Resist Fire	Faster Run/Walk
Hsarus' Iron Fist	3	Damage Reduced by 2	+10 Strength
Hsarus' Iron Stay	3	+20% Resist Cold	+20 To Life

CLEGLAW'S BRACE			
Partial Set	+50 Defense		
Full Set	+100 Defense	6% Mana Steal	35% Crushing Blow
Cleglaw's Tooth	4	30% Bonus to Attack Rating	50% Deadly Strike
Cleglaw's Claw	4	+17 Defense	75% Reduced Poison Len
Cleglaw's Pincers	4	Knockback	Slows Target By 25%

IRATHA'S FINERY			
Partial Set	+50 Defense	Faster Run/Walk	
Full Set	+50 Defense	+20 Resist All	+10 To Max Fire Resist
Iratha's Collar	15	+30% Poison Resist	Poison Len Reduced by 75%
Iratha's Cuff	15	+30 To Resist Cold	Half Freeze Duration
Iratha's Coil	15	+30 To Resist Fire	+30 To Resist Lightning
Iratha's Cord	15	+25 Defense	+5 To Minimum Damage

ISENHART'S ARMORY			
Partial Set	+10 Strength	+10 Dexterity	
Full Set	+10 Dexterity	5% Life Steal	+10% Resist All
Isenhart's Lightbrand	8	+10 To Minimum Damage	Increased Attack Speed
Isenhart's Parry	8	+40 Defense	Attacker Takes Lght Dmg of 4
Isenhart's Case	8	+40 Defense	Magic Damage Reduced by 2
Isenhart's Horns	8	+6 Dexterity	Damage Reduced By 2

NOTE

Elite Items are found only when playing in Hell mode and is perhaps the most powerful equipment in the **Diablo II** universe.

+(21-22) Mana	+(25-26) Poison Resist			
+25% Cold Resist	+25 Defense			
+Damage/Level				
+25% Resist Lightning				
+Attack Rating (Based on Character Level)				
+Defense (Based on Character Level)				
+Defense (Based on Character Level)				
Increased Attack Speed				
+Damage(Based On Character Level)				
+15% Resist All				
+Attack Rating(Based On Character Level)				
+10 To Max Cold Resist	+10 To Max Lightning Resist	+10 To Max Poison Resist	+15 Dexterity	Faster Run/Walk
+15% Resist All				
Increased Attack Speed				
+Defense (Based On Character Level0				
+10 To Dexterity				
+35% Bonus to Attack Rating	+30% To Blocking	Faster Run/Walk	+10 Strength	
+Attack Rating (Based on Character Level)				
+8 Resist All				
+Defense (Based on Character Level)				
+8 Resist All				

VIDALA'S RIG			
Partial Set	+75 To Attack Rating	+15 To Dexterity	
Full Set	Freezes Target	Piercing Attack	+10 To Strength
Vidala's Barb	14	+1 Min Lightning Damage	+20 Max Lightning Damage
Vidala's Fetlock	14	+150 Stamina	Fastest Run/Walk
Vidala's Ambush	14	+50 Defense	+11 Dexterity
Vidala's Snare	14	+15 Life	+20% Resist Cold

MILABREGA'S REGALIA			
Partial Set	+75 To Attack Rating	+125 To Attack Rating	
Full Set	+2 To Paladin Skills	10% Mana Steal	+15% Resist Poison
Milabrega's Orb	17	+20% Magic Find	+25 Defense
Milabrega's Rod	17	+2 To Paladin Skills	+50% Damage
Milabrega's Diadem	17	+15 Life	+15 Mana
Milabrega's Robe	17	Attacker Takes Damage of 3	Damage Reduced by 2

CATHAN'S TRAPS			
Partial Set	+15-20 Fire Damage	+25% Resist Lightning	
Full Set	Magic Damage Reduced by 3	+25% Resist All	Fast Cast Rate
Cathan's Rule	11	+1 To Fire Skills	+10 To Max Fire Damage
Cathan's Mesh	11	+15 Defense	Requirements -50%
Cathan's Visage	11	+20 Mana	25% Cold Resist
Cathan's Sigil	11	Fast Hit Recovery	Attacker Takes lgt dmg of 5
Cathan's Seal	11	6% Life Steal	Damage Reduced By 2

TANCRED'S BATTLEGEAR			
Partial Set	5% Life Steal	+15 Lightning Damage	
Full Set	+10% Resist All	Slows Target by 25%	5% Mana Steal
Tancred's Crowbill	20	+75 Attack Rating	+80% Damage
Tancred's Spine	20	+40 Life	+15 Strength
Tancred's Hobnails	20	Heal Stamina By 25%	+10 Dexterity
Tancred's Weird	20	Damage Reduced By 2	Magic Damage Reduced By 1
Tancred's Skull	20	+10% Damage	+40 Attack Rating

SIGON'S COMPLETE STEEL			
Partial Set	+10% Life Steal	+100 Defense	
Full Set	Attacker Takes Damage of 12	Damage Reduced By 7	+24 Max Fire Damage
Sigon's Visor	6	+30 Mana	+25 Defense
Sigon's Shelter	6	+25% Defense	+30% Resist Lightning
Sigon's Gage	6	+10 Strength	+20 Attack Rating
Sigon's Sabot	6	Faster Run/Walk	+40% Resist Cold
Sigon's Wrap	6	+20 Fire Resist	+20 Life
Sigon's Guard	6	+1 To All Skills	+20% To Blocking

+15 To Dexterity	+75 To Attack Rating	+15-20 Cold Damage		
+Attack Rating(Based On Character Level)				
+8 Resist All				
+24% Fire Resist	+Defense(Based On Character Level)			
+50% Magic Find				

8% Life Steal	+200 To Attack Rating			
+50 To Life	+50% Defense			
+2 To Light Radius				
+40% Cold Resist				
+100% Defense				

+20 Mana	+60 To Attack Rating	+15-20 Fire Damage	+25% Resist Lightning	
+50 Mana	+10% Resist All			
Attacker Takes Damage of 5	+30% Resist Fire			
+Defense(Based On Character Level)				
+50 Attack Rating	+25% Magic Find			
+10 Strength				

+75% More Gold	5% Life Steal	+15 Lightning Damage		
+20 Mana	Increased Attack Speed			
+Defense(Based On Character Level)				
Fastest Run/Walk	+10 Strength			
+78% Magic Find	+60 Attack Rating			
+10% Resist All				

+20 Mana	12% Fire Resist	+100 Defense	+10% Life Steal	
+Attack Rating(Based On Character Level)				
Attacker Takes Damage of 20				
Greatly Increased Attack Speed				
+50 Attack Rating	+50% Magic Find			
+Defense(Based On Character Level)				

INFERNAL TOOLS			
Partial Set	+25 Poison Damage	+10 Mana	
Full Set	+20% Bonus to Attack Rating	+1Necromancer Skills	20% Open Wounds
Infernal Cranium	5	+10% Resist All	20% Damage goes To Mana
Infernal Torch	5	+8 Min Damage	+1 Necromancer Skills
Infernal Sign	5	+25 Defense	+20 Life

BERSERKER'S ARSENAL			
Partial Set	+50 Life		
Full Set	+50 Life	4-7 Poison Damage over 3 secs	Poison Len Reduced by 75%
Berserker's Headgear	3	+15 Defense	+25% Fire Resist
Berserker's Hauberk	3	Magic Damage Reduced by 2	+1 Barbarian Skills
Berserker's Hatchet	3	+30% Bonus to Attack Rating	5% Mana Steal

DEATH'S DISGUISE			
Partial Set			
Full Set	+10 Min Lighting Damage	+25% Resist All	+40% Bonus to Attack Rating
Death's Hand	6	+50% Resist Poison	Poison Len Reduced by 75%
Death's Guard	6	+20 Defense	Cannot Be Frozen
Death's Touch	6	+25% Damage	4% Life Steal

ANGELIC RAIMENT			
Partial Set	+10 Dexterity	+50 Mana	
Full Set	Half Freeze Duration	+40% Magic Find	Regenerate Mana +8%
Angelic Sickle	12	+75 Attack Rating	+350% Damage To Undead
Angelic Mantle	12	Damage Reduced By 3	+40% Defense
Angelic Halo	12	Replenish Life +6	+20 Life
Angelic Wings	12	+3 To Light Radius	20% Damage Goes To Mana

ARCTIC GEAR			
Partial Set	+5 Strength	+50 Life	
Full Set	+5 Strength	+50 Life	Cannot Be Frozen
Arctic Horn	2	+20% Bonus to Attack Rating	+50% Damage
Arctic Furs	2	+275-325 Defense	+10% Resist All
Arctic Binding	2	+40% Resist Cold	+30 Defense
Arctic Mitts	3	+20 Life	Slightly Increased Attack Speed

ARCANNA'S TRICKS			
Partial Set	+25 Mana	+50 Life	
Full Set	+50 Mana	+50 Life	5% Mana Steal
Arcanna's Sign	15	+15 Mana	Regenerate Mana +20%
Arcanna's Deathwand	15	+1 Sorceress Skills	25% Deadly Strike
Arcanna's Head	15	Replenish Life +4	Attacker Takes Damage of 2
Arcanna's Flesh	15	+2 To Light Radius	Damage Reduced By 3

6% Mana Steal				
+Defense(Based On Character Level)				
+Attack Rating(Based On Character Level)				
+25% Poison Resist	Half Freeze Duration			
+75 Defense				
+Attack Rating(Based On Character Level)				
+Defense(Based On Character Level)				
+50% Damage				
8% Life Steal				
Greatly Increased Attack Speed				
+15% Resist All				
+25-75 Cold Damage				
+25% Resist All	+10 Dexterity	+50 Mana		
+75% Damage	Greatly Increased Attack Speed			
+150 Defense	+50% Fire Resist			
+Attack Rating(Based On Character Level)	+50% Magic Find			
+75 Life	+1 To All Skills			
+6-14 Cold Damage				
+Attack Rating(Based On Character Level)	+20-30 Cold Damage			
+Defense(Based On Character Level)	+15% Resist Cold			
+40% Magic Find	+10% Resist Cold			
+50 Attack Rating	+10 Dexterity			
Fastest Cast Rate				
+50% Magic Find	+20% Resist Fire			
+50 Mana	Regenerate Mana +5%			
+Defense (Based On Character Level)	+15% Resist Lightning			
+100 Defense	+10 Energy			

NATALYA'S ODIUM

Partial Set	Magic Damage Reduced By 15	+200 Defense	
Full Set	Magic Damage Reduced By 15	+350 Defense	16% Life Steal
Natalya's Totem	59	+135 Defense	+25 Dexterity
Natalya's Mark	79	Greatly Increased Attack Speed	+200% Damage
Natalya's Shadow	73	+150 Defense	+Life(Based On Character Level)
Natalya's Soul	25	+75 Defense	Fastest Run/Walk

ALDUR'S WATCHTOWER

Partial Set	+100 Attack Rating	+50% Magic Find	
Full Set	+100 Attack Rating	+50% Magic Find	10% Life Steal
Aldur's Stony Gaze	36	+90 Defense	Regenerate Mana +17%
Aldur's Deception	76	+300 Defense	+1 Elemental Skills
Aldur's Rhythm	42	+200% Damage	+50-75 Lightning Damage
Aldur's Advance	45	Indestructible	Heal Stamina +32%

IMMORTAL KING

Partial Set	+50 Attack Rating	+75 Attack Rating	+125 Attack Rating
Full Set	+3 All Skills	+150 Life	Magic Damage Reduced By 10
Immortal King's Will	47	+125 Defense	+37% More Gold
Immortal King's Soul Cage	76	+400 Defense	5% Chance to Cast Level 4 Enchant When Struck
Immortal King's Detail	29	+36 Defense	+28% Resist Fire
Immortal King's Forge	30	+65 Defense	+20 Strength
Immortal King's Pillar	31	+75 Defense	Fastest Run/Walk
Immortal King's Stone Crusher	76	Indestructible	Greatly Increased Attack Speed

TAL RASHA'S WRAPPINGS

Partial Set	Replenish Life +10	+65% Magic Find	Fastest Hit Recovery
Full Set	Replenish Life +10	+65% Magic Find	Fastest Hit Recovery
Tal Rasha's Fine-Spun Cloth	53	Requirements -20%	+30 Mana
Tal Rasha's Adjudication	67	+33 Resist Lightning	+2 Sorceress Skills
Tal Rasha's Lidless Eye	65	+111 Life	+77 Mana
Tal Rasha's Guardianship	71	Requirements -60%	Magic Damage Reduced By 15
Tal Rasha's Horadric Crest	66	+30 Mana	+60 Life

GRISWOLD'S LEGACY

Partial Set	+20 Strength	+30 Dexterity	
Full Set	+20 Strength	+30 Dexterity	+150 Life
Griswold's Valor	69	+(50-70)% Defense	+5% Resist All
Griswold's Heart	45	+500 Defense	+2 Defense Auras
Griswolds's Redemption	53	+175% Damage	Greatly Increased Attack Speed
Griswold's Honor	68	+108 Defense	3 Sockets

16% Mana Steal	+50 Resist All	+3 All Skills		
+10 Strength	+10% Resist All	Magic Damage Reduced By 3		
Ignore's Target Defense	+50 Cold Damage	+12-17 Fire Damage	+300% Damage vs Undead	+300% Damage vs Demons
+2 Shadow Disciplines	Poison Len Reduced By 75%	+25% Poison Resist	+150 Defense	
+Heal Stamina(Based on Character Level)	+15% Resist Lightning	+15% Cold Resist		
+150 Mana	+50 Resist All	+3 All Skills	+150 Defense	+10% Mana Steal
+5 To Light Radius	Fastest Hit Recovery	+25% Resist Cold		
+20 Strength	+15 Dexterity	+30% Resist Lightning	Requirements -50%	+1 Shape Shifting Skills
10% Life Steal	Greatly Increased Attack Speed	+300% Damage vs Demons	5% Mana Steal	
+50 Life	10% Damage Goes To Mana	Fastest Run/Walk	+180 Stamina	
+200 Attack Rating				
+450 Attack Rating	+50% Resist All			
+2 Warcries	+4 To Light Radius	(25-40)% Magic Find		
+2 Combat Skills	+50% Resist Poison			
+31% Resist Lightning	+25 Strength			
+20 Dexterity	12% Chance to Cast Level 4 Charged Bolt When Struck			
+110 Attack Rating	+44 Life			
+300% Damage vs Demons	+350% Damge vs Undead	(35-40)% Crushing Blow	+200% Damage	
+50 Defense vs Missiles	+Life(Based on Character Level)	+3 All Skills	+150 Defense	+50 Resist All
+20 Dexterity	37% Damage Goes to Mana	10-15% Magic Find		
+50 Life	3-32 Lightning Damage	+42 Mana		
+10 Energy	Fastest Cast Rate	+1 Lightning Mastery	+2 Fire Mastery	+1 Cold Mastery
+88% Magic Find	+40% Resist Cold	+40% Fire Resist	+40% Resist Lightning	+400 Defense
+45 Defense	+15% Resist All	10% Life Steal	10% Mana Steal	
+50% Resist All	+3 All Skills	+200 Attack Rating		
2 Sockets	Requirements -40%	+(20-30)% Magic Find		
3 Sockets	+20 Strength	Requirements -40%		
+200% Damage vs Undead	Requirements -20%	3 sockets		
Faster Block Rate				

TRANG-OUL'S AVATAR			
Partial Set	Regenerate Mana +15%	Regenerate Mana +15%	Regenerate Mana +15%
Full Set	Regenerate Mana +60%	+100 Mana	+200 Defense
Trang-Oul's Guise	65	+80-100 Defense	Fastest Hit Recovery
Trang-Oul's Scales	49	Requirements -40%	+100 Defense vs Missiles
Trang-Oul's Wing	54	+125 Defense	+25 Strength
Trang-Oul's Claws	45	+30 Defense	Fastest Cast Rate
Trang-Oul's Girth	47	+75-100 Defense	+30 Stamina

M'AVINA'S BATTLE HYMN			
Partial Set	+20 Strength	+30 Dexterity	
Full Set	+20 Strength	+30 Dexterity	+100 Attack Rating
M'avina's True Sight	59	+150 Defense	Replenish Life +10
M'avina's Embrace	70	Requirements -30%	10% Chance To Cast level 3 Glacial Spike When Struck
M'avina's Icy Clutch	32	+(45-50) Defense	+6-18 Cold Damage
M'avina's Tenet	45	+50 Defense	Fastest Run/Walk
M'avina's Caster	70	+188% Damage	10% Chance To Cast Level 3 Nova When Struck

THE DISCIPLE			
Partial Set	+150 Defense	+21 Poison Damage over 3 secs	+10 Strength
Full Set	+150 Defense	+21 Poison Damage over 3 secs	+10 Strength
Telling of Beads	30	+(35-50)% Resist Poison	+1 To All Skills
Laying of Hands	63	+25 Defense	Increased Attack Speed
Rite of Passage	29	+25 Defense	Fastest Run/Walk
Dark Adherent	43	+(305-415) Defense	+24% Resist Fire
Credendum	65	+50 Defense	+10 Strength

HEAVEN'S BRETHREN			
Partial Set	Heal Stamina +50%	Replenish Life +20	
Full Set	Heal Stamina +50%	Replenish Life +20	+5 To Light Radius
Dangoon's Teaching	68	Greatly Increased Attack Speed	+Damage (Based On Character Level)
Taebaek's Glory	81	+50 Defense	+100 Mana
Haemosu's Adamant	44	+500 Defense	+35 To Missile Defense
Ondal's Almighty	69	+50 Defense	Requirements -40%

ORPHAN'S CALL			
Partial Set	+35 Life	Attacker Takes Damage of 5	
Full Set	+85 Life	Attacker Takes Damage of 5	+100 Defense
Guillaume's Face	34	+120% Defense	Fastest Hit Recovery
Wilhelm's Pride	42	+75% Defense	5% Mana Steal
Magnus' Skin	37	+50% Defense	+15% Resist Fire
Whitstan's Guard	29	+175% Defense	Fastest Block Rate

Replenish Life +5	+50% Resist All	+3 All Skills		
Attacker Takes Damage of 20	+150 Mana	Replenish Life +5		
+40% Poison Resist	+2 Summoning Skills	Fastest Run/Walk	+150% Defense	
+15 Dexterity	+(38-45) Resist Fire	+30% To Blocking	+40% Poison Resist	+2 Poison and Bone skills
+30% Cold Resist	+2 To Curses			
Replenish Life +5	+66 Life	Cannot Be Frozen	Requirements -40%	+(25-50) Mana

+100% Magic Find	+50% Resist All	+3 All Skills	+100 Defense	
Increased Attack Speed	+25 Mana			
Magic Damage Reduced By 5-12	+Defense (Based on Character Level)	+2 Passive and Magic Skills	+350 Defense	
Half Freeze Duration	+56% More Gold	+10 Strength	+15 Dexterity	
10-15% Mana Steal	+5 To Light Radius			
Greatly Increased Attack Speed	+50 Attack Rating			

+50 Resist All	+2 To All Skills	+100 Mana		
+18% Resist Cold	Attacker Takes Damage of 8-10			
+50% Absorb Fire	10% Chance to Cast Level 3 Holy Bolt On Attack	+350% Damage vs Demons		
Half Freeze Duration	+(15-25) Stamina			
24-34 Poison Damage over 3 secs	25% Chance to Cast Level 3 Nova When Struck			
+10 Dexterity	+15 Resist All			

+50% Resist All	+2 All Skills	Cannot Be Frozen		
+20-30 Fire Damage	10% Chance to cast Level 3 Frost Nova On Attack			
+30% Resist Lightning	Attacker Takes Damage of 30	Indestructible	+25% To Blocking	Block +30
+75 Life	+40 Defense vs Melee	Requirements -20%		
+10 Strength	10% Chance to cast Level 3 Weaken On Attack	+15 Dexterity	Fastest Hit Recovery	

+15% Resist All	+80% Magic Find	+10 Dexterity	+20 Strength	
35% Crushing Blow	15% Deadly Strike	+15 To Strength		
+10% Resist Cold	5% Life Steal			
Increased Attack Speed	+3 To Light Radius	+100 To Attack Rating		
+55% To Blocking	Half Freeze Duration	+5 To Light Radius		

HWANIN'S MAJESTY			
Partial Set	+100 Defense	+200 Defense	
Full Set	+300 Defense	Fastest Run/Walk	+30% Resist All
Hwanin's Splendor	45	Replenish Life +20	Magic Reduced By 10
Hwanin's Refuge	30	+200 Defense	+27% Poison Resist
Hwanin's Blessing	35	3-33 Lightning Damage	Prevent Monster Heal
Hwanin's Justice	28	+330 Attack Rating	Indestructible

SAZABI'S GRAND TRIBUTE			
Partial Set	Fastest Run/Walk		
Full Set	Fastest Run/Walk	+27% Life	+30% Resist All
Sazabi's Cobalt Redeemer	73	+150% Damage	+25-35 Cold Damage
Sazabi's Ghost Liberator	67	+400 Defense	Fastest Hit Recovery
Sazabi's Mental Sheath	43	+100 Defense	+1 All Skills

BUL-KATHOS' CHILDREN			
Partial Set			
Full Set	+2 All Skills	+200 Attack Rating	+25 Defense
Bul-Kathos' Sacred Charge	61	35% Crushing Blow	+20% Resist All
Bul-Kathos' Tribal Guardian	54	+50 Fire Resist	49 Poison Damage over 2 seconds

COW KING'S LEATHERS			
Partial Set	+25% Resist Poison		
Full Set	+25% Resist Poison	+100% More Gold	25% Chance to Cast level 5 Static Field When Struck
Cow King's Horns	25	+75 Defense	Half Freeze Duration
Cow King's Hide	18	+18% Resist All	+60% Defense
Cow King's Hoofs	13	+25-35 Defense	Fastest Run/Walk

NAJ'S ANCIENT SET			
Partial Set	+175 Defense		
Full Set	+175 Defense	+15 Dexterity	+50% Resist All
Naj's Puzzler	78	+35 Energy	+150% Damage
Naj's Light Plate	71	Requirements -60%	+65 Life
Naj's Circlet	28	+75 Defense	+25-35 Fire Damage

SANDER'S FOLLY			
Partial Set	+50 Defense	+75 Attack Rating	
Full Set	+50 Defense	+75 Attack Rating	4% Life Steal
Sander's Paragon	25	+35% Magic Find	+Defense (Based On Character Level)
Sander's Riprap	20	Fastest Run/Walk	+100 Attack Rating
Sander's Taboo	28	+20-25 Defense	Increased Attack speed
Sander's Superstition	25	+75% Damage	+25 Mana

+2 All Skills	20% Life Steal			
+37% Resist Cold	+100% Defense			
+100 Life	10% Chance to Cast Level 3 Static Field When Struck			
12% Damage Goes To Mana	+Defense (Based on Character Level)			
Greatly Increased Attack Speed	10% Chance to Cast Level 3 Ice Blast On Attack	5-25 Lightning Damage	+200% Damage	
15% Life Steal				
Greatly Increased Attack Speed	+418% Damage vs Demons	Indestructible	+15 Dexterity	+5 Strength
+25 Strength	+300 Attack Rating vs Demons	+50-75 Life		
+(15-20)% Fire Resist	+(15-20)% Resist Lightning			
+300% Damage vs Undead	+300% Damage vs Demons	+20 Fire Damage		
Increased Attack Speed	Knockback	+200% Damage		
Increased Attack Speed	+20 Strength	+200% Damage		
+100% Magic Find	Greatly Increased Attack Speed	+20 Strength	+100 Stamina	
+35% Damage Goes To Mana	Attacker Takes Damage of 10			
+30 Life	18% Chance to Cast Level 5 Chain Light When Struck			
+25% Magic Find	+20 Dexterity	+25-35 Fire Damage		
+20 Strength	+100 Mana	+1 All Skills	Replenish Life +10	
Greatly Increased Attack Speed	Fastest Cast Rate	6-45 Lightning Damage	+70 Mana	+1 All Skills
+25% Resist All	+45% Damage Goes to Mana	+1 All Skills	+300 Defense	
+5 To Light Radius	12% Chance to Cast Level 5 Chain Light When Struck	+15 Strength		
+50 Mana	+50% Magic Find	+1 All Skills		
Attacker Takes Damage of 8				
+5 Strength	+10 Dexterity			
+40 Life	8-10 Poison Damage over 3 seconds			
8% Mana Steal	Fastest Cast Rate	+25-75 Cold Damage		

RUNES (EXPANSION SET ONLY)

Runes are a great new addition to the expansion set. These scripted tablets can be inserted into Socketed items to give them special powers (much like Gems or Jewels). The fascinating thing about Runes is that they produce extra benefits if they are placed in a specific order into an item! Refer to the *Appendix* in the back of this guide for the complete list of Runes and Rune Word combinations.

NOTE

The Rune Word combinations table in the Appendix is based on the final Expansion Gold Master Version 1.07 of the single-player game (the one included in the Battle Chest). The formulae in the single-player game differ significantly from those in first patch of the expansion set (Version 1.08). If you're playing on Battle.net and have downloaded this patch, then visit Blizzard's web site to reference the current Battle.net Rune Word list and stay on top of all of the latest revisions to the Diablo II Realm.

JEWELS (EXPANSION SET ONLY)

Jewels are the new Gem-like items of the expansion set. They have predetermined abilities that, when placed into a socket, will be taken on by the socketed object. Jewels can be Magical or Rare (the Rare ones are limited to three properties). Jewels are created randomly from a table of prefixes and suffixes. Refer to the *Appendix* in the back of this guide for the complete list of Jewels.

UNIQUE ITEMS

Unique Items are just that, items that are unique in the game and can be found throughout the *Diablo II* Realm. Some of these are Weapons or Armor, while others are objects like Amulets. We've decided not to take up precious space in the guide by listing the Unique Items. This is because you'll either find or trade for the Unique Items, or you won't. Knowing what they are by listing them in this book won't help you because once you identify a Unique Item, you'll be able to mouse over it and see exactly what it is and what it can do. However, if you have an unsatiable curiosity and still wish to look at a complete list of Unique items in the game, then check out our website at www.bradygames.com.

Chapter 5

MULTIPLAYER

Multiplayer

The original *Diablo* game presented a multiplayer experience that was unique in the world of computer games. Indeed, *Diablo* encouraged players to cooperate, trade, and depend on each other to gain the most from the game. It has always been possible to simply kill each other, but the most profitable way to play in a multiplayer *Diablo* game is to help your fellow adventurers. With the assistance of your friends you can find more weapons, armor, spells, and potions than you could on your own, and you can gang-up on the toughest monsters using tactics that would make a seasoned war general proud.

For many fans of the game, Multiplayer *Diablo II* is where it's at.

Diablo II followed this tradition very closely. Although it is possible to play the game simply to kill other players, it is most beneficial to cooperate in quests and follow the game as it unfolds.

Following in the footsteps of its predecessors, *Diablo II: Lord of Destruction* is an extremely engrossing and compelling single-player game that can capture its audience for literally hundreds of hours of gameplay. As if the massive and captivating single-player gameplay isn't enough, the inclusion of a complex and rich multiplayer format for both *Diablo II* and the expansion set ensures that these games will be played by fans around the world for years to come. This chapter covers some of the intricacies of multiplayer action, including character-specific strategies for the Assassin and Druid. The game manual covers the basics of getting connected to Battle.net and TCP/IP connections, so we'll focus on real-life Battle.net multiplayer tactics—many of them gathered from insiders at Blizzard Entertainment!

BATTLE.NET

Battle.net is a great place to meet and play the expansion set with people from around the planet.

Battle.net launched in 1997 with the release of *Diablo*. Since its inception, Battle.net has registered millions of users, and there are as many as 200,000 people worldwide playing simultaneously on the *Diablo II* Realms! Battle.net has truly set the standard for gaming-only services. Remarkably, Battle.net is entirely free of charge for all users, bringing the world of games like *Diablo*, *StarCraft*, *WarCraft II: Battle.net Edition*, *Diablo II*, and now *Diablo II: Lord of Destruction* to millions of players who (through Battle.net's magic) can face an unlimited number of new adversaries every time they log on!

Indeed, with a single click you can log on to Battle.net and do battle against Diablo with other players (up to eight), or even choose to battle *against* other players. Battle.net also gives you the opportunity to chat, trade items, set up your own games, or join games created by other adventurers. For *Diablo II: Lord of Destruction*, Battle.net includes some cool new features. These new features are discussed in detail in the manual, but we'll still touch on them in this chapter just to make sure that you are getting everything you can out of the multiplayer realm.

NOTE

There have been very few changes to Battle.net with regard to what we talk about in a strategy guide. Why fix something that works?

LADDER

The Ladder system in *Diablo II* keeps track of the top-ranked players in each Realm.

The Ladder system provides a great way to see just how you stack up against the best *Diablo II* players in the world. The expansion set and Battle.net offer this service, which rates both regular and Hardcore characters. The Ladder system is based on experience, and applies to only one Realm—each Realm ranks and lists only the top-ranked players, so you'll have to be on your toes to make the cut on one of the ladders. When it comes to Hardcore players, they're listed on their ladders even if they die, but can still be removed from the ladder if other players exceed their experience level and bump them down enough rungs.

TRADING

The trade screen is a secure place to conduct business.

Trading in the expansion set is the same as in *Diablo II*, that is to say it must occur within the boundaries of a town; it cannot occur anywhere else outside of a player dropping an item that you may want to pick up. The Trading feature is a way for you to 'officially' trade with another player in a sanctioned way that protects both players from cheating or other less than honorable activities. Any time you wish to make a trade on a particularly valuable item or you want to be sure that an unrelated player doesn't hop in and pick up an item you're dropping for someone else, use the secure trading method to be absolutely safe. It may take a little more time to portal back to a town, but it's worth it if you're dealing with high-priced items.

PARTIES

When you join a multiplayer game, you can select other players in the game to form a team. When in a party, you and the other members of the team will work together with the common goal of getting through the quests in *Diablo II* and the expansion set. Along with your mutual endeavors, you will also share Experience with other party members during the course of your adventure. The method that the game uses to share Experience amongst many players of different levels is complicated, but suffice it to say that a level 3 character will not be receiving gobs of Experience just by hanging around with level 25 characters. Indeed, there is somewhat of a sliding scale that manages the disbursement of Experience. An important change in *Diablo II: Lord of Destruction* is the addition of a 35% bonus in Experience earned for those members of the same party who are in the same named area (game level) when the Experience is earned (that is, at the moment of monster death). The idea is to reward party members for working together. However, if you have to portal back to town in mid-battle, you should ask your teammates to wait for you to return before dealing the killing blow. Gold, on the other hand, is divided up equally among the members of the party (regardless of where they are) with any gold that doesn't divide equally by the party number going to the character who picked it up.

When you become hostile toward someone, any Skeletons, Valkyries, Golems, or Mercenaries also become hostile toward your enemies (and visa versa).

NOTE

When you ally with another player, you can see a small picture of your teammate and a read-out of their hit points. This allows you keep track of how everyone is doing and rush to the aid of someone who gets too busy to send a message for help.

MAP

The map displayed over the game screen shows you the location of the other players in the game when they are nearby. Each player's marker is labeled with their character name. Additional markers are displayed for any NPCs that are fighting for you or your teammates. When you team up with more than one Necromancer, you can expect the map display to be crowded!

The Automap shows where each of your party members is (if they're close enough to you).

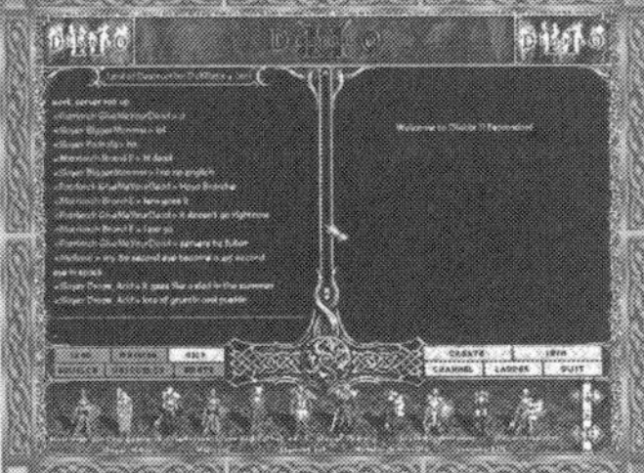

Chatting is the primary method of communication on Battle.net.

CHAT

The chat feature of *Diablo II* multiplayer games works much the same as in the original *Diablo*. You can press the ENTER key to bring up a prompt, then type in a message to send to everyone. *Diablo II* also lets you select players from whom to block messages received or sent, which is a good way to filter out distractions from other players not in your area. Refer to the manual for details on Chatting.

NOTE

The Horadic Cube's Crafted Item recipes may be changed by Blizzard in future patches (Version 1.08 or greater) to use scarcer ingredients. For example, instead of using just any quality gem, certain recipes may in the future require a perfect gem. Check out the Blizzard website for all the latest Battle.net updates.

Multiplayer Tactics

Like *Diablo II*, the expansion set has much more open space than the original game (in the original *Diablo*, the dungeon hallways and doors were sometimes too narrow for more than one player to fight monsters at a time), so staying together is more practical. On top of this, the expansion set has eliminated collisions between player characters and all player minions (hirelings plus pets). Thus, the Necromancer with his many skeletons will not feel crowded in any of the areas of the game and will even feel welcome to join large parties. Indeed, for the most part there's plenty of room to move around and attack parties of monsters from different angles.

NOTE

One of the problems with staying in the pack is that you must share the spoils of victory with whoever else is fighting in the same screen. It's sometimes frustrating when you come up against a particularly fierce opponent, finally manage to kill it, and then miss picking up the magic item it dropped because your teammate grabbed it first.

In order to keep comrades happy and your Inventory full, it is a good practice to venture into *Diablo II: Lord of Destruction* multiplayer games in small groups, or individually. You can select a central spot to collect unwanted items if you want. You should also try to work in the same general area—when someone needs help, they won't want to wait for you to find a waypoint and jog around looking for them. Staying one or two screen-widths apart will allow you fight your own battles and still have your friends nearby for safety.

Tips from the Experts

This section provides a collection of great tips straight from the mouths of the Blizzard QA (Quality Assurance) department. Keep in mind that these folks are experts in the *Diablo II* Realm, and have been playing it for years. These tips are well worth reading over—they come from the masters! Each member of the QA department is mentioned by name above each tip so you know where each kernel of knowledge originated. Some tips have been included from our *Diablo II Official Strategy Guide*, but there's plenty of new advice relating to the Druid and Assassin, too.

NOTE

There are plenty of tips relating to many of the skills' multiplayer attributes in *Chapter 2: The Characters* where each skill is examined in detail.

Ed Kang/Jason Hutchins

Use the Configure Controls menu. Although it may have been possible in *Diablo II* to consistently use one skill or a pair of skills, the two new character classes in the expansion set definitely benefit from their ability to layer skills on top of each other. To effectively manage this, however, the user must configure hotkeys in such a way that allows for quick and accurate switching of skills. We have assigned the keys "q, w, e, r" as our right-click hotkeys and "a, s, d, f" as our left-click hotkeys. Also, we use "z, x, c, v, b" for the mini-panel functions. Remember that *Diablo II: Lord of Destruction* now has 16 hotkeys, making it easier for you to rule supreme from the keyboard.

Jason Hutchins

Weapon Switching: A good example of a character that *greatly* benefits from this new feature is the Amazon. A spear-azon (as we like to call them) can have Weapon Group #1 filled with good Javelin-class weapons and Weapon Group #2 equipped with a high damage (but slower) spear. When Weapon Group #1 is active, you can then assign Throw or any of the various thrown Javelin skills and melee skills—especially Jab.

Druid: By the time you reach level 30, you'll be ready to learn Spirit of Barbs. This skill grants you, your Pets, and your party members something similar to the Paladin's Thorns Aura. If you have a lot of hit points, you will be well served by this Pet. Even the deadly monsters in Act V become a lot less devastating, regardless of your armor!

Spirit of Barbs is an awesome skill for the Druid and his party members.

Roger Eberhart

Assassin: The Assassin doesn't have any skills that benefit other party members directly. She can, however, add to the party with an extra NPC through Shadow Master and Shadow Warrior. In many ways, she is very similar to the Amazon, except with an emphasis on melee instead of missiles. This class will undoubtedly have an impact on player-versus-player, especially with her traps. The trick is to lure people into the area you have trapped. For example, you could trap the area directly outside of town, and then hide your Assassin nearby. As someone walks over the trapped area, you can turn on hostility for a nasty surprise!

Druid: The Druid ranks up there with the Paladin as a great party member. Many of his spirits and vines directly benefit other party members. He can also bring a host of summoned animals with him to distract and damage monsters. However, a Druid may not work as well with classes that rely heavily on corpses. For example, Barbarians use corpses for Find Potion and Find Item and Necromancers use corpses for Corpse Explosion. Sharing of corpses could become an issue if the Druid's Vines or Dire Wolves use up every corpse in the vicinity.

Ron Frybarger

Assassin: For the Assassin, it's all about hot-keying skills. I assign Charge-ups to my left mouse button with the first few hotkeys, and Finishing Moves to the right. Charge-up skills 'stack' so there are some powerful combinations to experiment with. Since eight hotkeys have been added, Traps and Shadow Disciplines can also be just a keystroke away, creating the perfect killing machine.

A combination of Cloak of Shadows and a trap like the Wake of Fire is very effective.

Robert Foote

Cloak 'em and Smoke 'em: One of the best combinations for the Assassin is the use of Cloak of Shadows with Traps. When approaching a group of monsters, cast Cloak of Shadows and blind them. Then, when they are standing there, throw down your traps. You should be able to decimate most monsters before they have a chance to attack you.

Michael Backus

Holding out: Hold out on your quest rewards if you can. An example of this is Charsi in Act I—you can delay your reward and return later to imbue a better item. Don't rush to use those up right away; just after you use them up, you'll find yourself wishing you hadn't. Give yourself a few levels of play to find something even more worthwhile to arm yourself with, then go back and see just how much better the reward has become. Some of those rewards can be based on level, or what item you choose to give them.

Dave Fried

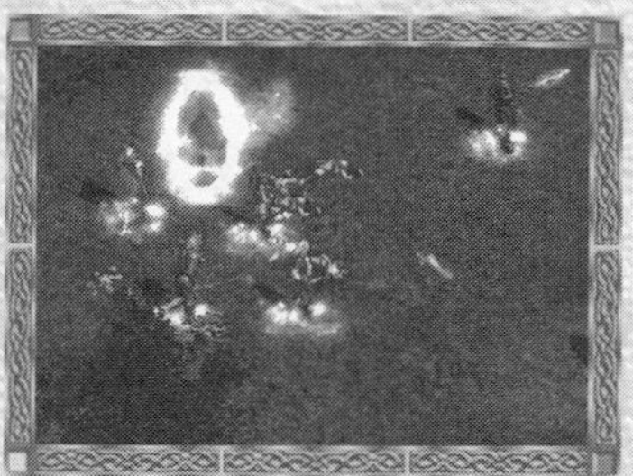

The Paladin's Auras are critical for party play in multiplayer *Diablo II*.

The Paladin: This is one of the best characters to party with. All of his aura skills have a radius that shows how far a fellow party member can be from the Paladin and still be under its effects. A group consisting of multiple Paladins can be very effective if they each specializes in a different aura. Holy Bolt has the ability to heal other party members. Simply select Holy Bolt as your right-click (Command + left-click on the Mac) skill, target a party member, and then right-click (Command + left-click) on them to fire healing bolts of energy.

The Sorceress: Area-affect spells are of prime importance with the Sorceress. You can often turn the tide of a large battle by using Frost Nova to slow the enemies.

The Barbarian: This character's Warcries are often overlooked in lieu of the direct damage skills. However, it is important to remember that when grouped with others, teamwork is very important and Warcries can have a huge impact. You can use Shout to increase the defense of party members within the range of its effects.

The Amazon: When playing the Amazon, remember that ranged attacks are her specialty. It's often better to stand back from combat while others get into melee range of the enemies, and then fire from a distance into the crowd. Remember that missiles will not harm allies, even if you aim directly at them.

Josh Kurtz

When playing as a Sorceress in a group, one of your best spells is the Frost Nova. Run into a group of monsters, let the Frost Nova fly, and then retreat as you watch your melee buddies walk through the frozen creatures with ease.

Also, I cannot stress enough the importance of the Town Portal scroll, or how effectively these can be used by a full group. Make sure someone has a full supply of Town Portal scrolls so that when you get in trouble they can open one up and allow everyone in the party to get to safety. The whole team can run through, get fully healed and Mana restored in town, and be back in the fray fairly swiftly. It's like a Full Rejuvenation potion for the whole team, just make sure the person who casts it is the last one back from town or the portal will close! Always have Town Portal assigned to a hotkey to make invoking this scroll quicker.

Make sure your melee fighter is carrying as many Health potions as possible. This character is the one who takes the brunt of the attacks by leading the charge into battle—the Barbarian is a good choice because he is much better at absorbing damage than the Sorceress or the Necromancer—so make sure he stays alive.

Conner Brandt

Golem, Amplify Damage, and Corpse Explosion are a great combination against large groups of monster in big multiplayer games. Necromancers working in concert can be deadly when using combinations of these skills.

Pete Underwood

Thorns is a powerful aura that, when used with a Necromancer's minions, is an awesome weapon.

Paladins and Necromancers using Zeal and Amplify Damage in a group are a force to be reckoned with. Auras such as Thorns in conjunction with a Necromancer's minions is also an incredibly potent combination.

A Paladin with Holy Fire or Holy Shock can draw the attention of the monsters to him while remaining out of melee range. Other characters may then attack those monsters with ranged weapons. These skills provide a great 'distract and damage' combination.

John Lagrave

Barbarians grouped together should each specialize in a different weapon class (one with Sword Mastery, one with Axe Mastery, etc.). This way, when it comes to weapons that the enemies give up, they can divide the loot and conquer their enemies more effectively without squabbling over who gets the unique item.

The Sorceress is the character you need in every party. Static Field can weaken even the toughest opponents quickly, allowing the melee class characters to mop up (remember that Static Field reduces the enemy's hit points by one-third). This is especially important in large multiplayer games because Diablo's minions are that much tougher. The importance of Hirelings/Mercenaries should also not be overlooked; they can provide distraction, or even the backup to turn the tide of the battle.

NOTE

The difficulty of a multiplayer game is dependent on how many players are participating. For example, a six-player game will feature monsters that are much tougher to defeat than a two-player game. This scaling of difficulty is a great feature that ensures that playing through *Diablo II* and the expansion set will be challenging enough even if there's a large party working in unison.

Derek Simmons

Rancid Gas potions give you the same effect as poison. Early in the game they provide an excellent means for killing several enemies while racking up Experience points.

Stick Together. The more players that are in the game, the tougher the monsters become—regardless of where the players are. Sticking together as a unit is the best way to survive and conquer your enemies. Diablo's minions will have a difficult time defeating a party of adventurers who support each other with auras, missile fire, and heavy armor.

Carlos Guerrero

Rancid Gas potions are very effective for taking out large groups of monsters in the Blood Moor, Cold Plains, or Stony Field. The key is to get the monsters to chase you and bunch into large groups, then simply throw a potion at them and they will all take substantial (if not fatal) poison damage, thus quickly boosting your (and your party's) Experience points.

APPENDIX

Character Skills & Other Tables

Runes

Runes	Level	Weapon	Armor	Helms	Shields
El Rune	11	+1 to light radius +50 to attack ratting	+1 to light radius +15 to defense	+1 to light radius +15 to defense	+1 to light radius +15 to defense
Eld Rune	11	+50 to attack ratting vs undead 175% damage vs undead	15% Stamina Drain	15% Stamina Drain	increased chance of blocking
Tir Rune	13	+2 Mana after each kill	+2 Mana after each kill	+2 Mana after each kill	+2 Mana after each kill
Nef Rune	13	knockback	+30 defense VS missile	+30 defense VS missile	+30 defense VS missile
Eth Rune	15	-25% Targets Defense	Regenerate Mana 15%	Regenerate Mana 15%	Regenerate Mana 15%
Ith Rune	15	+9 to Max damage	15% damage goes to Mana	15% damage goes to Mana	15% damage goes to Mana
Tal Rune	17	+19 Poison dmg/2 sec	Poison Resistance 30%	Poison Resistance 30%	Poison Resistance 30%
Ral Rune	19	Adds 5-30 Fire damage	Fire Resistance 30%	Fire Resistance 30%	Fire Resistance 30%
Ort Rune	21	Adds 1-50 Lightning Damage	Lightning Resistance 30%	Lightning Resistance 30%	Lightning Resistance 30%
Thul Rune	23	Adds 3-14 Cold Damage	Cold Resistance 30%	Cold Resistance 30%	Cold Resistance 30%
Amn Rune	25	7% life stolen per hit	Attacker takes damage of 14	Attacker takes damage of 14	Attacker takes damage of 14
Sol Rune	27	+9 to minimum damage	Damage reduced by 7	Damage reduced by 7	Damage reduced by 7
Shae/Shael Rune	29	Increased attack speed	Faster hit recovery	Faster hit recovery	Faster block rate
Dol Rune	31	Monster flee 32%	Replenish life +7	Replenish life +7	Replenish life +7
Hel Rune	1	Requirements -20%	Requirements -15%	Requirements -15%	Requirements -15%
Po/Io Rune	35	+10 to Vitality	+10 to Vitality	+10 to Vitality	+10 to Vitality
Lum Rune	37	+10 to Energy	+10 to Energy	+10 to Energy	+10 to Energy
Ko Rune	39	+10 to Dexterity	+10 to Dexterity	+10 to Dexterity	+10 to Dexterity
Fal Rune	41	+10 to Strength	+10 to Strength	+10 to Strength	+10 to Strength
Lem Rune	43	75% extra gold from monsters	50% extra gold from monsters	50% extra gold from monsters	50% extra gold from monsters
Pul Rune	45	+100 to attack rating against demons 175% damage to demons	30% enhanced defense	30% enhanced defense	30% enhanced defense
Um Rune	47	25% Open Wounds	All resistances +20%	All resistances +10%	All resistances +20%
Mal Rune	49	Prevent Monster heal	Magic damage reduced by 7	Magic damage reduced by 7	Magic damage reduced by 7
Ist Rune	51	+30% Magic Items	+25% Magic Find	+25% Magic Items	+25% Magic Items
Gul Rune	53	20% to attack ratting	3% to Max poison resist	3% to Max poison resist	3% to Max poison resist
Vex Rune	55	7% Mana stolen per hit	3% to Max fire resist	3% to Max fire resist	3% to Max fire resist
Ohm Rune	57	50% Enhanced Damage	3% to Max cold resist	3% to Max cold resist	3% to Max cold resist
Lo Rune	59	20% Deadly strike	3% to Max lightning resist	3% to Max lightning resist	3% to Max lightning resist
Sur Rune	61	Hit Blinds Target	Increases Max Mana 5%	increase Max Mana 5%	+50 to Mana
Ber Rune	63	20% Chance of Crushing Blow	Damage reduced by 8%	Damage reduced by 8%	Damage reduced by 8%
Jo/Cho Rune	65	Slows target by 25%	Increase Max life 5%	increase Max life 5%	+50 to Life
Cham Rune	67	Freeze Target	Cannot be frozen	Cannot be frozen	Cannot be frozen
Zod Rune	69	Indestructible	Indestructible	Indestructible	Indestructible

Rune Word Enhanced Items
(Expansion Gold Master Version 1.07)

Name	# of Runes	Items	Rune Word	Effect 1	Effect 2	Effect 3	Effect 4	Effect 5
Ancient's Pledge	3	Shields	Ral + Ort + Tal	+43% Cold Resist	+50% Defense	10% Damage goes to Mana	+13% Fire/Poison Resist	+13% Lightning Resist
Armageddon	6	Axes/Clubs/Pole-arms/ Hammers	Amn + Jo/Cho + Cham + Sol + Amn + Ith	+185% Damage	+300 Attack Rating	Increased Attack Speed	3% Life Steal	

Authority	3	Helms	Zod + Gul + Um	+100% Defense	+5 Resist All	+1 to All Skills	+20 Strength	
The Beast	5	Axes/Clubs/Hammers	Zod + Tir + Um + Mal + Lum	+200% Damage	25% Crushing Blow	25% Open Wounds	+150% Damage to Undead	+150 Damage to Demons
Beauty	3	Helms	El + Ral + Eth	+2 To Light Radius	+50% Magic Find	Faster Hit Recovery		
Black	3	Clubs/Hammers/Maces	Io/Po + Sol + Eld	+25% Damage to Undead	+50 AR vs Undead	7% Mana Steal	+133% Damage	7% Life Steal
Blood	4	Spears/Axes/Swords	Jo/Cho + Ber + El + Um	+175% Damage	+75% Open Wounds	25% Deadly Strike	13% Life Steal	+13 Strength
Bone	2	Spears	Lum + Eld	+200 AR vs Undead	+75% Damage to Undead	+180% Damage	9% Mana Steal	+4 to Poison and Bone Skills
Bound by Duty	4	Body Armor	Tir + Amn + El + Ort	+70% Defense	Fastest Hit Recovery	+2 Defensive Auras	+30 Life	
Bramble	2	Body Armor	Eth + Ral	+47% Defense	+3% Resist Fire	+33 Resist Lightning	Fast Run/Walk	
Brand	4	Scepters/Swords	El + Hel + Ral + Ith	+1 To Light Radius	10-30 Fire Damage	+100% Damage	+35% Resist Cold	
Breath of the Dying	6	Weapons	Po/Io + Tal + Lst + Lo + Ort + Lem	+100% Damage	Cold Damage 9-15	+5 Mana Per Kill		
Broken Promise	3	Weapons	Tal + Ohm + Dol	Adds 19-58 PD over 2 sec	Cold Damage 6-11	+250 to Attack Rating	+25% Damage	
Call to Arms	4	Weapons	Thul + Ith + Thul + Mal	+77% Damage	+200 Defense	+15 To Dexterity	Attacker takes dmg of +21	+200 Attack Rating
Chance	2	Weapons	Lo + Ral	+50% Magic Find	+100% More Gold	Hit Blinds Target	+42% Damage	
Chaos	4	Body Armor	Sur + Ort + Eld + Shae/Shael	+80% Defense	+30% Fire Resist	+15 Strength	50% Chance to Cast Level 7 Charged Bolt When Struck	
Crescent Moon	3	Axes/Swords/Pole-arms	El + Hel + Um	+100% Damage	7% Mana Steal	Greatly Increased Attack Speed	20% Bonus to Attack Rating	
Darkness	5	Melee Weapons	Tal + Amn + Gul + Nef + Thul	+120% Damage	3% Life Steal	Hit Blinds Target		
Daylight	3	Melee Weapons	Amn + Tir + Jo/Cho	+120% Damage	+3 To Light Radius	3% Mana Steal	33-99 Fire Damage	
Death	5	Weapons	Dol + Lem + Nef + Tal + Eth	33% Deadly Strike	+133% Damage	Prevent Monster Heal	Total of 87 Poison Damage over 3 sec	5% Life Steal
Deception	3	Knives	Ko + Dol + Eth	20 PD over 4 sec	10% Mana Steal	Ignore's Target Defense	+199% Damage	Slows Targets by 50%
Delirium	3	Helms	Lem + Ort + Io/Po	+77% Defense	+44% Resist Cold	+55% Resist Fire	+66% Resist Poison	+3% Resist Lightning

CRAFTED ITEMS

Crafted	Fixed Effect 1	Fixed Effect 2	Fixed Effect 3	Fixed Effect 4
Magic Weapon + Any Jewel + Ort Rune + Any Sapphire ➡ Hitpower Weapon	5% Chance to Cast Level 8 Frost Nova When Struck	Attacker Takes Damage (5-10)	(34-67)% Damage	
Magic Light Plated Boots + Any Jewel + Eld Rune + Any Ruby ➡ Blood Boots	(1-4)% Life Steal	Replenish Life +(5-10)	+(10-20) Life	
Magic Heavy Gloves + Any Jewel + Tir Rune + Any Ruby ➡ Blood Gloves	(1-4)% Life Steal	(5-10)% Crushing Blow	+(10-20) Life	
Magic Belt + Any Jewel + Nef Rune + Any Ruby ➡ Blood Belt	(1-4)% Life Steal	(5-10)% Open Wounds	+(10-20) Life	
Magic Boots + Any Jewel + Eld Rune + Any Amethyst ➡ Caster Boots	Regenerate Mana (4-12)%	+(10-20) Mana	Increase Maximum Mana (5-10)%	
Magic Chain Gloves + Any Jewel + Tir Rune + Any Amethyst ➡ Caster Gloves	Regenerate Mana (4-12)%	+(10-20) Mana	+(1-3) Mana Per Kill	
Magic Plate + Any Jewel + Ith Rune + Any Amethyst ➡ Caster Body	Regenerate Mana (4-12)%	+(10-20) Mana	+(1-3) Mana Per Kill	
Magic Breast Plate + Any Jewel + Ith Rune + Any Emerald ➡ Safety Body	Damage Reduced by (3-9)	Magic Damage Reduced By (2-5)	Half Freeze Duration	(10-33)% Defense
Magic Weapon + Any Jewel + Ort Rune + Any Emerald ➡ Safety Weapon	Damage Reduced by (3-9)	Magic Damage Reduced By (2-5)	+(34-67)% Damage	
Magic Vampirefang Belt + Any Jewel + Dol Rune + Any Sapphire ➡ Hitpower Belt	7% Chance to Cast Level 12 Frost Nova When Struck	Attacker Takes Damage (8-20)	(20-35%) Damage Goes to Mana	

continues on next page

CRAFTED ITEMS

Crafted	Fixed Effect 1	Fixed Effect 2	Fixed Effect 3	Fixed Effect 4
Magic Weapon + Any Jewel + Fal Rune + Any Sapphire ➡ Hitpower Weapon	7% Chance to Cast Level 12 Frost Nova When Struck	Attacker Takes Damage (8-20)	+(40-80)% Damage	
Magic Mirrored Boots + Any Jewel + Sol Rune + Any Ruby ➡ Blood Boots	(2-6%) Life Steal	+(15-25) Life	Replenish Life +(8-15)	
Magic Vampirebone Gloves + Any Jewel + Shae/Shael Rune + Any Ruby ➡ Blood Gloves	(2-6%) Life Steal	+(15-25) Life	(8-15)% Crushing Blow	
Magic Mithril Coil Belt + Any Jewel + Dol Rune + Any Ruby ➡ Blood Belt	(2-6%) Life Steal	+(15-25) Life	(8-15)% Open Wounds	
Magic Aegis Shield + Any Jewel + Hel Rune + Any Ruby ➡ Blood Shield	(2-6%) Life Steal	+(15-25) Life	Attacker Takes Damage of (8-15)	
Magic Kraken Shell + Any Jewel + Io/Po Rune + Any Ruby ➡ Blood Body	(2-6%) Life Steal	+(15-25) Life	+(1-3) Life Per Demon Kill	
Magic Amulet + Any Jewel + Lum Rune + Any Ruby ➡ Blood Amulet	(2-6%) Life Steal	+(15-25) Life	Fast Run/Walk	
Magic Ring + Any Jewel + Ko Rune + Any Ruby ➡ Blood Ring	(2-6%) Life Steal	+(15-25) Life	+(8-15) Strength	
Magic Weapon + Any Jewel + Fal Rune + Any Ruby ➡ Blood Weapon	(2-6%) Life Steal	+(15-25) Life	+(40-80)% Damage	
Magic Wyrmhide Boots + Any Jewel + Sol Rune + Any Amethyst ➡ Caster Boots	Regenerate Mana (7-21)%	+(15-25) Mana	Increase Maximum Mana (8-15)%	
Magic Vambraces + Any Jewel + Shae/Shael Rune + Amethyst ➡ Caster Gloves	Regenerate Mana (7-21)%	+(15-25) Mana	+(2-5) Mana Per Kill	
Magic Troll Belt + Any Jewel + Dol Rune + Any Amethyst ➡ Caster Belt	Regenerate Mana (7-21)%	+(15-25) Mana	Fast Cast Rate	
Magic Luna Shield + Any Jewel + Hel Rune + Any Amethyst ➡ Caster Shield	Regenerate Mana (7-21)%	+(15-25) Mana	Increased Chance of Blocking (8-15)	
Magic Hellforge Plate + Any Jewel + Io/Po Rune + Any Amethyst ➡ Caster Body	Regenerate Mana (7-21)%	+(15-25) Mana	+(2-5) Mana Per Kill	
Magic Amulet + Any Jewel + Lum Rune + Any Amethyst ➡ Caster Amulet	Regenerate Mana (7-21)%	+(15-25) Mana	Fast Cast Rate	
Magic Ring + Any Jewel + Ko Rune + Any Amethyst ➡ Caster Ring	Regenerate Mana (7-21)%	+(15-25) Mana	+(8-15) Energy	
Magic Weapon + Any Jewel + Fal Rune + Any Amethyst ➡ Caster Weapon	Regenerate Mana (7-21)%	+(15-25) Mana	+(40-80%) Damage	
Magic Great Hauberk+ Any Jewel + Io/Po Rune + Any Emerald ➡ Safety Body	Damage Reduced by (6-15)	Magic Damage Reduced By (3-10)	Half Freeze Duration	+(20-50)% Defense
Any Weapon + Any Jewel + Fal Rune + Any Emerald ➡ Safety Weapon	Damage Reduced by (6-15)	Magic Damage Reduced By (3-10)	+(40-80%) Damage	

JEWELS MAGIC PREFIXES

	Spawns	Bonus	Min	Max	Bonus 2	Max	Min	Level	Level Requirement
Blanched	Magic and Rare	Defense	5	8				1	1
Eburin	Magic and Rare	Defense	9	20				16	12
Bone	Magic and Rare	Defense	21	40				32	24
Ivory	Magic Only	Defense	41	64				64	56
Scarlet	Magic and Rare	Minimum Damage	1	4				8	6
Crimson	Magic and Rare	Minimum Damage	5	8				38	30
Carbuncle	Magic and Rare	Maximum Damage	1	5				12	9
Carmine	Magic and Rare	Maximum Damage	6	9				35	27
Vermilion	Magic Only	Maximum Damage	11	15				58	50
Cinnabar	Magic and Rare	+% Damage	5	10				1	1
Rusty	Magic and Rare	+% Damage	11	20				13	9
Realgar	Magic and Rare	+% Damage	21	30				45	37

	Spawns	Bonus 1	Min	Max	Bonus 2	Min	Max	Level	Level Requirement
Ruby	Magic Only	+% Damage	31	40				66	58
Dun	Magic and Rare	% Damage Goes To Mana	7	12				7	5
Brown	Magic and Rare	% Heal Stamina	10	15				39	31
Chestnut	Magic and Rare	Stamina	10	15				1	1
Maroon	Magic and Rare	Stamina	16	25				17	12
Nickel	Magic and Rare	Attack Rating	10	20				1	1
Tin	Magic and Rare	Attack Rating	21	40				8	6
Silver	Magic and Rare	Attack Rating	41	60				25	18
Argent	Magic Only	Attack Rating	61	100				44	36
Bright	Magic and Rare	+Light Radius	1	1				1	1
Emerald	Magic and Rare	% Magic Find	3	7				16	12
Zircon	Magic and Rare	Mana	5	10				3	2
Jacinth	Magic and Rare	Mana	11	15				17	12
Turquoise	Magic Only	Mana	16	20				29	21
Shimmering	Magic and Rare	% Resist All	5	10				16	12
Scintillating	Magic Only	% Resist All	11	15				34	26
Lapis Lazuli	Magic and Rare	% Resist Cold	5	15				2	1
Sapphire	Magic and Rare	% Resist Cold	16	30				19	14
Garnet	Magic and Rare	% Resist Fire	5	15				2	1
Ruby	Magic and Rare	% Resist Fire	16	30				18	13
Camphor	Magic and Rare	% Resist Lightning	5	15				2	1
Ambergris	Magic and Rare	% Resist Lightning	16	30				19	14
Beryl	Magic and Rare	% Resist Poison	5	15				2	1
Jade	Magic and Rare	% Resist Poison	16	30				19	14
Aureolic	Magic and Rare	+Mana Per Kill	1	3				22	16
Diamond	Magic and Rare	Attack Rating-demon	25	50	+% Damage vs Demons	25	40	26	19
Pearl	Magic and Rare	Attack Rating-undead	25	50	+% Damage vs Undead	25	50	18	13

Jewels Magic Suffixes

	Spawns	Bonus 1	Min	Max	Bonus 2	Min	Max	Level	Level Requirement
of Malice	Magic and Rare	Attacker Takes Damage of	1	5				37	29
of Fervor	Magic Only	Slightly Increased Attack Rating	15	15				39	31
of Frigidity	Magic and Rare	Cold Damage	1	5				16	12
of Passion	Magic and Rare	Minimum Fire Damage	1	3	Max Fire Damage	6	10	15	11
of Ennui	Magic and Rare	Minimum Lightning Damage	1	1	Max Lightning Damage	10	20	15	11
of Ire	Magic and Rare	Maximum Damage	2	5				4	3

continues on next page

JEWELS MAGIC SUFFIXES (CONTINUED)

	Spawns	Bonus 1	Min	Max	Bonus 2	Min	Max	Level	Level Requirement
of Wrath	Magic and Rare	Maximum Damage	6	9				11	8
of Carnage	Magic Only	Maximum Damage	11	15				25	18
of Joyfulness	Magic and Rare	Minimum Damage	1	4				5	3
of Bliss	Magic and Rare	Minimum Damage	5	10				43	37
of Envy	Magic and Rare	Minimum Poison Damage	48	48	Max Poison Damage	48	144	1	1
of Daring	Magic and Rare	Dexterity	1	3				7	5
of Truth	Magic and Rare	Fast Hit Recovery	7	7				44	36
of Honor	Magic and Rare	Replenish Life +	1	4				47	35
of Avarice	Magic and Rare	% More Gold	10	30				1	1
of Prosperity	Magic and Rare	% Magic Find	5	10				26	19
of Knowledge	Magic and Rare	Energy	1	5				9	6
of Spirit	Magic and Rare	Life	3	8				1	1
of Hope	Magic Only	Life	9	20				45	37
of Freedom	Magic and Rare	Requirements	-15	-15				1	1
of Virility	Magic and Rare	Strength	1	4			4	18	13
of the Icicle	Magic and Rare	Minimum Cold Damage	2	3	Max Cold Damage	6	10	37	29
of the Glacier	Magic Only	Minimum Cold Damage	4	5	Max Cold Damage	11	15	58	50
of Fire	Magic and Rare	Minimum Fire Damage	4	10	Max Fire Damage	11	30	36	28
of Burning	Magic and Rare	Minimum Fire Damage	11	25	Max Fire Damage	35	50	57	49
of Lightning	Magic and Rare	Minimum Lightning Damage	1	1	Max Lightning Damage	21	60	36	28
of Thunder	Magic and Rare	Minimum Lightning Damage	1	1	Max Lightning Damage	61	100	57	49
of Daring	Magic and Rare	Dexterity	4	6				19	14
of Daring	Magic and Rare	Dexterity	7	9				36	28
of Knowledge	Magic and Rare	Energy	4	6				24	18
of Knowledge	Magic and Rare	Energy	7	9				41	33
of Virility	Magic and Rare	Strength	5	6				33	25
of Virility	Magic and Rare	Strength	7	9				50	42

MAGIC ITEMS PREFIXES

	Spawns	Bonus	Min	Max	Bonus 2	Max	Min	Available On	Level	Level Req
Sturdy	Magic and Rare	% Defense	10	20				Armor	1	1
Sturdy	Magic and Rare	% Defense	21	30				Armor	4	3
Strong	Magic and Rare	% Defense	31	40				Armor	9	6

Glorious	Magic and Rare	% Defense	41	50				Armor	19	14
Blessed	Magic and Rare	% Defense	51	65				Armor	25	18
Saintly	Magic and Rare	% Defense	66	80				Armor	31	23
Holy	Magic and Rare	% Defense	81	100				Armor	36	27
Godly	Magic Only	% Defense	101	200				Armor	45	38
Jagged	Magic and Rare	% Damage	10	20				Circlets, Weapons	1	1
Deadly	Magic and Rare	% Damage	21	30				Circlets, Weapons	5	3
Vicious	Magic and Rare	% Damage	31	40				Weapons	8	6
Brutal	Magic and Rare	% Damage	41	50				Weapons	14	10
Massive	Magic and Rare	% Damage	51	65				Weapons	20	15
Savage	Magic and Rare	% Damage	66	80				Weapons	26	19
Merciless	Magic and Rare	% Damage	81	100				Weapons	32	24
Ferocious	Magic Only	% Damage	101	200				Weapons	41	33
Cruel	Magic Only	% Damage	201	300				Weapons	51	43
Vulpine	Magic and Rare	% Damage Goes To Mana	7	12				Amulets, Shields	9	6
Tireless	Magic and Rare	% Heal Stamina	25	25				Boots	6	4
Tireless	Magic and Rare	% Heal Stamina	50	50				Boots	14	10
Rugged	Magic and Rare	Stamina	5	10				Amulets, Belts, Boots, Circlets, Gloves, Rings	1	1
Rugged	Magic and Rare	Stamina	11	20				Belts, Boots	8	6
Rugged	Magic and Rare	Stamina	11	20				Amulets, Circlets, Rings	8	6
Vigorous	Magic and Rare	Stamina	21	30				Belts, Boots	16	12
Bronze	Magic and Rare	Attack Rating	10	20				Amulets, Circlets, Gloves, Rings, Weapons	1	1
Iron	Magic and Rare	Attack Rating	21	40				Circlets, Weapons, Rings	4	3
Steel	Magic and Rare	Attack Rating	41	60				Circlets, Weapons, Rings	8	6
Silver	Magic and Rare	Attack Rating	61	80				Circlets, Weapons, Rings	12	9
Gold	Magic and Rare	Attack Rating	81	100				Circlets, Weapons, Rings	17	12
Platinum	Magic and Rare	Attack Rating	101	120				Circlets, Weapons, Rings	22	16
Meteoric	Magic and Rare	Attack Rating	121	150				Weapons	27	20
Strange	Magic Only	Attack Rating	151	300				Weapons	32	24
Weird	Magic Only	Attack Rating	301	450				Weapons	37	27
Sharp	Magic and Rare	% Damage	10	20				Weapons	5	3
Fine	Magic and Rare	% Damage	21	30				Weapons	12	9
Warrior's	Magic and Rare	% Damage	31	40				Weapons	19	13
Soldier's	Magic and Rare	% Damage	41	50				Weapons	27	19
Knight's	Magic and Rare	% Damage	51	65				Weapons	38	30
Lord's	Magic and Rare	% Damage	66	80				Weapons	47	39
King's	Magic and Rare	% Damage	81	100				Weapons	56	48
Master's	Magic Only	% Damage	101	150				Weapons	56	48
Grandmaster's	Magic Only	% Damage	151	200				Weapons	69	61
Glimmering	Magic and Rare	Light Radius	1	1				Amulets, Armor, Orbs, Rings, Staves, Wands	1	1
Glowing	Magic and Rare	Light Radius	2	2				Amulets, Armor, Orbs, Rings, Staves, Wands	6	4
Screaming	Magic and Rare	Hit Causes Monster To Flee	32	32				Weapons	10	7
Howling	Magic and Rare	Hit Causes Monster To Flee	64	64				Weapons	16	12
Wailing	Magic and Rare	Hit Causes Monster To Flee	128	128				Weapons	20	13

continues on next page

	Spawns	Bonus	Min	Max	Bonus 2	Max	Min	Available On	Level	Level Req
Screaming	Magic and Rare	Hit Causes Monster To Flee	16	16				Bows and Crossbows	10	7
Howling	Magic and Rare	Hit Causes Monster To Flee	24	24				Bows and Crossbows	16	12
Wailing	Magic Only	Hit Causes Monster To Flee	32	32				Bows and Crossbows	24	18
Felicitous	Magic and Rare	% Magic Find	5	10				Amulets, Circlets, Rings	5	3
Fortuitous	Magic Only	% Magic Find	11	15				Amulets, Circlets, Rings	12	8
Lizard's	Magic and Rare	Mana	1	5				Amulets, Armor, Orbs, Rings, Rods	3	2
Snake's	Magic and Rare	Mana	5	10				Amulets, Belts, Circlets, Rings, Rods, Shields	6	4
Serpent's	Magic and Rare	Mana	11	20				Amulets, Belts, Circlets, Rings, Rods, Shields	14	10
Serpent's	Magic and Rare	Mana	11	20				Body Armor, Boots, Gloves, Orbs, Rods, Weapons	37	27
Drake's	Magic and Rare	Mana	21	30				Amulets, Circlets, Orbs, Rings, Rods	20	15
Dragon's	Magic and Rare	Mana	31	40				Amulets, Circlets, Orbs, Rings, Rods	24	18
Dragon's	Magic and Rare	Mana	31	40				Body Armor, Boots, Gloves	52	39
Wyrm's	Magic and Rare	Mana	41	60				Amulets, Circlets, Orbs, Rings, Rods	30	22
Great Wyrm's	Magic Only	Mana	61	90				Amulets, Circlets, Orbs, Rings, Rods	37	29
Bahamut's	Magic Only	Mana	91	120				Amulets, Circlets, Orbs, Rings, Rods	45	37
Shimmering	Magic and Rare	% Resist All	3	7				Shields	6	4
Rainbow	Magic and Rare	% Resist All	8	11				Shields	18	13
Scintillating	Magic and Rare	% Resist All	12	15				Shields	28	21
Prismatic	Magic and Rare	% Resist All	16	20				Shields	39	31
Chromatic	Magic Only	% Resist All	21	30				Shields	50	42
Shimmering	Magic and Rare	% Resist All	3	7				Amulets, Circlets	8	6
Rainbow	Magic and Rare	% Resist All	8	11				Amulets, Circlets	21	15
Scintillating	Magic and Rare	% Resist All	12	15				Amulets, Circlets	34	25
Prismatic	Magic and Rare	% Resist All	16	20				Amulets, Circlets	42	31
Chromatic	Magic Only	% Resist All	21	25				Amulets, Circlets	55	41
Shimmering	Magic and Rare	% Resist All	3	7				Rings	45	37
Rainbow	Magic and Rare	% Resist All	8	11				Rings	56	48
Scintillating	Magic Only	% Resist All	12	15				Rings	67	59
Azure	Magic and Rare	% Resist Cold	5	10				Amulets, Armor, Circlets, Orbs, Rings, Weapons	5	3
Lapis	Magic and Rare	% Resist Cold	11	20				Amulets, Armor, Circlets, Orbs, Rings	12	9
Lapis	Magic and Rare	% Resist Cold	11	20				Weapons	35	26
Cobalt	Magic and Rare	% Resist Cold	21	30				Amulets, Armor, Circlets, Orbs, Rings	18	13
Cobalt	Magic and Rare	% Resist Cold	21	30				Weapons	55	41
Sapphire	Magic and Rare	% Resist Cold	31	40				Amulets, Boots, Circlets, Orbs, Rods	25	18
Russet	Magic and Rare	% Resist Fire	11	20				Amulets, Armor, Circlets, Orbs, Rings	12	9
Russet	Magic and Rare	% Resist Fire	11	20				Weapons	35	26
Garnet	Magic and Rare	% Resist Fire	21	30				Amulets, Armor, Circlets, Orbs, Rings	18	13
Garnet	Magic and Rare	% Resist Fire	21	30				Weapons	55	41
Ruby	Magic and Rare	% Resist Fire	31	40				Amulets, Boots, Circlets, Orbs, Rods	25	18

Tangerine	Magic and Rare	% Resist Lightning	5	10				Amulets, Armor, Circlets, Orbs, Rings, Weapons	5	3
Ocher	Magic and Rare	% Resist Lightning	11	20				Amulets, Armor, Circlets, Orbs, Rings	12	9
Ocher	Magic and Rare	% Resist Lightning	11	20				Weapons	35	26
Coral	Magic and Rare	% Resist Lightning	21	30				Amulets, Armor, Circlets, Orbs, Rings	18	13
Coral	Magic and Rare	% Resist Lightning	21	30				Weapons	55	41
Amber	Magic and Rare	% Resist Lightning	31	40				Amulets, Boots, Circlets, Orbs, Rods	25	18
Beryl	Magic and Rare	% Resist Poison	5	10				Amulets, Armor, Circlets, Orbs, Rings, Weapons	5	3
Viridian	Magic and Rare	% Resist Poison	11	20				Amulets, Armor, Circlets, Orbs, Rings	12	9
Viridian	Magic and Rare	% Resist Poison	11	20				Weapons	35	26
Jade	Magic and Rare	% Resist Poison	21	30				Amulets, Armor, Circlets, Orbs, Rings	18	13
Jade	Magic and Rare	% Resist Poison	21	30				Weapons	55	41
Emerald	Magic and Rare	% Resist Poison	31	40				Amulets, Boots, Circlets, Orbs, Rods	25	18
Triumphant	Magic and Rare	Mana Per Kill	1	1				Circlets, Rings, Weapons	3	2
Victorious	Magic and Rare	Mana Per Kill	2	5				Circlets, Weapons	17	12
Mechanic's	Magic and Rare	Add Sockets	1					Body Armor, Circlets, Helms, Shields, Weapons	10	7
Artisan's	Magic Only	Add Sockets	3					Body Armor, Helms, Shields, Weapons	33	25
Jeweler's	Magic Only	Add Sockets	4					Body Armor, Helms, Shields, Weapons	55	47
Lunar	Magic and Rare	Attack Rating vs Demons	25	50	Damage vs. Demons	10	25	Circlets, Weapons	3	1
Arcadian	Magic and Rare	Attack Rating vs Demons	51	100	Damage vs. Demons	26	50	Circlets, Weapons	15	11
Unearthly	Magic and Rare	Attack Rating vs Demons	101	150	Damage vs. Demons	51	100	Weapons	25	18
Astral	Magic and Rare	Attack Rating vs Demons	151	200	Damage vs. Demons	101	150	Weapons	35	26
Elysian	Magic and Rare	Attack Rating vs Demons	201	300	Damage vs. Demons	151	200	Weapons	45	33
Celestial	Magic Only	Attack Rating vs Demons	301	400	Damage vs. Demons	201	300	Weapons	55	41
Fletcher's	Magic and Rare	Bow and Crossbow	1					Bows, Crossbows, Gloves	20	15
Bowyer's	Magic and Rare	Bow and Crossbow	2					Bows, Crossbows, Gloves	40	30
Archer's	Magic Only	Bow and Crossbow	3					Bows, Crossbows, Gloves	60	45
Acrobatic	Magic and Rare	Passive	1					Amulets, Circlets, Gloves	20	15
Gymnastic	Magic and Rare	Passive	2					Amulets, Circlets, Gloves	40	30
Athletic	Magic Only	Passive	3					Amulets, Circlets, Gloves	60	45
Harpoonist's	Magic and Rare	Javelin and Spear	1					Gloves, Spears	20	15
Spearmaiden's	Magic and Rare	Javelin and Spear	2					Gloves, Spears	40	30
Lancer's	Magic Only	Javelin and Spear	3					Gloves, Spears	60	45
Burning	Magic and Rare	Fire Spells	1					Amulets, Circlets, Orbs, Staves	20	15
Blazing	Magic and Rare	Fire Spells	2					Amulets, Circlets, Orbs, Staves	40	30
Volcanic	Magic Only	Fire Spells	3					Amulets, Circlets, Orbs, Staves	60	45
Sparking	Magic and Rare	Lightning Spells	1					Amulets, Circlets, Orbs, Staves	20	15
Charged	Magic and Rare	Lightning Spells	2					Amulets, Circlets, Orbs, Staves	40	30
Powered	Magic Only	Lightning Spells	3					Amulets, Circlets, Orbs, Staves	60	45
Chilling	Magic and Rare	Cold Spells	1					Amulets, Circlets, Orbs, Staves	20	15
Freezing	Magic and Rare	Cold Spells	2					Amulets, Circlets, Orbs, Staves	40	30
Glacial	Magic Only	Cold Spells	3					Amulets, Circlets, Orbs, Staves	60	45
Hexing	Magic and Rare	Curse Spells	1					Amultes, Circlets, Head, Wands	20	15

continues on next page

	Spawns	Bonus	Min	Max	Bonus 2	Max	Min	Available On	Level	Level Req
BLighting	Magic and Rare	Curse Spells	2					Amultes, Circlets, Head, Wands	40	30
Cursing	Magic Only	Curse Spells	3					Amultes, Circlets, Head, Wands	60	45
Fungal	Magic and Rare	Poison and Bone Spells	1					Amultes, Circlets, Head, Knives, Wands	20	15
Noxious	Magic and Rare	Poison and Bone Spells	2					Amultes, Circlets, Head, Knives, Wands	40	30
Venomous	Magic Only	Poison and Bone Spells	3					Amultes, Circlets, Head, Knives, Wands	60	45
Graverobber's	Magic and Rare	Summoning Spells	1					Amultes, Circlets, Head, Wands	20	15
Mojo	Magic and Rare	Summoning Spells	2					Amultes, Circlets, Head, Wands	40	30
Golemlord's	Magic Only	Summoning Spells	3					Amultes, Circlets, Head, Wands	60	45
Lion Branded	Magic and Rare	Combat Skills	1					Amulets, Circlets, Maces, PalShields, Scepters, Shields, Swords	20	15
Hawk Branded	Magic and Rare	Combat Skills	2					Amulets, Circlets, Maces, PalShields, Scepters, Shields, Swords	40	30
Rose Branded	Magic Only	Combat Skills	3					Amulets, Circlets, Maces, PalShields, Scepters, Shields, Swords	60	45
Captain's	Magic and Rare	Offensive Auras	1					Amulets, Circlets, Maces, PalShields, Scepters, Shields, Swords	20	15
Commander's	Magic and Rare	Offensive Auras	2					Amulets, Circlets, Maces, PalShields, Scepters, Shields, Swords	40	30
Marshal's	Magic Only	Offensive Auras	3					Amulets, Circlets, Maces, PalShields, Scepters, Shields, Swords	60	45
Preserver's	Magic and Rare	Defensive Auras	1					Amulets, Circlets, PalShields, Shields	20	15
Warden's	Magic and Rare	Defensive Auras	2					Amulets, Circlets, PalShields, Shields	40	30
Guardian's	Magic Only	Defensive Auras	3					Amulets, Circlets, PalShields, Shields	60	45
Sounding	Magic and Rare	Combat Skills	1					BarHelm, Helms, Weapons	20	15
Resonant	Magic and Rare	Combat Skills	2					BarHelm, Helms, Weapons	40	30
Echoing	Magic Only	Combat Skills	3					BarHelm, Helms, Weapons	60	45
Fanatic	Magic and Rare	Combat Masteries	1					Amulets, BarHelms, Weapons	20	15
Raging	Magic and Rare	Combat Masteries	2					Amulets, BarHelms, Weapons	40	30
Furious	Magic Only	Combat Masteries	3					Amulets, BarHelms, Weapons	60	45
Expert's	Magic and Rare	Warcries	1					Amulets, BarHelms, Weapons	20	15
Veteran's	Magic and Rare	Warcries	2					Amulets, BarHelms, Weapons	40	30
Master's	Magic Only	Warcries	3					Amulets, BarHelms, Weapons	60	45
Trainer's	Magic and Rare	Summoning Spells	1					Amulets, Circlets, Clubs, Pelts	20	15
Caretaker's	Magic and Rare	Summoning Spells	2					Amulets, Circlets, Clubs, Pelts	40	30
Keeper's	Magic Only	Summoning Spells	3					Amulets, Circlets, Clubs, Pelts	60	45
Spiritual	Magic and Rare	Shape Shifting	1					Amulets, Circlets, Clubs, Pelts	20	15
Feral	Magic and Rare	Shape Shifting	2					Amulets, Circlets, Clubs, Pelts	40	30
Communal	Magic Only	Shape Shifting	3					Amulets, Circlets, Clubs, Pelts	60	45
Natural	Magic and Rare	Elemental Spells	1					Amulets, Circlets, Clubs, Pelts	20	15
Terrene	Magic and Rare	Elemental Spells	2					Amulets, Circlets, Clubs, Pelts	40	30
Gaean	Magic Only	Elemental Spells	3					Amulets, Circlets, Clubs, Pelts	60	45
Entrapping	Magic and Rare	Traps	1					Amulets, Circlets, Katars	20	15
Trickster's	Magic and Rare	Traps	2					Amulets, Circlets, Katars	40	30

Cunning	Magic Only	Traps	3					Amulets, Circlets, Katars	60	45
Mentalist's	Magic and Rare	Shadow Disciplines	1					Amulets, Circlets, Helms, Katars	20	15
Psychic	Magic and Rare	Shadow Disciplines	2					Amulets, Circlets, Helms, Katars	40	30
Shadow	Magic Only	Shadow Disciplines	3					Amulets, Circlets, Helms, Katars	60	45
Shogukusha's	Magic and Rare	Martial Arts	1					Amulets, Circlets, Gloves, Katars	20	15
Sensei's	Magic and Rare	Martial Arts	2					Amulets, Circlets, Gloves, Katars	40	30
Kenshi's	Magic Only	Martial Arts	3					Amulets, Circlets, Gloves, Katars	60	45
Faithful	Magic and Rare	+Defense / Level	24					Body Armor	30	22
Faithful	Magic and Rare	+Defense / Level	4					Belts, Boots, Gloves, Shields	30	22
Fool's	Magic and Rare	+ Damage/Level	4					Weapons	50	37
Screaming	Magic and Rare	+ Damage/Level	6					Weapons	50	37
Hawkeye	Magic Only	Attack Rating/level	12					Weapons	35	26
Visionary	Magic and Rare	Attack Rating%/level	2					Bows, Crossbows, Helms	25	18
Mnemonic	Magic and Rare	Mana/level	4					Helms	25	18
Snowy	Magic Only	Minimum Cold Damage	6	9	Max Cold Damage	19	30	Circlets, Weapons	25	18
Shivering	Magic Only	Minimum Cold Damage	10	15	Max Cold Damage	31	45	Weapons	35	26
Boreal	Magic Only	Minimum Cold Damage	16	23	Max Cold Damage	46	90	Weapons	50	40
Hibernal	Magic Only	Minimum Cold Damage	24	45	Max Cold Damage	91	140	Weapons	70	60
Fiery	Magic Only	Minimum Fire Damage	16	25	Max Fire Damage	31	60	Circlets, Weapons	25	18
Smoldering	Magic Only	Minimum Fire Damage	26	50	Max Fire Damage	61	90	Weapons	35	26
Smoking	Magic Only	Minimum Fire Damage	51	80	Max Fire Damage	91	130	Weapons	47	37
Flaming	Magic Only	Minimum Fire Damage	81	120	Max Fire Damage	131	180	Weapons	61	51
Condensing	Magic Only	Minimum Fire Damage	121	170	Max Fire Damage	181	240	Weapons	77	67
Static	Magic Only	Minimum Lightning Damage	1	1	Max Lightning Damage	49	120	Circlets, Weapons	25	18
Glowing	Magic Only	Minimum Lightning Damage	1	1	Max Lightning Damage	121	180	Weapons	34	25
Buzzing	Magic Only	Minimum Lightning Damage	1	1	Max Lightning Damage	181	260	Weapons	46	36
Arcing	Magic Only	Minimum Lightning Damage	1	1	Max Lightning Damage	261	360	Weapons	60	50
Shocking	Magic Only	Minimum Lightning Damage	1	1	Max Lightning Damage	361	480	Weapons	76	66
Septic	Magic Only	Minimum Poison Damage	40	40	Max Poison Damage	40	40	Circlets, Weapons	1	1
Foul	Magic Only	Minimum Poison Damage	75	75	Max Poison Damage	75	75	Weapons	10	7
Corrosive	Magic Only	Minimum Poison Damage	150	150	Max Poison Damage	150	150	Weapons	20	15
Toxic	Magic Only	Minimum Poison Damage	200	200	Max Poison Damage	200	200	Weapons	35	26
Pestilent	Magic Only	Minimum Poison Damage	350	350	Max Poison Damage	350	350	Weapons	50	37
Maiden's	Magic and Rare	Amazon Skills	1	1				Amulets, Circlets	36	27
Valkyrie's	Magic Only	Amazon Skills	2	2				Amulets, Circlets	90	67
Maiden's	Magic and Rare	Amazon Skills	1	1				Bows, Crossbows, Spears	30	22
Valkyrie's	Magic Only	Amazon Skills	2	2				Bows, Crossbows, Spears	50	42
Monk's	Magic and Rare	Paladin Skills	1	1				Amulets, Circlets	36	27
Priest's	Magic Only	Paladin Skills	2	2				Amulets, Circlets	90	67
Monk's	Magic and Rare	Paladin Skills	1	1				PalShields, Scepters	30	22
Priest's	Magic Only	Paladin Skills	2	2				PalShields, Scepters	50	42
Monk's	Magic and Rare	Paladin Skills	1	1				Hammers, Maces, Shields, Swords	35	27
Priest's	Magic Only	Paladin Skills	2	2				Hammers, Maces, Shields, Swords	65	58
Summoner's	Magic and Rare	Necromancer Skills	1	1				Amulets, Circlets	36	27

continues on next page

MAGIC ITEMS PREFIXES (CONTINUED)

	Spawns	Bonus	Min	Max	Bonus 2	Max	Min	Available On	Level	Level Req
Necromancer's	Magic Only	Necromancer Skills	2	2				Amulets, Circlets	90	67
Summoner's	Magic and Rare	Necromancer Skills	1	1				Head, Knives, Wands	30	22
Necromancer's	Magic Only	Necromancer Skills	2	2				Head, Knives, Wands	50	42
Angel's	Magic and Rare	Sorceress Skills	1	1				Amulets, Circlets	36	27
Arch-Angel's	Magic Only	Sorceress Skills	2	2				Amulets, Circlets	90	67
Angel's	Magic and Rare	Sorceress Skills	1	1				Orbs, Staves	30	22
Arch-Angel's	Magic Only	Sorceress Skills	2	2				Orbs, Staves	50	42
Slayer's	Magic and Rare	Barbarian Skills	1	1				Amulets, Circlets	36	27
Berserker's	Magic Only	Barbarian Skills	2	2				Amulets, Circlets	90	67
Slayer's	Magic and Rare	Barbarian Skills	1	1				Axes, Clubs, Hammers, Javelins, Knives, Maces, Throwing Weapons, Spears, Swords	30	22
Berserker's	Magic Only	Barbarian Skills	2	2				Axes, Clubs, Hammers, Javelins, Knives, Maces, Throwing Weapons, Spears, Swords	50	42
Slayer's	Magic and Rare	Barbarian Skills	1	1				BarHelm	30	22
Berserker's	Magic Only	Barbarian Skills	2	2				BarHelm	50	42
Shaman's	Magic and Rare	Druid Skills	1	1				Amulets, Circlets	36	27
Hierophant's	Magic Only	Druid Skills	2	2				Amulets, Circlets	90	67
Shaman's	Magic and Rare	Druid Skills	1	1				Clubs, Pelts	30	22
Hierophant's	Magic Only	Druid Skills	2	2				Clubs, Pelts	50	42
Magekiller's	Magic and Rare	Assassin Skills	1	1				Amulets, Circlets	36	27
Witch-hunter's	Magic Only	Assassin Skills	2	2				Amulets, Circlets	90	67
Magekiller's	Magic and Rare	Assassin Skills	1	1				Katars	30	22
Witch-hunter's	Magic Only	Assassin Skills	2	2				Katars	50	42
Compact	Magic and Rare	+ Quantity	10	20				Throwing Weapons	2	1
Thin	Magic and Rare	+ Quantity	21	40				Throwing Weapons	17	12
Dense	Magic and Rare	+ Quantity	41	60				Throwing Weapons	38	30
Consecrated	Magic and Rare	Attack Rating vs. Undead	25	75	Damage vs. Undead	25	75	Weapons	1	1
Pure	Magic and Rare	Attack Rating vs. Undead	76	175	Damage vs. Undead	76	125	Weapons	15	11
Sacred	Magic and Rare	Attack Rating vs. Undead	175	250	Damage vs. Undead	126	200	Weapons	25	18
Hallowed	Magic and Rare	Attack Rating vs. Undead	251	325	Damage vs. Undead	201	275	Weapons	35	27
Divine	Magic Only	Attack Rating vs. Undead	326	450	Damage vs. Undead	276	350	Weapons	45	37

MAGIC ITEMS SUFFIXES

	Spawns	Bonus	Min	Max	Bonus 2	Max	Min	Available On	Level	Level Req
of Health	Magic and Rare	Damage Reduced By	1	1				Amulets, Body Armor, Circlets, Rings, Shields	7	5
of Protection	Magic and Rare	Damage Reduced By	2	2				Amulets, Circlets, Rings	18	13
of Absorption	Magic and Rare	Damage Reduced By	3	3				Amulets, Circlets	26	19
of Life	Magic and Rare	Damage Reduced By	4	4				Amulets, Circlets	35	26
of Life Everlasting	Magic Only	Damage Reduced By	10	25				Amulets, Circlets	45	37

of Protection	Magic and Rare	Damage Reduced By	2	2				Body Armor, Circlets, Shields	24	18
of Absorption	Magic and Rare	Damage Reduced By	3	3				Body Armor, Circlets, Shields	32	24
of Life	Magic and Rare	Damage Reduced By	4	7				Body Armor, Circlets, Shields	41	33
of Amicae	Magic Only	Damage Reduced By	8	15				Body Armor, Circlets, Shields	51	43
of Warding	Magic and Rare	Magic Damage Reduced By	1	1				Amulets, Body Armor, Circlets, Orbs, Rings, Shields	7	5
of the Sentinel	Magic and Rare	Magic Damage Reduced By	2	2				Amulets, Circlets, Orbs, Rings	18	12
of Guarding	Magic and Rare	Magic Damage Reduced By	3	3				Amulets, Circlets, Orbs	26	19
of Negation	Magic Only	Magic Damage Reduced By	4	6				Amulets, Circlets, Orbs	42	35
of the Sentinel	Magic and Rare	Magic Damage Reduced By	2	2				Body Armor, Circlets, Shields	24	18
of Guarding	Magic and Rare	Magic Damage Reduced By	3	3				Body Armor, Circlets, Shields	32	24
of Negation	Magic Only	Magic Damage Reduced By	4	6				Body Armor, Circlets, Shields	41	33
of Piercing	Magic and Rare	Ignore Target Defense						Katars, Knives, Rods	25	18
of Thorns	Magic and Rare	Attacker Takes Damage of	1	3				Belts, Body Armor, Circlets, Shields	14	10
of Spikes	Magic and Rare	Attacker Takes Damage of	4	6				Belts, Body Armor, Circlets, Shields	21	15
of Razors	Magic and Rare	Attacker Takes Damage of	7	9				Body Armor, Circlets, Shields	34	26
of Swords	Magic Only	Attacker Takes Damage of	10	20				Body Armor, Circlets, Shields	47	39
of Readiness	Magic and Rare	Slightly Increased Attack Speed	10	10				Weapons	5	3
of Alacrity	Magic and Rare	Increased Attack Speed	20	20				Weapons	25	17
of Swiftness	Magic and Rare	Increased Attack Speed	30	30				Melee Weapons	34	26
of Quickness	Magic and Rare	Greatly Increased Attack Speed	40	40				Melee Weapons	46	38
of Alacrity	Magic and Rare	Increased Attack Speed	20	20				Gloves	43	35
of Blocking	Magic and Rare	+ % Blocking	10	10				Shields	1	1
of Deflecting	Magic and Rare	+ % Blocking	20	20				Shields	11	8
of the Apprentice	Magic and Rare	Fast Cast Rate	10	10				Amulets, Circlets, Orbs, Rings, Rods	5	3
of the Magus	Magic and Rare	Fastest Cast Rate	20	20				Circlets, Orbs, Rods	29	21
of Frost	Magic and Rare	Minimum Cold Damage	1	1	Max Cold Damage	1	2	Weapons	4	3
of the Icicle	Magic and Rare	Minimum Cold Damage	1	1	Max Cold Damage	3	4	Weapons	13	9
of the Glacier	Magic and Rare	Minimum Cold Damage	2	4	Max Cold Damage	4	10	Melee Weapons	27	20
of Winter	Magic and Rare	Minimum Cold Damage	3	6	Max Cold Damage	11	25	Melee Weapons	30	22
of Frost	Magic and Rare	Minimum Cold Damage	1	1	Max Cold Damage	3	6	Amulets, Belts	55	41
of Thawing	Magic and Rare	Half Freeze Duration						Amulets, Boots, Circlets, Gloves, Orbs, Rings, Shields		
of Flame	Magic and Rare	Minimum Fire Damage	1	1	Max Fire Damage	2	5	Weapons	4	3
of Fire	Magic and Rare	Minimum Fire Damage	1	4	Max Fire Damage	6	11	Weapons	15	11
of Burning	Magic and Rare	Minimum Fire Damage	5	9	Max Fire Damage	10	20	Weapons	25	18
of Incineration	Magic and Rare	Minimum Fire Damage	10	15	Max Fire Damage	21	35	Weapons	32	24
of Flame	Magic and Rare	Minimum Fire Damage	1	1	Max Fire Damage	2	6	Amulets, Gloves, Rings	40	30
of Shock	Magic and Rare	Minimum Lightning Damage	1	1	Max Lightning Damage	6	8	Weapons	4	3
of Lightning	Magic and Rare	Minimum Lightning Damage	1	1	Max Lightning Damage	9	16	Weapons	15	11
of Thunder	Magic and Rare	Minimum Lightning Damage	1	1	Max Lightning Damage	17	32	Weapons	25	18
of Storms	Magic and Rare	Minimum Lightning Damage	1	6	Max Lightning Damage	33	48	Weapons	34	26
of Shock	Magic and Rare	Minimum Lightning Damage	1	1	Max Lightning Damage	11	23	Amulets, Boots, Rings	50	37

continues on next page

Magic Items Suffixes (Continued)

	Spawns	Bonus	Min	Max	Bonus 2	Max	Min	Available On	Level	Level Req
of Craftsmanship	Magic and Rare	Max Damage	1	1				Amulets, Rings, Weapons	1	1
of Quality	Magic and Rare	Max Damage	2	2				Weapons	4	3
of Maiming	Magic and Rare	Max Damage	3	4				Weapons	7	5
of Slaying	Magic and Rare	Max Damage	5	7				Weapons	11	8
of Gore	Magic and Rare	Max Damage	8	10				Weapons	14	10
of Carnage	Magic and Rare	Max Damage	11	14				Weapons	19	14
of Slaughter	Magic and Rare	Max Damage	15	20				Weapons	25	18
of Butchery	Magic Only	Max Damage	21	40				Weapons	35	27
of Evisceration	Magic Only	Max Damage	41	63				Weapons	45	37
of Maiming	Magic and Rare	Max Damage	3	4				Amulets, Rings, Shields	42	34
of Worth	Magic and Rare	Minimum Damage	1	2				Weapons	1	1
of Measure	Magic and Rare	Minimum Damage	3	4				Weapons	12	9
of Excellence	Magic and Rare	Minimum Damage	5	8				Weapons	24	18
of Performance	Magic and Rare	Minimum Damage	9	14				Weapons	48	40
of Transcendence	Magic and Rare	Minimum Damage	15	20				Weapons	76	68
of Worth	Magic and Rare	Minimum Damage	2	3				Amulets, Circlets, Rings	15	11
of Measure	Magic and Rare	Minimum Damage	4	5				Amulets, Circlets, Rings	37	29
of Excellence	Magic and Rare	Minimum Damage	6	9				Amulets, Circlets, Rings	59	51
of Performance	Magic Only	Minimum Damage	10	13				Amulets, Circlets, Rings	81	73
of Blight	Magic and Rare	Minimum Poison Damage	8	8	Max Poison Damage	24	24	Circlets, Weapons	5	3
of Venom	Magic and Rare	Minimum Poison Damage	16	16	Max Poison Damage	48	48	Circlets, Weapons	15	11
of Pestilence	Magic and Rare	Minimum Poison Damage	32	32	Max Poison Damage	72	72	Circlets, Weapons	25	18
of Anthrax	Magic and Rare	Minimum Poison Damage	64	64	Max Poison Damage	128	128	Weapons	33	25
of Blight	Magic and Rare	Minimum Poison Damage	8	8	Max Poison Damage	24	24	Amulets, Rings	45	33
of Dexterity	Magic and Rare	Dexterity	1	2				Amulets, Bows, Circlets, Crossbows	2	1
of Skill	Magic and Rare	Dexterity	3	5				Amulets, Bows, Circlets, Crossbows	11	8
of Accuracy	Magic and Rare	Dexterity	6	9				Amulets, Bows, Circlets, Crossbows	27	20
of Precision	Magic and Rare	Dexterity	10	15				Amulets, Bows, Circlets, Crossbows	43	35
of Perfection	Magic and Rare	Dexterity	16	20				Amulets, Bows, Circlets, Crossbows	59	51
of Nirvana	Magic Only	Dexterity	21	30				Amulets, Bows, Circlets, Crossbows	72	64
of Dexterity	Magic and Rare	Dexterity	1	2				Gloves, Rings	6	4
of Skill	Magic and Rare	Dexterity	3	5				Gloves, Rings	22	16
of Accuracy	Magic and Rare	Dexterity	6	9				Gloves, Rings	39	31
of Precision	Magic and Rare	Dexterity	10	15				Gloves, Rings	56	48
of Perfection	Magic Only	Dexterity	16	20				Gloves, Rings	75	67
of Dexterity	Magic and Rare	Dexterity	1	2				Body Armor, Boots	13	9
of Skill	Magic and Rare	Dexterity	3	5				Body Armor, Boots	34	26
of Accuracy	Magic and Rare	Dexterity	6	9				Body Armor, Boots	46	38
of Precision	Magic Only	Dexterity	10	15				Body Armor, Boots	60	52
of Balance	Magic and Rare	Fast Hit Recovery	10	10				Armor	5	3
of Equilibrium	Magic and Rare	Faster Hit Recovery	17	17				Belts, Body Armor, Shields	9	6
of Stability	Magic and Rare	Fastest Hit Recovery	24	24				Body Armor, Belts	18	13

of Regeneration	Magic and Rare	Replenish Life +	3	5				Amulets, Belts, Circlets, Rings, Scepters	10	7
of Regeneration	Magic and Rare	Replenish Life +	3	5				Gloves, Shields	40	30
of Regeneration	Magic and Rare	Replenish Life +	3	5				Body Armor, Boots, Weapons	70	52
of Regrowth	Magic and Rare	Replenish Life +	6	10				Amulets, Circlets, Scepters	17	12
of Regrowth	Magic and Rare	Replenish Life +	6	9				Belts, Rings	55	41
of Revivification	Magic Only	Replenish Life +	11	15				Amulets, Circlets, Scepters	38	30
of Vileness	Magic and Rare	Prevent Monster Heal						Melee Weapons	9	6
of Greed	Magic and Rare	% More Gold	25	40				Amulets, Circlets, Rings	2	1
of Wealth	Magic and Rare	% More Gold	41	80				Amulets, Belts, Boots, Circlets, Gloves	17	12
of Chance	Magic and Rare	% Magic Find	5	15				Amulets, Boots, Circlets, Gloves, Rings	12	9
of Fortune	Magic and Rare	% Magic Find	16	25				Amulets, Boots, Circlets, Gloves	16	12
of Fortune	Magic Only	% Magic Find	16	25				Rings	42	31
of Luck	Magic Only	% Magic Find	26	35				Amulets, Boots, Circlets	26	19
of Energy	Magic and Rare	Energy	1	3				Amulets, Circlets, Orbs, Staves, Wands	1	1
of the Mind	Magic and Rare	Energy	4	6				Amulets, Circlets, Orbs, Staves, Wands	7	3
of Brilliance	Magic and Rare	Energy	7	10				Amulets, Circlets, Orbs, Staves, Wands	13	9
of Sorcery	Magic and Rare	Energy	11	15				Amulets, Circlets, Orbs, Staves, Wands	21	16
of Wizardry	Magic and Rare	Energy	16	20				Amulets, Circlets, Orbs, Staves, Wands	31	23
of Enlightenment	Magic Only	Energy	21	30				Amulets, Circlets, Orbs, Staves, Wands	41	33
of Energy	Magic and Rare	Energy	1	3				Rings	7	5
of the Mind	Magic and Rare	Energy	4	6				Rings	13	9
of Brilliance	Magic and Rare	Energy	7	10				Rings	21	16
of Sorcery	Magic and Rare	Energy	11	15				Rings	31	23
of Wizardry	Magic Only	Energy	16	20				Rings	41	33
of Energy	Magic and Rare	Energy	1	3				Helms, Scepters	4	3
of the Mind	Magic and Rare	Energy	4	6				Helms, Scepters	10	7
of Brilliance	Magic and Rare	Energy	7	10				Helms, Scepters	16	12
of Sorcery	Magic Only	Energy	11	15				Helms, Scepters	26	21
of the Bear	Magic and Rare	Knockback						Melee Weapons	8	6
of Light	Magic and Rare	+ Light Radius	1	1				Amulets, Body Armor, Rings, Rods	6	4
of Radiance	Magic and Rare	+ Light Radius	3	3				Amults, Bows, Crossbows, Helms, Rings, Rods	15	11
of the Sun	Magic and Rare	+ Light Radius	5	5				Amulets, Bows, Crossbows, Gloves, Helms, Rings, Rods	17	12
of the Jackal	Magic and Rare	Life	1	5				Amulets, BarHelm, Belts, Body Armor, Circlets	1	1
of the Fox	Magic and Rare	Life	6	10				Amulets, BarHelm, Belts, Body Armor, Circlets	7	5
of the Wolf	Magic and Rare	Life	11	20				Amulets, BarHelm, Belts, Body Armor, Circlets	15	11
of the Tiger	Magic and Rare	Life	21	30				Amulets, BarHelm, Belts, Body Armor, Circlets	20	15
of the Mammoth	Magic and Rare	Life	31	40				Amulets, BarHelm, Belts, Body Armor, Circlets	25	18
of the Gargantuan	Magic and Rare	Life	41	60				Amulets, BarHelm, Belts, Body Armor, Circlets	30	22
of the Squid	Magic Only	Life	61	80				Amulets, BarHelm, Belts, Body Armor, Circlets	40	30
of the Whale	Magic Only	Life	81	100				Amulets, BarHelm, Belts, Body Armor, Circlets	50	37
of the Jackal	Magic and Rare	Life	1	5				DruPelts, Shields	4	3
of the Fox	Magic and Rare	Life	6	10				DruPelts, Shields	11	8
of the Wolf	Magic and Rare	Life	11	20				DruPelts, Shields	27	20

continues on next page

MAGIC ITEMS SUFFIXES (CONTINUED)

	Spawns	Bonus	Min	Max	Bonus 2	Max	Min	Available On	Level	Level Req
of the Tiger	Magic and Rare	Life	21	30				DruPelts, Shields	43	35
of the Mammoth	Magic and Rare	Life	31	40				DruPelts, Shields	59	51
of the Gargantuan	Magic Only	Life	41	60				DruPelts, Shields	75	67
of the Jackal	Magic and Rare	Life	1	5				Clubs, Hammers, Helms, Maces, Rings	8	6
of the Fox	Magic and Rare	Life	6	10				Clubs, Hammers, Helms, Maces, Rings	17	13
of the Wolf	Magic and Rare	Life	11	20				Clubs, Hammers, Helms, Maces, Rings	34	26
of the Tiger	Magic and Rare	Life	21	30				Clubs, Hammers, Helms, Maces, Rings	51	43
of the Mammoth	Magic and Rare	Life	31	40				Clubs, Hammers, Helms, Maces, Rings	68	60
of the Leech	Magic and Rare	% Life Steal	4	5				Weapons	6	4
of the Locust	Magic and Rare	% Life Steal	6	7				Melee Weapons	20	15
of the Lamprey	Magic and Rare	% Life Steal	8	9				Melee Weapons	55	43
of the Leech	Magic and Rare	% Life Steal	3	4				Circlets, Rings	14	10
of the Locust	Magic and Rare	% Life Steal	5	6				Circlets, Rings	47	35
of the Lamprey	Magic and Rare	% Life Steal	7	8				Circlets, Rings	77	65
of the Leech	Magic and Rare	% Life Steal	3	3				Gloves	34	26
of the Bat	Magic and Rare	% Mana Steal	4	5				Weapons	7	4
of the Wraith	Magic and Rare	% Mana Steal	6	7				Melee Weapons	21	16
of the Vampire	Magic and Rare	% Mana Steal	8	9				Melee Weapons	56	48
of the Bat	Magic and Rare	% Mana Steal	3	4				Amulets, Circlets	15	11
of the Wraith	Magic and Rare	% Mana Steal	5	6				Amulets, Circlets	58	40
of the Vampire	Magic and Rare	% Mana Steal	7	8				Amulets, Circlets	78	66
of the Bat	Magic and Rare	% Mana Steal	3	3				Gloves	35	27
of Defiance	Magic and Rare	Poison Length Reduced by %	75	75				Amulets, Body Armor, Circlets, Shields	25	18
of Amelioration	Magic and Rare	Poison Length Reduced by %	50	50				Amulets, Body Armor, Circlets, Shields	18	13
of Remedy	Magic and Rare	Poison Length Reduced by %	25	25				Amulets, Armor, Circlets, Rings	7	5
of Simplicity	Magic and Rare	Requirements -%	-30	-30				Body Armor, Shields, Weapons	25	18
of Ease	Magic and Rare	Requirements -%	-20	-20				Body Armor, Shields, Weapons	15	11
of Strength	Magic and Rare	Strength	1	2				Amulets, Belts, Circlets, Clubs, Hammers	1	1
of Might	Magic and Rare	Strength	3	5				Amulets, Belts, Circlets, Clubs, Hammers	10	8
of the Ox	Magic and Rare	Strength	6	9				Amulets, Belts, Circlets, Clubs, Hammers	26	19
of the Giant	Magic and Rare	Strength	10	15				Amulets, Belts, Circlets, Clubs, Hammers	42	34
of the Titan	Magic and Rare	Strength	16	20				Amulets, Belts, Circlets, Clubs, Hammers	58	50
of Atlas	Magic Only	Strength	21	30				Amulets, Belts, Circlets, Clubs, Hammers	71	63
of Strength	Magic and Rare	Strength	1	2				Body Armor, Maces, Rings, Scepters	5	3
of Might	Magic and Rare	Strength	3	5				Body Armor, Maces, Rings, Scepters	21	15
of the Ox	Magic and Rare	Strength	6	9				Body Armor, Maces, Rings, Scepters	38	30
of the Giant	Magic and Rare	Strength	10	15				Body Armor, Maces, Rings, Scepters	55	47
of the Titan	Magic Only	Strength	16	20				Body Armor, Maces, Rings, Scepters	74	66
of Strength	Magic and Rare	Strength	1	2				Gloves, Melee Weapons, Shields	12	8
of Might	Magic and Rare	Strength	3	5				Gloves, Melee Weapons, Shields	33	25
of the Ox	Magic and Rare	Strength	6	9				Gloves, Melee Weapons, Shields	45	37
of the Giant	Magic Only	Strength	10	15				Gloves, Melee Weapons	59	51
of Pacing	Magic and Rare	Fast Run/Walk	10	10				Boots, Circlets	2	1

of Haste	Magic and Rare	Faster Run/Walk	20	20				Boots, Circlets	22	16
of Speed	Magic and Rare	Fastest Run/Walk	30	30				Boots, Circlets	37	29
of Transportation	Magic Only	Fastest Run/Walk	30	30	stamdrain	80	90	Boots	65	57
of Acceleration	Magic Only	Fastest Run/Walk	40	40				Boots	51	43
of Self-Repair	Magic and Rare	Repair Durability	3					Armor, Weapons	3	1
of Restoration	Magic and Rare	Repair Durability	5					Armor, Weapons	20	12
of Ages	Magic Only	Indestructible						Armor, Weapons	50	42
of Replenishing	Magic and Rare	Replenish Quantity	2					Throwing Weapons	5	3
of Propogation	Magic and Rare	Replenish Quantity	4					Throwing Weapons	24	18
of the Centaur	Magic Only	Life/Level	4					Amulets, BarHelms, Body Armor, DruPelts	20	1
of Memory	Magic Only	Mana/Level	4					Amulets, Circlets, DruPelts	20	1
of the Elephant	Magic Only	Life/Level	2		Mana/Level	2		Circlets, DruPelts	37	7

PROCING SPELLS/SKILLS

	Spawns	Bonus	Min	Max	Bonus 2	Max	Min	Available On	Level	Level Req
of Firebolts	Magic and Rare	10% Chance To Cast Level 8 On Hit	10	8	8			Weapons	16	12
of Firebolts	Magic and Rare	5% Chance To Cast Level 3 On Attack	5	3	3			Weapons	6	4
of Firebolts	Magic and Rare	10% Chance To Cast Level 4 On Attack	10	4	4			Weapons	20	1
of Charged Bolt	Magic and Rare	10% Chance To Cast Level 3 When Struck	10	3				Amulets, Armor, Rings	6	4
of Charged Bolt	Magic and Rare	12% Chance To Cast Level 4 When Struck	12	4				Amulets, Armor, Rings	16	12
of Charged Bolt	Magic and Rare	14% Chance To Cast Level 5 When Struck	14	5				Amulets, Armor, Rings	26	19
of Icebolt	Magic and Rare	5% Chance To Cast Level 3 On Attack	5	3				Weapons	6	4
of Frost Shield	Magic and Rare	5% Chance To Cast Level 3 When Struck	5	3				Amulets, Armor	12	9
of Nova	Magic and Rare	10% Chance To Cast Level 3 On Hit	10	3				Weapons	18	13
of Nova	Magic and Rare	12% Chance To Cast Level 4 On Hit	12	4				Weapons	28	21
of Nova Shield	Magic and Rare	10% Chance To Cast Level 3 When Struck	10	3				Armor, Rings	18	13
of Nova Shield	Magic and Rare	12% Chance To Cast Level 4 When Struck	12	4				Armor, Rings	28	21
of Nova Shield	Magic and Rare	14% Chance To Cast Level 5 When Struck	14	5				Armor, Rings	38	28
of Lighting	Magic and Rare	5% Chance To Cast Level 3 On Attack	5	3				Weapons	18	13
of Chain Lightning	Magic and Rare	5% Chance To Cast Level 3 On Attack	5	3				Amulets, Rings, Weapons	25	18
of Chain Lightning	Magic and Rare	8% Chance To Cast Level 3 On Attack	8	3				Amulets, Rings, Weapons	35	26
of Chain Lightning	Magic and Rare	8% Chance TO Cast Level 5 On Attack	8	5				Amulets, Rings, Weapons	45	33
of Hydra Shield	Magic and Rare	10% Chance To Cast Level 3 On Hit	10	3				Amulets	40	30
of Amplify Damage	Magic and Rare	5% Chance To Cast Level 1 On Hit						Weapons	3	1

continues on next page

CHARGED SKILL SPELLS/SKILLS

	Spawns	Bonus	Min	Max	Bonus 2	Max	Min	Available On	Level	Level Req
of Magic Arrow	Magic and Rare	Charged Skill	-30	-10				AmaBow, Bows, Crossbows	12	11
of Fire Arrow	Magic and Rare	Charged Skill	-20	-6				Gloves	40	32
of Inner Sight	Magic and Rare	Charged Skill	-30	-6				Amulets, AmaBows, AmaSpears, AmaJavelins, Circlets	18	14
of Inner Sight	Magic and Rare	Charged Skill	-20	-4				Gloves	50	42
of Cold Arrow	Magic and Rare	Charged Skill	-30	-8				AmaBows, Bows, Crossbows	15	16
of Cold Arrow	Magic and Rare	Charged Skill	-20	-5				Gloves	47	39
of Multiple Shot	Magic and Rare	Charged Skill	-30	-8				AmaBows, Bows, Crossbows	18	19
of Multiple Shot	Magic and Rare	Charged Skill	-20	-4				Gloves	63	55
of Power Strike	Magic and Rare	Charged Skill	-60	-6				AmaSpears, Spears	12	13
of Power Strike	Magic and Rare	Charged Skill	-20	-4				Gloves	55	47
of Exploding Arrow	Magic and Rare	Charged Skill	-30	-6				AmaBows, Bows, Crossbows	30	26
of Exploding Arrow	Magic and Rare	Charged Skill	-20	-4				Gloves	69	61
of Ice Arrow	Magic and Rare	Charged Skill	-30	-5				AmaBows, Bows, Crossbows	36	28
of Ice Arrow	Magic and Rare	Charged Skill	-20	-3				Gloves	72	64
of Charged Strike	Magic and Rare	Charged Skill	-60	-5				AmaSpears, Spears	33	25
of Charged Strike	Magic and Rare	Charged Skill	-20	-3				Gloves	68	60
of Freezing Arrow	Magic and Rare	Charged Skill	-30	-4				AmaBows, Bows, Crossbows	50	42
of Freezing Arrow	Magic and Rare	Charged Skill	-20	-2				Gloves	94	86
of Lightning Strike	Magic and Rare	Charged Skill	-60	-4				AmaSpears, Spears	47	39
of Lightning Strike	Magic and Rare	Charged Skill	-20	-2				Gloves	90	82
of Fire Bolt	Magic and Rare	Charged Skill	-30	-10				Orbs, Staves	7	7
of Fire Bolt	Magic and Rare	Charged Skill	-20	-6				Circlets, Rings, Swords	14	14
of Charged Bolt	Magic and Rare	Charged Skill	-30	-10				Orbs, Staves	7	7
of Charged Bolt	Magic and Rare	Charged Skill	-20	-6				Circlets, Hammers, Maces, Rings, Scepters	14	14
of Ice Bolt	Magic and Rare	Charged Skill	-30	-10				Orbs, Staves	7	7
of Ice Bolt	Magic and Rare	Charged Skill	-20	-6				Knives	14	14
of Telekinesis	Magic and Rare	Charged Skill	-30	-8				Orbs, Staves	12	12
of Telekinesis	Magic and Rare	Charged Skill	-20	-5				Circlets, Hammers, Maces, Rings, Scepters	24	24
of Frost Nova	Magic and Rare	Charged Skill	-30	-8				Orbs, Staves	12	12
of Frost Nova	Magic and Rare	Charged Skill	-20	-5				Amulets, Circlets, Knives	24	24
of Ice Blast	Magic and Rare	Charged Skill	-30	-8				Orbs, Staves	12	12
of Ice Blast	Magic and Rare	Charged Skill	-20	-5				Circlets, Hammers, Maces, Rings, Scepters	24	24
of Fire Ball	Magic and Rare	Charged Skill	-30	-7				Orbs, Staves	18	18
of Fire Ball	Magic and Rare	Charged Skill	-20	-4				Spears, Wands	36	36
of Nova	Magic and Rare	Charged Skill	-30	-7				Orbs, Staves	18	18
of Nova	Magic and Rare	Charged Skill	-20	-4				Shields	36	36
of Lightning	Magic and Rare	Charged Skill	-30	-7				Orbs, Staves	18	18
of Lightning	Magic and Rare	Charged Skill	-20	-4				Axes, Hammers	36	36
of Enchantment	Magic and Rare	Charged Skill	-20	-3				Orbs, Staves	24	24
of Enchantment	Magic and Rare	Charged Skill	-10	-1				Melee Weapons	48	48
of Chain Lightning	Magic and Rare	Charged Skill	-30	-6				Orbs, Staves	24	24

of Chain Lightning	Magic and Rare	Charged Skill	-20	-3				Spears	48	48
of Teleportation	Magic and Rare	Charged Skill	-30	-6				Orbs, Staves	24	24
of Teleportation	Magic and Rare	Charged Skill	-20	-3				Amulets, Circlets	48	48
of Glacial Spike	Magic and Rare	Charged Skill	-30	-6				Orbs, Staves	24	24
of Glacial Spike	Magic and Rare	Charged Skill	-20	-3				Knives	48	48
of Meteor	Magic and Rare	Charged Skill	-30	-5				Orbs, Staves	30	30
of Meteor	Magic and Rare	Charged Skill	-20	-2				Clubs, Knives	60	60
of Blizzard	Magic and Rare	Charged Skill	-30	-5				Orbs, Staves	30	30
of Blizzard	Magic and Rare	Charged Skill	-20	-2				Knives	60	60
of Frozen Orb	Magic and Rare	Charged Skill	-30	-3				Orbs, Staves	36	36
of Frozen Orb	Magic and Rare	Charged Skill	-20	-1				Knives	72	72
of Dim Vision	Magic and Rare	Charged Skill	-60	-8				Head, Knives, Wands	12	12
of Dim Vision	Magic and Rare	Charged Skill	-20	-5				Circlets, Rings	24	24
of Weaken	Magic and Rare	Charged Skill	-60	-8				Head, Knives, Wands	12	12
of Weaken	Magic and Rare	Charged Skill	-20	-5				Gloves	24	24
of Poison Dagger	Magic and Rare	Charged Skill	-60	-8				Head, Knives	12	12
of Poison Dagger	Magic and Rare	Charged Skill	-20	-5				Circlets, Gloves, Rings	24	24
of Iron Maiden	Magic and Rare	Charged Skill	-60	-7				Head, Knives, Wands	18	18
of Iron Maiden	Magic and Rare	Charged Skill	-20	-4				Shields	36	36
of Terror	Magic and Rare	Charged Skill	-60	-7				Head, Knives, Wands	18	18
of Terror	Magic and Rare	Charged Skill	-20	-4				Shields	36	36
of Confusion	Magic and Rare	Charged Skill	-60	-6				Head, Knives, Wands	24	24
of Confusion	Magic and Rare	Charged Skill	-20	-3				Circlets, Rings	48	48
of Life Tap	Magic and Rare	Charged Skill	-60	-6				Head, Knives, Wands	24	24
of Life Tap	Magic and Rare	Charged Skill	-20	-3				Axes	48	48
of Bone Spear	Magic and Rare	Charged Skill	-60	-6				Head, Knives, Wands	24	24
of Bone Spear	Magic and Rare	Charged Skill	-20	-3				Spears	48	48
of Attract	Magic and Rare	Charged Skill	-60	-5				Head, Knives, Wands	30	30
of Attract	Magic and Rare	Charged Skill	-20	-2				Amults, Circlets, Rings	60	60
of Lower Resistance	Magic and Rare	Charged Skill	-60	-3				Head, Knives, Wands	36	36
of Lower Resistance	Magic and Rare	Charged Skill	-20	-1				Staves	72	72
of Poison Nova	Magic and Rare	Charged Skill	-60	-3				Head, Knives, Wands	36	36
of Poison Nova	Magic and Rare	Charged Skill	-20	-1				Gloves	72	72
of Bone Spirit	Magic and Rare	Charged Skill	-60	-3				Head, Knives, Wands	36	36
of Bone Spirit	Magic and Rare	Charged Skill	-20	-1				Amulets, Circlets	72	72
of Sacrifice	Magic and Rare	Charged Skill	-30	-10				PalShield, Scepters	7	7
of Sacrifice	Magic and Rare	Charged Skill	-20	-6				Melee Weapons	14	14
of Holy Bolt	Magic and Rare	Charged Skill	-30	-8				PalShield, Scepters	12	12
of Holy Bolt	Magic and Rare	Charged Skill	-20	-5				Amulets, Circlets	24	24
of Zeal	Magic and Rare	Charged Skill	-30	-7				PalShield, Scepters	18	18
of Zeal	Magic and Rare	Charged Skill	-20	-4				Melee Weapons	36	36
of Vengeance	Magic and Rare	Charged Skill	-30	-6				PalShield, Scepters	24	24
of Vengeance	Magic and Rare	Charged Skill	-20	-3				Axes, Swords	48	48

continues on next page

MAGIC ITEMS SUFFIXES (CONTINUED)

	Spawns	Bonus	Min	Max	Bonus 2	Max	Min	Available On	Level	Level Req
of Blessed Hammer	Magic and Rare	Charged Skill	-30	-6				PalShield, Scepters	24	24
of Blessed Hammer	Magic and Rare	Charged Skill	-20	-3				Hammers	48	48
of Bashing	Magic and Rare	Charged Skill	-60	-10				BarHelm	7	7
of Stun	Magic and Rare	Charged Skill	-60	-7				BarHelm	18	18
of Concentration	Magic and Rare	Charged Skill	-60	-6				BarHelm	24	24
of Grim Ward	Magic and Rare	Charged Skill	-60	-5				BarHelm	30	30
of Firestorm	Magic and Rare	Charged Skill	-30	-10				Clubs	7	7
of Firestorm	Magic and Rare	Charged Skill	-20	-6				Staves	14	14
of Fissure	Magic and Rare	Charged Skill	-30	-7				Clubs	18	18
of Fissure	Magic and Rare	Charged Skill	-20	-4				Staves	36	36
of Twister	Magic and Rare	Charged Skill	-30	-6				Clubs	24	24
of Twister	Magic and Rare	Charged Skill	-20	-3				Amulets, Circlets	48	48
of Volcano	Magic and Rare	Charged Skill	-30	-6				Clubs	30	30
of Volcano	Magic and Rare	Charged Skill	-20	-3				Hammers	60	60
of Tornado	Magic and Rare	Charged Skill	-30	-5				Clubs	30	30
of Tornado	Magic and Rare	Charged Skill	-20	-2				Amulets, Circlets	60	60

NECROMANCER SKILLS

SUMMONING SPELLS

RAISE SKELETON - REQUIRED LEVEL 1

Raise a skeleton from monster corpse to fight for you.

Level	1	2	3	4	5	6	7	8	9	10	11	12	13	14	15	16	17	18	19	20
Life	21	21	21	21	21	21	21	21	21	21	21	21	21	21	21	21	21	21	21	21
Damage	1-2	1-2	1-2	1-2	1-2	1-2	1-2	1-2	1-2	1-2	1-2	1-2	1-2	1-2	1-2	1-2	1-2	1-2	1-2	1-2
Number of Skeletons																				
	1	2	3	4	5	6	7	8	9	10	11	12	13	14	15	16	17	18	19	20
Mana Cost	6	7	8	9	10	11	12	13	14	15	16	17	18	19	20	21	22	23	24	25

SKELETON MASTERY - REQUIRED LEVEL 1

Passive - Raise the life and damage of skeletons and revived creatures.

Level	1	2	3	4	5	6	7	8	9	10	11	12	13	14	15	16	17	18	19	20
Skeleton Life (+pts)																				
	7	14	21	28	35	42	49	56	63	70	77	84	91	98	105	112	119	126	133	140
Skeleton Damage (+pts)																				
	2	4	6	8	10	12	14	16	18	20	22	24	26	28	30	32	34	36	38	40

Monster Life +%																				
	7	14	21	28	35	42	49	56	63	70	77	84	91	98	105	112	119	126	133	140
Monster Damage +%																				
	2	4	6	8	10	12	14	16	18	20	22	24	26	28	30	32	34	36	38	40

CLAY GOLEM - REQUIRED LEVEL 6

Raise a clay golem to fight for you.

Level	1	2	3	4	5	6	7	8	9	10	11	12	13	14	15	16	17	18	19	20
Golem Life	100	135	170	205	240	275	310	345	380	415	450	485	520	555	590	625	660	695	730	765
Golem Damage																				
	2-5	2-6	3-8	4-10	4-12	5-13	6-15	6-17	7-19	8-20	9-22	9-24	10-26	11-27	11-29	12-31	13-33	13-34	14-36	15-38
Mana Cost	15	18	21	24	27	30	33	36	39	42	45	48	51	54	57	60	63	66	69	72

GOLEM MASTERY - REQUIRED 12

Enhances the speed and life of all your golems.

Level	1	2	3	4	5	6	7	8	9	10	11	12	13	14	15	16	17	18	19	20
Life +%	20	40	60	80	100	120	140	160	180	200	220	240	260	280	300	320	340	360	380	400
Walk/Run Speed +%																				
	6	10	14	17	20	22	23	24	26	27	28	29	30	30	31	32	32	32	33	33

RAISE SKELETAL MAGE - REQUIRED LEVEL 12

Raise a skeletal mage from enemy corpse to fight for you.

Level	1	2	3	4	5	6	7	8	9	10	11	12	13	14	15	16	17	18	19	20
Life	61	61	61	61	61	61	61	61	61	61	61	61	61	61	61	61	61	61	61	61
Number of Skeletal Mages																				
	1	2	3	4	5	6	7	8	9	10	11	12	13	14	15	16	17	18	19	20
Mana Cost	8	9	10	11	12	13	14	15	16	17	18	19	20	21	22	23	24	25	26	27

BLOOD GOLEM - REQUIRED LEVEL 18

A golem that shares with you the life it steals and the damage it receives.

Level	1	2	3	4	5	6	7	8	9	10	11	12	13	14	15	16	17	18	19	20
Life	201	201	201	201	201	201	201	201	201	201	201	201	201	201	201	201	201	201	201	201
Convert X% Damage to Life																				
	86	95	102	108	112	116	119	121	124	126	128	129	131	132	133	134	135	136	137	138
Blood Golem Damage																				
	6-16	8-21	10-27	12-32	14-38	15-44	18-49	20-55	22-60	24-66	27-72	29-77	31-83	33-88	35-94	37-100	39-105	41-111	43-116	45-122
Mana Cost	25	29	33	37	41	45	49	53	57	61	65	69	73	77	81	85	89	93	97	101

IRON GOLEM - REQUIRED LEVEL 24

A metal golem that takes on the properties of the metal item from which you have raised it.

Level	1	2	3	4	5	6	7	8	9	10	11	12	13	14	15	16	17	18	19	20
Life	306	306	306	306	306	306	306	306	306	306	306	306	306	306	306	306	306	306	306	306
Golem Damage																				
	7-19	7-19	7-19	7-19	7-19	7-19	7-19	7-19	7-19	7-19	7-19	7-19	7-19	7-19	7-19	7-19	7-19	7-19	7-19	7-19

continues on next page

Thorns Damage (%)																				
	N/A	150	165	180	195	210	225	240	255	270	285	300	315	330	345	360	375	390	405	420
Mana Cost	35	35	35	35	35	35	35	35	35	35	35	35	35	35	35	35	35	35	35	35

SUMMON RESIST - REQUIRED LEVEL 24

Passive - Raises the resistance of your summoned monsters/minions.

Level	1	2	3	4	5	6	7	8	9	10	11	12	13	14	15	16	17	18	19	20
Resistance Raised (%)																				
	28	34	39	44	47	50	52	54	56	57	59	60	61	62	62	64	64	65	65	66

FIRE GOLEM - REQUIRED LEVEL 30

Fire golem that converts the damage it receives from fire into life.

Level	1	2	3	4	5	6	7	8	9	10	11	12	13	14	15	16	17	18	19	20
Life	313	313	313	313	313	313	313	313	313	313	313	313	313	313	313	313	313	313	313	313
Absorbs X% Fire Damage																				
	36	45	52	58	62	66	69	71	74	76	78	79	81	82	83	85	85	86	87	88
Fire Golem Damage																				
	10-27	12-33	15-40	17-47	20-54	22-60	25-67	27-74	30-81	32-87	35-94	37-101	40-108	42-114	45-121	47-128	50-135	52-141	55-148	57-155
Mana Cost	50	60	70	80	90	100	110	120	130	140	150	160	170	180	190	200	210	220	230	240

REVIVE - REQUIRED LEVEL 30

Revives a slain monster to fight for you.

Level	1	2	3	4	5	6	7	8	9	10	11	12	13	14	15	16	17	18	19	20
Duration (seconds)																				
	180	180	180	180	180	180	180	180	180	180	180	180	180	180	180	180	180	180	180	180
Life (% of the monsters' original amount of life)																				
	200	200	200	200	200	200	200	200	200	200	200	200	200	200	200	200	200	200	200	200
Number of Revived																				
	1	2	3	4	5	6	7	8	9	10	11	12	13	14	15	16	17	18	19	20
Mana Cost	45	45	45	45	45	45	45	45	45	45	45	45	45	45	45	45	45	45	45	45

CURSES

AMPLIFY DAMAGE - REQUIRED LEVEL 1

Curse - Amplify damage taken by enemies; Damge +100%.

Level	1	2	3	4	5	6	7	8	9	10	11	12	13	14	15	16	17	18	19	20
Radius in yards																				
	2	2.6	3.3	4	4.6	5.3	6	6.6	7.3	8	8.6	9.3	10	10.6	11.3	12	12.6	13.3	14	14.6
Duration in seconds																				
	8	11	14	17	20	23	26	29	32	35	38	41	44	47	50	53	56	59	62	65
Mana Cost	4	4	4	4	4	4	4	4	4	4	4	4	4	4	4	4	4	4	4	4

DIM VISION - REQUIRED LEVEL 6

Curse - Temporarily blinds targets.

Level	1	2	3	4	5	6	7	8	9	10	11	12	13	14	15	16	17	18	19	20

Radius in yards																				
	2.6	3.3	4	4.6	5.3	6	6.6	7.3	8	8.6	9.3	10	10.6	11.3	12	12.6	13.3	14	14.6	15.3
Duration in seconds																				
	7	9	11	13	15	17	19	21	23	25	27	29	31	33	35	37	39	41	43	45
Mana Cost	9	9	9	9	9	9	9	9	9	9	9	9	9	9	9	9	9	9	9	9

WEAKEN - REQUIRED LEVEL 6

Curse - Temporarily lowers damge done by target; Damage reduced -33%.

Level	1	2	3	4	5	6	7	8	9	10	11	12	13	14	15	16	17	18	19	20
Radius in yards																				
	6	6.6	7.3	8	8.6	9.3	10	10.6	11.3	12	12.6	13.3	14	14.6	15.3	16	16.6	17.3	18	18.6
Duration in seconds																				
	14	16.4	18.8	21.2	23.6	[illegible]	28.4	30.8	33.2	35.6	38	40.4	42.8	45.2	47.6	50	52.4	54.8	57.2	59.6
Mana Cost	4	4	4	4	4	4	4	4	4	4	4	4	4	4	4	4	4	4	4	4

IRON MAIDEN - REQUIRED LEVEL 12

Curse - Enemies Damage themselves.

Level	1	2	3	4	5	6	7	8	9	10	11	12	13	14	15	16	17	18	19	20
% Damage returned																				
	200	225	250	275	300	325	350	375	400	425	450	475	500	525	550	575	600	625	650	675
Radius in yards																				
	4.6	4.6	4.6	4.6	4.6	4.6	4.6	4.6	4.6	4.6	4.6	4.6	4.6	4.6	4.6	4.6	4.6	4.6	4.6	4.6
Duration in seconds																				
	12	14.4	16.8	19.2	21.6	24	26.4	28.8	31.2	33.6	36	38.4	40.8	43.2	45.6	48	50.4	52.8	55.2	57.6
Mana Cost	5	5	5	5	5	5	5	5	5	5	5	5	5	5	5	5	5	5	5	5

TERROR - REQUIRED LEVEL 12

Curse - Causes enemies to flee.

Level	1	2	3	4	5	6	7	8	9	10	11	12	13	14	15	16	17	18	19	20
Radius in yards																				
	2.6	2.6	2.6	2.6	2.6	2.6	2.6	2.6	2.6	2.6	2.6	2.6	2.6	2.6	2.6	2.6	2.6	2.6	2.6	2.6
Duration in seconds																				
	8	9	10	11	12	13	14	15	16	17	18	19	20	21	22	23	24	25	26	27
Mana Cost	7	7	7	7	7	7	7	7	7	7	7	7	7	7	7	7	7	7	7	7

CONFUSE - REQUIRED LEVEL 18

Curse - Causes monsters to attack random targets.

Level	1	2	3	4	5	6	7	8	9	10	11	12	13	14	15	16	17	18	19	20
Radius in yards																				
	4	4.6	5.3	6	6.6	7.3	8	8.6	9.3	10	10.6	11.3	12	12.6	13.3	14	14.6	15.3	16	16.6
Duration in seconds																				
	10	12	14	16	18	20	22	24	26	28	30	32	34	36	38	40	42	44	46	48
Mana Cost	13	13	13	13	13	13	13	13	13	13	13	13	13	13	13	13	13	13	13	13

continues on next page

LIFE TAP - REQUIRED LEVEL 18

Curse - Damaging cursed monster give the attacker life; Heals 50% damge inflicted on monster.

Level	1	2	3	4	5	6	7	8	9	10	11	12	13	14	15	16	17	18	19	20
Radius in yards																				
	2.6	3.3	4	4.6	5.3	6	6.6	7.3	8	8.6	9.3	10	10.6	11.3	12	12.6	13.3	14	14.6	15.3
Duration in seconds																				
	16	18.4	20.8	23.2	25.6	28	30.4	32.8	35.2	37.6	40	42.4	44.8	47.2	49.6	52	54.4	56.8	59.2	61.6
Mana Cost	9	9	9	9	9	9	9	9	9	9	9	9	9	9	9	9	9	9	9	9

ATTRACT - REQUIRED LEVEL 24

Curse - Causes the monster to be targeted by nearby monsters.

Level	1	2	3	4	5	6	7	8	9	10	11	12	13	14	15	16	17	18	19	20
Radius in yards																				
	6	6	6	6	6	6	6	6	6	6	6	6	6	6	6	6	6	6	6	6
Duration in seconds																				
	12	15.6	19.2	22.8	26.4	30	33.6	37.2	40.8	44.4	48	51.6	55.2	58.8	62.4	66	69.6	73.2	76.8	80.4
Mana Cost	17	17	17	17	17	17	17	17	17	17	17	17	17	17	17	17	17	17	17	17

DECREPIFY - REQUIRED LEVEL 24

Curse - Greatly slows and weakens enemies.

Level	1	2	3	4	5	6	7	8	9	10	11	12	13	14	15	16	17	18	19	20
Radius in yards																				
	4	4	4	4	4	4	4	4	4	4	4	4	4	4	4	4	4	4	4	4
Duration in seconds																				
	4	4.6	5.2	5.8	6.4	7	7.6	8.2	8.8	9.4	10	10.6	11.2	11.8	12.4	13	13.6	14.2	14.8	15.4
Mana Cost	11	11	11	11	11	11	11	11	11	11	11	11	11	11	11	11	11	11	11	11

LOWER RESIST - REQUIRED LEVEL 24

Curse - Lowers enemies resistances.

Level	1	2	3	4	5	6	7	8	9	10	11	12	13	14	15	16	17	18	19	20
Radius in yards																				
	4.6	5.3	6	6.6	7.3	8	8.6	9.3	10	10.6	11.3	12	12.6	13.3	14	14.6	15.3	16	16.6	17.3
Duration in seconds																				
	20	22	24	26	28	30	32	34	36	38	40	32	44	46	48	50	52	54	56	58
Mana Cost	22	22	22	22	22	22	22	22	22	22	22	22	22	22	22	22	22	22	22	22
Resist all reduced by %																				
	31	37	41	44	47	49	51	52	54	55	56	57	58	59	60	61	61	61	62	62

BONE AND POISON SPELLS

TEETH - REQUIRED LEVEL 1

Fires a barrage of summoned barbed teeth.

Level	1	2	3	4	5	6	7	8	9	10	11	12	13	14	15	16	17	18	19	20
Mana	3	3.5	4	4.5	5	5.5	6	6.5	7	7.5	8	8.5	9	9.5	10	10.5	11	11.5	12	12

Magic Damage	2-4	3-5	4-6	5-7	6-8	7-9	8-10	9-11	10-12	11-13	12-14	13-15	14-16	15-17	16-18	17-19	18-20	19-21	20-22	21-23
# of teeth	2	3	4	5	6	7	8	9	10	11	12	13	14	15	16	17	18	19	20	21

BONE ARMOR - REQUIRED LEVEL 1

Creates an orbiting shield of bone that absorbs mele damage.

Level	1	2	3	4	5	6	7	8	9	10	11	12	13	14	15	16	17	18	19	20
Damage absorbed	20	30	40	50	60	70	80	90	100	110	120	130	140	150	160	170	180	190	200	210
Mana	11	12	13	14	15	16	17	18	19	20	21	22	23	24	25	26	27	28	29	30

CORPSE EXPLOSION - REQUIRED LEVEL 6

Cast on the corpse of a slain monster, it explodes, damaging nearby enemies.

Damage 60-100% of corpse life

Level	1	2	3	4	5	6	7	8	9	10	11	12	13	14	15	16	17	18	19	20
Range in yards	2.6	3	3.3	3.6	4	4.3	4.6	5	5.3	5.6	6	6.3	6.6	7	7.3	7.6	8	8.3	8.6	9
Mana	15	16	17	18	19	20	21	22	23	24	25	26	27	28	29	30	31	32	33	34

POISON DAGGER - REQUIRED LEVEL 6

Adds poison to your dagger attacks.

Level	1	2	3	4	5	6	7	8	9	10	11	12	13	14	15	16	17	18	19	20
Mana	3	3.2	3.5	3.7	4	4.2	4.5	4.7	5	5.2	5.5	5.7	6	6.2	6.5	6.7	7	7.2	7.5	7.7
Bonus attack %	15	25	35	45	55	65	75	85	95	105	115	125	135	145	155	165	175	185	195	205
Poison Damage/2 sec	7-15	10-19	14-23	18-27	22-31	26-35	30-39	34-42	40-48	46-54	51-60	57-66	63-72	69-78	75-83	81-89	89-97	96-105	104-113	112-121

BONE WALL - REQUIRED LEVEL 12

Creates an impassible barrier of bone and debris.

Level	1	2	3	4	5	6	7	8	9	10	11	12	13	14	15	16	17	18	19	20
Mana	17	17	17	17	17	17	17	17	17	17	17	17	17	17	17	17	17	17	17	17
Life	19	23	28	33	38	42	47	52	57	61	66	71	76	80	85	90	95	99	104	109
Duration in seconds	48	48	48	48	48	48	48	48	48	48	48	48	48	48	48	48	48	48	48	48

BONE SPEAR - REQUIRED LEVEL 18

Summons a deadly spike of bone to impale your enemies.

Level	1	2	3	4	5	6	7	8	9	10	11	12	13	14	15	16	17	18	19	20
Mana	7	7.2	7.5	7.7	8	8.2	8.5	8.7	9	9.2	9.5	9.7	10	10.2	10.5	10.7	11	11.2	11.5	11.7
Magic Damage	16-24	24-32	32-40	40-48	48-56	56-64	64-72	72-80	80-88	88-96	96-104	104-112	112-120	120-128	128-136	136-144	144-152	152-160	160-168	168-176

POISON EXPLOSION - REQUIRED LEVEL 18

Cast on the corpse of a slain monster, toxic gas is released that poisons nearby monsters.

Level	1	2	3	4	5	6	7	8	9	10	11	12	13	14	15	16	17	18	19	20
Mana	8	8	8	8	8	8	8	8	8	8	8	8	8	8	8	8	8	8	8	8

continues on next page

NECROMANCER SKILLS (CONTINUED)

Poison Damage/ 2 sec																				
	25-50	31-56	37-62	43-68	50-75	56-81	62-87	68-93	81-106	93-118	106-131	118-143	131-156	143-168	156-181	168-193	187-212	206-231	225-250	243-268

BONE PRISON - REQUIRED LEVEL 24

Creates a barrier of fossilized bone around your target.

Level	1	2	3	4	5	6	7	8	9	10	11	12	13	14	15	16	17	18	19	20
Mana	27	26	25	24	23	22	21	20	19	18	17	16	15	14	13	12	11	10	9	8
Life	19	23	28	33	38	42	47	52	57	61	66	71	76	80	85	90	95	99	104	109
Duration in seconds																				
	48	48	48	48	48	48	48	48	48	48	48	48	48	48	48	48	48	48	48	48

BONE SPIRIT - REQUIRED LEVEL 30

Releases a spirit of the restless undead that tracks its target or finds one of its own.

Level	1	2	3	4	5	6	7	8	9	10	11	12	13	14	15	16	17	18	19	20
Mana	12	12	13	13	14	14	15	15	16	16	17	17	18	18	19	19	20	20	21	21
Magic Damage																				
	20-30	36-46	52-62	68-78	84-94	100-110	116-126	132-142	149-159	166-176	183-193	200-210	217-227	234-244	251-261	268-278	286-296	304-314	322-332	340-350

POISON NOVA - REQUIRED LEVEL 30

Emits an expanding ring of concentrated poison.

Level	1	2	3	4	5	6	7	8	9	10	11	12	13	14	15	16	17	18	19	20
Mana	20	20	20	20	20	20	20	20	20	20	20	20	20	20	20	20	20	20	20	20
Poison Damage/2 sec																				
	43-78	56-90	68-103	81-115	93-128	106-140	118-153	131-165	146-181	162-196	178-212	193-228	209-243	225-259	240-275	256-290	281-315	306-340	331-365	356-390

AMAZON SKILLS

JAVELIN & SPEAR

JAB - REQUIRED LEVEL 1

Rapid attacks with a thrusting weapon.

Level	1	2	3	4	5	6	7	8	9	10	11	12	13	14	15	16	17	18	19	20
Mana Cost	2	2.2	2.5	2.7	3	3.2	3.5	3.7	4	4.2	4.5	4.7	5	5.2	5.5	5.7	6	6.2	6.5	6.7
Attack Rating																				
	+10%	+15%	+20%	+25%	+30%	+35%	+40%	+45%	+50%	+55%	+60%	+65%	+70%	+75%	+80%	+85%	+90%	+95%	+100%	+105%
Damage per Target																				
	-15%	-12%	-9%	-6%	-3%	-0%	+3%	+6%	+9%	+12%	+15%	+18%	+21%	+24%	+27%	+30%	+33%	+36%	+39%	42%

POWER STRIKE - REQUIRED LEVEL 6

Adds Lightning damage to attacks with Spear or Javelin class weapons.

Level	1	2	3	4	5	6	7	8	9	10	11	12	13	14	15	16	17	18	19	20
Mana Cost	2	2.2	2.5	2.7	3	3.2	3.5	3.7	4	4.2	4.5	4.7	5	5.2	5.5	5.7	6	6.2	6.5	6.7
Attack Rating																				
	+10%	+15%	+20%	+25%	+30%	+35%	+40%	+45%	+50%	+55%	+60%	+65%	+70%	+75%	+80%	+85%	+90%	+95%	+100%	+105%

Lightning Damage

1-16	7-22	13-28	19-34	25-40	31-46	37-52	43-58	51-66	59-74	67-82	75-90	83-98	91-106	99-114	107-122	117-132	127-142	137-152	147-162

POISON JAVELIN - REQUIRED LEVEL 6

Magically enhances your javelin to leave a trail of poison clouds.

Level	1	2	3	4	5	6	7	8	9	10	11	12	13	14	15	16	17	18	19	20
Mana Cost	4	4.2	4.5	4.7	5	5.2	5.5	5.7	6	6.2	6.5	6.7	7	7.2	7.5	7.7	8	8.2	8.5	8.7
Poison Damage over 3 seconds																				
	9-14	14-18	18-23	23-28	28-32	32-37	37-42	42-46	46-51	51-56	56-60	60-65	65-70	70-75	75-79	79-84	84-89	89-93	93-98	98-103

IMPALE - REQUIRED LEVEL 12

Increases Attack Damage, but rapidly degrades the weapon.

Level	1	2	3	4	5	6	7	8	9	10	11	12	13	14	15	16	17	18	19	20
Mana Cost	3	3	3	3	3	3	3	3	3	3	3	3	3	3	3	3	3	3	3	3
Attack Rating																				
	+25%	+32%	+39%	+46%	+53%	+60%	+67%	+74%	+81%	+88%	+95%	+102%	+109%	+116%	+123%	+130%	+137%	+144%	+151%	+158%
Damage	+300%	+305%	+310%	+315%	+320%	+325%	+330%	+335%	+340%	+345%	+350%	+355%	+360%	+365%	+370%	+375%	+380%	+385%	+390%	+395%
Chance of losing durability																				
	46%	42%	40%	37%	35%	34%	33%	32%	31%	30%	29%	29%	28%	27%	27%	26%	26%	26%	26%	25%

LIGHTNING BOLT - REQUIRED LEVEL 12

Magically converts your Javelin into a lightning bolt.

Level	1	2	3	4	5	6	7	8	9	10	11	12	13	14	15	16	17	18	19	20
Mana Cost	6	6.2	6.5	6.7	7	7.2	7.5	7.7	8	8.2	8.5	8.7	9	9.2	9.5	9.7	10	10.2	10.5	10.7
Lightning Damage																				
	1-40	1-48	1-56	1-64	1-72	1-80	1-88	1-96	1-104	1-112	1-120	1-128	1-136	1-144	1-152	1-160	1-168	1-176	1-184	1-192

CHARGED STRIKE - REQUIRED LEVEL 18

Adds Lightning damage to attacks with spear or Javelin class weapons and released charged bolts.

Level	1	2	3	4	5	6	7	8	9	10	11	12	13	14	15	16	17	18	19	20
Mana Cost	4	4.2	4.5	4.7	5	5.2	5.5	5.7	6	6.2	6.5	6.7	7	7.2	7.5	7.7	8	8.2	8.5	8.7
Lightning Damage																				
	1-30	11-40	21-50	31-60	41-70	51-80	61-90	71-100	83-112	95-124	107-136	119-148	131-160	143-172	155-184	167-196	181-210	195-224	209-238	223-252

PLAGUE JAVELIN - REQUIRED LEVEL 18

Magically Enhances your Javelin to release expanding clouds of poison upon impact.

Level	1	2	3	4	5	6	7	8	9	10	11	12	13	14	15	16	17	18	19	20
Mana Cost	7	8	9	10	11	12	13	14	15	16	17	18	19	20	21	22	23	24	25	26
Poison Damage over three seconds																				
	23-37	30-44	37-51	44-58	51-65	58-72	65-79	72-86	84-98	96-110	107-121	119-133	131-145	142-157	154-168	166-180	185-199	203-217	222-236	241-255

FEND - REQUIRED LEVEL 24

Attacks all adjacent targets.

Level	1	2	3	4	5	6	7	8	9	10	11	12	13	14	15	16	17	18	19	20
Mana Cost	5	5	5	5	5	5	5	5	5	5	5	5	5	5	5	5	5	5	5	5
Attack +%	+40%	+50%	+60%	+70%	+80%	+90%	+100%	+110%	+120%	+130%	+140%	+150%	+160%	+170%	+180%	+190%	+200%	+210%	+220%	+230%
Damage	+70%	+80%	+90%	+100%	+110%	+120%	+130%	+140%	+150%	+160%	+170%	+180%	+190%	+200%	+210%	+220%	+230%	+240%	+250%	+260%

continues on next page

LIGHTNING STRIKE - REQUIRED LEVEL 30

Enchants a thrusting weapon with chain lightning.

Level	1	2	3	4	5	6	7	8	9	10	11	12	13	14	15	16	17	18	19	20
Mana Cost	9	9	9	9	9	9	9	9	9	9	9	9	9	9	9	9	9	9	9	9
Hits	2	3	4	5	6	7	8	9	10	11	12	13	14	15	16	17	18	19	20	21
Lightning Damage																				
	5-25	15-35	25-45	35-55	45-65	55-75	65-85	75-95	85-105	95-115	105-125	115-135	125-145	135-155	145-165	155-175	165-185	175-195	185-205	195-215

LIGHTNING FURY - REQUIRED LEVEL 30

Lightning bolt that splits on impact.

Level	1	2	3	4	5	6	7	8	9	10	11	12	13	14	15	16	17	18	19	20
Mana Cost	10	10.5	11	11.5	12	12	13	13	14	14	15	15	16	16	17	17	18	18	19	19
# of Bolts	2	3	4	5	6	7	8	9	10	11	12	13	14	15	16	17	18	19	20	21
Lightning Damage																				
	1-40	11-50	21-60	31-70	41-80	51-90	61-100	71-110	84-123	97-136	110-149	123-162	136-175	149-188	162-201	175-214	191-230	207-246	223-262	239-278

PASSIVE AND MAGIC SKILLS

INNER SIGHT - REQUIRED LEVEL 1

Illuminates nearby enemies, making them easier to hit for you and your party.

Level	1	2	3	4	5	6	7	8	9	10	11	12	13	14	15	16	17	18	19	20
Mana Cost	5	5	5	5	5	5	5	5	5	5	5	5	5	5	5	5	5	5	5	5
Duration in seconds																				
	8	12	16	20	24	28	32	36	40	44	48	52	56	60	64	68	72	76	80	84
Lowers enemy defense																				
	-46	-50	-54	-57	-60	-62	-63	-64	-66	-67	-68	-69	-70	-70	-71	-72	-72	-72	-73	-73
Radius	13.3 yrds	13.3 yrds	13.3 yrds	13.3 yrds	13.3 yrds	13.3 yrds	13.3 yrds	13.3 yrds	13.3 yrds	13.3 yrds	13.3 yrds	13.3 yrds	13.3 yrds	13.3 yrds	13.3 yrds	13.3 yrds	13.3 yrds	13.3 yrds	13.3 yrds	13.3 yrds

CRITICAL STRIKE - REQUIRED LEVEL 1

Passive-your attacks have a chance to do double damage.

Level	1	2	3	4	5	6	7	8	9	10	11	12	13	14	15	16	17	18	19	20
Chance to Critical																				
	16%	25%	32%	38%	42%	46%	49%	51%	54%	56%	58%	59%	61%	62%	63%	65%	65%	66%	67%	68%

DODGE - REQUIRED LEVEL 6

Passive-You have a chance to dodge melee attacks while attacking or standing still.

Level	1	2	3	4	5	6	7	8	9	10	11	12	13	14	15	16	17	18	19	20
Chance to Dodge																				
	18%	24%	29%	34%	37%	40%	42%	44%	46%	47%	49%	50%	51%	52%	52%	54%	54%	55%	55%	56%

SLOW MISSILES - REQUIRED LEVEL 12

Slow enemy ranged attacks to 33%.

Level	1	2	3	4	5	6	7	8	9	10	11	12	13	14	15	16	17	18	19	20
Mana Cost	5	5	5	5	5	5	5	5	5	5	5	5	5	5	5	5	5	5	5	5

Duration in seconds																				
	12	18	24	30	36	42	48	54	60	66	72	78	84	90	96	102	108	114	120	126
Radius	13.3 yrds	13.3 yrds	13.3 yrds	13.3 yrds	13.3 yrds	13.3 yrds	13.3 yrds	13.3 yrds	13.3 yrds	13.3 yrds	13.3 yrds	13.3 yrds	13.3 yrds	13.3 yrds	13.3 yrds	13.3 yrds	13.3 yrds	13.3 yrds	13.3 yrds	13.3 yrds

AVOID - REQUIRED LEVEL 12

Passive-You have a Chance to dodge ranged attacks while attacking or standing still.

Level	1	2	3	4	5	6	7	8	9	10	11	12	13	14	15	16	17	18	19	20
Chance to Avoid																				
	24%	31%	36%	41%	45%	48%	50%	52%	54%	55%	57%	58%	60%	61%	61%	63%	63%	64%	64%	65%

PENETRATE - REQUIRED LEVEL 18

Increases your Attack Rating.

Level	1	2	3	4	5	6	7	8	9	10	11	12	13	14	15	16	17	18	19	20
Bonus to Attack Rating																				
	+35%	+45%	+55%	+65%	+75%	+85%	+95%	+105%	+115%	+125%	+135%	+145%	+155%	+165%	+175%	+185%	+195%	+205%	+215%	+225%

DECOY - REQUIRED LEVEL 24

Creates a duplicate of yourself that draws fire from your enemies.

Level	1	2	3	4	5	6	7	8	9	10	11	12	13	14	15	16	17	18	19	20
Mana Cost	19	18	17	16	16	15	14	13	13	12	11.5	10.7	10	9.2	8.5	7.7	7	6.2	5.5	4.7
Duration in seconds																				
	10	15	20	25	30	35	40	45	50	55	60	65	70	75	80	85	90	95	100	105

EVADE - REQUIRED LEVEL 24

Passive-You have a chance to dodge a missile or melee attack while walking or running.

Level	1	2	3	4	5	6	7	8	9	10	11	12	13	14	15	16	17	18	19	20
Chance to Evade																				
	18%	24%	29%	34%	37%	40%	42%	44%	46%	47%	49%	50%	51%	52%	52%	54%	54%	55%	55%	56%

VALKYRIE - REQUIRED LEVEL 30

Summon a powerful Valkyrie ally.

Level	1	2	3	4	5	6	7	8	9	10	11	12	13	14	15	16	17	18	19	20
Mana Cost	25	29	33	37	41	45	49	53	57	61	56	69	73	77	81	85	89	93	97	101
Life	362	422	483	543	604	664	724	785	845	906	966	1026	1087	1147	1208	1268	1328	1389	1449	1510
Damage bonus																				
		+20%	+40%	+60%	+80%	+100%	+120%	+140%	+160%	+180%	+200%	+220%	+240%	+260%	+280%	+300%	+320%	+340%	+360%	+380%
Attack Rating bonus																				
		+5%	+10%	+15%	+20%	+25%	+30%	+35%	+40%	+45%	+50%	+55%	+60%	+65%	+70%	+75%	+80%	+85%	+90%	+95%
Defense Bonus																				
		+5%	+10%	+15%	+20%	+25%	+30%	+35%	+40%	+45%	+50%	+55%	+60%	+65%	+70%	+75%	+80%	+85%	+90%	+95%

PIERCE - REQUIRED LEVEL 30

Passive-Your missiles have a chance to pass through the enemies they hit.

Level	1	2	3	4	5	6	7	8	9	10	11	12	13	14	15	16	17	18	19	20
Chance to Pierce																				
	23%	34%	42%	49%	55%	59%	63%	65%	69%	71%	73%	75%	77%	79%	80%	82%	82%	83%	84%	85%

continues on next page

Bow and Crossbow Skills

Magic Arrow - Required Level 1

Creates a Magical Arrow that adds to damage.

Level	1	2	3	4	5	6	7	8	9	10	11	12	13	14	15	16	17	18	19	20
Mana Cost	1.5	1.3	1.2	1.1	1	.8	.7	.6	.5	.3	.2	.1	0	0	0	0	0	0	0	0
Damage Bonus																				
	0	+1	+2	+3	+4	+5	+6	+7	+8	+9	+10	+11	+12	+13	+14	+15	+16	+17	+18	+19

Fire Arrow - Required Level 1

Magically enhance your arrow or bolt with Fire; always hits.

Level	1	2	3	4	5	6	7	8	9	10	11	12	13	14	15	16	17	18	19	20
Mana Cost	3	3.2	3.5	3.7	4	4.2	4.5	4.7	5	5.2	5.5	5.7	6	6.2	6.5	6.7	7	7.2	7.5	7.7
Fire Damage																				
	1-4	3-6	5-8	7-10	9-12	11-14	13-16	15-18	17-20	19-22	21-24	23-26	25-28	27-30	29-32	31-34	33-36	35-38	37-40	39-42

Cold Arrow - Required Level 6

Magically enhances your arrow or bolt with cold damage and a slowing effect; Cold Arrows only do half or their regular damage; always hits.

Level	1	2	3	4	5	6	7	8	9	10	11	12	13	14	15	16	17	18	19	20
Mana Cost	3	3.2	3.5	3.7	4	4.2	4.5	4.7	5	5.2	5.5	5.7	6	6.2	6.5	6.7	7	7.2	7.5	7.7
Cold Length in seconds																				
	4	5.2	6.4	7.6	8.8	10	11.2	12.4	13.6	14.8	16	17.2	18.4	19.6	20.8	22	23.2	24.4	25.6	26.8
Cold Damage																				
	3	5	7	9	11	13	15	17	19	21	23	25	27	29	31	33	35	37	39	41

Multiple Shot - Required Level 6

Magically splits your arrow or bolt into many, Multiple shot does

Level	1	2	3	4	5	6	7	8	9	10	11	12	13	14	15	16	17	18	19	20
Mana Cost	4	5	6	7	8	9	10	11	12	13	14	15	16	17	18	19	20	21	22	23
Arrows	2	3	4	5	6	7	8	9	10	11	12	13	14	15	16	17	18	19	20	21

Exploding Arrow - Required Level 12

Enchants an arrow or bolt that explodes on contact, damaging nearby enemies; always hits.

Level	1	2	3	4	5	6	7	8	9	10	11	12	13	14	15	16	17	18	19	20
Mana Cost	5	5.5	6	6.5	7	7.5	8	8.5	9	9.5	10	10.5	11	11.5	12	12	13	13	14	14
Fire Damage																				
	2-4	7-9	12-14	17-19	22-24	27-29	32-34	37-39	42-44	47-49	52-54	57-59	62-64	67-69	72-74	77-79	82-84	87-89	92-94	97-99

Ice Arrow - Required Level 18

Magically enhances your Arrow or Bolt to freeze your enemies; always hits.

Level	1	2	3	4	5	6	7	8	9	10	11	12	13	14	15	16	17	18	19	20
Mana Cost	4	4.2	4.5	4.7	5	5.2	5.5	5.7	6	6.2	6.5	6.7	7	7.2	7.5	7.7	8	8.2	8.5	8.7
Freeze Length in seconds																				
	2	2.2	2.4	2.6	2.8	3	3.2	3.4	3.6	3.8	4	4.2	4.4	4.6	4.8	5	5.2	5.4	5.6	5.8
Cold Damage																				
	6-10	10-14	14-18	18-22	22-28	26-30	30-34	34-38	38-42	42-46	46-50	50-54	54-58	58-62	62-66	66-70	70-74	74-78	78-82	82-86

Magically enhances your arrow to hit your target or find one of its own; always hits.

Level	1	2	3	4	5	[illegible]	7	8	9	10	11	12	13	14	15	16	17	18	19	20
Mana Cost	8	7.7	7.5	7.2	7	3.7	6.5	6.2	6	5.7	5.5	5.2	5	4.7	4.5	4.2	4	3.7	3.5	3.2
Damage bonus																				
	0	+5%	+10%	+15%	+20%	+25%	+30%	+35%	+40%	+45%	+50%	+55%	+60%	+65%	+70%	+75%	+80%	+85%	+90%	+95%

STRAFE - REQUIRED LEVEL 24

Enchants arrows to strike multiple targets.

Level	1	2	3	4	5	[illegible]	7	8	9	10	11	12	13	14	15	16	17	18	19	20
Mana Cost	11	11	11	11	11	1	11	11	11	11	11	11	11	11	11	11	11	11	11	11
Targets attacked																				
	5	6	7	8	9	0	10	10	10	10	10	10	10	10	10	10	10	10	10	10
Damage bonus																				
	+5%	+10%	+15%	+20%	+25%	30%	+35%	+40%	+45%	+50%	+55%	+60%	+65%	+70%	+75%	+80%	+85%	+90%	+95%	+100%

IMMOLATION ARROW - REQUIRED LEVEL 24

Enchants an arrow or bolt to cause severe fire damage and create a pyre on impact; always hits.

Level	1	2	3	4	5	[illegible]	7	8	9	10	11	12	13	14	15	16	17	18	19	20
Mana Cost	6	7	8	9	10	1	12	13	14	15	16	17	18	19	20	21	22	23	24	25
Fire Explosion Damage																				
	4-10	10-16	16-22	22-28	28-34	[illegible]4-40	40-46	46-52	52-58	58-64	64-70	70-76	76-82	82-88	88-94	94-100	100-106	106-112	112-118	118-124
Fire Duration in seconds																				
	4.6	5.6	6.6	7.6	8.6	[illegible].6	10.6	11.6	12.6	13.6	14.6	15.6	16.6	17.6	18.6	19.6	20.6	21.6	22.6	23.6
Fire Damage per second																				
	8-10	14-16	19-22	25-28	31-33	[illegible]7-39	43-45	49-51	55-57	60-63	66-69	72-75	78-80	84-86	90-92	96-98	101-104	107-110	113-116	119-121

FREEZING ARROW - REQUIRED LEVEL 30

Level	1	2	3	4	5	[illegible]	7	8	9	10	11	12	13	14	15	16	17	18	19	20
Mana Cost	9	10	11	12	13	4	15	16	17	18	19	20	21	22	23	24	25	26	27	28
Cold Damage	40-45	50-[illegible]0	60-70	70-80	80-90	[illegible]0-100	100-110	110-120	125-135	140-150	155-165	170-108	185-195	200-210	215-225	230-240	250-260	270-280	290-300	310-320

Duration: 2 seconds; Radius: 3.3 Yards

PALADIN SKILLS

DEFENSIVE AURAS

PRAYER - REQUIRED LEVEL 1

Gradually heals you and your party members' life.

Level	1	2	3	4	5	[illegible]	7	8	9	10	11	12	13	14	15	16	17	18	19	20
Radius (yards)																				
	7.3	8.6	10	11.3	12.6	4	15.3	16.6	18	19.3	20.6	22	23.3	24.6	26	27.3	28.6	30	31.3	32.6
Heals	2	3	4	5	6	[illegible]	8	9	10	11	12	13	14	15	16	17	18	19	20	21
Mana Cost	1	1.1	1.3	1.5	1.7	.9	2.1	2.3	2.5	2.6	2.8	3	3.2	3.4	3.6	3.8	4	4.1	4.3	4.5

RESIST FIRE - REQUIRED LEVEL 1

Aura reducing fire damage to your party.

Level	1	2	3	4	5	[illegible]	7	8	9	10	11	12	13	14	15	16	17	18	19	20
Radius (yards)																				
	7.3	8.6	10	11.3	12.6	4	15.3	16.6	18	19.3	20.6	22	23.3	24.6	26	27.3	28.6	30	31.3	32.6

continues on next page

Fire Resistance +%																				
	52	66	76	85	92	98	102	106	110	113	116	118	121	123	124	127	128	129	130	131

DEFIANCE - REQUIRED LEVEL 6

Aura increasing defense rating for your party.

Level	1	2	3	4	5	6	7	8	9	10	11	12	13	14	15	16	17	18	19	20
Radius (yards)	7.3	8.6	10	11.3	12.6	14	15.3	16.6	18	19.3	20.6	22	23.3	24.6	26	27.3	28.6	30	31.3	32.6
Defense Bonus +%	70	80	90	100	110	120	130	140	150	160	170	180	190	200	210	220	230	240	250	260

RESIST COLD - REQUIRED LEVEL 6

Aura reducing cold damage to your party.

Level	1	2	3	4	5	6	7	8	9	10	11	12	13	14	15	16	17	18	19	20
Radius (yards)	7.3	8.6	10	11.3	12.6	14	15.3	16.6	18	19.3	20.6	22	23.3	24.6	26	27.3	28.6	30	31.3	32.6
Cold Resistance +%	52	66	76	85	92	98	102	106	110	113	116	118	121	123	124	127	128	129	130	131

CLEANSING - REQUIRED LEVEL 12

Aura reducing the amount of time your party is cursed or poisoned.

Level	1	2	3	4	5	6	7	8	9	10	11	12	13	14	15	16	17	18	19	20
Radius (yards)	7.3	8.6	10	11.3	12.6	14	15.3	16.6	18	19.3	20.6	22	23.3	24.6	26	27.3	28.6	30	31.3	32.6
Duration Reduced (%)	39	46	51	56	60	63	65	67	69	70	72	73	75	76	76	78	78	79	79	80

LIGHTNING RESIST - REQUIRED LEVEL 12

Aura reducing lightning damage to your party.

Level	1	2	3	4	5	6	7	8	9	10	11	12	13	14	15	16	17	18	19	20
Radius (yards)	7.3	8.6	10	11.3	12.6	14	15.3	16.6	18	19.3	20.6	22	23.3	24.6	26	27.3	28.6	30	31.3	32.6
Lightning Resistance +%	52	66	76	85	92	98	102	106	110	113	116	118	121	123	124	127	128	129	130	131

VIGOR - REQUIRED LEVEL 18

Increases Stamina Recovery Rate, Max Stamina, and Walk/Run Speed of your party.

Level	1	2	3	4	5	6	7	8	9	10	11	12	13	14	15	16	17	18	19	20
Radius (yards)	10	12	14	16	18	20	22	24	26	28	30	32	34	36	38	40	42	44	46	48
Walk/Run Speed	13	18	22	25	28	30	32	33	35	36	37	38	39	40	40	41	41	42	42	43
Stamina Bonus (%)	50	75	100	125	150	175	200	225	250	275	300	325	350	375	400	425	450	475	500	525
Stamina Recovery Rate (%)	50	75	100	125	150	175	200	225	250	275	300	325	350	375	400	425	450	475	500	525

MEDITATION - REQUIRED LEVEL 24

Increases Mana recovery rate of your party.

Level	1	2	3	4	5	[illegible]	7	8	9	10	11	12	13	14	15	16	17	18	19	20
Radius (yards)																				
	7.3	8.6	10	11.3	12.6	[illegible]4	15.3	16.6	18	19.3	20.6	22	23.3	24.6	26	27.3	28.6	30	31.3	32.6
Mana Recovery Rate (%)																				
	300	325	350	375	400	[illegible]25	450	475	500	525	550	575	600	625	650	675	700	725	750	775

REDEMPTION - REQUIRED LEVEL 30

Redeems slain monsters for Life and Mana to your party.

Level	1	2	3	4	5	[illegible]	7	8	9	10	11	12	13	14	15	16	17	18	19	20
Radius (yards)																				
	7.3	7.3	7.3	7.3	7.3	[illegible].3	7.3	7.3	7.3	7.3	7.3	7.3	7.3	7.3	7.3	7.3	7.3	7.3	7.3	7.3
Chance to Redeem (%)																				
	23	34	42	49	55	[illegible]9	63	65	69	71	73	75	77	79	80	82	82	83	84	85
Amount of Life/Mana Redeemed (points)																				
	25	30	35	40	45	[illegible]0	55	60	65	70	75	80	85	90	95	100	105	110	115	120

SALVATION - REQUIRED LEVEL 30

Aura that raises your resistance to elemental damages.

Level	1	2	3	4	5	[illegible]	7	8	9	10	11	12	13	14	15	16	17	18	19	20
Radius (yards)																				
	7.3	8.6	10	11.3	12.6	[illegible]4	15.3	16.6	18	19.3	20.6	22	23.3	24.6	26	27.3	28.6	30	31.3	32.6
% Resistance to Fire, Cold, Lightning Raised																				
	60	68	75	80	85	[illegible]8	91	93	96	97	99	101	102	103	104	106	106	107	108	108

OFFENSIVE AURAS

MIGHT - REQUIRED LEVEL 1

Aura increases the damage done by your party.

Level	1	2	3	4	5	[illegible]	7	8	9	10	11	12	13	14	15	16	17	18	19	20
Radius (yards)																				
	7.3	8.6	10	11.3	12.6	[illegible]4	15.3	16.6	18	19.3	20.6	22	23.3	24.6	26	27.3	28.6	30	31.3	32.6
Damage +%	40	50	60	70	80	[illegible]0	100	110	120	130	140	150	160	170	180	190	200	210	220	230

HOLY FIRE - REQUIRED LEVEL 6

Aura inflicting fire damage on nearby enemies.

Level	1	2	3	4	5	[illegible]	7	8	9	10	11	12	13	14	15	16	17	18	19	20
Radius (yards)																				
	4	4.6	5.3	6	6.6	[illegible].3	8	8.6	9.3	10	10.6	11.3	12	12.6	13.3	14	14.6	15.3	16	16.6
Fire Damage	1-3	1.5-3.5	2.5-4.5	3-5	4-6	[illegible].5-6.5	5.5-7.5	6-8	7-9	8-10	9-11	10-12	11-13	12-14	13-15	14-16	15.5-17.5	16.5-18.5	18-20	19-21

THORNS - REQUIRED LEVEL 6

Aura returning damage back to enemies based on the damage they have done.

Level	1	2	3	4	5	[illegible]	7	8	9	10	11	12	13	14	15	16	17	18	19	20
Radius (yards)																				
	7.3	8.6	10	11.3	12.6	[illegible]4	15.3	16.6	18	19.3	20.6	22	23.3	24.6	26	27.3	28.6	30	31.3	32.6

continues on next page

% Damage Returned																				
	250	290	330	370	410	450	490	530	570	610	650	690	730	770	810	850	890	930	970	1010
BLESSED AIM - REQUIRED LEVEL 12																				
Aura increasing the attack rating for you and your party.																				
Level	1	2	3	4	5	6	7	8	9	10	11	12	13	14	15	16	17	18	19	20
Radius (yards)																				
	7.3	8.6	10	11.3	12.6	14	15.3	16.6	18	19.3	20.6	22	23.3	24.6	26	27.3	28.6	30	31.3	32.6
Attack Rating +%																				
	75	90	105	120	135	150	165	180	195	210	225	240	255	270	285	300	315	330	345	360
CONCENTRATION - REQUIRED LEVEL 18																				
Aura increasing the damage done and the chance your party's attack is uninterruptible.																				
Level	1	2	3	4	5	6	7	8	9	10	11	12	13	14	15	16	17	18	19	20
Chance for Uninterruptible Attack (%)																				
	20	20	20	20	20	20	20	20	20	20	20	20	20	20	20	20	20	20	20	20
Damage +%	60	75	90	105	120	135	150	165	180	195	210	225	240	255	270	285	300	315	330	345
HOLY FREEZE - REQUIRED LEVEL 18																				
Aura freezes and slows nearby enemies.																				
Level	1	2	3	4	5	6	7	8	9	10	11	12	13	14	15	16	17	18	19	20
Radius (yards)																				
	4	4.6	5.3	6	6.6	7.3	8	8.6	9.3	10	10.6	11.3	12	12.6	13.3	14	14.6	15.3	16	16.6
Enemies Slowed X%																				
	30	34	37	40	42	44	45	46	48	48	49	50	51	51	52	53	53	53	54	54
HOLY SHOCK - REQUIRED LEVEL 24																				
Aura that adds lightning damage to your party's attack and damages nearby monsters with lightning damage.																				
Level	1	2	3	4	5	6	7	8	9	10	11	12	13	14	15	16	17	18	19	20
Radius (yards)																				
	7.3	7.3	7.3	7.3	7.3	7.3	7.3	7.3	7.3	7.3	7.3	7.3	7.3	7.3	7.3	7.3	7.3	7.3	7.3	7.3
Lightning Damaged Added to Attack																				
	1-20	1-27	1-34	1-41	1-48	1-55	1-62	1-69	1-76	1-83	1-90	1-97	1-104	1-111	1-118	1-125	1-132	1-139	1-146	1-153
Lightning Damage to Nearby Monsters																				
	1-10	4-13	7-16	10-19	13-22	16-25	19-28	22-31	26-35	30-39	34-43	38-47	42-51	46-55	50-59	54-63	59-68	64-73	69-78	74-83
SANCTUARY - REQUIRED LEVEL 24																				
Aura that damages the undead and knocks them back.																				
Level	1	2	3	4	5	6	7	8	9	10	11	12	13	14	15	16	17	18	19	20
Radius (yards)																				
	3.3	4	4.6	5.3	6	6.6	7.3	8	8.6	9.3	10	10.6	11.3	12	12.6	13.3	14	14.6	15.3	16
Damage (Melee)																				
	150	180	210	240	270	300	330	360	390	420	450	480	510	540	570	600	630	660	690	720
Magic Damage (points)																				
	8-16	12-20	16-24	20-28	24-32	28-36	32-40	36-44	40-48	44-52	48-56	52-60	56-64	60-68	64-72	68-76	72-80	76-84	80-88	84-92

FANATICISM - REQUIRED LEVEL 30

Aura that increases damage, attack speed, and attack rating for your party.

Level	1	2	3	4	5	[illegible]	7	8	9	10	11	12	13	14	15	16	17	18	19	20
Radius (yards)																				
	7.3	7.3	7.3	7.3	7.3	[illegible]	7.3	7.3	7.3	7.3	7.3	7.3	7.3	7.3	7.3	7.3	7.3	7.3	7.3	7.3
Damage +%	50	67	84	101	118	[illegible]	152	169	186	203	220	237	254	271	288	305	322	339	356	373
Attack Speed +%																				
	14	18	20	23	25	[illegible]	27	28	29	30	31	31	32	33	33	34	34	34	34	35
Attack Rating +%																				
	40	45	50	55	60	[illegible]	70	75	80	85	90	95	100	105	110	115	120	125	130	135

CONVICTION - REQUIRED LEVEL 30

Aura that lowers the defense and resistance of nearby enemies.

Level	1	2	3	4	5	[illegible]	7	8	9	10	11	12	13	14	15	16	17	18	19	20
Radius (yards)																				
	13.3	13.3	13.3	13.3	13.3	[illegible]	13.3	13.3	13.3	13.3	13.3	13.3	13.3	13.3	13.3	13.3	13.3	13.3	13.3	13.3
Defense Lowered by X%																				
	49	56	61	66	70	[illegible]	75	77	79	80	82	83	85	86	86	88	88	89	89	90
Resistance Lowered by X%																				
	30	35	40	45	50	[illegible]	60	65	70	75	80	85	90	95	100	105	110	115	120	125

COMBAT SKILLS

SACRIFICE - REQUIRED LEVEL 1

Increased Attack Rating and Damage at the cost of Life.

Level	1	2	3	4	5	[illegible]	7	8	9	10	11	12	13	14	15	16	17	18	19	20
Damage to Self (%)																				
	8	8	8	8	8	[illegible]	8	8	8	8	8	8	8	8	8	8	8	8	8	8
Attack Rating +%																				
	20	25	30	35	40	[illegible]	50	55	60	65	70	75	80	85	90	95	100	105	110	115
Damage +%	180	192	204	216	228	[illegible]	252	264	276	288	300	312	324	336	348	360	372	384	396	408

SMITE - REQUIRED LEVEL 1

Stun and hurt your enemy by bashing them with your shield.

Level	1	2	3	4	5	[illegible]	7	8	9	10	11	12	13	14	15	16	17	18	19	20
Damage +%	15	30	45	60	75	[illegible]	105	120	135	150	165	180	195	210	225	240	255	270	285	300
Stun length (seconds)																				
	0.6	0.8	1	1.2	1.4	[illegible]	1.8	2	2.2	2.4	2.6	2.8	3	3.2	3.4	3.6	3.8	4	4.2	4.4
Mana Cost	2	2	2	2	2	[illegible]	2	2	2	2	2	2	2	2	2	2	2	2	2	2

HOLY BOLT - REQUIRED LEVEL 6

Divine bolt that damages undead enemies or heals allies.

Level	1	2	3	4	5	[illegible]	7	8	9	10	11	12	13	14	15	16	17	18	19	20

continues on next page

Magic Damage

	8-16	14-22	20-28	26-34	32-40	38-46	44-52	50-58	56-64	62-70	68-76	74-82	80-88	86-94	92-100	98-106	104-112	110-118	116-124	122-130
Heals	1-6	3-8	5-10	7-12	9-14	11-16	13-18	15-20	17-22	19-24	21-26	23-28	25-30	27-32	29-34	31-36	33-38	35-40	37-42	39-44
Mana Cost	4	4.2	4.5	4.7	5	5.2	5.5	5.7	6	6.2	6.5	6.7	7	7.2	7.5	7.7	8	8.2	8.5	8.7

ZEAL - REQUIRED LEVEL 12

Attack multiple adjacent targets with a single attack.

Level	1	2	3	4	5	6	7	8	9	10	11	12	13	14	15	16	17	18	19	20
Attack Bonus (%)																				
	10	20	30	40	50	60	70	80	90	100	110	120	130	140	150	160	170	180	190	200
Number of Hits																				
	2	3	4	5	5	5	5	5	5	5	5	5	5	5	5	5	5	5	5	5
Mana Cost	2	2	2	2	2	2	2	2	2	2	2	2	2	2	2	2	2	2	2	2

CHARGE - REQUIRED LEVEL 12

Charge and attack an enemy.

Level	1	2	3	4	5	6	7	8	9	10	11	12	13	14	15	16	17	18	19	20
Damage +%	100	125	150	175	200	225	250	275	300	325	350	375	400	425	450	475	500	525	550	575
Attack Rating +%																				
	50	65	80	95	110	125	140	155	170	185	200	215	230	245	260	275	290	305	320	335
Mana Cost	9	9	9	9	9	9	9	9	9	9	9	9	9	9	9	9	9	9	9	9

VENGEANCE - REQUIRED LEVEL 18

Adds elemental damage to attack.

Level	1	2	3	4	5	6	7	8	9	10	11	12	13	14	15	16	17	18	19	20
Attack Bonus (%)																				
	20	30	40	50	60	70	80	90	100	110	120	130	140	150	160	170	180	190	200	210
Cold Length (seconds)																				
	1.2	1.8	2.4	3	3.6	4.2	4.8	5.4	6	6.6	7.2	7.8	8.4	9	9.6	10.2	10.8	11.4	12	12.6
Elemental Damage +%																				
	70	76	82	88	94	100	106	112	118	124	130	136	142	148	154	160	166	172	178	184
Mana Cost	4	4.2	4.5	4.7	5	5.2	5.5	5.7	6	6.2	6.5	6.7	7	7.2	7.5	7.7	8	8.2	8.5	8.7

BLESSED HAMMER - REQUIRED LEVEL 18

Ethereal hammer that damages enemy.

Level	1	2	3	4	5	6	7	8	9	10	11	12	13	14	15	16	17	18	19	20
Damage to Undead																				
	150%	150%	150%	150%	150%	150%	150%	150%	150%	150%	150%	150%	150%	150%	150%	150%	150%	150%	150%	150%
Magic Damage																				
	12-16	20-24	28-32	36-40	44-48	52-56	60-64	68-72	76-80	84-88	92-96	100-104	108-112	116-120	124-128	132-136	140-144	148-152	156-160	164-168
Mana Cost	5	5.2	5.5	5.7	6	6.2	6.5	6.7	7	7.2	7.5	7.7	8	8.2	8.5	8.7	9	9.2	9.5	9.7

CONVERSION - REQUIRED LEVEL 24

Convert enemies to fight for you.

Level	1	2	3	4	5	6	7	8	9	10	11	12	13	14	15	16	17	18	19	20

Chance to Convert (%)																				
	7	13	18	22	25	27	29	31	33	34	35	36	37	38	39	40	40	41	41	42
Duration (seconds)																				
	16	16	16	16	16	16	16	16	16	16	16	16	16	16	16	16	16	16	16	16
Mana Cost	4	4	4	4	4	4	4	4	4	4	4	4	4	4	4	4	4	4	4	4

HOLY SHIELD - REQUIRED LEVEL 24

Enhances your shield.

Level	1	2	3	4	5	6	7	8	9	10	11	12	13	14	15	16	17	18	19	20
Smite Damage																				
	3-6	5-8	7-10	9-12	11-14	13-16	15-18	17-20	20-23	23-26	26-29	29-32	32-35	35-38	38-41	41-44	45-48	49-52	53-56	57-60
Duration (seconds)																				
	30	40	50	60	70	80	90	100	110	120	130	140	150	160	170	180	190	200	210	220
Defense Bonus +%																				
	25	40	55	70	85	100	115	130	145	160	175	190	205	20	235	250	265	280	295	310
Blocking +%	8	10	12	13	15	16	16	17	18	18	19	19	20	20	20	21	21	21	21	21
Mana Cost	35	35	35	35	35	35	35	35	35	35	35	35	35	35	35	35	35	35	35	35

FIST OF THE HEAVENS - REQUIRED LEVEL 30

Lightning bolt strikes your target as holy bolt seeks out nearby enemies.

Level	1	2	3	4	5	6	7	8	9	10	11	12	13	14	15	16	17	18	19	20
Holy Bolt Damage																				
	40-50	46-56	52-62	58-68	64-74	70-80	76-86	82-92	92-102	102-112	112-122	122-132	132-142	142-152	152-162	162-172	178-188	194-204	210-220	226-236
Lightning Damage																				
	150-200	160-210	170-220	180-230	190-240	200-250	210-260	220-270	232-282	244-294	256-306	268-318	280-330	292-342	304-354	316-366	330-380	344-394	358-408	372-422
Mana Cost	25	25	25	25	25	25	25	25	25	25	25	25	25	25	25	25	25	25	25	25

SORCERESS SKILLS

FIRE SPELLS

FIRE BOLT - REQUIRED LEVEL 1

Creates a magical flaming missile.

Level	1	2	3	4	5	6	7	8	9	10	11	12	13	14	15	16	17	18	19	20
Mana	2.5	2.5	2.5	2.5	2.5	2.5	2.5	2.5	2.5	2.5	2.5	2.5	2.5	2.5	2.5	2.5	2.5	2.5	2.5	2.5
Fire Damage																				
	3-6	4-7	6-9	7-10	9-12	10-13	12-15	13-16	16-19	18-21	21-24	23-26	26-29	28-31	31-34	33-36	37-40	40-43	44-47	47-50

WARMTH (PASSIVE) - REQUIRED LEVEL 1

Passive - Increases the rate at which you recover Mana.

Level	1	2	3	4	5	6	7	8	9	10	11	12	13	14	15	16	17	18	19	20
Recovery Rate																				
	30%	42%	54%	66%	78%	90%	102%	114%	126%	138%	150%	162%	174%	186%	198%	210%	222%	234%	246%	258%

continues on next page

INFERNO - REQUIRED LEVEL 6

Creates a continuous jef of flame to scorch your enemies.

Minimum Mana required to cast: 6

Level	1	2	3	4	5	6	7	8	9	10	11	12	13	14	15	16	17	18	19	20
Mana per second	7	7	8	9	10	10	11	12	13	14	14	15	16	17	17	18	19	20	21	21
Range in yards	3.3	3.3	4	4.6	5.3	5.3	6	6.6	7.3	7.3	8	8.6	9.3	9.3	10	10.6	11.3	11.3	12	12.6
Fire Damage	12-25	21-34	31-43	40-53	50-62	59-71	68-81	78-90	88-100	98-110	108-121	118-131	128-141	139--151	149-161	159-171	170-182	181-193	192-204	203-215

BLAZE - REQUIRED LEVEL 12

Creates a wall of fire in your wake to scorch your enemies.

Level	1	2	3	4	5	6	7	8	9	10	11	12	13	14	15	16	17	18	19	20
Mana	11	11.5	12	12	13	13	14	14	15	15	16	16	17	17	18	18	19	19	20	20
Fire duration in seconds	4.6	5.6	6.6	7.6	8.6	9.6	10.6	11.6	12.6	13.6	14.6	15.6	16.6	17.6	18.6	19.6	20.6	21.6	22.6	23.6
Avg fire dmg/sec	18-37	28-46	37-56	46-65	56-75	65-84	75-93	84-103	98-117	112-131	126-145	140-159	154-173	168-187	182-201	196-215	215-234	234-253	253-271	271-290

FIRE WALL - REQUIRED LEVEL 18

Creates a wall of flame that blocks or burns your enemies.

Level	1	2	3	4	5	6	7	8	9	10	11	12	13	14	15	16	17	18	19	20
Mana	22	23	24	25	26	27	28	29	30	31	32	33	34	35	36	37	38	39	40	41
Duration in seconds	3.6	3.6	3.6	3.6	3.6	3.6	3.6	3.5	3.6	3.6	3.6	3.6	3.6	3.6	3.6	3.6	3.6	3.6	3.6	3.6
Range in yards	4	6	7	8	10	11	12	14	15	16	18	19	20	22	23	24	26	27	28	30
Avg fire dmg/sec	60-93	93-121	121-150	150-178	178-206	206-234	234-262	262-290	295-323	328-256	360-389	393-421	426-454	459-487	492-520	525-553	567-595	609-637	651-679	693-721

FIRE BALL - REQUIRED LEVEL 12

Creates an explosive sphere of firery death to engulf your enemies. Radius: 2 yards

Level	1	2	3	4	5	6	7	8	9	10	11	12	13	14	15	16	17	18	19	20
Mana	5	5.5	6	6.5	7	7.5	8	8.5	9	9.5	10	10.5	11	11.5	12	12	13	13	14	14
Avg fire dmg/sec	65-93	93-121	121-150	150-178	178-206	206-234	234-262	262-290	295-323	328-256	360-389	393-421	426-454	459-487	492-520	525-553	567-595	609-637	651-679	693-721

METEOR - REQUIRED LEVEL 24

Summons a meteor from the heavens to crush and incinerate your enemies.

Level	1	2	3	4	5	6	7	8	9	10	11	12	13	14	15	16	17	18	19	20
Mana	17	17	18	18	19	19	20	20	21	21	22	22	23	23	24	24	25	25	26	26
Fire Damage	80-100	104-124	128-148	152-172	176-196	200-220	224-244	248-268	288-308	328-348	368-388	408-428	448-468	488-508	528-548	568-588	648-668	728-748	808-828	888-908

Avg fire dmg/sec																				
	35-58	44-67	53-77	63-86	72-96	[illegible]2-105	91-114	100-124	112-135	124-147	135-159	147-171	159-182	171-194	182-206	194-217	208-232	222-246	236-360	250-274
Range in yards																				
	4	4	4	4	4	[illegible]	4	4	4	4	4	4	4	4	4	4	4	4	4	4

ENCHANT - REQUIRED LEVEL 18

Enchants equipped weapon of targeted character or minion. Adds fire damage to melee weapon. Adds one-third fire damage to ranged weapons.

Level	1	2	3	4	5	[illegible]	7	8	9	10	11	12	13	14	15	16	17	18	19	20
Mana	25	27	29	31	33	[illegible]5	37	39	41	43	45	47	49	51	53	55	57	59	61	63
Fire Damage																				
	8-10	10-12	12-14	14-16	16-18	[illegible]8-20	20-22	22-24	26-28	30-32	34-36	38-40	42-44	46-48	50-52	54-56	60 62	66-68	72-74	78-80
Duration in seconds																				
	144	168	192	216	240	[illegible]64	288	312	336	360	384	408	432	456	480	504	528	552	576	600

HYDRA - REQUIRED LEVEL 30

Summons a multi-headed beast of flame to reduce your enemies to ashes.

Level	1	2	3	4	5	[illegible]	7	8	9	10	11	12	13	14	15	16	17	18	19	20
Mana	20	20	21	21	22	[illegible]2	23	23	24	24	25	25	26	26	27	27	28	28	29	29
Fire Damage																				
	12-17	17-22	22-27	27-32	32-37	[illegible]7-42	42-47	47-52	54-59	61-66	68-73	75-80	82-87	89-94	96-101	103-108	112-117	121-126	130-135	139-144
Duration in seconds																				
	10	10	10	10	10	[illegible]0	10	10	10	10	10	10	10	10	10	10	10	10	10	10

FIRE MASTERY - REQUIRED LEVEL 30

Passive - Increases all damage caused by your fire spells.

Level	1	2	3	4	5	[illegible]	7	8	9	10	11	12	13	14	15	16	17	18	19	20
% Damage Increase																				
	30%	37%	44%	51%	58%	[illegible]5%	72%	79%	86%	93%	100%	107%	114%	121%	128%	135%	142%	149%	156%	163%

COLD SPELLS

ICE BOLT - REQUIRED LEVEL 1

Creates a magical bolt of ice that damages and slows your enemies.

Level	1	2	3	4	5	[illegible]	7	8	9	10	11	12	13	14	15	16	17	18	19	20
Mana	3	3	3	3	3	[illegible]	3	3	3	3	3	3	3	3	3	3	3	3	3	3
Cold Damage																				
	3-5	4-6	5-7	6-8	7-9	[illegible]-10	9-11	10-12	12-14	14-16	16-18	18-20	20-22	22-24	24-26	26-28	29-31	32-34	35-37	38-40
Duration in seconds																				
	6	7.4	8.8	10.2	11.6	[illegible]3	14.4	15.8	17.2	18.6	20	21.4	22.8	24.2	25.6	27	28.4	29.8	31.2	32.6

FROZEN ARMOR - REQUIRED LEVEL 1

Increases your defense rating and freezes enemies that hit you.

Level	1	2	3	4	5	[illegible]	7	8	9	10	11	12	13	14	15	16	17	18	19	20
Mana	7	7	7	7	7	[illegible]	7	7	7	7	7	7	7	7	7	7	7	7	7	7
+% Defense Bonus																				
	30	35	40	45	50	[illegible]5	60	65	70	75	80	85	90	95	100	105	110	115	120	125

continues on next page

Armor Duration																				
	120	132	144	156	168	180	192	204	216	228	240	252	264	276	288	300	312	324	336	348
Freeze duration in seconds																				
	1.2	1.3	1.4	1.5	1.6	1.8	1.9	2	2.1	2.2	2.4	2.5	2.6	2.7	2.8	3	3.1	3.2	3.3	3.4

ICE BLAST - REQUIRED LEVEL 6

Creates a magical sphere of ice that damages and freezes your enemy.

Level	1	2	3	4	5	6	7	8	9	10	11	12	13	14	15	16	17	18	19	20
Mana	6	6.5	7	7.5	8	8.5	9	9.5	10	10.5	11	11.5	12	12	13	13	14	14	15	15
Cold Damage																				
	10	17	24	31	38	45	52	59	66	73	80	87	94	101	108	115	122	129	136	143
Freeze duration in seconds																				
	3	3.2	3.4	3.6	3.8	4	4.2	4.4	4.6	4.8	5	5.2	5.4	5.6	5.8	6	6.2	6.4	6.6	6.8

SHIVER ARMOR - REQUIRED LEVEL 12

Increases your defense rating. Freezes and damages enemies that hit you.

Level	1	2	3	4	5	6	7	8	9	10	11	12	13	14	15	16	17	18	19	20
Mana	11	11	11	11	11	11	11	11	11	11	11	11	11	11	11	11	11	11	11	11
Duration in seconds																				
	120	132	144	156	168	180	192	204	216	228	240	252	264	276	288	300	312	324	336	348
Defense Bonus %																				
	45	51	57	63	69	75	81	87	93	99	105	111	117	123	129	135	141	147	153	159
Cold Damage																				
	6-8	8-10	10-12	12-14	14-16	16-18	18-20	20-22	23-25	26-28	29-31	32-34	35-37	38-40	41-43	44-46	48-50	52-54	56-58	60-62
Cold length in seconds																				
	4	4	4	4	4	4	4	4	4	4	4	4	4	4	4	4	4	4	4	4

FROST NOVA - REQUIRED LEVEL 6

Creates an expanding ring of ice that damages and slows all nearby enemies.

Level	1	2	3	4	5	6	7	8	9	10	11	12	13	14	15	16	17	18	19	20
Mana	9	10	11	12	13	14	15	16	17	18	19	20	21	22	23	24	25	26	27	28
Cold Damage																				
	2-4	4-6	6-8	8-10	10-12	12-14	14-16	16-18	19-21	22-24	25-27	28-30	31-33	34-36	37-39	40-42	44-46	48-50	52-54	56-58
Cold length in seconds																				
	8	9	10	11	12	13	14	15	16	17	18	19	20	21	22	23	24	25	26	27

GLACIAL SPIKE - REQUIRED LEVEL 18

Creates a magical ice comet that freezes or kills nearby enemies. Radius: 2.6 yards

Level	1	2	3	4	5	6	7	8	9	10	11	12	13	14	15	16	17	18	19	20
Mana	10	10.5	11	11.5	12	12	13	13	14	14	15	15	16	16	17	17	18	18	19	19
Cold Damage																				
	16-24	23-31	30-38	37-45	44-52	51-59	58-66	65-73	72-80	79-87	86-94	93-101	100-108	107-115	114-122	121-129	128-136	135-143	142-150	149-157
Freeze duration/seconds																				
	2	2.1	2.2	2.3	2.4	2.6	2.7	2.8	2.9	3	3.2	3.3	3.4	3.5	3.6	3.8	3.9	4	4.1	4.2

CHILLING ARMOR - REQUIRED LEVEL 24

Increases defense and discharges an ice bolt in retaliation against ranged attackers.

Level	1	2	3	4	5	6	7	8	9	10	11	12	13	14	15	16	17	18	19	20
Mana	17	17	17	17	17	17	17	17	17	17	17	17	17	17	17	17	17	17	17	17
Defense % bonus																				
	45	50	55	60	65	70	75	80	85	90	95	100	105	110	115	120	125	130	135	140
Duration in seconds																				
	144	150	156	162	168	174	180	186	192	198	204	210	216	222	228	234	240	246	252	258
Cold Damage																				
	4-6	5-7	6-8	7-9	8-10	9-11	10-12	11-13	13-15	15-17	17-19	19-21	21-23	23-25	25-27	27-29	30-32	33-35	36-38	39-41

BLIZZARD - REQUIRED LEVEL 24

Summons massive shards of ice to destroy your enemies.

Level	1	2	3	4	5	6	7	8	9	10	11	12	13	14	15	16	17	18	19	20
Mana	23	24	25	26	27	28	29	30	31	32	33	34	35	36	37	38	39	40	41	42
Cold Damage																				
	30-50	42-62	54-74	66-86	78-98	90-110	102-122	114-134	139-159	164-184	189-209	214-234	239-259	264-284	289-309	314-334	354-374	394-414	434-454	474-494
Cold duration in seconds																				
	3	3	3	3	3	3	3	3	3	3	3	3	3	3	3	3	3	3	3	3

FROZEN ORB - REQUIRED LEVEL 30

Creates a magical globe that sprays a torrent of ice bolts to lay waste to your enemies.

Level	1	2	3	4	5	6	7	8	9	10	11	12	13	14	15	16	17	18	19	20
Mana	25	25	26	26	27	27	28	28	29	29	30	30	31	31	32	32	33	33	34	34
Cold Damage																				
	35-40	41-46	47-52	53-58	59-64	65-70	71-76	77-82	87-92	97-102	107-112	117-122	127-132	137-142	147-152	157-162	171-176	185-190	199-204	213-218
Cold length in seconds																				
	8	9	10	11	12	13	14	15	16	17	18	19	20	21	22	23	24	25	26	27

COLD MASTERY - REQUIRED LEVEL 30

Passive- Increases the damage of your cold attacks by piercing enemies resistances to cold.

Level	1	2	3	4	5	6	7	8	9	10	11	12	13	14	15	16	17	18	19	20
% bonus	23	34	42	49	55	59	63	65	69	71	73	75	77	79	80	81	82	83	84	85

LIGHTNING SPELLS

CHARGED BOLT - REQUIRED LEVEL 1

Creates multiple, randomly directed bolts of electrical energy.

Level	1	2	3	4	5	6	7	8	9	10	11	12	13	14	15	16	17	18	19	20
Mana	3	3.5	4	4.5	5	5.5	6	6.5	7	7.5	8	8.5	9	9.5	10	10.5	11	11.5	12	12
Lightning Damage																				
	2-4	2-4	3-5	3-5	4-6	4-6	5-7	5-7	6-8	6-8	7-9	7-9	8-10	8-10	9-11	9-11	10-12	11-13	12-14	13-15
# of bolts	3	4	5	6	7	8	9	10	11	12	13	14	15	16	17	18	19	20	21	22

continues on next page

TELEKINESIS - REQUIRED LEVEL 6

Uses the power of your mind to pick up items, use objects, and knock back enemies.

Level	1	2	3	4	5	6	7	8	9	10	11	12	13	14	15	16	17	18	19	20
Lightning Damage																				
	1-2	2-3	3-4	4-5	5-6	6-7	7-8	8-9	9-10	10-11	11-12	12-13	13-14	14-15	15-16	16-17	17-18	18-19	19-20	20-21
Mana	7	7	7	7	7	7	7	7	7	7	7	7	7	7	7	7	7	7	7	7

STATIC FIELD - REQUIRED LEVEL 6

Creates an electrical field that reduces life of all nearby enemies. Weakens enemies by 25%.

Level	1	2	3	4	5	6	7	8	9	10	11	12	13	14	15	16	17	18	19	20
Range in yards																				
	3.3	4	4.6	5.3	6	6.6	7.3	8	8.6	9.3	10	10.6	11.3	12	12.6	13.3	14	14.6	15.3	16
Mana	9	9	9	9	9	9	9	9	9	9	9	9	9	9	9	9	9	9	9	9

NOVA - REQUIRED LEVEL 12

Creates an expanding ring of lightning to shock nearby enemies.

Level	1	2	3	4	5	6	7	8	9	10	11	12	13	14	15	16	17	18	19	20
Lightning Damage																				
	1-20	8-27	15-34	22-41	29-48	39-55	43-62	50-69	57-76	64-83	71-90	78-97	85-104	92-111	99-118	106-125	113-132	120-139	127-146	134-153
Mana	15	16	17	18	19	20	21	22	23	24	25	26	27	28	29	30	31	32	33	34

LIGHTNING - REQUIRED LEVEL 12

Creates a powerful lightning bolt to lay waste to your enemies.

Level	1	2	3	4	5	6	7	8	9	10	11	12	13	14	15	16	17	18	19	20
Lightning Damage																				
	1-40	1-48	1-56	1-64	1-72	1-80	1-88	1-96	1-104	1-112	1-120	1-128	1-136	1-144	1-152	1-160	1-168	1-176	1-184	1-192
Mana	8	8.5	9	9.5	10	10.5	11	11.5	12	12	13	13	14	14	15	15	16	16	17	17

CHAIN LIGHTNING - REQUIRED LEVEL 18

Creates a bolt of lightning that arcs through several targets.

Level	1	2	3	4	5	6	7	8	9	10	11	12	13	14	15	16	17	18	19	20
Lightning Damage																				
	1-40	1-51	1-62	1-73	1-84	1-95	1-106	1-117	1-130	1-143	1-156	1-169	1-182	1-195	1-208	1-221	1-236	1-251	1-266	1-281
Mana	9	10	11	12	13	14	15	16	17	18	19	20	21	22	23	24	25	26	27	28
# of hits	5	5	5	5	6	6	6	6	6	7	7	7	7	7	8	8	8	8	8	9

THUNDERSTORM - REQUIRED LEVEL 24

Summons a deadly thunderstorm that strikes your enemies with bolts of lightning.

Level	1	2	3	4	5	6	7	8	9	10	11	12	13	14	15	16	17	18	19	20
Lightning Damage																				
	1-100	11-110	21-120	31-130	41-140	51-150	61-160	71-170	81-180	91-190	101-200	111-210	121-220	131-230	141-240	151-250	162-261	173-272	184-283	195-294
Duration in seconds																				
	32	40	48	56	64	72	80	88	96	104	112	120	128	136	144	152	160	168	176	184
Mana	19	19	19	19	19	19	19	19	19	19	19	19	19	19	19	19	19	19	19	19

TELEPORT - REQUIRED LEVEL 18

Instantly move to a destination within your line of sight.

Level	1	2	3	4	5	[illegible]	7	8	9	10	11	12	13	14	15	16	17	18	19	20
Mana	24	23	22	21	20	19	18	17	16	15	14	13	12	11	10	9	8	7	6	5

ENERGY SHIELD - REQUIRED LEVEL 24

Creates a magical shield that consumes Mana instead of health when you take damage.

Level	1	2	3	4	5	[illegible]	7	8	9	10	11	12	13	14	15	16	17	18	19	20
Damage Absorbed %																				
	15	23	30	35	40	43	46	48	51	52	54	56	57	58	59	61	61	62	63	63
Duration in seconds																				
	144	192	240	288	336	384	432	480	528	576	624	672	720	768	816	864	912	960	1008	1056
Mana	5	5	5	5	5	[illegible]	5	5	5	5	5	5	5	5	5	5	5	5	5	5

LIGHTNING MASTERY - REQUIRED LEVEL 30

Passive- Increases all damage caused by your lightning spells.

Level	1	2	3	4	5	[illegible]	7	8	9	10	11	12	13	14	15	16	17	18	19	20
% bonus	50	62	74	86	98	110	122	134	146	158	170	182	194	206	218	230	242	254	266	278

BARBARIAN SKILLS

WARCRIES

HOWL - REQUIRED LEVEL 1

Sends nearby enemies running away.

Level	1	2	3	4	5	[illegible]	7	8	9	10	11	12	13	14	15	16	17	18	19	20
Enemy runs up to X yards																				
X	16	19.3	22.6	26	29.3	32.6	36	39.3	42.6	46	49.3	52.6	56	59.3	62.6	66	69.3	72.6	76	79.3
Duration	3	4	5	6	7	[illegible]	9	10	11	12	13	14	15	16	17	18	19	20	21	22
Mana Cost	4	4	4	4	4	[illegible]	4	4	4	4	4	4	4	4	4	4	4	4	4	4

FIND POTION - REQUIRED LEVEL 1

Find potions from slain monster corpses.

Level	1	2	3	4	5	[illegible]	7	8	9	10	11	12	13	14	15	16	17	18	19	20
Chance to Find Potion (%)																				
	15	27	36	44	50	55	59	62	66	68	71	73	75	77	78	80	81	82	83	84
Mana Cost	2	2	2	2	2	[illegible]	2	2	2	2	2	2	2	2	2	2	2	2	2	2

TAUNT - REQUIRED LEVEL 6

Enrages the monster into relentlessly attacking.

Level	1	2	3	4	5	[illegible]	7	8	9	10	11	12	13	14	15	16	17	18	19	20
Target Damage Lowered (%)																				
	5	7	9	11	13	15	17	19	21	23	25	27	29	31	33	35	37	39	41	43

continues on next page

BARBARIAN SKILLS (CONTINUED)

Target Attack Rating Lowered (%)	5	7	9	11	13	15	17	19	21	23	25	27	29	31	33	35	37	39	41	43
Mana Cost	3	3	3	3	3	3	3	3	3	3	3	3	3	3	3	3	3	3	3	3

SHOUT - REQUIRED LEVEL 6

Increases the Defense Rating of you and your party.

Level	1	2	3	4	5	6	7	8	9	10	11	12	13	14	15	16	17	18	19	20
Defense Rating (improves X %)	100	110	120	130	140	150	160	170	180	190	200	210	220	230	240	250	260	270	280	290
Duration	16	18	20	22	24	26	28	30	32	34	36	38	40	42	44	46	48	50	52	54
Mana Cost	6	6	6	6	6	6	6	6	6	6	6	6	6	6	6	6	6	6	6	6

FIND ITEM - REQUIRED LEVEL 12

Find items from slain monster corpses.

Level	1	2	3	4	5	6	7	8	9	10	11	12	13	14	15	16	17	18	19	20
Chance to Find Item (%)	13	19	24	29	32	35	37	39	41	42	44	45	46	47	47	49	49	50	50	51
Mana Cost	7	7	7	7	7	7	7	7	7	7	7	7	7	7	7	7	7	7	7	7

BATTLE CRY - REQUIRED LEVEL 18

Lower enemy Defense Rating and Damage.

Level	1	2	3	4	5	6	7	8	9	10	11	12	13	14	15	16	17	18	19	20
Duration	12	14.4	16.8	19.2	21.6	24	26.4	28.8	31.2	33.6	36	38.4	40.8	43.2	45.6	48	50.4	52.8	55.2	57.6
Lower Defense Rating (%)	50	52	54	56	58	60	62	64	66	68	70	72	74	76	78	80	82	84	86	88
Lower Damage (%)	25	26	27	28	29	30	31	32	33	34	35	36	37	38	39	40	41	42	42	44
Mana Cost	5	5	5	5	5	5	5	5	5	5	5	5	5	5	5	5	5	5	5	5

BATTLE ORDERS - REQUIRED LEVEL 18

Improves Life, Mana, and Stamina of you and your party.

Level	1	2	3	4	5	6	7	8	9	10	11	12	13	14	15	16	17	18	19	20
Duration	30	36	42	48	54	60	66	72	78	84	90	96	102	108	114	120	126	132	138	144
Stamina/Life/Mana Increase (%)	35	38	41	44	47	50	53	56	59	62	65	68	71	74	77	80	83	86	89	92
Mana Cost	7	7	7	7	7	7	7	7	7	7	7	7	7	7	7	7	7	7	7	7

GRIM WARD - REQUIRED LEVEL 24

Use monster corpse to erect totem to cause nearby monsters to flee.

Level	1	2	3	4	5	6	7	8	9	10	11	12	13	14	15	16	17	18	19	20
Duration (seconds)	40	40	40	40	40	40	40	40	40	40	40	40	40	40	40	40	40	40	40	40
Radius (yards)	2	2.6	3.3	4	4.6	5.3	6	6.6	7.3	8	8.6	9.3	10	10.6	11.3	12	12.6	13.3	14	14.6
Mana Cost	4	4	4	4	4	4	4	4	4	4	4	4	4	4	4	4	4	4	4	4

BATTLE COMMAND - REQUIRED LEVEL 30

Increase Skill Level for you and your party.

Level	1	2	3	4	5	6	7	8	9	10	11	12	13	14	15	16	17	18	19	20
Duration	12	16	20	24	28	32	36	40	44	48	52	56	60	64	68	72	76	80	84	88
Mana Cost	11	11	11	11	11	11	11	11	11	11	11	11	11	11	11	11	11	11	11	11

WARCRY - REQUIRED LEVEL 30

Stun and damage enemy.

Level	1	2	3	4	5	6	7	8	9	10	11	12	13	14	15	16	17	18	19	20
Damage	20-30	26-36	32-42	38-48	44-54	50-60	55-66	62-72	69-79	76-86	83-93	90-100	97-107	104-114	111-121	118-128	126-136	134-144	142-152	150-160
Stun Length (seconds)																				
	1	1.2	1.4	1.6	1.8	[illegible]	2.2	2.4	2.6	2.8	3	3.2	3.4	3.6	3.8	4	4.2	4.4	4.6	4.8
Mana Cost	10	11	12	13	14	15	16	17	18	19	20	21	22	23	24	25	26	27	28	29

COMBAT MASTERIES

SWORD MASTERY - REQUIRED LEVEL 1

Better Damage, Attack Rating, and Chance for Critical Strike using Sword.

Level	1	2	3	4	5	6	7	8	9	10	11	12	13	14	15	16	17	18	19	20
Damage (%)	28	33	38	43	48	53	53	63	68	73	78	83	88	93	98	103	108	113	118	123
Attack Rating (%)																				
	28	36	44	52	60	68	76	84	92	100	108	116	124	132	140	148	156	164	172	180
Chance for Critical Strike																				
	3	6	9	11	12	13	14	15	16	17	17	18	18	19	19	20	20	20	20	21

AXE MASTERY - REQUIRED LEVEL 1

Better Damage, Attack Rating, and Chance for Critical Strike using Axe.

Level	1	2	3	4	5	6	7	8	9	10	11	12	13	14	15	16	17	18	19	20
Damage (%)	28	33	38	43	48	53	53	63	68	73	78	83	88	93	98	103	108	113	118	123
Attack Rating (%)																				
	28	36	44	52	60	68	76	84	92	100	108	116	124	132	140	148	156	164	172	180
Chance for Critical Strike																				
	3	6	9	11	12	13	14	15	16	17	17	18	18	19	19	20	20	20	20	21

MACE MASTERY - REQUIRED LEVEL 1

Better Damage, Attack Rating, and Chance for Critical Strike using Mace.

Level	1	2	3	4	5	6	7	8	9	10	11	12	13	14	15	16	17	18	19	20
Damage (%)	28	33	38	43	48	53	53	63	68	73	78	83	88	93	98	103	108	113	118	123
Attack Rating (%)																				
	28	36	44	52	60	68	76	84	92	100	108	116	124	132	140	148	156	164	172	180
Chance for Critical Strike																				
	3	6	9	11	12	13	14	15	16	17	17	18	18	19	19	20	20	20	20	21

continues on next page

POLE-ARM MASTERY - REQUIRED LEVEL 6

Better Damage, Attack Rating, and Chance for Critical Strike using Pole-Arm.

Level	1	2	3	4	5	6	7	8	9	10	11	12	13	14	15	16	17	18	19	20
Damage (%)	30	35	40	45	50	55	60	65	70	75	80	85	90	95	100	105	110	115	120	125
Attack Rating (%)																				
	30	38	46	54	62	70	78	86	94	102	110	118	126	134	142	150	158	166	174	182
Chance for Critical Strike																				
	3	6	9	11	12	13	14	15	16	17	17	18	18	19	19	20	20	20	20	21

THROWING MASTERY - REQUIRED LEVEL 6

Better Damage, Attack Rating, and Chance for Critical Strike using Throwing Weapons.

Level	1	2	3	4	5	6	7	8	9	10	11	12	13	14	15	16	17	18	19	20
Damage (%)	28	33	38	43	48	53	58	63	68	73	78	83	88	93	98	103	108	113	118	123
Attack Rating (%)																				
	28	36	44	52	60	68	76	84	92	100	108	116	124	132	140	148	156	164	172	180
Chance for Critical Strike																				
	3	6	9	11	12	13	14	15	16	17	17	18	18	19	19	20	20	20	20	21

SPEAR MASTERY - REQUIRED LEVEL 6

Better Damage, Attack Rating, and Chance for Critical Strike using Spears.

Level	1	2	3	4	5	6	7	8	9	10	11	12	13	14	15	16	17	18	19	20
Damage (%)	30	35	40	45	50	55	60	65	70	75	80	85	90	95	100	105	110	115	120	125
Attack Rating (%)																				
	30	38	46	54	62	70	78	86	94	102	110	118	126	134	142	150	158	166	174	182
Chance for Critical Strike																				
	3	6	9	11	12	13	14	15	16	17	17	18	18	19	19	20	20	20	20	21

INCREASED STAMINA - REQUIRED LEVEL 12

Level	1	2	3	4	5	6	7	8	9	10	11	12	13	14	15	16	17	18	19	20
Stamina Increases (%)																				
	30	45	60	75	90	105	120	135	150	165	180	195	210	225	240	255	270	285	300	315

IRON SKIN - REQUIRED LEVEL 18

Improves Defensive Rating.

Level	1	2	3	4	5	6	7	8	9	10	11	12	13	14	15	16	17	18	19	20
Defense Rating (%)																				
	30	40	50	60	70	80	90	100	110	120	130	140	150	160	170	180	190	200	210	220

INCREASED SPEED - REQUIRED LEVEL 24

Increased walk and run speed.

Level	1	2	3	4	5	6	7	8	9	10	11	12	13	14	15	16	17	18	19	20

Walk/Run Faster (%)																				
	13	18	22	25	28	30	32	33	35	36	37	38	39	40	40	41	41	42	42	43

NATURAL RESISTANCE - REQUIRED LEVEL 30

Increased Resistance to all elemental and poison attacks.

Level	1	2	3	4	5	6	7	8	9	10	11	12	13	14	15	16	17	18	19	20
Resistance % Raised																				
	12	21	28	35	40	44	47	49	52	54	56	58	60	61	62	64	64	65	66	67

COMBAT SKILLS

BASH - REQUIRED LEVEL 1

Increased Damage, Attack Rating, and Knockback.

Level	1	2	3	4	5	6	7	8	9	10	11	12	13	14	15	16	17	18	19	20
Damage +	1	2	3	4	5	6	7	8	9	20	11	12	13	14	15	16	17	18	19	20
Damage +%	50	55	60	65	70	75	80	85	90	95	100	105	110	115	120	125	130	135	140	145
Attack Rating +%																				
	20	25	30	35	40	45	50	55	60	65	70	75	80	85	90	95	100	105	110	115
Mana Cost	2	2	2	2	2	2	2	2	2	2	2	2	2	2	2	2	2	2	2	2

LEAP - REQUIRED LEVEL 6

Leap away from or into the enemies.

Level	1	2	3	4	5	6	7	8	9	10	11	12	13	14	15	16	17	18	19	20
Distance (yards)																				
	4.6	7.3	8.6	10	11.3	12	12.6	13.3	14	14	14.6	14.6	15.3	16	16	16	16.6	16.6	16.6	16.6
Mana Cost	2	2	2	2	2	2	2	2	2	2	2	2	2	2	2	2	2	2	2	2

DOUBLE SWING - REQUIRED LEVEL 6

When equipped with two weapons, attack two targets at once, or one target twice.

Level	1	2	3	4	5	6	7	8	9	10	11	12	13	14	15	16	17	18	19	20
Attack Rating +%																				
	15	20	25	30	35	40	45	50	55	60	65	70	75	80	85	90	95	100	105	110
Mana Cost	2	2	2	2	2	2	2	2	2	2	2	2	2	2	2	2	2	2	2	2

STUN - REQUIRED LEVEL 12

Stun target and increase attack rating.

Level	1	2	3	4	5	6	7	8	9	10	11	12	13	14	15	16	17	18	19	20
Attack Rating +%																				
	15	20	25	30	35	40	45	50	55	60	65	70	75	80	85	90	95	100	105	110
Stun Length	1.2	1.4	1.6	1.8	2	2.2	2.4	2.6	2.8	3	3.2	3.4	3.6	3.8	4	4.2	4.4	4.6	4.8	5
Mana Cost	2	2	2	2	2	2	2	2	2	2	2	2	2	2	2	2	2	2	2	2

DOUBLE THROW - REQUIRED LEVEL 12

Allows you to throw two different weapons at the same time.

Level	1	2	3	4	5	6	7	8	9	10	11	12	13	14	15	16	17	18	19	20

continues on next page

Attack Rating +%																				
	20	30	40	50	60	70	80	90	100	110	120	130	140	150	160	170	180	190	200	210
Mana Cost	2	2	2	2	2	2	2	2	2	2	2	2	2	2	2	2	2	2	2	2

LEAP ATTACK - REQUIRED LEVEL 18

Leap and attack enemy all with one swift move.

Level	1	2	3	4	5	6	7	8	9	10	11	12	13	14	15	16	17	18	19	20
Damage +%	100	130	160	190	220	250	280	310	340	370	400	430	460	490	520	550	580	610	640	670
Attack Rating +%																				
	50	65	80	95	110	125	140	155	170	185	200	215	230	245	260	275	290	305	320	335
Mana Cost	9	9	9	9	9	9	9	9	9	9	9	9	9	9	9	9	9	9	9	9

CONCENTRATE - REQUIRED LEVEL 18

Uninterruptible attack that improves attack and defensive rating.

Level	1	2	3	4	5	6	7	8	9	10	11	12	13	14	15	16	17	18	19	20
Defense Rating +%																				
	100	110	120	130	140	150	160	170	180	190	200	210	220	230	240	250	260	270	280	290
Attack Rating +%																				
	60	70	80	90	100	110	120	130	140	150	160	170	180	190	200	210	220	230	240	250
Damage +%	70	75	80	85	90	95	100	105	110	115	120	125	130	135	140	145	150	155	160	165
Mana Cost	2	2	2	2	2	2	2	2	2	2	2	2	2	2	2	2	2	2	2	2

FRENZY - REQUIRED LEVEL 24

Each successful attack increases attack speed and damage.

Must be equipped with two weapons.

Level	1	2	3	4	5	6	7	8	9	10	11	12	13	14	15	16	17	18	19	20
Damage +%	90	95	100	105	110	115	120	125	130	135	140	145	150	155	160	165	170	175	180	185
Attack Rating +%																				
	100	107	114	121	128	135	142	149	156	163	170	177	184	191	198	205	212	219	226	233
Attack Speed +%																				
	7	7-13	7-18	7-22	7-25	7-27	7-29	7-31	7-33	7-34	7-35	7-36	7-37	7-38	7-39	7-40	7-40	7-41	7-41	7-42
Walk/Run Speed +%																				
	47	47-68	47-84	47-99	47-110	47-119	47-126	47-131	47-138	47-142	47-147	47-151	47-155	47-158	47-160	47-164	47-165	47-167	47-169	47-171
Mana Cost	3	3	3	3	3	3	3	3	3	3	3	3	3	3	3	3	3	3	3	3

WHIRLWIND - REQUIRED LEVEL 30

Cuts through the enemies with a dance of death.

Level	1	2	3	4	5	6	7	8	9	10	11	12	13	14	15	16	17	18	19	20
Damage +%																				
	-50	-42	-34	-26	-18	-10	-2	6	14	22	30	38	46	54	62	70	78	86	94	102
Attack Rating +%																				
	0	5	10	15	20	25	30	35	40	45	50	55	60	65	70	75	80	85	90	95
Mana Cost	25	25	26	26	27	27	28	28	29	29	30	30	31	31	32	32	33	33	34	34

BERSERK - REQUIRED LEVEL 30

Reckless attack that increases damage and attack rating but decrease defense rating

Level	1	2	3	4	5	6	7	8	9	10	11	12	13	14	15	16	17	18	19	20
Attack Rating +%																				
	100	115	130	145	160	175	190	205	220	235	250	265	280	295	310	325	340	355	370	385
Magic Damage +%																				
	150	165	180	195	210	225	240	255	270	285	300	315	330	345	360	375	390	405	420	435
Duration (seconds)																				
	2.7	2.4	2.2	2.1	2	1.9	1.8	1.7	1.6	1.6	1.6	1.5	1.5	1.4	1.4	1.4	1.4	1.3	1.3	1.3
Mana Cost	4	4	4	4	4	4	4	4	4	4	4	4	4	4	4	4	4	4	4	4

ASSASSIN SKILLS

TRAPS

FIRE BLAST - REQUIRED LEVEL 1

Throw a firebomb to blast your enemies to bits.

Level	1	2	3	4	5	6	7	8	9	10	11	12	13	14	15	16	17	18	19	20
Mana	3	3.1	3.2	3.3	3.5	3.6	3.7	3.8	4	4.1	4.2	4.3	4.5	4.6	4.7	4.8	5	5.1	5.2	5.3
Fire Damage	3-4	5-6	7-8	9-10	11-12	13-14	15-16	17-18	21-22	25-26	29-30	33-34	37-38	41-42	45-46	49-50	54-55	59-60	64-65	69-70

SHOCK WEB - REQUIRED LEVEL 6

Throw a web of lightning.

Level	1	2	3	4	5	6	7	8	9	10	11	12	13	14	15	16	17	18	19	20
Mana	6	6	6	6	6	6	6	6	6	6	6	6	6	6	6	6	6	6	6	6
Spikes	6	6	6	6	7	7	7	7	8	8	8	8	9	9	9	9	10	10	10	10
Duration in Seconds																				
	3.6	3.6	3.6	3.6	3.6	3.6	3.6	3.6	3.6	3.6	3.6	3.6	3.6	3.6	3.6	3.6	3.6	3.6	3.6	3.6
Lightning Damage																				
	5-6	6-7	7-8	8-9	9-10	10-11	11-12	12-13	14-15	17-18	19-20	22-23	24-25	27-28	29-30	32-33	35-36	39-40	42-43	46-47

BLADE SENTINEL - REQUIRED LEVEL 6

Set a Spinning Blade to patrol between you and your target point.

Level	1	2	3	4	5	6	7	8	9	10	11	12	13	14	15	16	17	18	19	20
Mana	7	7	7	7	7	7	7	7	7	7	7	7	7	7	7	7	7	7	7	7
Duration in Seconds																				
	4	4	4	4	4	4	4	4	4	4	4	4	4	4	4	4	4	4	4	4
Damage	6-10	9-13	12-16	15-19	18-22	21-25	24-28	27-31	31-35	35-39	39-43	43-47	47-51	51-55	55-59	59-63	64-68	69-73	74-78	79-83

CHARGED BOLT SENTRY - REQUIRED LEVEL 12

A trap that emits charged bolts at enemies that pass near. Shoots five bolts five times.

Level	1	2	3	4	5	6	7	8	9	10	11	12	13	14	15	16	17	18	19	20
Mana	13	13	13	13	13	13	13	13	13	13	13	13	13	13	13	13	13	13	13	13

continues on next page

Lightning Damage																				
	1-7	2-8	4-10	5-11	7-13	8-14	10-16	11-17	13-19	15-21	17-23	19-25	21-27	23-29	25-31	27-33	30-36	33-39	36-42	39-45

WAKE OF FIRE - REQUIRED LEVEL 12

A trap that emits waves of fire. Shoots five times.

Level	1	2	3	4	5	6	7	8	9	10	11	12	13	14	15	16	17	18	19	20
Mana	13	13	13	13	13	13	13	13	13	13	13	13	13	13	13	13	13	13	13	13
Fire Damage																				
	5-10	7-12	9-14	11-16	13-18	15-20	17-22	19-24	22-27	25-30	28-33	31-36	34-39	37-42	40-45	43-48	47-52	51-56	55-60	59-64

BLADE FURY - REQUIRED LEVEL 18

Throws Spinning blades to slice your enemies.

Minimum of 3 Mana to cast

Level	1	2	3	4	5	6	7	8	9	10	11	12	13	14	15	16	17	18	19	20
Mana cost per Blade																				
	1	1	2	2	3	3	3	4	4	5	5	5	6	6	7	7	7	8	8	8
Damage per Blade																				
	8-10	11-13	14-16	17-19	20-22	23-25	26-28	29-31	34-36	39-41	44-46	49-51	54-56	59-61	64-66	69-71	77-79	85-87	93-95	101-103

LIGHTNING SENTRY - REQUIRED LEVEL 24

A trap that shoots lightning to scorch passing enemies. Shoots ten times.

Level	1	2	3	4	5	6	7	8	9	10	11	12	13	14	15	16	17	18	19	20
Mana	20	20	20	20	20	20	20	20	20	20	20	20	20	20	20	20	20	20	20	20
Lightning Damage																				
	10-20	15-25	20-30	25-35	30-40	35-45	40-50	45-55	52-62	59-69	66-76	73-83	80-90	87-97	94-104	101-111	111-121	121-131	131-141	141-151

WAKE OF INFERNO - REQUIRED LEVEL 24

A trap that sprays fire at passing enemies. Shoots ten times.

Level	1	2	3	4	5	6	7	8	9	10	11	12	13	14	15	16	17	18	19	20
Mana	20	20	20	20	20	20	20	20	20	20	20	20	20	20	20	20	20	20	20	20
Fire Damage per second																				
	8-21	16-29	24-37	32-45	40-53	48-61	56-69	63-77	73-86	83-96	92-105	102-115	112-125	121-134	131-144	140-154	153-166	166-178	177-190	189-203

DEATH SENTRY - REQUIRED LEVEL 30

A trap that shoots lightning or explodes nearby corpses to lay waste to more nearby enemies.

Corpse Explosion Damage: 40-80% of the corpses damage. Shoots five times.

Level	1	2	3	4	5	6	7	8	9	10	11	12	13	14	15	16	17	18	19	20
Mana	20	20	20	20	20	20	20	20	20	20	20	20	20	20	20	20	20	20	20	20
Lightning Damage																				
	20-30	24-34	28-38	32-42	36-46	40-50	44-54	48-58	53-63	58-68	63-73	68-78	73-83	78-88	83-93	88-98	96-106	104-114	112-122	120-130
Corpe Explosion Radius in yards																				
	3.3	3.6	4	4.3	4.6	5	5.3	5.6	6	6.3	6.6	7	7.3	7.6	8	8.3	8.6	9	9.3	9.6

BLADE SHIELD - REQUIRED LEVEL 30

Spinning blades slice enemies who stray too close.

Level	1	2	3	4	5	6	7	8	9	10	11	12	13	14	15	16	17	18	19	20
Mana	27	29	31	33	35	37	39	41	43	45	47	49	51	53	55	57	59	61	63	65

Duration in seconds																				
	20	24	28	32	36	40	44	48	52	56	60	64	68	72	76	80	84	88	92	96
Damage	1-30	6-35	11-40	16-45	21-50	25-55	31-60	36-65	42-71	48-77	54-83	60-89	66-95	72-101	78-107	84-113	91-120	98-127	105-134	112-141

SHADOW DISCIPLINES

CLAW MASTERY - REQUIRED LEVEL 1

Passive-Improves your skill with claw-class weapons.

Level	1	2	3	4	5	6	7	8	9	10	11	12	13	14	15	16	17	18	19	20
Damage Bonus																				
	+35%	+39%	+43%	+47%	+51%	+55%	+59%	+63%	+67%	+71%	+75%	+79%	+83%	+87%	+91%	+95%	+99%	+103%	+107%	+111%
Attack Rating Bonus																				
	+30%	+40%	+50%	+60%	+70%	+80%	+90%	+100%	+110%	+120%	+130%	+140%	+150%	+160%	+170%	+180%	+190%	+200%	+210%	+220%

PSYCHIC HAMMER - REQUIRED LEVEL 1

Use the power of your mind to create a psychic blast to crush and knock back your enemies.

Level	1	2	3	4	5	6	7	8	9	10	11	12	13	14	15	16	17	18	19	20
Mana	4	4.2	4.5	4.7	5	5.2	5.5	5.7	6	6.2	6.5	6.7	7	7.2	7.5	7.7	8	8.2	8.5	8.7
damage	2-5	3-6	4-7	5-8	6-9	7-10	8-11	9-12	10-13	12-15	13-16	15-18	16-19	18-21	19-22	21-24	23-26	25-28	27-30	29-32

BURST OF SPEED - REQUIRED LEVEL 6

Increases attack and movement speed for a period of time.

Level	1	2	3	4	5	6	7	8	9	10	11	12	13	14	15	16	17	18	19	20
Mana	10	10	10	10	10	10	10	10	10	10	10	10	10	10	10	10	10	10	10	10
Attack Speed Bonus																				
	+21%	+27%	+31%	+34%	+37%	+39%	+41%	+42%	+44%	+45%	+46%	+47%	+48%	+49%	+50%	+51%	+51%	+51%	+52%	+53%
Walk/Run Speed bonus																				
+23%	+29%	+34%	+39%	+42%	+45%	+47%	+49%	+51%	+52%	+54%	+55%	+56%	+57%	+57%	+59%	+59%	+60%	+60%	+61%	
Duration in Seconds																				
	120	132	144	156	168	180	192	204	216	228	240	252	264	276	288	300	312	324	336	348

WEAPON BLOCK - REQUIRED LEVEL 12

Passive-Chance to block when using dual claw-class weapons.

Level	1	2	3	4	5	6	7	8	9	10	11	12	13	14	15	16	17	18	19	20
Chance to Block																				
	26	32	36	39	42	44	46	47	49	50	51	52	53	54	55	56	56	56	57	57

CLOAK OF SHADOWS - REQUIRED LEVEL 12

Cast a shadow to blind nearby enemies, lowering their defense for a period of time.

Level	1	2	3	4	5	6	7	8	9	10	11	12	13	14	15	16	17	18	19	20
Mana	13	13	13	13	13	13	13	13	13	13	13	13	13	13	13	13	13	13	13	13
Range	20 yards	20 yards	20 yards	20 yards	20 yards	20 yards	20 yards	20 yards	20 yards	20 yards	20 yards	20 yards	20 yards	20 yards	20 yards	20 yards	20 yards	20 yards	20 yards	20 yards
Duration in Seconds																				
	8	8	8	8	8	8	8	8	8	8	8	8	8	8	8	8	8	8	8	8
Enemies Defense																				
	-21%	-27%	-31%	-34%	-37%	-39%	-41%	-42%	-44%	-45%	-46%	-47%	-48%	-49%	-50%	-51%	-51%	-51%	-52%	-52%

continues on next page

FADE - REQUIRED LEVEL 18

Raises all resistances and resist curses for a period of time.

Level	1	2	3	4	5	6	7	8	9	10	11	12	13	14	15	16	17	18	19	20
Mana	10	10	10	10	10	10	10	10	10	10	10	10	10	10	10	10	10	10	10	10
Curse Duration Reduced by X																				
X	47%	53%	58%	62%	65%	67%	69%	71%	73%	74%	75%	76%	77%	78%	79%	80%	80%	81%	81%	82%
Resist All	19%	27%	33%	38%	42%	45%	48%	50%	52%	54%	56%	57%	58%	60%	60%	62%	62%	63%	63%	64%
Duration in Seconds																				
	120	132	144	156	168	180	192	204	216	228	240	252	264	276	288	300	312	324	336	348

SHADOW WARRIOR - REQUIRED LEVEL 18

Summons a shadow of yourself that mimics your skills and fights by your side.

Level	1	2	3	4	5	6	7	8	9	10	11	12	13	14	15	16	17	18	19	20
Mana	27	29	31	33	35	37	39	41	43	45	47	49	51	53	55	57	59	61	63	65
Life	124	138	153	168	183	198	213	228	243	257	272	287	302	317	332	347	362	376	391	406
Attack Rating																				
		+15%	+30%	+45%	+60%	+75%	+90%	+105%	+120%	+135%	+150%	+165%	+180%	+195%	+210%	+225%	+240%	+255%	+270%	285%
Duration in Seconds																				
		+12%	+24%	+36%	+48%	+60%	+72%	+84%	96%	+	+120%	+132%	+144%	+156%	+168%	+180%	+192%	+204%	+216%	+228%

MIND BLAST - REQUIRED LEVEL 24

Uses the power of your mind to stun a group of enemies and convert the feeble-minded.

Level	1	2	3	4	5	6	7	8	9	10	11	12	13	14	15	16	17	18	19	20
Mana	15	15	15	15	15	15	15	15	15	15	15	15	15	15	15	15	15	15	15	15
Duration in Seconds																				
	6-10	6-10	6-10	6-10	6-10	6-10	6-10	6-10	6-10	6-10	6-10	6-10	6-10	6-10	6-10	6-10	6-10	6-10	6-10	6-10
Damage	10-20	12-22	14-24	16-26	18-28	20-30	22-32	24-34	29-39	34-44	39-49	44-54	49-59	54-64	59-69	64-74	72-82	80-90	88-98	96-106
Chance to convert																				
	18%	21%	24%	26%	27%	28%	29%	30%	31%	32%	32%	33%	33%	34%	34%	35%	35%	35%	35%	36%

VENOM - REQUIRED LEVEL 30

Adds Poison Damage to your weapons.

Level	1	2	3	4	5	6	7	8	9	10	11	12	13	14	15	16	17	18	19	20
Mana	12	12	12	12	12	12	12	12	12	12	12	12	12	12	12	12	12	12	12	12
Poison Damage over 2 seconds																				
	37-78	50-90	62-103	75-115	87-128	100-140	112-153	125-165	143-184	162-203	181-221	200-240	218-259	237-278	256-296	275-315	300-340	325-365	350-390	375-415
Duration in Seconds																				
	120	124	128	132	136	140	144	148	152	156	160	164	168	172	176	180	184	188	192	196

SHADOW MASTER - REQUIRED LEVEL 30

Summon a Powerful Shadow of yourself to fight by your side.

Level	1	2	3	4	5	6	7	8	9	10	11	12	13	14	15	16	17	18	19	20
Mana	40	40	40	40	40	40	40	40	40	40	40	40	40	40	40	40	40	40	40	40
Life	188	216	244	272	300	329	357	385	413	441	470	498	526	554	582	611	639	667	695	723

Attack Rating																				
		+15%	+30%	+45%	+60%	+75%	+90%	+105%	+120%	+135%	+150%	+165%	+180%	+195%	+210%	+225%	+240%	+255%	+270%	285%
Duration in Seconds																				
		16	25	32	38	[illegible]	46	49	51	54	56	58	59	61	62	63	65	65	66	67

MARTIAL ARTS

TIGER STRIKE - REQUIRED LEVEL 1

Charge-up Skill—Adds Damage bonus to Finishing Moves.

Level	1	2	3	4	5	6	7	8	9	10	11	12	13	14	15	16	17	18	19	20
Mana	1	1	1	1	1	1	1	1	1	1	1	1	1	1	1	1	1	1	1	1
Attack Rating Bonus																				
	+40%	+50%	+60%	+70%	+80%	-90%	+100%	+110%	+120%	+130%	+140%	+150%	+160%	+170%	+180%	+190%	+200%	+210%	+220%	+230%
Charge 1 Damage Bonus																				
	+100%	+120%	+140%	+160%	+160%	+200%	+220%	+240%	+260%	+280%	+300%	+320%	+340%	+360%	+380%	+400%	+420%	+440%	+460%	+480%
Charge 2 Damage Bonus																				
	+200%	+240%	+280%	+320%	+360%	+400%	+440%	+480%	+520%	+560%	+600%	+640%	+680%	+720%	+760%	+800%	+840%	+880%	+920%	+960%
Charge 3 Damage Bonus																				
	+300%	+360%	+420%	+480%	+540%	+600%	+660%	+720%	+780%	+840%	+900%	+960%	+1020%	+1080%	+1140%	+1200%	+1260%	+1320%	+1380%	+1440%

DRAGON TALON - REQUIRED LEVEL 1

Finishing Move—Kick your enemies out of your way.

Level	1	2	3	4	5	[illegible]	7	8	9	10	11	12	13	14	15	16	17	18	19	20
Mana	6	6	6	6	6	[illegible]	6	6	6	6	6	6	6	6	6	6	6	6	6	6
Number of Kicks																				
	1	1	1	1	1	[illegible]	2	2	2	2	2	3	3	3	3	3	3	3	3	3
Kick Damage																				
	0	+7%	+14%	+21%	+28%	-35%	+42%	+49%	+56%	+63%	+70%	+77%	+84%	+91%	+98%	+105%	+112%	+119%	+126%	+133%
Attack Rating																				
	+40%	53%	+64%	+76%	+88%	-100%	+112%	+124%	+136%	+148%	+160%	+172%	+184%	+196%	+208%	+220%	+232%	+244%	+256%	+268%

FISTS OF FIRE - REQUIRED LEVEL 6

Charge-up Skill—Adds Fire Damage to Finishing Move.

Level	1	2	3	4	5	[illegible]	7	8	9	10	11	12	13	14	15	16	17	18	19	20
Mana	2	2	2	2	2	[illegible]	2	2	2	2	2	2	2	2	2	2	2	2	2	2
Attack +%	+50%	+60%	+70%	+80%	+90%	-100%	+110%	+120%	+130%	+140%	+150%	+160%	+170%	+180%	+190%	+200%	+210%	+220%	+230%	+240%
Fire Damage: All charges																				
	6-10	11-15	16-20	21-25	26-30	31-35	36-40	41-45	50-54	59-63	68-72	77-81	86-90	95-99	104-108	113-117	129-133	145-149	161-165	177-181
Charge 2 Fire Radius																				
	2 yards	2 yards	2 yards	2 yards	2 yards	[illegible] yards	2 yards	2 yards	2 yards	2 yards	2 yards	2 yards	2 yards	2 yards	2 yards	2 yards	2 yards	2 yards	2 yards	2 yards
Charge 3 fire burn length in seconds																				
	2.5	2.5	2.5	2.5	2.5	2.5	2.5	2.5	2.5	2.5	2.5	2.5	2.5	2.5	2.5	2.5	2.5	2.5	2.5	2.5

continues on next page

ASSASSIN SKILLS (CONTINUED)

DRAGON CLAW - REQUIRED LEVEL 6

Finishing Move - Double Claw Attack

Level	1	2	3	4	5	6	7	8	9	10	11	12	13	14	15	16	17	18	19	20
Mana	2	2	2	2	2	2	2	2	2	2	2	2	2	2	2	2	2	2	2	2
Damage Bonus																				
	+50%	+55%	+60%	+65%	+70%	+75%	+80%	+85%	+90%	+95%	+100%	+105%	+110%	+115%	+120%	+125%	+130%	+135%	+140%	+145%
Attack Rating bonus																				
	+50%	+60%	+70%	+80%	+90%	+100%	+110%	+120%	+130%	+140%	+150%	+160%	+170%	+180%	+190%	+200%	+210%	+220%	+230%	+240%

COBRA STRIKE - REQUIRED LEVEL 12

Charge-up Skill—Adds Life and Mana Steal to Finishing Moves.

Level	1	2	3	4	5	6	7	8	9	10	11	12	13	14	15	16	17	18	19	20
Mana	2	2	2	2	2	2	2	2	2	2	2	2	2	2	2	2	2	2	2	2
Attack Rating bonus																				
	+60%	+75%	+90%	+105%	+120%	+135%	+150%	+165%	+180%	+195%	+210%	+225%	+240%	+255%	+270%	+285%	+300%	+315%	+330%	+345%
Charge 1 Life Stealing																				
	40%	45%	50%	55%	60%	65%	70%	75%	80%	85%	90%	95%	100%	105%	110%	115%	120%	125%	130%	135%
Charge 2 Life and Mana Steal																				
	40%	45%	50%	55%	60%	65%	70%	75%	80%	85%	90%	95%	100%	105%	110%	115%	120%	125%	130%	135%
Charge 3 Life and Mana Steal																				
	80%	90%	100%	110%	120%	130%	140%	150%	160%	170%	180%	190%	200%	210%	220%	230%	240%	250%	260%	270%

CLAWS OF THUNDER - REQUIRED LEVEL 18

Charge-up Skill—Adds Lightning Damage to Finishing Moves.

Level	1	2	3	4	5	6	7	8	9	10	11	12	13	14	15	16	17	18	19	20
Mana	4	4	4	4	4	4	4	4	4	4	4	4	4	4	4	4	4	4	4	4
Attack Rating Bonus																				
	+80%	+95%	+110%	+125%	+140%	+155%	+170%	+185%	+200%	+215%	+230%	+245%	+260%	+275%	+290%	+305%	+320%	+335%	+350%	+365%
Charge 1 Lightning Damage																				
	1-80	11-90	21-100	31-110	41-120	51-130	61-140	71-150	91-170	111-190	131-210	151-230	171-250	191-270	211-290	231-310	261-340	291-370	321-400	351-430
Charge 2 Nova Damage																				
	1-20	1-27	1-34	1-41	1-48	1-55	1-62	1-69	1-76	1-83	1-90	1-97	1-104	1-111	1-118	1-125	1-132	1-139	1-146	1-153
Charge 3 Charged Bolt Damage																				
	1-40	1-51	1-62	1-73	1-84	1-95	1-106	1-117	1-130	1-143	1-156	1-169	1-182	1-195	1-208	1-221	1-236	1-251	1-266	1-281

DRAGON TAIL - REQUIRED LEVEL 18

Finishing Move—Explosive kick attack.

Level	1	2	3	4	5	6	7	8	9	10	11	12	13	14	15	16	17	18	19	20
Mana	10	10	10	10	10	10	10	10	10	10	10	10	10	10	10	10	10	10	10	10
Fire Damage																				
	+50%	+60%	+70%	+80%	+90%	+100%	+110%	+120%	+130%	+140%	+150%	+160%	+170%	+180%	+190%	+200%	+210%	+220%	+230%	+240%
Explosion Radius																				
	4 yards	4 yards	4 yards	4 yards	4 yards	4 yards	4 yards	4 yards	4 yards	4 yards	4 yards	4 yards	4 yards	4 yards	4 yards	4 yards	4 yards	4 yards	4 yards	4 yards

BLADES OF ICE - REQUIRED LEVEL 24

Charge-up Skill—Adds Cold Damage to Finishing Moves.

Level	1	2	3	4	5	6	7	8	9	10	11	12	13	14	15	16	17	18	19	20
Mana	3	3	3	3	3	3	3	3	3	3	3	3	3	3	3	3	3	3	3	3
Attack Rating Bonus																				
	+70%	+80%	+90%	+100%	+110%	+120%	+130%	+140%	+150%	+160%	+170%	+180%	+190%	+200%	+210%	+220%	+230%	+240%	+250%	+260%
Charge 1 Cold Damage																				
	15-35	23-43	31-51	39-59	47-67	55-75	63-83	71-91	81-101	91-111	101-121	111-131	121-141	131-151	141-161	151-171	171-191	191-211	211-231	231-251
Charge 2 Cold Radius																				
	3.3 yards	3.3 yards	3.3 yards	3.3 yards	3.3 yards	3.3 yards	3.3 yards	3.3 yards	3.3 yards	3.3 yards	3.3 yards	3.3 yards	3.3 yards	3.3 yards	3.3 yards	3.3 yards	3.3 yards	3.3 yards	3.3 yards	3.3 yards
Charge 3 Freeze Duration in Seconds																				
	4	4.4	4.8	5.2	5.6	6	6.4	6.8	7.2	7.6	8	8.4	8.8	9.2	9.6	10	10.4	10.8	11.2	11.6

DRAGON FLIGHT - REQUIRED LEVEL 24

Fnishing Move—Teleports you to kick your enemy.

Level	1	2	3	4	5	6	7	8	9	10	11	12	13	14	15	16	17	18	19	20
Mana	15	15	15	15	15	15	15	15	15	15	15	15	15	15	15	151	15	15	15	15
Attack Rating Bonus %																				
	100	120	140	160	180	200	220	240	260	280	300	320	340	360	380	400	420	440	460	480
Kick Damage Bonus %																				
	100	125	150	175	200	225	250	275	300	325	350	375	400	425	450	475	500	525	550	575

PHOENIX STRIKE - REQUIRED LEVEL 30

Charge-up Skill—Adds Elemental Moves to Finishing Moves.

Level	1	2	3	4	5	6	7	8	9	10	11	12	13	14	15	16	17	18	19	20
Mana	4	4	4	4	4	4	4	4	4	4	4	4	4	4	4	4	4	4	4	4
Attack Rating Bonus																				
	70	85	100	115	130	145	160	175	190	205	220	235	250	265	280	295	310	325	340	355
Charge 1 Meteor Damage																				
	20-40	26-46	32-52	38-58	44-64	50-70	56-76	62-82	74-94	86-106	98-118	110-130	122-142	134-154	146-166	158-178	178-198	198-218	218-238	238-258
Charge 2 Chain Lightning Damage																				
	1-40	1-51	1-62	1-73	1-84	1-95	1-106	1-117	1-130	1-143	1-156	1-169	1-182	1-195	1-208	1-221	1-236	1-251	1-266	1-281
Charge 3 Chaos Ice Bolt Damage																				
	16-32	30-36	24-40	28-44	32-48	36-52	40-56	44-60	50-66	56-72	62-78	68-84	74-90	80-96	86-102	92-108	100-116	108-124	116-132	124-140

DRUID SKILLS

ELEMENTAL

FIRESTORM - REQUIRED LEVEL 1

Unleash fiery chaos to burn your enemies.

Level	1	2	3	4	5	6	7	8	9	10	11	12	13	14	15	16	17	18	19	20
Mana	4	4	4	4	4	4	4	4	4	4	4	4	4	4	4	4	4	4	4	4

continues on next page

Average Fire Damage per second																				
	3-7	7-10	10-14	14-17	17-21	21-24	24-28	28-31	32-36	37-41	42-45	46-50	51-55	56-59	60-64	65-69	71-75	77-80	83-86	89-92

MOLTEN BOULDER - REQUIRED LEVEL 6

Launch a boulder of flaming hot magma that knocks back your enemies.

Level	1	2	3	4	5	6	7	8	9	10	11	12	13	14	15	16	17	18	19	20
Mana	10	10.5	11	11.5	12	12	13	13	14	14	15	15	16	16	17	17	18	18	19	19
Average Fire Damage per second																				
	11-16	19-24	28-32	36-41	44-49	52-57	60-65	69-73	79-84	90-94	100-105	111-116	121-126	132-137	142-147	153-158	166-171	179-183	192-196	205-209

ARCTIC BLAST - REQUIRED LEVEL 6

Blast a continuous jet of Ice to burn your enemies with frost.

Level	1	2	3	4	5	6	7	8	9	10	11	12	13	14	15	16	17	18	19	20
Mana	4	5	6	7	7	8	9	10	10	11	12	13	14	14	15	16	17	17	18	19
Cold Damage per Second																				
	8-15	14-21	20-28	26-34	33-40	39-46	45-53	51-59	58-66	65-72	71-79	78-85	85-92	91-99	98-105	105-112	112-119	119-126	126-133	133-140
Cold Length in seconds																				
	4	4.6	5.2	5.8	6.4	7	7.6	6.8	7.2	7.6	8	8.4	8.8	9.2	9.6	10	10.4	10.8	11.2	11.6
Range in yards																				
	5.3	6	6	6.6	6.6	7.3	7.3	8	8	8.6	8.6	9.3	9.3	10	10	10.6	10.6	11.3	11.3	12

FISSURE - REQUIRED LEVEL 12

Open volcanic vents below your enemies, burning them to a crisp.

Level	1	2	3	4	5	6	7	8	9	10	11	12	13	14	15	16	17	18	19	20
Mana	15	15	15	15	15	15	15	15	15	15	15	15	15	15	15	15	15	15	15	15
Duration in seconds																				
	3.2	3.2	3.2	3.2	3.2	3.2	3.2	3.2	3.2	3.2	3.2	3.2	3.2	3.2	3.2	3.2	3.2	3.2	3.2	3.2
Fire Damage																				
	15-25	21-31	27-37	33-43	39-49	45-55	51-61	57-67	69-79	81-91	93-103	105-115	117-127	129-139	141-151	153-163	169-179	185-195	201-211	217-227

CYCLONE ARMOR - REQUIRED LEVEL 12

Shield yourself from Damage caused by fire, cold, or lightning.

Level	1	2	3	4	5	6	7	8	9	10	11	12	13	14	15	16	17	18	19	20
Mana	5	6	7	8	9	10	11	12	13	14	15	16	17	18	19	20	21	22	23	24
Damage Absorbed																				
	40	52	64	76	88	100	112	124	136	148	160	172	184	196	208	220	232	244	256	268

TWISTER - REQUIRED LEVEL 18

Release several small whirlwinds that cut a path through your enemies.

Level	1	2	3	4	5	6	7	8	9	10	11	12	13	14	15	16	17	18	19	20
Mana	7	7	7	7	7	7	7	7	7	7	7	7	7	7	7	7	7	7	7	7
Stun length in seconds																				
	.4	.4	.4	.4	.4	.4	.4	.4	.4	.4	.4	.4	.4	.4	.4	.4	.4	.4	.4	.4
Fire Damage																				
	6-8	8-10	10-12	12-14	14-16	16-18	18-20	20-22	23-25	27-29	30-32	34-36	37-39	41-43	44-46	48-50	52-54	57-59	61-63	66-68

VOLCANO - REQUIRED LEVEL 24

Summon forth a volcano to rain fiery death upon your enemies.

Level	1	2	3	4	5	6	7	8	9	10	11	12	13	14	15	16	17	18	19	20
Mana	25	25	25	25	25	25	25	25	25	25	25	25	25	25	25	25	25	25	25	25
Fire Damage																				
	15-20	19-24	23-28	27-32	31-36	35-40	39-44	43-48	51-56	59-64	67-72	75-80	83-88	91-96	99-104	107-112	119-124	131-136	143-148	155-160

TORNADO - REQUIRED LEVEL 24

Create a funnel of wind and debris to blast your enemies.

Level	1	2	3	4	5	6	7	8	9	10	11	12	13	14	15	16	17	18	19	20
Mana	10	10	10	10	10	10	10	10	10	10	10	10	10	10	10	10	10	10	10	10
Damage	25-35	33-43	41-51	49-59	57-67	65-75	73-83	81-91	95-105	109-119	123-133	137-147	151-161	165-175	179-189	193-203	213-223	233-243	253-263	273-283

ARMAGEDDON - REQUIRED LEVEL 30

Create a meteor shower to rain fiery death upon your enemies.

Level	1	2	3	4	5	6	7	8	9	10	11	12	13	14	15	16	17	18	19	20
Mana	35	35	35	35	35	35	35	35	35	35	35	35	35	35	35	35	35	35	35	35
Duration in seconds																				
	10	10	10	10	10	10	10	10	10	10	10	10	010	10	10	10	10	10	10	10
Fire Damage																				
	25-75	40-90	55-105	70-120	85-135	100-150	115-165	130-180	150-200	170-220	190-240	210-260	230-280	250-300	270-320	290-340	315-365	340-390	365-415	390-440
Radius in yards																				
	5.3	5.3	5.3	5.3	5.3	5.3	5.3	5.3	5.3	5.3	5.3	5.3	5.3	5.3	5.3	5.3	5.3	5.3	5.3	5.3

HURRICANE - REQUIRED LEVEL 30

Create a massive wind storm.

Level	1	2	3	4	5	6	7	8	9	10	11	12	13	14	15	16	17	18	19	20
Mana	30	30	30	30	30	30	30	30	30	30	30	30	30	30	30	30	30	30	30	30
Duration in seconds																				
	10	10	10	10	10	10	10	10	10	10	10	10	010	10	10	10	10	10	10	10
Damage	25-50	32-57	39-64	46-71	53-78	60-85	67-92	74-99	84-109	94-119	104-129	114-139	124-149	134-159	144-169	154-179	166-191	178-203	190-215	202-227
Radius in yards																				
	5.3	5.3	5.3	5.3	5.3	5.3	5.3	5.3	5.3	5.3	5.3	5.3	5.3	5.3	5.3	5.3	5.3	5.3	5.3	5.3

SHAPE SHIFTING

WEREWOLF - REQUIRED LEVEL 1

Transform into a Werewolf. Life +25%, Stamina +25%

Level	1	2	3	4	5	6	7	8	9	10	11	12	13	14	15	16	17	18	19	20
Mana	15	15	15	15	15	15	15	15	15	15	15	15	15	15	15	15	15	15	15	15
Duration in seconds																				
	40	40	40	40	40	40	40	40	40	40	40	40	40	40	40	40	40	40	40	40
Attack Rating Bonus %																				
	50	65	80	95	110	125	140	155	170	185	200	215	230	245	260	275	290	305	320	335

continues on next page

Attack Speed Bonus %																				
	20	28	35	40	45	48	51	53	56	57	59	61	62	63	64	66	66	67	68	68
LYCANTHROPY - REQUIRED LEVEL 1																				
Passive-Improve shapeshifting ability.																				
Level	1	2	3	4	5	6	7	8	9	10	11	12	13	14	15	16	17	18	19	20
Max Life Bonus %																				
	20	25	30	35	40	45	50	55	60	65	70	75	80	85	90	95	100	105	110	115
Duration in seconds																				
	40	60	80	100	120	140	160	180	200	220	240	260	280	300	320	340	360	380	400	420
WEREBEAR - REQUIRED LEVEL 6																				
Transform into a Werebear. Life+100%.																				
Level	1	2	3	4	5	6	7	8	9	10	11	12	13	14	15	16	17	18	19	20
Mana	15	15	15	15	15	15	15	15	15	15	15	15	15	15	15	15	15	15	15	15
Duration in seconds																				
	40	40	40	40	40	40	40	40	40	40	40	40	40	40	40	40	40	40	40	40
Damage Bonus %																				
	50	57	64	71	78	85	92	99	106	113	120	127	134	141	148	155	162	169	176	183
Defense Bonus %																				
	25	30	35	40	45	50	55	60	65	70	75	80	85	90	95	100	105	110	115	120
FERAL RAGE - REQUIRED LEVEL 12																				
When in Werewolf form, go into a frenzied rage to steal increasing amounts of life from your enemies with successive hits.																				
Level	1	2	3	4	5	6	7	8	9	10	11	12	13	14	15	16	17	18	19	20
Mana	3	3	3	3	3	3	3	3	3	3	3	3	3	3	3	3	3	3	3	3
Duration in seconds																				
	20	20	20	20	20	20	20	20	20	20	20	20	20	20	20	20	20	20	20	20
Damage Bonus %																				
	50	55	60	65	70	75	80	85	90	95	100	105	110	115	120	125	130	135	140	145
Attack Rating Bonus %																				
	20	30	40	50	60	70	80	90	100	110	120	130	140	150	160	170	180	190	200	210
Life Steal %																				
	2-6	2-8	2-8	2-10	2-10	2-12	2-12	2-14	2-14	2-16	2-16	2-18	2-18	2-20	2-20	2-22	2-22	2-24	2-24	2-26
Walk/Run Speed % Bonus																				
	19-31	19-36	19-36	19-40	19-40	19-43	19-43	19-45	19-45	19-47	19-47	19-49	19-49	19-50	19-50	19-52	19-52	19-53	19-53	19-55
MAUL - REQUIRED LEVEL 12																				
When in Werebear form, maul your enemies for increasing damage with successive hits.																				
Level	1	2	3	4	5	6	7	8	9	10	11	12	13	14	15	16	17	18	19	20
Mana	3	3	3	3	3	3	3	3	3	3	3	3	3	3	3	3	3	3	3	3
Duration in seconds																				
	20	20	20	20	20	20	20	20	20	20	20	20	20	20	20	20	20	20	20	20
Damage Bonus %																				
	25-75	25-100	25-100	25-125	25-125	25-150	25-150	25-175	25-175	25-200	25-200	25-225	25-225	25-250	25-250	25-275	25-275	25-300	25-300	25-325

Attack Rating Bonus %																				
	20	30	40	50	60	70	80	90	100	110	120	130	140	150	160	170	180	190	200	210
Stun length in seconds																				
	1.7-2.8	1.7-3.2	1.7-3.2	1.7-3.4	1.7-3.4	1.7-3.7	1.7-3.7	1.7-3.9	1.7-3.9	1.7-4.0	1.7-4.0	1.7-4.2	1.7-4.2	1.7-4.4	1.7-4.4	1.7-4.5	1.7-4.5	1.7-4.6	1.7-4.6	1.7-4.7

RABIES - REQUIRED LEVEL 18

While in Werewolf form, bite your enemies to inflict them disease that they spread to other monsters.

Level	1	2	3	4	5	6	7	8	9	10	11	12	13	14	15	16	17	18	19	20
Mana	10	10	10	10	10	10	10	10	10	10	10	10	10	10	10	10	10	10	10	10
Poison Damage over 4 seconds																				
	18-43	31-56	43-68	56-81	68-93	81-106	93-118	106-131	121-146	137-162	153-178	168-193	184-209	200-225	215-240	231-256	250-275	268-293	287-312	306-331
Attack Rating Bonus %																				
	50	57	64	71	78	85	92	99	106	113	120	127	134	141	148	155	162	169	176	183

FIRE CLAWS - REQUIRED LEVEL 18

In Werewolf or Werebear form, maul your enemies with a fiery claw attack.

Level	1	2	3	4	5	6	7	8	9	10	11	12	13	14	15	16	17	18	19	20
Mana	4	4	4	4	4	4	4	4	4	4	4	4	4	4	4	4	4	4	4	4
Fire Damage																				
	15-20	21-26	27-32	33-38	39-44	45-50	51-56	57-62	69-74	81-86	93-98	105-110	117-122	129-134	141-146	153-158	173-178	193-198	213-218	233-238
Attack Rating Bonus %																				
	50	65	80	95	110	125	140	155	170	185	200	215	230	245	260	275	290	305	320	335

HUNGER - REQUIRED LEVEL 24

In Werewolf or Werebear form, bite your enemies to regain Life and Mana. -75% normal attack damage.

Level	1	2	3	4	5	6	7	8	9	10	11	12	13	14	15	16	17	18	19	20
Mana	3	3	3	3	3	3	3	3	3	3	3	3	3	3	3	3	3	3	3	3
Attack Rating Bonus %																				
	50	60	70	80	90	100	110	120	130	140	150	160	170	180	190	200	210	220	230	240
% Life Stolen																				
	72	90	104	116	125	132	138	143	149	152	156	159	162	165	167	170	171	173	174	176
% Mana Stolen																				
	72	90	104	116	125	132	138	143	149	152	156	159	162	165	167	170	171	173	174	176

SHOCK WAVE - REQUIRED LEVEL 24

When in Werebear form, stomp to create a shockwave that stuns nearby enemies.

Level	1	2	3	4	5	6	7	8	9	10	11	12	13	14	15	16	17	18	19	20
Mana	7	7	7	7	7	7	7	7	7	7	7	7	7	7	7	7	7	7	7	7
Damage	10-20	13-23	16-26	19-29	22-32	25-35	28-38	31-41	36-46	41-51	46-56	51-61	56-66	61-71	66-76	71-81	78-88	85-95	92-102	99-109
Stun length in seconds																				
	1.6	2.2	2.8	3.4	4	4.6	5.2	5.8	6.4	7	7.6	8.2	8.8	9.4	10	10.6	11.2	11.8	12.4	13

FURY - REQUIRED LEVEL 30

In Werewolf form, attack severcl opponents or one opponent several times.

Level	1	2	3	4	5	6	7	8	9	10	11	12	13	14	15	16	17	18	19	20
Mana	4	4	4	4	4	4	4	4	4	4	4	4	4	4	4	4	4	4	4	4

continues on next page

Attack Rating Bonus %																				
	50	57	64	71	78	85	92	99	106	113	120	127	134	141	148	155	162	169	176	183
Damage Bonus %																				
	100	117	134	151	168	185	202	219	236	253	270	287	304	321	338	355	372	389	406	423
Hits	2	3	4	5	5	5	5	5	5	5	5	5	5	5	5	5	5	5	5	5

SUMMONING

RAVEN - REQUIRED LEVEL 1

Summon Ravens

Level	1	2	3	4	5	6	7	8	9	10	11	12	13	14	15	16	17	18	19	20
Mana	6	6	6	6	6	6	6	6	6	6	6	6	6	6	6	6	6	6	6	6
Ravens	1	2	3	4	5	5	5	5	5	5	5	5	5	5	5	5	5	5	5	5
Hits	12	13	14	15	16	17	18	19	20	21	22	23	24	25	26	27	28	29	30	31
Damage	2-4	3-5	4-6	5-7	6-8	7-9	8-10	9-11	10-12	11-13	12-14	13-15	14-16	15-17	16-18	17-19	18-20	19-21	20-22	21-23

POISON CREEPER - REQUIRED LEVEL 1

Summon a vine that spreads disease.

Level	1	2	3	4	5	6	7	8	9	10	11	12	13	14	15	16	17	18	19	20
Mana	8	8	8	8	8	8	8	8	8	8	8	8	8	8	8	8	8	8	8	8
Life	15	18	21	24	27	30	33	36	39	42	45	48	51	54	57	60	63	66	69	72
Poison Damage over 4 seconds																				
	4-6	7-8	10-11	12-14	15-17	18-19	21-22	23-25	28-30	33-34	37-39	42-44	47-48	51-53	56-58	61-62	57-68	73-74	78-80	84-86

OAK SAGE - REQUIRED LEVEL 6

Summon a Spirit that adds to life of you and your party.

Level	1	2	3	4	5	6	7	8	9	10	11	12	13	14	15	16	17	18	19	20
Mana	15	16	17	18	19	20	21	22	23	24	25	26	27	28	29	30	31	32	33	34
Life	30	39	48	57	66	75	84	93	102	111	120	129	138	147	156	165	174	183	192	201
Life Bonus %																				
	30	35	40	45	50	55	60	54	70	75	80	85	90	95	100	105	110	115	120	125

SUMMON SPIRIT WOLF - REQUIRED LEVEL 6

Summons a teleporting wolf to fight by your side; Life 35.

Level	1	2	3	4	5	6	7	8	9	10	11	12	13	14	15	16	17	18	19	20
Mana	15	15	15	15	15	15	15	15	15	15	15	15	15	15	15	15	15	15	15	15
Wolves	1	2	3	4	5	5	5	5	5	5	5	5	5	5	5	5	5	5	5	5
Damage	2-5	3-6	4-8	5-9	6-10	8-11	9-12	10-13	12-16	14-18	17-20	19-23	21-25	24-27	26-29	28-32	33-36	37-41	42-46	47-50
Passive Attack Rating Bonus %																				
	50	65	80	95	110	125	140	155	170	185	200	215	230	245	260	275	290	305	320	335
Passive Defense Bonus %																				
	50	65	80	95	110	125	140	155	170	185	200	215	230	245	260	275	290	305	320	335

CARRION VINE - REQUIRED LEVEL 12

Summons a vine that eats corpses and replenishes your Life.

Level	1	2	3	4	5	6	7	8	9	10	11	12	13	14	15	16	17	18	19	20
Mana	10	10	10	10	10	10	10	10	10	10	10	10	10	10	10	10	10	10	10	10
Life	47	56	65	75	84	94	103	112	122	131	141	150	159	169	178	188	197	206	216	225
Heals %	4	5	6	6	7	7	8	8	8	9	9	9	9	9	10	10	10	10	10	10

HEART OF WOLVERINE - REQUIRED LEVEL 18

Summons a spirit that adds to the attack rating and damage of you and your party.

Level	1	2	3	4	5	6	7	8	9	10	11	12	13	14	15	16	17	18	19	20
Mana	20	21	22	23	24	25	26	27	28	29	30	31	32	33	34	35	36	37	38	39
Radius	20 yard	20 yard	20 yard	20 yard	20 yard	20 yard	20 yard	20 yard	20 yard	20 yard	20 yard	20 yard	20 yard	20 yard	20 yard	20 yard	20 yard	20 yard	20 yard	20 yard
Life	68	81	95	108	122	136	149	163	176	190	204	217	231	244	258	272	285	299	312	326
Bonus % to Damage																				
	20	27	34	41	48	55	62	69	76	83	90	97	104	111	118	125	132	139	146	153
Bonus % to Attack Rating																				
	25	32	39	46	53	60	67	74	81	88	95	102	109	116	123	130	137	144	151	158

SUMMON DIRE WOLF - REQUIRED LEVEL 18

Summons a wolf that increases its damage by eating corpses; Life 57.

Level	1	2	3	4	5	6	7	8	9	10	11	12	13	14	15	16	17	18	19	20
Mana	20	20	20	20	20	20	20	20	20	20	20	20	20	20	20	20	20	20	20	20
Wolves	1	2	3	3	3	3	3	3	3	3	3	3	3	3	3	3	3	3	3	3
Life (with passive bonus added)																				
	85	99	114	128	142	156	171	185	199	213	228	242	256	270	285	299	313	327	342	356
Passive life % bonus to bears and wolves																				
	50	75	100	125	150	175	200	225	250	275	300	325	350	375	400	425	450	475	500	525

SOLAR CREEPER - REQUIRED LEVEL 24

Summons a vine that eats corpses and replenishes your Mana.

Level	1	2	3	4	5	6	7	8	9	10	11	12	13	14	15	16	17	18	19	20
Mana	14	15	16	17	18	19	20	21	22	23	24	25	26	27	28	29	30	31	32	33
Life	82	98	114	131	147	164	180	196	213	229	246	262	278	295	311	328	344	360	377	393
Heals %	2	2	3	4	4	4	5	5	5	5	5	6	6	6	6	6	6	6	6	6

SPIRIT OF BARBS - REQUIRED LEVEL 30

Summons a spirit that adds a Thorns aura to you and your party.

Level	1	2	3	4	5	6	7	8	9	10	11	12	13	14	15	16	17	18	19	20
Mana	25	26	27	28	29	30	31	32	33	34	35	36	37	38	39	40	41	42	43	44
Life	106	127	148	169	190	212	233	254	275	296	318	339	360	381	402	424	445	466	487	508
% of Damage Returned																				
	50	60	70	80	90	100	110	120	130	140	150	160	170	180	190	200	210	220	230	240

continues on next page

SUMMON GRIZZLY - REQUIRED LEVEL 30

Summons a bear; Base Life 142, Base Damage 34-69.

Level	1	2	3	4	5	6	7	8	9	10	11	12	13	14	15	16	17	18	19	20
Mana	40	40	40	40	40	40	40	40	40	40	40	40	40	40	39	40	41	42	43	44
Damage (passive bonus added)																				
	37-75	54-94	72-116	93-139	115-165	140-192	166-222	195-253	235-297	279-344	326-393	376-446	428-502	484-561	543-622	605-687	684-769	767-855	854-945	945-1039
Passive % Damage Bonus to wolves and bears																				
	25	35	45	55	65	75	85	95	105	115	125	135	145	155	165	175	185	195	205	215